Clichés and Coinages

THE LANGUAGE LIBRARY

EDITED BY DAVID CRYSTAL

The Articulate Computer	*Michael McTear*
The Artificial Language Movement	*Andrew Large*
Children's First School Books	*Carolyn D. Baker & Peter Freebody*
Children's Writing and Reading	*Katharine Perera*
A Child's Learning of English	*Paul Fletcher*
Clichés and Coinages	*Walter Redfern*
A Companion to Old and Middle English Studies	*A. C. Partridge*
A Dictionary of Literary Terms (revised)	*J. A. Cuddon*
Early Modern English	*Charles Barber*
A Dictionary of Linguistics and Phonetics (second edition)	*David Crystal*
The Foreign-Language Barrier	*J. A. Large*
A History of the English Language	*G. L. Brook*
A History of Foreign-Language Dictionaries	*R. L. Collison*
How Conversation Works	*Ronald Wardhaugh*
An Informal History of the German Language	*W. B. Lockwood*
Language and Class in Victorian England	*K. C. Phillipps*
The Language of *1984*	*W. F. Bolton*
Language, Society and Identity	*John Edwards*
Languages in Competition	*Ronald Wardhaugh*
Modern Englishes: Pidgins and Creoles	*Loreto Todd*
Non-Standard Language in English Literature	*N. F. Blake*
Puns	*Walter Redfern*
Rhetoric: The Wit of Persuasion	*Walter Nash*
Sense and Sense Development (revised)	*R. A. Waldron*
The Study of Dialect	*K. M. Petyt*
Thomas Hardy's English	*Ralph W. V. Elliott*
The Treatment of Sounds in Language and Literature	*Raymond Chapman*
Words in Time	*Geoffrey Hughes*
The Writing Systems of the World	*Florian Coulmas*

CLICHÉS AND COINAGES

Walter Redfern

Basil Blackwell

First published 1989

Basil Blackwell Ltd
108 Cowley Road, Oxford, OX4 1JF, UK

Basil Blackwell Inc.
3 Cambridge Center
Cambridge, MA 02142, USA

British Library Cataloguing in Publication Data

A CIP catalogue record for this book is available from the British Library.

Library of Congress Cataloging in Publication Data

Redfern, W. D.
Clichés and coinages/Walter Redfern.
p. cm.
Bibliography: p.
Includes index.
ISBN 0–631–15691–7
1. English language – Terms and phrases. 2. French language – Terms and phrases. 3. English language – Usage. 4. French language – Usage. 5. Words, New – English. 6 Words, New – French. I. Title.
PE1442.R38 1989
427 – dc19   89–30937
                                                                              CIP

Typeset in 10½ on 12½ Ehrhardt
by Footnote Graphics, Warminster, Wilts
Printed in Great Britain by
The Camelot Press Ltd, Southampton

*To Angela, my far better half,
who gives the kiss of life
to the deadest things.*

Imprimatur
'Quid humani a te alienum putes (sic)?'
'Nihil (Et quid obstat? Nihil)'

Myles na Gopaleen

'Wonderful!' I ejaculated.
'Commonplace,' said Holmes.
Conan Doyle, *passim*.

Let's have some new clichés.
Sam Goldwyn

Qu'on ne dise pas que je n'ai rien dit de nouveau: la
disposition des matières est nouvelle; quand on joue à la
paume, c'est une même balle dont joue l'un et l'autre, mais
l'un la place mieux. (Let no one say that I have said nothing
new; the arrangement of the subject is new. When we play
tennis, both partners use the same ball, but one of them
has a better aim.)

Pascal

Les lieux communs ne se révèlent qu'à ceux qui les
étudient humblement et avec une grande pureté de coeur.
(The meaning of commonplaces is revealed only to those
who study them with humility and great purity of heart.)

Léon Bloy

Times there are when I forget the world exists,
and yet, and yet,
come the next day,
keep I must the trodden way.

W. D. Redfern (16¾)

Contents

Acknowledgements		x
1	*Declaring an Interest*	1
2	Language Schools, or Grounding in Cliché	7
3	Howling with the Wolves	16
4	Swinging Between the Poles	26
5	Scaling the Heights	41
6	Plumbing the Depths: Plagiarism	65
7	The Modes of Plagiarism	85
8	Letdowns	97
9	A Few Well-Chosen Words	109
10	Habits of Mind/Odious Comparisons	130
11	Pop Eyes	144
12	A Dead-and-Alive Hole	155
13	Change of Gear in the Melting-Pot	180
14	First Words	183
15	Illustration of Defence	187
16	New Words Home and Abroad	204
17	Subtle Blends	216
18	Controlled Appellations	227
19	High Neologism	234
20	Looking Round the Bend	241
21	When All is Said and Done	253
Notes		257
Bibliography		294
Index		299

Acknowledgements

I dedicate this book to the lot of us, for where would it have been without our conjoined, unstinting, competing and ubiquitous contributions to the dead and the quick in language?

Within this greater structure, the microcosm: my wife, Angela. Herself indoors or outdoors, she has aided my self to evolve in life and on paper.

More locally, Patrick Hughes, whose fascination with the overlap of all things frequently criss-crosses mine, and whose visual spectacles correct my short sight. Keith Foley, who generously shared his neologbook with me. We keep each other going by neologrolling. Doug Pye, who gave me hints about the rhythm method. Geoffrey Strickland, who reminded me of what I tend to neglect: context.

Ken Gladdish, Dr Jean Bobon, André Blavier, Gaston Ferdière kindly provided tips, sources and examples.

I am indebted, indeed desperately in hock, to Michel Schneider's powerfully suggestive *Voleurs de mots*. I am a plagiarist, said the Cretan plagiarist.

And of course, to close the family circle, my universal uncle, Tom Cobbleigh.

Any unattributed neologisms or twists on clichés are, as far as I can tell or remember, my own. As are all translations. I supply the original only when its language is remarkable in some way. All puns and the occasional Gallicism are intended and remorse-free.

1

Declaring an Interest

I will use I a good deal in this book. Partly because we is too conspiratorial, regal or editorial: presumptuous.[1] I is, strangely, more modest. I will use we when I feel more confident that my views are shared by others – how many, though, I could never dare to guess. One of the sporadic premisses, then, is that some people think at times approximately like me. This assumption seems relatively sane. Without it, I would only be burbling into a bottle launched from a desert island. While that situation does bear thinking about, I mainly prefer not to. (The cliché skulking here is Vigny's 'Une bouteille à la mer': it is a champagne-bottle carrying the proudly unkillable message in the poem). If you disagree when I use we, you will possibly mutter: 'Speak for yourself'. I promise, in what follows, to do that; and hope that it is catching.

I went to grammar school, then to Cambridge and the Ecole Normale Supérieure, Paris. I was born the wrong side of many things in Bootle. My mind and my prose reflect these varied facts of life. I am interested in (that is, intrigued by and caught up in) both common and elite culture. I am drawn to clichés, as I hate debts and prize freedom from influence. Born in a would-be free port, hostile to automatic 'pietas erga parientes' or towards *almae matres*, not much of a patriot, a blind fan neither of the present age nor of any previous one, still less hankering for any imaginary one, as a teenager I wanted vainly to be the admiral of my soul, if I was too pessimistic to aim to be master of my fate. Largely because my chief rival at school, and subsequently one of my most durable friends, submitted proudly to letting the style of leading poets infiltrate his first attempts at writing poetry, for my parallel first shots I refused on principle even to read any such mentors. Talk about the anxiety of influence. In middle age, both his and my poems are recognizably individual. The whole complex, known variously as irony, 'la contre-finalité', Sod's Law, or Resistentialism, seems to me to rule the world. In wanting to distance myself from my competitor, I backed into parody, pastiche: knocking-jobs on him and his several begetters. My independence depended. It was all an impossible dream, but it helped to make me what I am. For my sins. For what it's worth. The premature existentialist, the only self-begetter, has come roughly down to earth.

After my previous study (*Puns*) – and a Nandi proverb holds that 'there is no saying without a double meaning'[2] – what drew me to clichés and neologisms? Without being in the remotest a spiritualist, I am permanently fascinated by the spirit more than the letter: the implied, the buried, the inadvertently revealed, the second degree. Already in *Puns* I had briefly examined clichés and neologisms for their connections with puns: rejuvenation, recycling, creativity, or at least activity. If the pun is, at its infrequent best, a 'sudden bright idea', clichés are long-lasting, possibly eternal, grown dull ideas. Neologisms are something else. A sign that there is still life (still life!) in the old dog (or, to accommodate feminists and equity, bitch). That language and creative thinking have not yet given up the ghost. A few lines, already raddled with clichés – though a slight change is as good as a rest. Does your heart sink? Hopefully, stick with me. I could say just as well: listen to yourselves. We are all more parasitic, and more inventive, than we credit. And there might be some loose connection between the two. Clichés and neologisms: strange bedfellows, you might think. I am arranging a shotgun wedding. This book is about passive and active borrowing, uninventive or creative parasitism. A bipartite study, it resembles a centaur, a mermaid, or a pantomime horse. My target is diffuse, squashy. I leave precision to watchmakers, or to statisticians and economic forecasters, those digital poets. John Gross called *Puns* an omnium-gatherum.[3] Clichés, too, are hold-alls, as are portmanteau words. Until the contents of all our brains are filed and instantly updated on some umpteenth-generation computer, I cannot possibly check whether my clichés are yours, or vice versa. I have to take shots in the dark.

Though by temperament and choice I am sedentary and love my wife, in words I can hardly resist taking off. Friends speak charitably of my 'glancing' approach. More honestly, I know that each time I light on a word or an idea I feel the need to take off from it, often in several directions. I land as a pheasant; I take off as a covey.

Taxonomy, the naming of parts, opposes my favoured approximation. I like aiming at being approximately to the point. Besides, language itself has anarchist tendencies, which chafe under, throw off or wriggle around any would-be imprisonment by rigid rules. I do not share the penis-envy that the so-called soft sciences feel towards the so-called hard. Nor do I want to shelter behind the riot-shields of OK names. Take me as you find me. In intellectual matters I prefer unhappy families, more varied and idiosyncratic. Though here and there I will try to give the kiss of life to the suspendedly animated terms of traditional rhetoric, I would echo Paul de Man (once in a while won't hurt): 'Not only are tropes, as their name implies [turns], always on the move – more like quicksilver than like flowers or butterflies which one can at least hope to pin down and insert in a neat taxonomy – but they can disappear altogether, or at least appear to disappear.'[4] My atheism is of the catholic variety: I want to corral rather than to pigeonhole. If I interchangeably use the varied terms for clichés (and neologisms), it is not because I wish to fudge matters, but because I value overlap and embracingness. Rhetoric itself is notably incestuous, so much so that chiasmus seems the quintessential rhetorical operation. I stand in the shadow of Sir Thomas Browne: 'There are many things delivered Rhetorically, many expressions therein merely Tropicall [i.e. speaking figuratively], and as they best illustrate my intention.'[5]

We apply two basic metaphors to language: as clothes ('threadbare'), and as organism ('dead languages', 'the sick state of the language'). The one is superficial and secondary, the second central; but both can mislead by freezing the topic. Speaking or thinking clichés is as easy as riding, or falling off, a bike. Some people believe that thinking or talking *about* clichés, or indeed about any of the multiple aspects of language, will make you fall off your bike. This is the common fear, especially in England, of analysis; analysis is breakdown, as in the old joke about the man who, once told of the anatomical intricacies involved in getting out of a chair, was ever after unable to rise from his. I am not a linguistic scientist. I do not take sides in the following confrontation: 'It is better to be a doorkeeper in the house of philology than to dwell in the tents of the rhetoricians.'[6] My favourite French expression is *à cheval*. Not in the sense of 'on horseback', where (to use an idiom from my native Liverpool), I feel about as comfortable as a cow on a bike. But rather in the sense of straddling, bridging the gap. Or, given the tendency to fiasco that marks much human enterprise, falling between two stools. I do have a tongue in my head, and differing quantities of other tongues. Many linguistic scientists reinvest the dogmatism they have withdrawn from value-judgements about language use in taxonomic obsession. As T.E. Hope said, 'for 99 per cent of the population language is not something one views detachedly at all, but an essential item of man's make-up like the use of his limbs or his senses. Philologists, on the other hand, [are] used to conceiving of language as a discrete entity.'[7] I only sometimes believe that ignorance is bliss. Obscurantism never opened anyone's eyes. Why, the more thoughtful infant-school teachers today begin the process of teaching tots to be critical about language. We all are so instinctively, besides, and just need reminding. 'Mark my words', 'to watch one's tongue': whether in ultimatums or self-censoring nervousness, everybody's doing it.

> If people are bright enough to learn the language of money – as they must be if they are to pay their taxes and buy their goods without falling prey to legal or illegal con artists – they are bright enough to learn the language of language – with a bit of help from linguists who have acquired a sense of their social responsibilities.[8]

Engagingly, Bolinger had earlier defined the linguist as 'the metaperson par excellence', and compared such activity to 'a physician's healing himself, to repairing a boat while remaining afloat in it, and to lifting oneself by one's own bootstraps'.[9] The first two of these are feasible, if not the third. Often we talk unthinkingly of clichés. The very fact that so many people shrink from scrutinizing language suggests how central it is to everything. It is the fear of narcissism, navel-reviews, that makes many shy away from analysis.

The first part of my book is not, like Eric Partridge's, a dictionary of clichés, but rather an analysis of the *idea* of cliché. Examples will be mainly conspicuous by their absence, despite the good-sense warning of a colleague, Christie Davies, that readers will feel cheated if denied instances. (As he is a collector and student of ethnic jokes, perhaps his reflexes differ from mine.) I am implicitly inviting readers to fill in the gaps themselves. If my insights are valid, this should be easy. If they are askew, no amount of examples will save me. A related reason is the hope of not dating too badly. Clichés, besides, abolish the barriers between the individual and the mass. Even Barthes speaks of 'all the codes which constitute me, so that in the end my subjectivity takes on the generality of stereotypes'.[10] As in *Puns*, I will call on English, French and American approaches to my topic. After inventing the term and (it often seems) the habit or practice, many French writers have disowned clichés more cuttingly than their British/American counterparts have. They represent, therefore, an extreme case, a yardstick. I take what examples I have from both literature and everyday speech. While books and chat obviously differ, all of us can and do misuse our powers of speech and thought.

> Much written and spoken expression these days is equivalent to the background music that incessantly encroaches on us ... It thumps and tinkles

away, mechanical, without colour, inflection, vigour, charm or distinction. People who work in the presence of background music often tell you and sometimes with pride that they don't hear it anymore. The parallel with language is alarming.[11]

Thus Edwin Newman, speaking strictly. I myself want to moralize as little as possible. One of the many dangers of studying clichés is of sounding like a reactionary snob, lamenting a finer age, however mythical, and higher standards ('more means worse'). Whereas we are all vulgarians. When it comes to clichés, the whole of humanity is the scapegoat; all humans are beyond the pale. So who shall give the first shove? It is always others, it does not go without saying, who mouth clichés. Yet even the most moderately honest teacher, parent, friend, person in the street or at workplace, must have many a time winced and wished briefly to be struck dumb, because of the horrors they have just uttered. Is it possible to be original, or even relatively fresh, about clichés? If I let myself be paralysed in advance, even though I recognize the risk of brain-damage by dwelling on them, would I not be surrendering to the inert in life?

They get everywhere. Especially into sports reporting: why, for instance, do sinistropedal footballers alone have an 'educated foot'? Unavoidably, to think and write about clichés, I have to emulate the page of Good King Wenceslas, and put my feet into ready-made tracks. I will put my foot in, no doubt, in more ways than one, but, like that boy, boldly. 'Something old, something new, something borrowed, something blue': a motto for brides, stand-up comedians, and many writers. I would like to feel that every cliché is here used knowingly, but I can never be sure that I am always vigilant or putting them productively to work. The study of clichés is inescapably a study of knowledge (and of ignorance), of how we transmit or acquire it, and of what difference it makes to us.

My reluctance to classify, as distinct from circumscribing or hinting, is due to my belief that it is wrong strategically and maybe ethically to tranquillize the spirited. And clichés *are* spirited: vestiges of life, haunting the present, and still able to trouble and direct it. So many studies of clichés I've read – especially by psychologists, linguisticians, or sociologists – end up by mechanizing the quarry, thus giving themselves sitting ducks. They do not give the subject its head, or its due. So I am not just being evasive (though I don't mind being elusive), when I say, in effect: don't fence me in; let me ride over the wide open country that I love. Clichés are alive, and surprisingly free. I seek to get under their skin.

Just as an impersonator can point up what is peculiar and significant in a famous public figure, so my kind of mimicking, intended to be critical (for impersonation, at its best, is a comment), may illuminate this other kind of well-known public figure: the cliché.

2

Language Schools, or Grounding in Cliché

Although exploring every avenue suggests pith-helmets in suburbia, I will try, however lacunically, to do that. There will be no compelling logic about the sequence of the chapters, for clichés have the knack of curling back on themselves, perhaps to ensure survival. If I had to plot the curves of my arguments, they would be at very best a series of interlooping circles. The Olympics Committee partakes, however, more of the internecine than of the ecumenical. Clichés are varied. They can take the form of writing up (exaggeration, embroidering), or of writing down (taking the steam or the barb out of menace, simplifying knottiness). What they often lack (as current English lacks this word) is *adéquation*. This does not mean (there is literally a cliché for every occasion) that they are dispensable or irrelevant.

Whereas we have the capacity for second thoughts – adaptation, twists, questioning – clichés are first thoughts, unexamined, in fact often non-thoughts or automatisms. This common knowledge represented by cliché sustains the status quo. Thus, 'relate to' and 'identify with', splendidly good-hearted as ideals, too seldom involve a courageous leap of imagination, too often a diminishing of the target. Putting yourself in someone else's shoes can be an act of annexation rather than of surrender and sympathy. The current cliché of the 'System', whether the system is that of *1984*, intergalactic science-fiction, job-networks, or any everyday experience of frustration, got its boost from Rousseau and his persecution-mania. Systems can be tackled and subverted, if not over-thrown, head-on or deviously, as can clichés, which are piecemeal systems of thought and expression. I agree with Lerner that frequent use is not a criterion.[1] A lavatory is not more of a cliché than Christmas-tree lights. Perhaps it is less of one, as it is not pretending, unless beribboned and bewigged, to be anything but what it is, whereas those glass cartridges carry a heavy cargo of obligatory meanings (fête and fellowship).

The archetypal student essay cautiously begins with a definition of terms. Like a good part of our language, we borrowed the word *cliché* from the French. It may be an echoic word, like 'click' and 'clack' in English. Because of its origins, together with 'stereotype' in printing, and its later extension to photography, the term parallels the development of modern technology. Imitation, identical reproduction (cloning, before its time), such associations led on to the figurative meaning (because reproducibility entails wear-and-tear) of mechanized mental processes and textural fatigue. If modern culture is indeed moving away from print towards pictures, a present-day updating of the term would be 'image': something fixed (though air-brushable), inspectable and influential. I start, as we all do, with education, where we receive our first formal grounding in set ways of thinking and expression.

Even when we have graduated from our cradles or carry-cots, we go on using cribs for the rest of our natural. 'Nous sommes chacun plus riche que nous ne pensons; mais on nous dresse à l'emprunt et à la queste; on nous duict à nous servir plus de l'autruy que du nostre'. (We are all of us richer than we think, but we are brought up to beg and borrow; we are drilled to make more use of what is another's than of our own).[2] The French word *répétition* means both reiteration and rehearsal. We all repeat by way of learning our lines for a future performance, whether on the theatrical or the social stage. Repetition, indeed, is the most basic characteristic of life, for what is more repetitive than breathing, eating, excreting and sleeping? The most endlessly usable particle is re-. Repetition ties us in knots. From an examination-script I recall: 'This avoidance of repetition represents the author's obsession with the repetitive pattern of life'. The very fact that humankind relies on generation to perpetuate itself ensures the centrality of repetition. Each new generation needs to be told and to rediscover old ideas. Much of the time we live off left-overs – often tastier than the real thing.

'The cliché leaves us staring banality straight in the eye',[3] and is therefore troubling and educational. The instance reminds us of the generality, or it would if education more frequently worked to lead out rather than to stuff in. There is a long history of the teaching of rhetoric in French schools, above all in Jesuit establishments, for this order makes no bones about catching early. Normative education easily becomes force-feeding, well-known to French geese. The alimentary metaphor is apt. The seventeenth-century novelist, Charles Sorel, in his *Francion*, tells of his studies, when the boys were obliged to make a *capilotade* (a pot-pourri or ragout) of selected passages from authors, instead of being encouraged to develop their own thoughts and expression.[4] What was unwillingly swallowed by a boy could be gladly pursued by the adult. Concurrently, the sieur de Richesource (appropriately named) ran courses in plagiarism, which he called Plagianism[5] – only one letter away from Pelagianism; presumably he too disbelieved in original sin, or rather thought originality was a sin. The whole stress of his teaching fell on disguise: the tyro plagiarist was taught to launder his stolen property. It was truly French without tears. A leading pulpit orator of the age, Fléchier, attended his lectures when a youth.

Nineteenth-century French education really systematized such methods. Historians of the practice describe how the main instrument of indoctrination was *le discours*: the composing of written speeches, based on the model of writers from Antiquity, in which noble-sounding and predeterminedly appropriate words were placed by pupils in the abstract mouths of famous figures from the past. It was, in effect, inbred ventriloquism, in which the master fed the dummy. The kind of prose most favoured by teachers was abstract, or conventionally metaphorical, moralistic, and strewn with maxims. It is clear where French public oratory, however small-scale the occasion, even today springs (or rather seeps) from. Girls, while they make equally good barrack-room lawyers, were generally spared rhetorical induction, and saved for the kitchen or the marriage-couch; but boys were browbeaten into concocting ideas and sentiments not their own, nor even within their comprehension. Michel Bréal, a professor of comparative grammar at the Collège de France, commented that this practice was symptomatic of an intellectual malady which consisted in contenting oneself with fine words, locking oneself into a role and dragging out of oneself passions one did not feel.[6] Thus teenage French schoolboys were taught formal rhetoric before they had had enough experience to wax rhetorical about. It was back-to-front: words came first. As Jules Vallès's hapless hero Jacques Vingtras so rightly complains in *Le Bachelier*: how can I impersonate Mucius Scaevola without the benefit of a charred wrist? (Yet, in protesting stereotyped exemplarity in a spirit of serious play, in addressing the dangers inherent in not having a style to call your own, Vallès ended up inventing a self and a style that are inimitable. Yet again, for he was vitally full of contradictions, whereas the *lycée* taught *abondance*, Vallès's hero exemplifies Diderot's remark in *Jacques le fataliste* that the only riches the poor enjoy is the gift of the gab. Yet thirdly, as Vingtras is fiasco-prone, it should be the gift of the gabble, for he has a lot of trouble, and sport, with the pitfalls of enunciation and delivery.) No true love of Antiquity was fostered, no real curiosity about other cultures: everything was annexed to Gallocentric, xenophobic French purposes. Hence the pedantic dread of barbarisms and solecisms. The distaste for freshness betrays a fear of life itself. Invention and imagination were frowned upon. What was demanded was amplification, the padding-out of ingurgitated (but not digested) material. Amplification – adornment, window-dressing – provides another well-stocked pool of clichés. A critic of the system, Albalat, details it thus: 'Make two ideas out of one; seek out the antithesis of an idea; double up the point of view; add on striking details; go over what you have already said; increase the detail while avoiding prolixity; turn aridity into fertility'.[7] Extension should be personal, should be what we bring to a text or an idea. To teach such extensions, to impress models of them on waxy young minds, can only artificialize a reasonably natural habit.

Such stylistic regimentation had everything to do with the production of set-pieces, and the churning-out of pre-formed members of the liberal professions and of state servants trained to operate by the letter of the law. Even the most rebellious students were often scarred for life, retaining indelible vestiges of what they strove mightily to cast off. A culture became, however much contested, a partial second nature. I might coin a proverb: 'Péroraison n'est pas raison', for not only comparisons are odious.

Of course, the opposite view is also incontrovertible. How can we learn anything except by copying? But to make it the principal mode of learning is stultifying. Albalat says of the *cahier d'expressions* (the schoolboy version of the commonplace book, an album of quotes): 'C'est encore une façon mécanique de meubler la mémoire, de bibeloter la littérature' (It is one more mechanical means of packing the memory and of turning literature into a hoard of trinkets).[8] All this produced was pupils 'habiles à plaquer la banalité'.[9] *Plaquer*: to plaster down hair, to veneer, to plonk down (colours or paint); indiscriminate emphasis, the result of inculcated plagiarism. When Vallès confesses to stitching together filched phrases, he was going along with the system, playing ball. In these circumstances of a vicious circle, the larcenist robs himself, of a personal voice. Behind the whole practice, developing capitalism was instructing the young how to capitalize on the already established (*l'acquis: vivre sur son acquis* means to mark time, though *vitesse acquise* signifies impetus, momentum). The past can be a trampoline or starting-blocks. By the 1930s, not much of significance had changed. Claude Duneton recounts how in rural schools the emphasis still fell, with a heavy hand, on stylized *rédaction*.[10] It was borrowed plumes, in both senses, for it was fancy writing that country lads were rewarded for aping. Céline beefs persuasively about *le français de lycée:*

Ils n'ont jamais eu d'émotions … Ils n'ont jamais éprouvé que des émotions lycéennes, des émotions livresques … Tout ce qu'ils élaborent par la suite, au cours de leurs 'oeuvres' ne peut être que le rafistolage d'emprunts, de choses vues à travers un pare-brise … ou simplement volées au tréfonds des bibliothèques'. (They've never had any feelings. They've only ever had *lycée* feelings, book-feelings. Anything they cook up later in their 'works' can only be the patching-together of things seen through windscreens, or just stolen from the bowels of libraries.)[11]

As well as indicting, Céline also typifies a culture where words often come cheap, where they are easily mistaken for deeds, where a policeman's report is *une verbalisation*, where so much in life seems to be *un procès-verbal*. Yet every nation confuses the shadow with the substance in its own inimitable way. In the old grammar schools, the English equivalent of *amplification* was 'abundance' (*copia*). *Copia* and copying were elided. Boys were trained to use 'proverbs and sententious quotations from the poets as amplifying matter in the development of some commonplace'. Such methods 'instilled in the boys the habit of discovering everything that might be said for or against a general proposition, but it did not set out expressly to develop originality'.[12] A masterly understatement. In fact, English miniloquence, though not plugged with the same rigour as French orotundity, is a hidden, part abashed and part arrogant, rhetoric: the rhetoric of litotes and anti-intellectualism. Like amplification, it too is a high-infidelity system. On a more common-or-garden level, pupils in Britain and the United States have long been requested, as an exercise, to complete series of set expressions ('black as a …'), which is designed to promote respect for clichés. (I once completed such a test myself, scored 69.3 per cent: a borderline first.[13] My fate is to play with the stiffs.) It is argued that the teaching and learning of clichés is a major part of our apprenticeship as social animals. 'Say after me' is what every parent, elocution tutor or classroom teacher instructs. What we have learned, except when it falls through our memory-holes, weighs on our minds. As well as correction (as in 'house of correction'), there is also discipline: either a code or an instrument for punishing its infringers. 'Teaching a lesson': we all are familiar with the punitive aspect of education. Pedantry is heavy, though some, like Lamb, find it restful: 'I love to lose myself in other men's minds. When I am not walking, I am reading; I cannot sit and think. Books think for me.'[14] Famously, Churchill said of magisterial corrections: 'This is the kind of pedantry up with which I will not put'. A cliché by now, but a living one: many truths have to be repeated if there is to be any hope of affecting attitudes.[15]

As if school were not enough, instructional manuals have been a constant since Antiquity, e.g. rhetorical treatises seeking to codify material and to mould practitioners. An influential minority has always tried to set the rest of us on tramlines, to make us toe the line. In those treatises proliferate lists of recommended, permitted or vetoed figures, or lists of epithets suitable for partnering nouns. Decorum and décor go together in such enterprises. In the modern age, the United States' back-handed gift to the world, how-to or know-how books, derives from the conviction that there is a formula, and a solution, for everything, success or failure. The native Sioux said 'How', the latecoming Yankee 'How to'. Despite having passed the hundred-mark, Samuel Smiles on and on. As Dwight Macdonald points out in *Against the Grain*, quoting as an example a manual entitled *Teach Your Wife to be a Widow* (presumably by putting ideas into her head): 'Howto authors make a living by taking in each other's washing, or even their own – quoting from each other or from their own earlier works (and padding).'[16] His explanation is that the Americans are

> an active, ingenious, pragmatic race, concerned with production rather than enjoyment, with practicality rather than contemplation, with efficiency rather than understanding, and with information rather than wisdom. Our frontier past and our industrialised present both incline us towards a pre-occupation with technique, with know-how rather than know-why.[17]

The tellingly forenamed Orison Swett Marden – effort and prayer – and his book *Heading for Victory* typify inspirational literature. In recoil, we might turn to Flaubert's *Bouvard et Pécuchet*, a great how-not-to book, though its cataloguing of failure makes no attempt to suggest how success might be achieved.

One suggestion at least potentially fertile was that of Ludwig Börne, a German writer who in 1823 wrote *The Art of Becoming an Original Writer in Three Days*. A great admirer of the punning and dreaming and highly productive Jean Paul, Börne argued, no doubt with his tongue in his cheek but his hand on his heart, that what mankind needed most today were unthinking books. On the premiss that the true act of self-education lay in the art of making oneself unwitting, Börne advised the aspiring original to take some paper and for three days on end to write down 'without fabrication or hypocrisy, everything that comes into your head'. After the three days, 'you will be quite out of your senses with astonishment at the new and unheard-of thoughts you have had'. It is easy to see why Freud pricked up his ears on reading this around the age of fourteen. Freud's memory, he confessed himself, was haunted by this text throughout his life, especially by the phrase: 'The censorship of governments is less oppressive than the censorship exercised by public opinion over our intellectual productions.' Freud admitted that Börne's text first suggested to him the concept of free association. So, Börne's free-play of ideas set off in Freud a train of thought which later enabled him to pin down his patients' neuroses, and then, on a good day, to release them from their psychic bonds. That particular, ironic manual encouraged creative thinking.[18]

Slogans are less 'how to' than 'what to'. They telescope and simplify, as we will see later. Jargon, however, very much at home in pedagogy, veers more towards ornament and pomposity, like much earlier educational practice. Today educational discourse is prolific in jargoneering. Initially, jargon is closely related to neologism, for it is a new, special language. That is, when it is necessary, in order to service the expressive needs of a new science or form of behaviour. Many versions, however, innovate less than they obfuscate: 'Obscuranto' or 'Eurospeak'. Raymond Queneau's variation is 'l'européen vernaculaire ou le néo-babélien ... Vous ferchtéer l'iouropéen?' (Compristand Uropean?).[19] On an even wider stage, Clare Booth Luce coined a beauty when she said: 'Much of what Mr. [Vice-President, Henry] Wallace calls his global thinking is, no matter how you slice it, still Globaloney.'[20]

Originally, jargon meant avian warbling; and the rigmarole of rabid feminists might be aptly called bird-song. Philip Howard, a devoted student of the whole phenomenon, analyses it into three main components: esoteric (short-hand, an in-language); hybrid discourse (pidgin); and falsely inflated style (preciosity, pedantry): the 'borborygm of obfuscation'.[21] Jargon, cant, slang all seek to create a private, exclusive enclave in language, to talk secretly, as twins often do. This pulling the blanket to one side of the communal bed is self-evidently selfish, and anti-social. Though it appeals to a homogeneous group it is, viewed from outside, non-cooperative. Yet strangely, as Mencken puts it, it is prevalent among all varieties of 'sucklers at the public teat'.[22] State-servants are often self-serving, with mainly tribal loyalties. Jargon functions as a charlatan's disguise of platitude. 'The metaphors of scientism tempt us with a sham authority; they keep the ordinary from sounding commonplace.'[23] They can also cloak dangerous subjects in euphemism. Sounding precise, jargon often promotes vagueness. 'Imprecision offers scope.'[24] Above all, it betrays a fear of simplicity, of plain speech. An example: 'Summarising, the vehicle of a stock simile can metaphorically motivate its tertium in two separate ways: one due to domain incongruency and another due to salience imbalance with consequent hyperbole.'[25] Is this attempt to sound 'scientific', this catch-all lingo, any less secretive, in effect if not perhaps in intention, than thieves' cant?

Sexologists should have by now convinced us that length has no connection with quality (even if gimcrack tailors take the opposite line), so why do people anxiously prefer the longer word, thinking it more impressive? Why do students write longer essays, and teachers longer books, than they generally need? To talk like a book is known in old slang (and it sounds like fellatio) as 'to swallow the dick'. Insiders do not see the dead metaphors which, in their community, are the accepted tokens of communication, and so are blind to their frequent collision or mismatch in their shop-talk. Bolinger traces the evolution of this process in 'Johnny', the archetypal schoolchild:

> Writing is such an alien activity that he overreaches himself. Stepping into a written paragraph for him is like stepping into a Paris salon – to play safe he dons the most formal style he can lay hands on, and since he has little acquaintance with formal styles, he combines purple tails with a frilled shirt and forgets that he is still wearing his work trousers. As more and more Johnnies spread by capillary action through the professions, the level of prose sinks with a dead weight. By sheer numbers, Johnny's ineptitudes are transformed. The more Johnnies there are in contact with one another and performing the same activities, the more their altered language becomes a badge of their class. Jargon takes on the function of a SOCIOLECT ... A solidarity of Bureaucrats, whose bureaucratese is their password.[26]

This 'barnacular' (a nice blend: barnacled vernacular), this parasitic growth on the body linguistic, parallels cliché in its fostering of a formulaic, repeatable discourse, applicable willy-nilly and automatically. It too is unthinking. Psychobabble, that distinctively Californian promotion, affords us a view of what I would call shrink-wrapping in action. Just as Eric Partridge found commercialese self-defeating – 'Business English, in short, is extremely un-businesslike'[27] – so psychobabble can be seen as 'a set of repetitive verbal formalities that kills off the very spontaneity, candor, and understanding it pretends to promote'.[28] Nor is it a uniquely twentieth-century phenomenon, for Kierkegaard a century ago was already observing that 'our age ... demands, if not lofty then at least loud-voiced pathos, if not speculation then surely results, if not truth then conviction, if not honesty then certainly affidavits to that effect, if not emotion then incessant talk about it.'[29] As we have already noted with manuals, self-help attracts foreign aid. Of one such supplier, Rosen comments (though this would be equally true, at a self-congratulatingly higher level, of many academic works): 'Viscott ... evidently trusts the public's insatiable need to be reminded of the obvious'.[30] It goes near my juvenile knuckle when Rosen quotes Viscott's proclaimed refusal to read in his field: '"I find", he says, "that in reading other people I forfeit my originality", when it would be closer to the truth to say that in not reading others, he forfeits the chance to appreciate his own lack of it'.[31] The damage of such cabalistic jargon is not merely private, bad enough as that would be. '*Est* may be an amphetamine for the spirit, but it's a Mickey Finn for the body politic.'[32]

Such 'bafflegab' comes from private enterprise and from governments.[33] The superbly named Maury Maverick coined 'gobbledygook' in 1944 after decreeing to his subordinates that anyone using the words 'activation' or 'implementation' would be shot. He explained: 'Perhaps I was thinking of the old bearded turkey back in Texas who was always gobbledy-gobbling and strutting with ludicrous pomposity. At the end of this gobble there was a sort of gook.'[34] Perhaps Texans have always wanted to shoot gooks. Yet it is the energy of the United States that we import, along with the verbals. That unusually humane linguistician, Dwight Bolinger, reminds us that we are all in the same boat. 'To catch jargon aimed at us we must understand our own all too easy retreat into it. Words pass for solutions because we permit language to become automatic ... we have convenience foods and we want a convenience language, one with a formula for every occasion.'[35] More positively, he adds his conviction that 'along with slang, [jargon] is part of the exuberance of language always striving to keep one jump ahead of reality.'[36] And he makes a nice final distinction: 'The familiar jargon is the alcohol of our verbal drug culture, the unfamiliar jargon is its marijuana.'[37]

3

Howling with the Wolves

Language is by its very nature a communal thing; that is it expresses never the exact thing but a compromise – that which is common to you, me and everybody.

T. E. Hulme

I imagine no seducer has ever bored the pants off his or her prey. Physical, emotional or mental tiredness means that we cannot be forever on the alert to what we or others write or say. Boredom, switching-off, threatens all human intercourse. The eyes glaze, vacancy appears where once there was a full-up notice: the mental regions witness emigration. It is perhaps true that most grievances against clichés attach themselves to literary discourse, which is not where most people live. But all people can identify boredom, provoked by having to listen to mindless, repetitive talk. Supposedly less articulate citizens still have a vocabulary of critique: baloney, balls, rubbish, crap, tripe, guff. All of these state that the receiver is not taken in by specious words, words for words' sake, formal nonentity.

The central feature of clichés is dependence. Where do we get our ideas from? Even if some proudly think that they are self-created, such an attitude presupposes the existence of others to react against. Mostly we know that life means interaction, interchange, interplay. Still, who makes up whose mind? 'Ai-je lu cela ou l'ai-je pensé' (Did I read that somewhere, or think it up by myself?), asks Camus's anguished Clamence, trapped in the excruciating posture and imposture of his *malconfort*.[1] Even the most dogmatic of us still have open minds, are still pregnable. We are all secondhand dealers: would you buy a used idea from me? Dogma and clichés are things to cling to: life-belts, guide-rails, straws. Even when less desperate, we carry a heavy burden of excess baggage, foreign aid. Many of our brain-children are bastards. Mental contagion, Jung believed, sprang from over-close living and working; he honestly included the infection of the therapist by the patient. Montaigne was being similarly egalitarian when he proposed that 'nous ne faisons que nous entregloser'.[2] Plagiarism and intertextuality are not just legal or literary concerns; they are consubstantial with our very being, every man Jack and woman Jill of us. If such parasitism seems more widespread today it is because we live so much more in each other's pockets, in more ways than one. Pirating and hacking are only the commercial application of well-established habits.

Like the pun, though less fruitfully, the cliché is a labour-saving device. Everybody loves bargains, getting things on the cheap, with minimal expense and effort. Clichés are the lazy option, the line of least resistance, the easy way out or in. Even the word itself is often a convenient shorthand for 'an idea I do not like', so that, although past cultures lacked the term 'cliché' or cognates, the hostile attitude towards them must stretch across time and at least some societies. When we talk or pen them, we doff our thinking caps. They form one area where, for their users at least, familiarity does not breed contempt. Old favourites, old slippers, the Good Old Daze: clichés are comfortable. They furnish intellectual comfort, in Marcel Aymé's two-faced use of that term: mindless bandwaggoning, and the very necessary refusal to gambol on the wilder shores of whatever – the virtues of the peaceful mind. Many attacks on them are comfortable attempts to discomfit. Accompanied by this Musak of the mind, we cosset pet ideas. Many feel that, if these went astray, or were run over, the sense of loss would be grievous because of the dependence.

Although much divides us all, we share a great deal. 'In modern life nothing produces such an effect as a good platitude. It makes the whole world kin.'[3] Wilde was being automatically ironic. In outlook, he was less of a socialist, more akin to the fastidious elitism of Sartre's Roquentin observing his fellow-bourgeois pus-like at their gatherings: 'Pour exister, il faut qu'ils se mettent à plusieurs' (To feel alive they have to gang together).[4] Or Michel Schneider's variation: 'On s'assemble le plus souvent pour ne pas penser' (People get together generally so as not to think).[5] Cliché is, for Jonathan Raban, 'the most gregarious form of language'.[6] It becomes so ingrained that it might be likened to the collective unconscious of Jung, which was a spontaneous, mythopoeic level of mind, shared by both normals and psychotics, and common to all epochs and cultures. It fosters clannishness and clubbability (and we will see later how slogans and other rallying-calls and passwords relate to cliché). If a camel is a horse designed by a committee, then consensus is most often an idea settled on by a group. Chiming in with others' views recalls the klang-effects of manic punning. Similarly, consensualists look for family-likenesses, as if they wanted to make society a big happy family, to throw bridges between the islands. 'That rings a bell', we say, making the obvious association. Follow My Leader, Simon Says: even (or especially) games make us toe the line, fall into step (unless, like Thoreau, we choose to hear a different drummer. Yet even this sounds like directed action, and could easily become another kind of automatism). By common consent, most often, we do as in Rome. Clichés seek to promote euphoria, not unsettling. To this end, they flatter, appeal to fellowship, do not brook contradiction. They reject dialogue, like Camus's Clamence, and feign that they speak for all right-minded persons. Even great minds think alike, though this reach-me-down phrase is most often uttered ironically, for surely great minds are independent. 'Birds of a feather flock together' rarely operates as praise. The yes-man is one who always 'stoops to concur'.[7]

How could we be of one mind? Is unanimity ever more than mathematical? Even though bones of contention are frequently made of rubber, and fit only for lap-dogs, surely we agree truly less often than we pretend to. 'Orthodoxy', said the ill-mannered, swashbuckling Bishop Warburton, 'is my doxy – heterodoxy is another man's doxy.'[8] Doxy has meant whore for centuries, and it refreshes to hear a bishop preaching a lesson against pietism. Juntas, cabales, governments, academies, inspectorates: there are more than enough imposers of set opinions. Do we have to be a captive market or audience, play second-fiddle? A sociologist determinedly analyses the determinism of cliché: 'We could view clichés as micro-institutions, while the institutions of modernized society tend to grow into macro-clichés.'[9] Zijderveld coins the neologism of the 'clichégenic society' (more on the analogy, I imagine, of 'carcinogenic' than of 'photogenic').[10] His text repeats itself endlessly, like a mantra. Eloquently, if not plausibly, he reduces our contemporary complexities to 'Gnostic ideologies':

> Science-without-universities, religion-without-churches, medicare-without-hosptials, performing arts-without-theatres or concert-halls – all of them floating 'freely', 'creatively', liberated from tradition and traditional bonds. The individual is promised that thus he will discover his 'real' Self. But what such gnostic ideologies really promise are swimming-pools-with-water.[11]

'Gnostic', here, clearly equals content-less. As Christopher Ricks has astutely diagnosed, Zijderveld's 'fear of clichés is inordinate. Countless times he warns of their tyranny ... "It is a kind of brainwashing, and in order to be successful, a rather crass kind of behaviourism has to be applied." I doubt whether clichés do in fact work by a "rather crass kind of behaviourism", but I am sure that this argument about them does'.[12] As if recognizing the perils of overloading, the sociologist periodically finds useful employment for clichés, for instance as 'beacons in this vagueness, instability and uncertainty'.[13] Yet his overall theme is that of a conspiracy-theory. Clichés '[massage] people's consciousness incessantly rather like brainwashing'.[14] He does not distinguish between the probable intention and the likely results of such an enterprise. As with TV licence (and even the government thinks that nobody should be without it) and street violence, we become blasé about, if not inured to, strong language: it becomes clichéic, as does much discourse about cliché.

Clichés are so often the talk of the town, though when condensed ideas take to the streets in the form of revolutionary, or counter-revolutionary, rhetoric, we then see their energizing powers. By definition, they live longer than mere vogue-words or phrases, which have their season. Partridge: 'The cliché springs from the true, deep soil of language, the vogue-word from the top-soil. The cliché, in short, is natural, the vogue-phrase artificial.'[15] Clothes, and thinking or speaking or writing: in French 'le prêt-à-porter' (off-the-peg clothes) begets *le prêt-à-penser* (ready-made ideas). Inevitably middle-aged thoughts turn to youth: passing phases, stages to go through, built-in obsolescence, rapid turn-over; all of these convenient concepts attach themselves to the doings and wearings of the younger generation. The lack of historical sense unsurprisingly found in youth means that they have too short a cultural memory to realize how commonplace much of what they believe new really is. Turn this round: they have a sharper sense of the clichéic, hence their urge towards rapid and frequent change. They see perhaps what formerly it took several generations to perceive: that something is played out. The generation-gap is mainly a matter of timing. Besides, think-alikes may be more noxious than look-alikes (and the young easily distinguish between their own sub-groups).

Camus's *La Chute* is a most stylish, if fudged, attack on intellectual modishness and its potentially lethal consequences. A great fetishist himself in private life, Flaubert in his *Education sentimentale* belittles both revolutionary and reactionary fetishes. It is easy of course to mock the committed, but I cannot myself refrain from joy at the spectacle of gurus like Barthes or Derrida outdistancing their camp-followers, leaving them for dead. I would loathe, however, to kow-tow to that backlash which weariness with novelty whips some towards. When Schneider wonders whether plagiarism might be the concern only of intellectuals, he obviously stresses that the complainant must have something that is worth stealing.[16] But he seems to discount other forms: copying fashion in dress or décor, keeping up with the Joneses; or, of course, behaving as *badly* as others, as in hooliganism. Though vogues are short-lived, there are revivals (the *rétro* cult in France). Recycling (which will come, as it must, later) breathes life into the dormant. Of course, even when renewing itself, fashion still appeals to the herd-instinct, rhinoceritis, as Ionesco called it. Upward mobility animates peer-groups. People are often rushed into cliché with no time to think. Maintenance predominates in longer-lived groups. The book of common prayer enables elect or self-selected individuals to submerge themselves gladly. 'Unless the words are the same, there can be a strong feeling that they may not be valid, any more than the incantation of a magician is valid unless the proper words are used.'[17] Rituals are collective, consecrated clichés, and even such a recent attempt at conversion, the turning of Remembrance Sunday into a pacifist demonstration, had to borrow from the model. Rituals as clichés, clichés as rituals, the clichés of rituals next have their place.

While stereotyped utterances at funerals are maybe all that drained and strained people can summon or cope with – 'And common is the commonplace/And vacant chaff well meant for grain'[18] – the equally stilted words engraved after due deliberation on many gravestones or congregations suggest that consolation is one large area of human existence where novelty is out of place. The attempts to be witty or cheerful about death are generally black humour. Yet even the Old Testament allows for resistance to the trite, when Job's hymn of protest draws from his would-be comforters slavish repetition of worn-out songs of praise for what is. Only the resolutely strong-hearted would jeer at this example:

> A French peasant, taking his last farewell of his deceased wife as she lay in the open coffin, was overheard saying to her: 'Goodbye, dear, and take care of yourself'. The comfortable rumble of a conventional commonplace had diverted his mind from reality, and although the meaning of the words was lost their hypnotic power remained.[19]

In his study of irony, where he coins the splendid term 'wrought-ironic' for the more elaborately sophisticated variety of this figure, D.J. Enright truthfully states: 'Face to face, we resort to harmless banalities which the sufferer understands in the spirit intended. This is a shared, almost you could say sacred, acknowledgement of inadequacy, and irony would never invade it.'[20] In a different slant on the same target, Haig says this of the appropriateness of clichés for disaster-situations: 'In the face of disaster, words console exactly to the extent that they are non-specific and thus may be appropriated for the incomprehensible and the unassimilable. The cliché is fate, for it is predetermined and thus consoling in its unalterability.'[21] This strikes me as too neat a pattern, and I prefer the criss-cross of Diderot's *Jacques le fataliste*, where Jacques's Master, who thinks he is master of his fate, is a walking, or more often sitting, cliché, whereas his talkative servant, the self-styled fatalist, can surprise us, his Master and himself. For their part, most love-letters are famously rich to the sender and the recipient, enigmatic or excruciating to the outsider. These are would-be private clichés, whereas most are public. Even so, many lovers, like Emma Bovary's inadequate Léon, must have been reduced to copying out ready-made material and passing it off as their own spontaneous feeling; or even more pathetically, like Rodolphe in the same novel, dropping water on a farewell letter to simulate the expected tears he is incapable of shedding.

In less fraught social interchange, knowing on what occasion to utter clichés (by analogy with *savoir-faire: savoir-dire* – we still treat French as it once was: the language of diplomatic tact) reveals socio-cultural competence. On some set occasions, clichés act as a shibboleth, distinguishing those who know how to behave and speak from those held to be ignorant. They are wellnigh unavoidable not only in stress-situations but in highly formal ones, like the writing of testimonials or references – where we can so easily sound like obituarists – or in letters of protest, when we get on our high horse. A large area of comedy relies on misplacing or mistiming conventionalities. Some of the few better pages of Bergson's *Le Rire* study professional deformation and verbal automatisms, gaffes and other forms of fiasco. Trying so hard to get things right, we can get them comically wrong. In Proust, Dr Cottard moves eventually from missing his cues to a confident mastery of the appropriate use of lenitive language (salon as well as bedside manner), necessary for a man who had always been an accomplished medical practitioner. Proust was realist enough, even while ridiculing cliché, to recognize its inescapability. The whole business fuels some of the best comedy in his novel. The ham-actress, Mme Verdurin, has the habit of literalizing figurative expressions, yet by her equally strong hyperbolizing bent she wallows in the figurative. Thus, laughing so hard at her own literalizations, she has to have her jaw reset by Dr Cottard. It is as if her split sides had to be stitched up. She enacts metaphors physically, bringing everything down to her level, as her hypochondria does on the psychosomatic one. But down here is up: her art is that of 'faire accroire': this self-deluder ensnares her faithful *habitués*.

'Men are seldom more commonplace than on supreme occasions.'[22] It is well known that most famous last words are invented after the event, as if we needed to think that great people had significant messages to bequeath us. The awkward fact of life is that many of our most spontaneous utterances are clichés. It is only reflection, second thoughts, that even begins to make us see the played-out nature or the incongruity of what we have said – and we here is all-embracing. In the most charitable view, at such moments we re-invent clichés, invest them with fresh feeling; but the vehicle still cannot help looking ramshackle. At the other extreme, where most people mostly live, chatter (enshrined now in television chat-shows) indicates the dread of silence: clichés stop us thinking of nothing, of nothingness. If not life-enhancing, they are life-preservers. 'Phatic speech', speech used as social cement and relying heavily on stereotyped language, is not necessarily empty speech, hollow words. The phatic can be emphatic. It can be sorely missed, conspicuous by its absence. 'Er' and 'um' are not only meaningless but essential fillers, stopgaps, of sentences; they pay more than lip-service to dialogue. Interjections and curses seek to overcome hesitation. As Pierre Guiraud argues, they embody a will-to-power, though one that is generally frustrated or impotent. Really tough people act, and say little.[23] As such, curses in particular are a basic part of our confrontation with others.

Redundancy is crucial. Listening and communicating would be exhausting if speech were packed only with essentials. As our attention flags or extraneous sounds interfere, we need extra help to understand each other. 'Is he *still* doing the *same old routine as before*?' – this phrase re-enacts what it protests in order to underline. Redundancy of course generates tedium, forecastability, but how often, when someone has expressed himself succinctly, do others need to request that the ideas be spelt out or rephrased. As an alert watchdog, Rémy de Gourmont, admitted: 'Une page sans clichés est une suite d'énigmes; cela rebute l'esprit le plus curieux, l' "oedipe" le plus patient' (A page free of clichés is a series of enigmas; it puts off the most inquisitive reader, the most patient puzzler).[24] Jean Paulhan reminds that the so-called dead meanings of words are necessary if we are not to trip over an excess of connotation.[25] Phatic speech, as well as cement, is lubrication. In its sphere of influence, administrative and legal language has to use padding, repetition of synonyms, in order to block loopholes. It takes a deal of verbal caulking to make a document watertight and proof against litigation. All the same, recent attempts to eradicate mumbo-jumbo in official publications prove that not only high literature is hermetic to many people, but also the laws supposed to protect us.

Chatter can be harmless, some form of padding useful, some varieties of phatic speech essential for psychic health – but what about rumour? If much speaking derives from the panicky fear of silence, in gossip and rumour we jabber, fill the air, populate the empty spaces; rumours kill time, and sometimes human beings. In chain or poison-pen letters, rumour is anonymous cliché, in that a dubious claim is congealed, presented as consecrated, but no source is offered. Just as 'popular etymology' is practised at all intellectual levels, from deconstructionists to the man in the street, or in Grub Street, rumour can be up-market. How much knowledge is hearsay, or look-write? Rumour, as is statistically natural, is sometimes accurate ('no smoke without fire'), for example in the question of the illness of leading figures.[26] This oldest mass-media, word-of-mouth, is also the most elusive of social phenomena; legends can be seen as rumours about the past. Not only does it distort facts, it creates them. Many muck-spreaders try to exculpate themselves by claiming only to act as intermediaries. As Napoleon magisterially decreed: 'Les crimes collectifs n'engagent personne' (collective crimes are no one person's responsibility).[27] Despite the financial metaphor in 'common currency', such generalizers seek to be non-accountable. They want safety in numbers. Our common laziness about checking up ensures that we take far too much on trust. Often, circulating rumours is akin to proselytizing, and it frequently crops up in censorious milieux. More passively, rumours are 'collective chewing-gum'.[28] Notoriously, this loses its flavour on the bedpost overnight. When, comparing shopping-malls with old-time markets, Kapferer claims that they have become the common places of solitary consumerdom, and no longer the exchanges of sociability, he seems to reduce the possibilities for gossip; but he goes on to stress that the mass media, including telephones, can transmit rumours even quicker.[29] The 1987 world stock-market crisis may well have been triggered by computer nerves, rather than the grapevine of wine-bars. Whether on universal or local levels, disinformation can destabilize.

Our swallowing of rumours, for Kapferer, is partly explicable by an increasingly abstract connection with much of external reality. We hear of it mainly via words or images rather than by direct contact. Less parochial, we are strangely more naïve. Our hunger for meaningfulness, our cowardly fear of the fragmentary, which in earlier ages shanghaied people to God, makes us still look for a hidden order behind chaos, an explanation for what happens. However old-hat the particular rumour, it is always news to someone.[30] There are born-again rumours. Many outbreaks of anti-semitism spring from this. Rumours often seem caricatural, and some laugh, but their Manichean view of the world means that the sick joke is often on the victim. Like clichés, rumours reveal a fear of the new, which envelops the outsider or the foreigner. Just occasionally, they can approximate to oral literature, to a form of collective poetry, in that they chance their arm and ask, in effect: 'But *what if* something were true?' Such liberating tendencies are rare. As Kapferer relates, converging rumours more often construct a no-win situation. Accused of multiple murders on hearsay, Marie Besnard was found by psychiatrists to be 'abnormally normal.'[31] Rumours can make conspiracy-theories come true or at least about. In political terms, they can sometimes be the revenge of the marginal, the disfavoured. Just as leaks can begin a chain of disclosures, so rumours can be pilot-balloons or feelers. When the targets of rumour issue disclaimers, a common response is to treat these as clichés. 'They would say that, wouldn't they?' Certainly, to an avid public, denials seem like non-news, whereas rumours present themselves as scoops. Several times, Kapferer quotes the saying: 'Se non è vero è bene trovato' (if it's not true, it ought to be), as the presupposition or rationalization before or after rumours. Shop-talk or small-talk, as government propaganda dins home in wartime, can have disastrous consequences. The progress of a rumour illustrates the growth and spread of a stereotype, an unquestioned opinion.

Flaubert spoke of '"l'opinion publique", l'éternel et exécrable *on*'.[32] This all-purpose pronoun seems tailor-made for anonymous, smug and arrogant proclamations. It is, of course, ambiguous, for if it were truly impersonal, how could non-persons opine anything? As it is, it often stands in for one of the personal pronouns, but the question of who exactly is thinking or saying these things remains unresolved. It can be inclusive, or exclusive ('on ne fait pas cela!' = you are out of step). Much the same could be said of *man* in German, or reflexive verbs used in the third person in Spanish or Italian. The use of the infinitive for instructions in some languages has similar militaristic designs on the receiver. In Flaubert's *Dictionnaire des idées reçues*, it is used to mock the practice of opinionating. Where cook-books use it to promote success, Flaubert uses it as a recipe, for disaster, or so he hoped. Whereas a straight imperative is just one person ordering another or several about, the infinitive-imperative sounds like the will of God. As we have seen, the varieties of we – regal, editorial, co-optive or evasive – appearing to shoulder responsibility, displace it by sharing it out. Though in more colloquial French speech *on* = a real *we*, in general it is a cognitive vacuum, a black hole, a cop-out.

In this chapter I have looked at some of the varying ways people try to swim with the stream, to run with the hares and hunt with the hounds, to howl (as the French say) with the wolves: social dependency and opportunism. The ways that these practices are natural, reprehensible, or natural *and* reprehensible. Havelock Ellis speaks nobly but somewhat unforgivingly when he says: 'All progress in literary style lies in the heroic resolve to cast aside accretions ... all the conventions of a past age that were once beautiful because alive and are now false because dead.'[33] The polarities are too rigid. As we will see later, the urge towards the opposite reaction, iconoclasm, is equally widespread, mainly in the form of humour. Challenging clichés, conventional beliefs, easily provokes violence and certainly shock. But we cannot think of them as bad language or bad thinking. If they had no seduction, no apparent rightness, they would never catch on. Chamfort wrote it was a safe bet that every received idea is stupid for it has been agreed on by the greatest number.[34] The very idea of commonplaces brings out the aristocrat, the anti-egalitarian, in many people. Yet every one of us exists by taking in: food, air, drink, ideas, experience. Only the sadly autistic resist this take-in, tack-on, tuck-in; only they are walled off.

4

Swinging Between the Poles

To realize the nature of a cliché is not only to indulge in literary criticism, but to deal with one of its central problems.

Laurence Lerner

To write poems on a girl's leg is romanticism; to ban poems on a girl's leg is classicism.

D. J. Enright

I aim in this chapter to examine the stereotypes that have gathered around Classicism and Romanticism, or which their respective champions have talked themselves into supporting. When I discuss them I try to keep Paul Valéry's bottle in mind. No one, he reminded us, has ever got drunk on a wine-label.[1] I use these tags, then, as a shorthand for permanent or recurring types of responses, mentalities, personalities, and as a way into the habitual binary and polarized patterns of human thinking.

Nowadays, we talk of classics of popular or middlebrow culture; the term has been partially democratized, extended to big-occasion sporting events or to successful jokes. Clearly, the deciding factor is durability and assent: classics are agreed upon, unquestioned. Classics are central to any idea of a canon or tradition. There is indisputably an organic continuity between all humans since the beginning of mankind, and beyond that, residually, with our less-than-human forebears. So why not also in the products of the mind? Such a continuum would not rule out throw-backs, sports or jumps, any more than biological evolution does. Just as species and nations struggle for survival, so iconoclasm is as much a part of tradition as is maintenance of the status quo. As Norman Bryson has remarked: 'The relation of neophyte to precursor is in fact one of intrinsic antagonism ... Neo-classicism [in art] is a deadly style.'[2] Its opponents would agree. Classicism has its enemies as well as acting hostilely itself towards predecessors. Its dominant feature is, however, well described by Walter Gropius: 'In all great epochs the existence of standards – that is the conscious adoption of type-forms – has been the criterion of a polite and well-ordered society; for it is a commonplace that repetition of the same things for the same purpose exercises a settling and civilising influence on men's minds.'[3] The great cliché of classicism is that imitation is the surest way to fruitful achievement. It needs to be distinguished from straight copying (plagiarism), in that it stresses selection and rearrangement: inventive imitation. Art should resay the already said, or in the slogan of St Vincent of Lérins: 'Non nova sed nove' (not new ideas but new expression). Writers, no doubt, have always wanted to be the last word, the *nec plus ultra*. They carry out capping in its two contrasting senses of putting the lid or ceiling on a development, while going one better than forerunners.

One staunch defender of imitation, Roger Ascham, declared: 'Learning teacheth more in one year than experience in twenty, and learning teacheth safely, when experience maketh more miserable than wise.'[4] Where Romantics want to feel life on their very pulse, in their bones, traditionalists such as Ascham pleaded strongly for the vicarious experience afforded by books and instruction: distance learning. Both boys and adult writers were taught in an *éducation permanente* to submit to precedence. The justification, as for so much else, came from Aristotle: 'Imitation is natural to man from childhood, one of his advantages over the lower animals being this, that he is the most imitative creature in the world, and learns at first by imitation.'[5] The repetition seeks to drive the point home. Green has the apt term for this: 'sacramental imitation', that is, totally trustful acceptance (such as St Ignatius Loyola demanded of his Jesuits, *perinde ac cadaver*). This attitude 'reifies the energy of a venerated classic and thus loses touch with it'.[6] The chief pedagogic instrument was the *topos*, which pupils were obliged to keep spinning. In reality, *topoi* were static, however, and have often been likened to pigeonholes. Richard Rainolde defined them thus: 'This Oracion is called a common place, because the matter contained in it, doeth agree universally to all menne, which are partakers of it, and giltie [conscious] of the same.'[7] Such instruction inevitably produced much empty formalism, and centuries before St Augustine had already protested this tendency in Roman rhetoric. Yet the doctrine of the *places* (or *loci*) had its own, built-in ineluctability: 'Wherever the human mind turns, whatever thoughts it considers, it refers of necessity to one of the commonplaces listed above.'[8] While no doubt more thoughtful teachers treated commonplaces as both reins and goad, many pupils must have fretted restively. Despite all the emphasis on assimilation, instructors tried to justify their approach by talking of spontaneity. What they meant was well-rehearsed performance, art-concealing-art. The set-pieces should be so well digested that they could be reproduced 'naturally'. The arguable pedagogic value of the system was that it aimed to improve the memory.

So many agreed with this whole discipline, such a massed choir, that I wonder if they genuinely felt their lesson was self-evidently true. Were they preaching to the unconverted? In the same era Montaigne, picking his way thoughtfully through mazes of quotations, had the precious gift of seeming rarely to preach or to mouth a script laid down by others. Rather he offers a running commentary on a match which lasts over a lifetime and whose result is not rigged. As Lechner, after her sympathizing analysis of the whole phenomenon, concludes: 'Mental concepts are not neatly isolated in compartments ... But the commonplace tradition ... did not concern itself with explaining its own presuppositions, many of which, if not all, were highly contestable.'[9] A Jesuit, but in the present day, Walter Ong, writes engagingly of this tradition: '"O tempora! O mores!" – this piece which Cicero put down in the Catalinarian orations he must have used elsewhere any number of times. It was the "things-are-going-to-pot" *topos* or "bit".'[10] He divides the method into analytic and cumulative commonplaces – the latter the more common, and describable as purple patches or set-pieces, but always prefabricated. Rhetoric and oratory lorded it over the entire tradition, to the extent that literature and education were conducted and structured in rhetorical terms. Ong points out that it centres on two basic, binary themes: virtue and vice, praise/blame.[11] Hagiography and knocking-jobs (or whipping-topos): a computer programme already in the early days of the print-culture. Perhaps it is significant that the antonym of *topos, atopy* ('unusualness') is only in restricted medical use. And utopia or eutopia (no place or lovely place) are hardly of this world at all. *Topos* rules the roost.

The equivalent French tradition is, as befits that culture, even more intellectually incestuous. La Bruyère, towards the end of the seventeenth century, formulated the classic statement of the mood or sense which lay behind such readiness to imitate. 'Tout est dit, et l'on vient trop tard depuis plus de sept mille ans qu'il y a des hommes, et qui pensent' (Everything has already been said, and we come too late to a world where men have been thinking for seven thousand years).[12] Nearly three hundred years later, Lautréamont, brazenly plagiarizing for his poetic fuel, turns that declaration back-to-front: 'Rien n'est dit. L'on vient trop tôt, depuis plus de sept mille ans qu'il y a des hommes' (Nothing has yet been said. We come too early in the seven-thousand year history of mankind.)[13] The Romantic boasting twist here rings hollow. About the same time, the Goncourt brothers recorded in their diary: 'Tout est unique, rien n'arrive qu'une fois dans la vie ... Rien ne se recommence et tout n'est qu'une fois' (Everything is unique, anything happens but once in a lifetime. Nothing restarts and everything is once and once only).[14] The hiccuping pleonasms here wreck the pretty claim. A few years later, and with good cause, Maupassant enlarged pathetically on La Bruyère's tight-lipped complaint:

> Qui peut se vanter, parmi nous, d'avoir écrit une page, une phrase qui ne se trouve déjà, à peu près pareille, quelque part? Quand nous lisons, nous, si saturés d'écriture que notre corps entier nous donne l'impression d'être une pâte faite avec des mots ... (Who amongst us can boast of ever having written a page, a sentence, which does not already exist, more or less identical, somewhere else? When we read, we, who are so saturated with French writing that our whole body seems to us to be like a paste made of words ...)[15]

The twin of 'tout est dit' is 'tout est arrivé'. Not only are there no new things to say, there are no new experiences to be had. In 1880, the director of the Prussian patent office petitioned the government to dissolve his department, on the grounds that nothing new remained to be discovered. In our own century, for a fulcrum writer like James Joyce, no material is ever irrevocably old or new, but rather both simultaneously or alternately – in a state of flux and overlap. The dead can come to life, the newborn temporarily die.

I confessed in the opening my teenage defensive strategies against take-over. Harold Bloom plagiarized my obscure life, out in the Styx. 'The covert subject of most poetry from the last three centuries has been the anxiety of influence, each poet's fear that no proper work remains for him to perform.'[16] He calls it a mode of melancholy, yet omits to say that melancholy has traditionally been felt to be the most creative of the old humours, so that a heavy awareness of mighty precursors can spur as well as cripple; these can be seen as trail-blazers instead of as monopolists. Tracking the mutating meaning of the word 'influence', from ethereal fluid to its present sense, Bloom neglects the side-shoot, *influenza*. When they contemplate their forefathers, writers tend to suffer from a chill in the head. Bacon, Bloom adds, saw influence as health. Montaigne, of course, was already a healthy commentator on influence, and the proper response to and exploitation of it. Bloom lines up the great deniers of influence: Goethe, Nietzsche, Emerson, Blake, Rousseau, Hugo; and its great affirmers: Samuel Johnson, Coleridge, Ruskin.[17] I will concentrate on the French tradition of classicism, for 'les classiques [français] avaient l'emprunt facile et gai' (wore their borrowed gear lightly).[18]

Already in the sixteenth century, humanists steeped in the writings of Antiquity were quarrelling about how best to use the common stock: as a corset, or as a trampoline. The growth of nationalistic feeling made many claim that their country was as great as the ancient states, and of course greater than rivals of the day.[19] Should writers imitate or emulate? A commonplace quickly established itself: the Ancients had lied about their achievements, and scrupulous modern criticism must set the records straight. The consensus in the seventeenth century was that obeisance was due to predecessors, though even a champion of the classical outlook, Remy de Gourmont, finds in this cult of deference a certain delectable falsity:

> La mode était à se défier de soi-même; il en fallait au moins la feinte. L'imitation des anciens n'est, au dix-septième siècle, qu'un prétexte à des créations dont on n'osait prendre la responsabilité. Jamais, en somme, l'originalité du style ne fut plus nette qu'à cette époque merveilleuse où des maîtres naïfs se traitaient humblement en pauvres écoliers. (It was the fashion to lack confidence, or to pretend to. In the seventeenth century, imitation of the Ancients is a mere pretext for works that no one wanted to take responsibility for. Never indeed was originality of style more pronounced than in that splendid era when naïve masters posed humbly as wretched schoolboys.)[20]

A child of a different age, sensibility and ethos like me wants to ask why writers were not then braver, why they joined in the chorus. Some, it is true, fought a running battle with the party-line of the Académie Française, but the process of centralization of power and the imposition of authoritarian government joined forces with conservative cultural values to make resistance difficult. The writers of the time, the best of them intelligent beings, were fully aware of cliché, despite the commonplace tradition. Much satire was directed against preciosity and other forms of futile exaggeration. French uses *phébus* to mean farrago, whereas the English form, Phoebus, is used only in an honorific sense for the patron of poetry. It was viewed as upper-class vulgarization ('My sugar is so refined'). Above all, subscribers to the classical ethos found its constrictions both challenging and convenient. The avoidance of the particular and the search for the universal was, however, a fertile breeding-ground for the commonplace. As was the cult of reduction, which led to stylish streamlining at its best, and loss at its worst. Pared-down vocabulary led to both poverty and allusiveness. The dominant cliché of *unité* (of tone and genre in particular) made subversion, or even maverickhood, both more difficult and more necessary.[21] The fondness for demarcation-disputes, the love of classification and of hierarchy, led to impatience with the messiness of the here-and-now. A kind of Platonic cliché prospered, which saw the material world as low and as an unfit subject for art. French classicists became the first abstract artists.

Always, if nature is evoked, it is the *idea* of nature. As Michel Tournier says elsewhere: 'L'idée est plus que la chose, et l'idée de l'idée plus que l'idée. En vertu de quoi l'imitation est plus que la chose imitée.' (The idea is greater than the thing, and the notion of the idea greater than the idea. Therefore imitation is greater than the thing imitated.)[22] Lovers in French classical plays use phrases like 'allumer la flamme' (lighting the flame), 'briser les chaînes' (severing the chains), 'moissonner des lauriers' (harvesting laurel-crowns). Sometimes, by a curious mixture of clichés, they would speak of 'couronner une flamme' (crowning a flame), as if the words involved had totally shed their material base and were floating like counters, to be combined at will. After stressing, sensibly, that clichés are thought banal only when originality is the fashionable ethic, Michel Riffaterre, whose insightful asides make up for the recurrent longing for systematization which afflicts him like so many recent critics, quotes the case of Fénelon, whose *Télémaque* was one of the most widely read of all French neo-classical texts: 'Horrible danger, passer de la plus amère douleur à la plus vive joie' (Horrible peril, to pass from the bitterest woe to the most acute joy). We have here, Riffaterre says:

> une esthétique de la plénitude qui répugne à exprimer les états inter-médiaires, inachevés ou rarement expérimentés du réel; et à des formes tautologiques ou très structurées (descriptions, comme la périphrase; devinettes, comme la synecdoque) qui contrôlent étroitement l'interpréta-tion du lecteur.' (An aesthetic of plenitude reluctant to express intermedi-ary, incomplete or rarely encountered experiences; and tautological or highly structured forms (descriptions, as in periphrasis; guessing-games, as in synecdoche) which keep a tight control on the reader's inter-pretation.)[23]

Plénitude, here, clearly means authoritarian strategy. Strange how the anti-pluralistic classical mind, favouring the one over the many, so often produced the opposite, especially in circumlocutions. Reductionism was often long-winded. One repeated defence of classical cliché is that it does not interfere with the reader's registering of the import of what is said: such style is transparent. We can see a modern hankering for this in Pasternak: 'It had been the dream of his life to write with an originality so covert, so discreet, as to be outwardly unrecognisable ... an unnoticeable style.'[24] In fact, the style of *Dr Zhivago* veers on the surrealistic at times, and it is unsurprising that Yury is appalled to find how far he remained from his ideal.

It is well to remind ourselves, with Genette, that, in the course of French literary development, classicism was an episode, a reaction against an earlier ethos, and not a founding father.[25] The struggle known as the battle of the Ancients and Moderns, while most acute in both France and England in the seventeenth century, is obviously a permanent war. This binary polarity derives from the urge to compare (then and now, there and here, them and us), from political choice (conservatism or progressivism), from religious preferences (original sin, or belief in human perfectibility), and from the conflict between generations. As with all such antitheses, it begat a great deal of overlap, shuttling or changing camps. Schneider puts the opposition blithely but starkly:

> Dans un livre, tout est volé. Le sujet, le titre et le nom de l'auteur. Et la différence entre les Anciens et les Modernes, c'est que ceux-ci le taisent et font les originaux, tandis que ceux-là le savaient et le disaient.' (In a book, everything is stolen. The subject-matter, the title and the [real] author's name. And the difference between Ancients and Moderns is that the latter hush the matter up and pose as originals, whereas the former were fully aware of it and said so).[26]

Classical poets tend to confess their larcenies. Romantic poets, if nabbed, blame theirs on a broken home. Many have always wanted to turn the clock back. Advised to 'write for the age', Charles Lamb riposted: 'Damn the age! I will write for Antiquity!'[27]

At about the same time, Colton was remarking: 'To look back to antiquity is one thing, to go back to it another. If we look backwards to antiquity, it should be as those that are winning a race.'[28] Reflecting less in terms of competition and thinking more shrewdly, he wrote: 'If we steal thoughts from the moderns, it will be cried down as plagiarism; if, from the ancients, it will be cried up as erudition.'[29] The idea of the decay or senility of the world was at the heart of this age-old, ageless controversy. If you are convinced the world is going to the dogs, you look backwards for your reference-points; if the world is deteriorating, worship the peaks of the past, the *loci classici*. Bacon's paradox – that the moderns are the true ancients, because of the greater length of human history behind them – asked the awkward question: how could the men of old have said it all, if humanity was still in its infancy? If, on the other hand, the world is still in the making, let us think afresh, keep pace with its evolution. This response was often that of scientists, for experimental science sought to escape reliance on classical authority. Was learning static or incremental (or, as some would say today, exponential)?

Central to the whole argument was the venerable cliché that men were dwarfs standing on the shoulders of giants. Merton's superb study of this topos backtracks progressively, so to speak, through the multiple exploiters of this image (originated, Merton concludes, by St Bernard). The Saint who is now better known as a brandy-toting rescue-dog: clichés have some mobility. It is self-evidently a very basic idea, for it encapsulates the crucial question: where do we get our ideas from? And secondly: is there any progress in understanding over time? Physically, the image is less one of a piggy-back than of that human pyramid much beloved of police motor-cycle teams at exhibitions. The giants clearly stand for the stock-pile: accumulated knowledge. Even champions of the Ancients were occasionally perspicacious enough to see that the topos was not unambiguously flattering, as latecomers could say the giants are our footstools.[30] The image represents a calling to order, or as Merton puts it in an erudite pun, 'a mnemonic gnome about gnomes'.[31] He relates how the Moderns twisted the cliché to suit their own cause, making the ancients the puny ones. As a matter of fact we know there are pygmies. There have never been giants, except as figments. The superiority of the past exists only in some men's minds. Merton's seems the sanest response. His book is a defence of plagiarism honestly conducted. Just as the topos combines humility and self-confidence, his own stance is self-mockingly boastful; he parades both his erudition and his ignorance. The thought his study provokes is that the whole question is not so much 'Which came first, the chicken or the egg?' but rather, 'Which came first, the cliché or the original idea?' For it is often the latecomer using a topos who sounds most original, by providing the most telling support, context or formulation, or merely by lending his/her glamour, if he/she happens to become more famous than paltry forerunners. Marx, who knew very well how much of progress is farce, said that every giant spawns a dwarf. That is the common pattern, but it does not rule out the occasional birth of a giant, in whatever era.

Continuing the investigation of polarities and overlap; remembering the wise man (or guy) who said: 'The world is divided into two types of people. Those who believe you can make generalizations like this, and those who do not;' and wondering whether what most distinguishes us from computers is our ability to say Yo or Nes, I turn to embrace Romanticism. If the truest message of the classical credo is that we must learn from others, the worst feature of Romanticism is the belief that the singular self is the only source and arbiter of everything valuable. I speak as a descendant of Romanticism. In one of his more pussy-footing moments, T. S. Eliot declared: 'To be original with the minimum of alteration is sometimes more distinguished than to be original with the maximum of alteration.'[32] If not hedging his bets, he is here measuring out his preferences with a pipette. Much of the opposition between the two modes rests on an unexamined cliché. Why is it assumed that writers in pre-Romantic cultures were not every bit as vainglorious, as propriet-orial about their ideas or their language, as more modern authors? How could writers in the age of the 'Sun King', Louis XIV, obsessed as they were with *gloire* and *honneur*, not have cared about protecting their own particularity? Is not a modest author, in any age, an oxymoron, a contradiction in terms? Romanticism aimed, in theory at least, to take off the straitjacket of the classical concept of *bienséance*, decorum, for why should the social prejudices of a limited class dominate the products of the intellect? But then the more provocative Romantics insulted and helped to call into being the class of philistines. How different is this from classical elitism? Not only Eliot, but his French counterpart and partial model, Paul Valéry saw fit to issue a mugwump statement: 'Two dangers threaten the world: order and disorder.'

Henry Miller best typifies the latter peril: 'The new always carries with it the sense of violation, of sacrifice. What is dead is sacred; what is new, that is, *different*, is evil, dangerous, or subversive.'[33] But perhaps it was the seventy-five-year-old Young who made the classic statement of the anti-classical case. To this end he recycles the Baconian paradox based on the dwarfs/giants topos, and confronts the anxiety of influence:

> Why are Originals so few? not because the writer's harvest is over, the great reapers of antiquity having left nothing to be gleaned after them ... but because illustrious examples engross, prejudice and intimidate ... Too formidable an idea of their superiority, like a spectre, would fright us out of a proper use of our wits; and dwarf our understanding, by making a giant of theirs.[34]

His own paradox is: 'The less we copy the renowned antients, we shall resemble them the more' (p. 11), and he asks the crucial question: 'Born Originals, how comes it to pass that we die Copies?' (p. 20). And the rhetorical: 'Who hath fathomed the mind of man?' to which he replies: 'Its bounds are as unknown as those of the creation' (p. 22). The open-ended versus the end-stopper.

It has often been remarked that the French Romantics' desire to write only personal accounts were often couched in clichés, or, as Amossy and Rosen prefer, the discourse of the Other intrudes when they wish to say

'I'.[35] Perhaps it was a way of admitting that asocialism was, after all, impossible. The overhang, or hang-over, of classical rhetoric into Romantic writing is notorious. Musset illustrates all this well. He pens a letter warning a friend that if he does not take steps to avoid platitudes, he will become one himself, 'un lieu commun, un carrefour où les idées les plus rebattues traîneront comme autant de prostituées déguenillées' (a commonplace, a crossroads where the most shopworn ideas will hang around like so many ragged whores).[36] He had lifted the image from Gautier. He suffered from suppressed clichés:

> Je hais comme la mort l'état de plagiaire;
> Mon verre n'est pas grand mais je bois dans mon verre.
> (I have a mortal hatred of plagiarism: I drink out of my own
> glass even though it is small.)[37]

This was his response to the charge that he had filched from Byron in another work. In 'Namouna', Musset counter-attacked; Byron had stolen from the Italians: 'Even planting cabbages is an imitation of someone.'[38] As Lerner comments, Romantics tend to bully commonplaces, instead of parading them serenely.[39] They refused to countenance the long tradition of seeing commonplaces as the norm and not as a deviation. More than ironically, it was the allegedly subservient and conservative half of the human race who were to prove significantly responsible for introducing individualism, the private viewpoint, principally via the novels they wrote, into literature.

Of course, even in the olden days, a common counter-topos existed to the reverence for precedence: the boast of saying things never before expressed (as in Milton's 'things unattempted yet in Prose or Rhime').[40] As Curtius stresses, the commonplace of the world upside-down or out-of-joint is also ancient.[41] If we say that twisting is thus built into tradition, does this make it only a licensed fool, a reversal of roles about as revolutionary as Christmas Day in the Army? When Curtius adds that 'comic motifs have more vitality than others',[42] can we take this to mean that, to boggle a metaphor, piss-taking is unquenchable? He is alert to the fact that tradition is not linear, but can also involve leapfrogging or backtracking. Pointing out that the moderns were sometimes called 'neoterics', he mentions the variant: 'neuterics', those who were *neither* of both.[43] Dr Johnson shows more worked-for measure than the Eliot or Valéry lines quoted above: 'What is new is opposed, because most are unwilling to be taught; and what is known is rejected, because it is not sufficiently considered, that men more frequently require to be reminded than informed.'[44] No doubt our forename distinguishes us; our surname indebts us. Samuel Butler makes up my mind for me on this question: 'If a person would understand either the Odyssey or any other ancient work, he must never look at the dead without seeing the living in them, nor at the living without thinking of the dead. We are too fond of seeing the ancients as one thing and the moderns as another.'[45] But then no doubt it is easier for moderns to have 20/20 hindsight.

What of those who see themselves in an overlap position? The French group OULIPO operates as latter-day classicists, rejigging the idea that constraints can be fertile. Corsets, or cod-pieces, set off the hemmed-in flesh, or are in themselves eye-catching; rhubarb can be palatably forced. (Constraints can equally be devoted to pettiness, as in the old Chinese practice of binding feet to keep them attractively small.) As George Steiner remarks:

> We know now that the modernist movement ... was, at critical points, a strategy of conservation, of custodianship. Stravinsky's genius developed through phases of recapitulation ... The history of Picasso is marked by retrospection ... Had we only Picasso's sculptures, graphics, and paintings, we could reconstruct a fair portion of the development of the arts from the Minoan to Cézanne.

Then, in a nice, and appropriate, reprise of Eliot's famous lines, Steiner proceeds lugubriously: 'The apparent iconoclasts have turned out to be more or less anguished custodians racing through the museum of civilization, seeking order and sanctuary for its treasures, *before closing time*.'[46]

Are clichés specific to a culture (and a *lingua franca* within it), and to an epoch? Surely each age has its own, but each is differently aware of them. 'A cliché, says Geoffrey Strickland, 'is only a cliché in a certain context and when uttered in a certain state of mindlessness', which seems to me true in large part.[47] We should not too hastily label something as hackneyed. This is clear when we think that parody of cliché is sometimes difficult to distinguish from straight statement. If often happens that only the whole development of a text, or section of one, signals that parody has been at work. At any moment, in whatever dimension of life, we can wonder whether someone is pulling our leg, having us on. Yet anyone, of whatever degree of education, is capable of spotting the inert or the unmeant in a statement. I would add 'intention to deceive' to Geoffrey Stickland's 'mindlessness'. Such intention can naturally be self-deception as well as other-directed deceit. Certain nostalgics spend so much time looking in the rear-view mirror that they court a crash against onrushing reality. Reverence for the past can attach

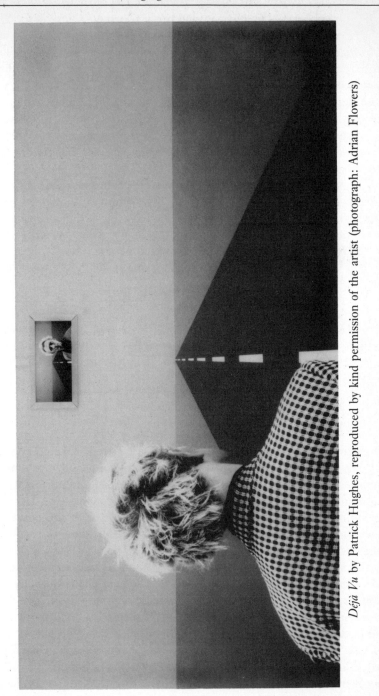

Déjà Vu by Patrick Hughes, reproduced by kind permission of the artist (photograph: Adrian Flowers)

too much importance to longevity and become gerontophiliac. The rapid turn-over characteristic of present-day life presents its own dangers. 'We have learned so well how to absorb novelty that receptivity itself has turned into a kind of tradition – "the tradition of the new". Yesterday's avant-garde experiment is today's chic and tomorrow's cliché.'[48] The older depress the younger by telling them their bright ideas are old hat ('I fell out of my cradle laughing at that one'). The wrong premiss of clichéists is to seek to deny change, when the physical world, human ideas and language are all in a state of flux. Perhaps it is the very dread of this flux which makes people adhere to clichés.

It is salutary to recall that 'invention' once meant refinding what already existed. When Du Bellay in his *Défense et Illustration de la langue française* (1550) said: 'Je me vante d'avoir inventé ce que j'ai mot à mot traduit des autres', he meant that he was proud to recycle what he had translated word by word from foreign writers. Howell comments on this ethos according to which ordering takes precedence over topic:

> It really is a way of saying that subject matter presents fewer difficulties than organisation, so far as composition is concerned. A society which takes such an attitude must be by implication a society that is satisfied with its traditional wisdom and knows where to find it. It must be a society that does not stress the virtues of an exhaustive examination of nature so much as the virtues of clarity of form. No guilt should be attached to either of these tendencies. Each is of value, and each is with us at any moment of time, guarding us against the excesses of the other.[49]

The present needs the past, if only to subvert it or to take off from it: nothing comes *ex nihilo*. While few might want to enjoy the smugly phrased bliss of Eliot, 'an easy commerce of the old and new',[50] we do know in our bones that they are mutually dependent. The Japanese distinguish nicely: for our one word 'new' they have two – 'pleasantly new' and 'repugnantly new', which no doubt reflect their twin cults of progress and tradition.

It must be the case that much of our thinking entails reinventing the wheel, either through ignorance, self-delusion or inability to see the same in a different guise. 'One may hazard the guess', says Chase, 'that erroneous identifications in human beings are pickled and preserved in words, and so not subject to the constant check of the environment, as in the case of cats or elephants.' Though he goes on to exclaim: 'How firmly the child believes in the reality of the word! It comes first; it is strong in its own right',[51] we must not blame language. 'It is through words that we are made human', writes Ashley Montagu, 'and it is through words that we are dehumanised.'[52] Either by our efforts or laziness, or those of others. Language is Janus Bifrons, Mr Facing-Both-Ways. This is very much the burden of Jean Paulhan's splendid study of clichés in his *Fleurs de Tarbes*. Like Queneau closer in spirit to the classical than to the post-Romantic tradition, for him the opposite of the 'Terrorist' that he analyses acutely is 'le Mainteneur'. We could say the Remembrancer, who keeps alive what is best from the past. He is a modern classic. He stresses that the same cliché word means different things to different people. Against linguistic prescriptivism, as his gratitude for the creations of popular etymology shows, Paulhan is no snob. The whole book is a supple example of lateral thinking, that is: thinking for himself about clichés. (And thinking properly for yourself makes you accessible to others.) One of his favourite structures is? but what if? The honesty is not diminished by the frequent rhetorical questions which drag in the reader to consent to the argument. He admits the need of the diagnostician to heal himself: 'Nous avons été nous-même ce que nous poursuivons. Nous sommes nous-même en jeu' (We have been what we attack. We are on trial too).[53] Unusual frankness, from this sleek Ahab of a rhetorician. In proof of his even-handedness, Paulhan admits, with the Terrorist, that words, or at least an obsessive concern with them, can take charge and destroy communication, in a short-circuiting of meaning.[54] He recognizes, above all, that clichés are slippery customers, 'une langue étrange, et comme double, que nous possédons tout à la fois et ne possédons pas' (a strange language, almost a doublespeak, that we both have and don't have).[55] When, however, he concludes by calling the cliché the 'site of incomprehension', he means that obsession with clichés leads to misunderstandings and sets up barriers.[56]

If he had lived to read it, I think he would have relished Schneider's wondering question as to whether we can ever identify a cliché in itself. Was Homer's 'wine-dark sea' already a commonplace, or a novelty?

> L'impression du déjà dit, comme celle du déjà vu, reconstruit un passé à l'image du présent, en une sorte d'hallucination inverse. Le nouveau déforme l'ancien en lui donnant la forme intelligible qu'il prend à chaque temps de sa répétition. (The impression of the already-said, like that of the *déjà-vu*, reconstructs a past in the image of the present, in a kind of inverted hallucination. The new deforms the old by giving it the intelligible shape it assumes each time it is repeated).

Lerner says he has stopped thinking that some phrase was *originally* brilliant and has since suffered eclipse; this is, he claims, a 'hypothesis for talking about the present'.[58] It has been maintained that the first person to compare tears to diamonds was a genius, but the umpteenth a fool or a parasitic knave.[59]

5

Scaling the Heights

i never think at all when i write
nobody can do two things at the same time
and do them both well

Don Marquis

Was uns alle bändigt, das Gemeine
(The universal subjugator, the commonplace)

Goethe

In this chapter I will not attempt a comprehensive chronological overview. I have picked certain significant figures from two literatures, who all typify, and complicate, diverse attitudes towards and exploitation of cliché. The cliché is the *reductio ad absurdum* of the work of art. It too enjoys a definitive form and general recognition. A Russian Formalist critic even argues that poetry is most consistently rehash: 'Poets are much more concerned with arranging images than with creating them. Images are given to poets; the ability to remember them is far more important than the ability to create them.'[1] Most works come down to most readers in highly compacted forms, for instance, often inaccurately remembered quotations. Our memory, too, often reduces to absurdity. Famous quotations become clichés when they are trivialized by inappropriate use, for example: 'To be or not to be' parroted when a footling decision has to be taken. On the other hand, my game father's favourite, 'On with the motley', uttered before he trekked off to his often tedious factory-work, retained point. Like Pagliacci, no less, he was grinning, and bearing it. On yet another hand, the mocking re-use of famous lines proves that all of us have a psychological need occasionally to deflate pomposity, to remind the literati that fine words butter no parsnips. Within high culture, a celebrated refrain like 'X is a sphere whose centre is everywhere and circumference nowhere' has enjoyed a lengthy history, complete with variants, stretching from Parmenides and Plato, through Alain de Lille, Rabelais, Bruno and Pascal to Marshall

McLuhan. Sometimes it is given a divine, and sometimes a lay, colouring. Schneider sees this as an instance of how an idea in a certain self-contained and apparently perfect formulation can take on a life of its own and pass with ease from age to age.[2] For me, it is also or even more an example of the perils of euphony and pattern-making, the first part summoning the second ineluctably, and therefore suspectly. A mental knee-jerk, of the highest order.

Since the late nineteenth century, a good many writers have been attracted to an aesthetics of banality, a prosaics to match the ancient poetics. Whereas soap-operas truly borrow romance, plug the exotic and the melodramatic, a sizeable part of serious literature has tried to take romance out of contention, or to offer a critique, as in *Madame Bovary*, an anybody dreaming of being a somebody, of borrowed romance. Titles like Henri Céard's *Une Journée* (when nothing of any note happens), Emile Guillaumin's *Life of a Simple Man*, Grossmith's *Diary of a Nobody*, or Jules Romains's *Mort de quelqu'un* (Death of Nobody in Particular) give the tone to this counter-tradition, a down-market extension of the Romantic cult of the superfluous man. It does not spring only from perverseness, but from a sense that 'banality, oddly enough, is what most escapes our grasp'.[3] While it can take the guise of simulated banality (mock-heroic, po-faced irony, condescension), it more profoundly addresses itself to the existential cliché, a life of stereotype. Then writers produce cliché-plots, overarching cliché, just as puns can steer a whole narrative, or public entertainment such as wrestling can be shaped into an enthralling catch, for, love it or hate it, cliché enthrals.

What can I say about Shakespeare that he or his myriad commentators have not already said? He makes the case for our joint dependence and initiative conclusively:

> The sun's a thief, and with his great attraction
> Robs the vast sea; the moon's an arrant thief,
> And her pale fire she snatches from the sun:
> The sea's a thief, whose liquid surge resolves
> The moon into salt tears; the earth's a thief,
> That feeds and breeds by a composture stolen
> From general excrement: each thing's a thief.[4]

Shakespeare's debtors have varied in frankness, but Edward Ravenscroft in the prologue to his revamping of *Titus Andronicus* contortedly confesses his garnering:

Like other poets, he'll not proudly scorn
To own that he but winnowed Shakespeare's corn.[5]

In a nice illustration of the sliding sense of 'original', Landor said of Shakespeare: 'Yet he was more original than his originals.'[6] Shakespeare is self-evidently the great remembrancer, 'a skilled conservator and reflector of the amassed wisdom of a sizeable portion of the human race.'[7] Because of the extent of his recyclings, Robert Greene called him 'Johannes Fac-totum'.[8]

By the late nineteenth century, Tennyson was cramming into one line a far more leery, self-conscious but not perhaps self-critical attitude: 'Staled by frequence, shrunk by usage into commonest commonplace'.[9] Eighty-odd years earlier, Wordsworth was less stroppily addressing the daisy as 'Thou unassuming Common-place/of Nature'.[10] Wordsworth tended to go misty-eyed and soft-brained over commonplaces. That line could pass for an original idea, as commonplaces are usually less unassuming than self-important. But Wordsworth was himself part of a daisy-chain, as is indicated by his epigraph to his third poem on the flower from George Wither (who was himself considered until the late eighteenth century as a by-word for the hack):

That from everything I saw
I could some instruction draw
And raise pleasure to the height
Through the meanest object's sight.[11]

The daisy assuredly is a commonplace, as there are billions of them. 'Unassuming' is an anthropomorphic epithet (or gynomorphic, given the stereotyped implications of the word). Why did he want to give the ordinary saliency, by addressing it, surrounding its evocation by ennobling white space; why did he campaign to make banality momentous? A 'daisy', in slang, can mean a first-rate person, or a chamber-pot (presumably because of the floral design often decorating the valley of the po); marguerite comes from the Greek word for pearl: the daisy has always wedded the rare and the common. In his poem 'Unité', Hugo likens the daisy to the sun, and, as Sabin persuasively demonstrates, the flower here is less a natural growth than a figure of speech, a rhetorical formula of praise, to the extent that the poet ignores the facts of a daisy's life, for instance that it closes its petals at sundown. 'Hugo's figurative style gives natural symbols a dogmatic, almost ecclesiastical authority rather than the force of inward persuasion.' In short, 'Nature's lesson in this poem is as pedantic and doctrinaire as a Sunday School lesson'.[12]

Another yea-saying, confident writer was Balzac, who suffered from a plentiful lack of doubt.[13] Though Joubert thought that Balzac's bombast was only a game, for he was never taken in by it, Proust felt sure that Balzac was in fact a dupe of the social glitter he often described. Balzac shows how the eye-catching can be just as mindless as the mundane: 'Tout est bilatéral dans le domaine de la pensée. Les idées sont binaires. Janus est le mythe de la critique et le symbole du génie. Il n'y a que Dieu de triangulaire' (Everything in thinking is bilateral. Ideas are binary. Janus is the myth of criticism and the symbol of genius. God alone is triangular).[14] Balzac commonly compares ordinary folk with extra-ordinary figures (a shop-owner is 'The Napoleon of finance', and, as Baudelaire noted, even the concierges are geniuses). This is a short-cut way of aggrandizing the petty, and of elevating the nineteenth century to the glamorous status of other ages. He no more kept faith with what he observed than minimalists who report that all is quiet on any front. With Flaubert, ambitions detumesce, and become principally negative, spoiling.

> Littérature: occupation des oisifs (Literature: hobby for people with time on their hands)[15]

Flaubert's recording of this received idea mocks both those who mindlessly spout it and, self-woundingly, himself who was able to devote his entire life to such a commonly disfavoured pursuit. From an early age, he thus parasitically exploited his enemies to justify himself, generally in a masochistic fashion. Apart from his own temperamental aversions, he received the nudge from the type created by Henry Monnier, Monsieur Prudhomme. A sketch-writer with a taste for English deadpan humour and Nonsense, an illustrator of Balzac, Monnier seems to have become willy-nilly his comic creation:[16] a type designed to capture typecast thinking, pomposity, truisms, Irish Bulls. A well-known example is: 'Ah! what woes are caused by ambition. It ruined Napoleon. If he had stayed an artillery lieutenant he would still be on the throne.'[17] Gradually M. Prudhomme swelled in significance the more Monnier wrote of him, and he was taken over by other writers and illustrators. He came to be seen as the quintessential Bourgeois, and is thus a spiritual and material father to much later writing (Flaubert, Queneau, Ionesco). Largely non-problematic in the original texts (he was meant to be a figure of fun only), he now seems complex; his myth seems to pose questions about the nature of thought and language. Monnier wrote a text, then light-hearted, now sinister: *Les Diseurs de rien* (Empty Talkers/Nothing-speakers).

Flaubert's take-up of this type, 'le Garçon', is also a ham, propelled by belligerent clichés, yet differentiating himself from his fellow-bourgeois by his sadistic revelling in shocking them. ('Epater le bourgeois' is of course *the* great literary cliché of the nineteenth century and our own.) In an excruciating twist he turns himself into a laughing-stock so as to make his targets, involuntarily, objects of derision. As Culler perceptively notes, le Garçon, like Rameau's Nephew for Diderot, achieves a kind of freedom through apparently signing it away.[18] It remains a desperately dangerous game, exaggerating so as to belittle, though Rabelais had played a similar one centuries before.

He is reborn as Homais in *Madame Bovary*, to which cliché is the dead centre. The dominant theme of secondhand living, whether the prop be a romanticized lover or ready-made discourse, ensures that cliché is the leading character. Even the conception of the novel threatened to be still-born. 'Bien écrire *le médiocre*' (to give a good account of mediocrity),[19] that is, to slave over trivial conversations: this was the founding oxymoron and the resulting strain. Yet Flaubert felt proud of his perverse ambition (like Beckett boasting quietly that nobody had written of powerlessness before him); he knew the aim to produce distinguished banality was monstrous.[20] Within the text, Homais's platitudes would cause him, every time he opens his mouth, to put his foot in it, but would also eventually secure him the wider fame he craves. In Homais, we see cliché leading to propaganda and self-boosting. If inadequate for the expression of emotion, language functions well for profiteering. This is illustrated by the differing ways in which Emma is seduced by Léon and by Rodolphe. The discourse of the official speechifier at the Agricultural Show, Lieuvain (*lieu vain*: empty space) fulfils the expectations of the listening crowd, as, simultaneously, at a higher elevation but on the same even level of successful meaningless-ness, Rodolphe's urgent clichés have their way of the receptive Emma. Convinced that human speech acts as *un laminoir*, a rolling-mill, Flaubert levelled much of what he touched. In the course of their affair, Rodolphe manipulates clichés, while Emma tries to feed off their insubstantial calories. She finds the platitudes of adultery relaying those of marriage.

Clichés create their own fugal patterns in this novel. The criss-cross of platitudes at the Yonville inn (those of Emma and Léon, and those of Homais) is itself paralleled, and upped, by the seducer's spiel at the Cattle Show, when Emma's unoriginal responses, and the droning officialese of prize-giving speeches are counterpointed with the lowing of cows, clucking of poultry and grunts of pigs. Homais chooses the conventional Latin inscription ('Sta viator: amabilem conjugem calcas': Hold your step, wayfarer, for you tread on a beloved wife), and recommends the archetypal weeping willow, for Emma's tomb. From the start readers are informed that Emma could not believe in anything which did not show itself in conventional forms, yet the clichés of domestic life are incompatible with her romantic ones. Even Homais's rhetoric is pseudo-literary. Only her semi-articulate father, the dumb servant Catherine at the Show, and her bumbling husband, Charles, seem to escape the contagion of misleading language. Towards the end, under the pressure of reality, Emma sheds much of her Romantic dross. After her months of sinning, her late-found dignity, and her briefer and more relevant speech, make something like an honest woman of her. We must never forget that clichés *energize* her. They get her, and keep her, going, until she exhausts her capacity for self-delusion. Clichés, like military harangues in the trenches, send her over the top.

For all his would-be implacable onslaught on clichés, Flaubert occasionally relents. In a key passage ('as if the plenitude of the soul did not sometimes emerge in the emptiest metaphors'), he reminds us of what clichés *conceal*. As Emma cannot break through Rodolphe's fake pleas of passion to the emotional anaemia behind, she thinks he secretes love; he does not see that she does secrete love: they pass each other by. The passage just quoted goes on to compare human speech to a cracked pot on which we beat out tunes fit only to set a bear dancing, whereas we want to move the heavens themselves.[21] A strange metaphor to describe a common failing, and of course a great Romantic topos: the ineffable. Harry Levin recognizes that 'eloquent banality' which Flaubert hoped to achieve.[22] Indeed, Emma and Léon speak volumes. They talk like books, but, at least in her case, she means better than she says. We as readers, anyway, need to believe this, for, if nothing distinguishes her from her fellow-platitudinizers, why is she singled out for special attention? A few strikingly lovely metaphors stand out from the general rout or rigor mortis of language. To this I would add what few rarely mention – the frequent clumsiness, despite the trumpeted concern for *le mot juste*, of Flaubert's style. As if a great choreographer kept treading on his own toes: it is a saving gracelessness. Otherwise, the perfection of the embalming done to language might chill off any reader.

Flaubert's correspondence was the drain, sewer or chamber-pot he refused to allow his fiction to become: a confessional outlet.[23] It is there that he can state openly, because privately, that, while the earth has its bounds, human stupidity is infinite, or that the bourgeois is, for him, something measureless.[24] Closed minds can, therefore, open up vast vistas; you can learn from stupidity. *Bouvard et Pécuchet* was to detail the lessons to be learnt from *la bêtise humaîne*. Taking off from a story by another writer, *Les Deux Greffiers* (The Two Clerks), *Bouvard et Pécuchet* is by its very constitution a parasitic text, so that its heroes' solution to their problems, a joint return to copy-clerking, is entirely fitting. How do they come to close the circle, to shape their existences into a big 0 (a cypher is both zero and a mystery)? Like all of Flaubert's heroes they could say, as Flaubert once put in a letter: 'I am too small for myself', a poignantly self-splitting admission. They are in their own way pilgrims who eventually discover that pilgrimage, retracing the steps of supposedly illustrious predecessors in the quest for knowledge, is only imitation. Indeed, throughout they have originated next to nothing. Their main activity has been to comment on and try out others' proposals, and to re-order them, messily in most cases (think of their hotchpotch garden). Their final stage will be the ordering (or simply the pell-mell registering) of the accumulated unwisdom of the experts, the recording of the mind's failures. They will be citing *ad infinitum*, and thus will resign themselves to monotonous work instead of from it as at the outset. Copying will be a relief from thinking, or at least trying to absorb, a welcome empty-headedness. But also, as with le Garçon, a revenge on those other writers whose idiocies they will put down and who will thus condemn themselves out of their own mouths or pens. In this way, Bouvard and Pécuchet might attain that 'perseverance in being' spoken of by Spinoza.[25] Two foolish men show up stupidity. This reveals both Flaubert's modesty (he often felt dangerously close to cretinism himself) and the clever strategy of homeopathy: treating like with like, instead of importing an alien intelligence of whose existence he besides had his doubts. His heroes find that copying (that is, acting out, putting others' ideas into practice) is impossible; knowledge is non-transferable, unassimilable. So the only kind of copying left is copying down on paper, reproducing textually: *clichage*. They learn the bitter lesson, forced down Emma Bovary's protesting throat, that it does not pay to carry over into everyday reality what they read in books.

Books, for Flaubert, were marvellous, indispensable, but useless. Hence his frequent equation of masterpieces with stupidity: 'Les chefs d'oeuvre sont bêtes; ils ont la mine tranquille … comme les grands animaux et les montagnes' (Works of art are stupid; they have the serene appearance of large animals or mountains).[26] 'Stupid' is ambiguous in Flaubert; it can also mean stupefied with joy or astonishment, as when he says of Shakespeare's works that they fill him with stupefaction and exaltation like thinking about the solar system.[27] This was the only kind of system to captivate him, for *l'esprit de système* dictated his obsession with clichés. His real black beast is pontification: bar-room bores, barrack-room lawyers, who, having nothing to say, say it *ad nauseam*. He once confessed that discussions about Voltaire, magnetism, Napoleon, revolution, Catholicism, whether for or against, got his goat equally. It was the very act of coming to a conclusion, end-stopping thought, that enraged him.[28] The later nineteenth century witnessed the start of a loss of faith in unified knowledge, after the ambitious schemes of Comte, Fourier and Saint-Simon in the first half, and the proliferation of mad encyclopaedic systems by those *fous littéraires* that a spiritual son of Flaubert, Raymond Queneau, spent years studying in appalled fascination. When you try to embrace everything, you grasp nothing.

It is ironic, if logical, that two of the great in-takers of French literature, Flaubert and Sartre, should protest so copiously ingestion.[29] Indeed, in his *La Nausée*, where the Self-Taught Man re-enacts the futile odyssey of Bouvard et Pécuchet, Sartre offers a *vomitif* to replace the smug *digestif* supplied by more consoling literature. It may be that Sartre's massive, yet even so uncompleted, homage-cum-critique, *l'Idiot de la famille*, acted as a purgative for Sartre's long-standing love–hate relationship with Flaubert. In it he forces himself to rehearse Flaubert's fascination with and horror of stupidity. In Sartre's analysis, the leitmotif is that stupidity is thing-like, concretized.[30] The reason for Flaubert's obsession, or neurosis (for Sartre treats Flaubert as a pathological case, though one of great complexity), is the passivity inculcated into the child Gustave; his father had induced him to believe he was 'l'idiot de la famille'.[31] Flaubert was indeed much taken with the state of stupor: the phenomenon in which, in a kind of mental lockjaw, any of us can stare (or read) and take nothing in; not so much absorbed in what we contemplate as sucked into it. Vertigo can result. Stupidity, however, was not only a bottomless pit (one of his favourite images) which Flaubert plumbed, it could also be a high column inspiring awe. In Egypt, Flaubert was deeply impressed by the act of a certain Thompson of Sunderland, who had carved his name in letters six feet high on Pompey's column; 'Ce crétin s'est incorporé au monument et se perpétue avec lui.'[32] A perfect case of mineral stupidity, an everlasting inscription of human egomania. As Henry James commented, to find a perfect example of stupidity like this was for Flaubert 'his nearest approach to natural bliss'.[33] The registering of absurdity depends on the refusal to allow meaning to another's gestures or words; a hardening of the heart, mind and imagination. In another travel-book, Flaubert describes seeing a telegraphist's cabin perched high up, and reflects that the operator relays messages he does not comprehend. The incident swells into a meditation on human incommunicability.[34] When Camus, comparably, described the dumb-show of a man in a phone-kiosk, Sartre's brisk response was to say that this was only relatively absurd, and that the broken circuit could be restored by the mere opening of the door.[35] The weird gesticulator (or the glass-partitioned telegraphist) is not as inhuman as the observer who refuses to bridge the gap, and indeed desires to accentuate it.

> Je sens monter contre la bêtise de mon époque des flots de haine qui m'étouffent. Il me monte de la merde à la bouche comme dans les hernies étranglées. Mais je veux la garder, la figer, la durcir; j'en veux faire une pâte dont je barbouillerai le dix-neuvième siècle, comme on dore de bouse de vache les pagodes indiennes; et qui sait? Cela durera peut-être? (I can feel floods of hatred for the age I live in rise up and choke me. Shit comes up into my mouth like in strangulated hernias. But I want to hang on to it, and let it set to a hard consistency; I want to make a paste with it to daub the nineteenth century, like the cow-pats they decorate Indian pagodas with; and who knows? Perhaps it will last for years?)[36]

Congealed crap to be made marmoreal: it sounds like Baudelaire's 'Tu m'as donné ta boue et j'en ai fait de l'or' (You gave me your slime and I made gold out of it).[37] Uncomfortably like that Geordie Thompson, Flaubert wanted to leave a monument scarred by himself to posterity, but the medium is the stupidity of others. From at least the age of nine he had collected samples: 'Comme il y a une dame qui vient chez papa et qui nous contes toujours des bêtises, je les écrirait' (There's a lady who comes to our house and she's always talking nonsense, so I will write it down).[38] Flaubert does not differentiate (the greatest fault of his muddling heroes, too) between 'les bêtises' and 'la Bêtise': incidental foolishness and profound stupidity; he makes mountains out of molehills and gets hugely angry over nonentities. Stupidly, he plugged away at sitting ducks he had set up himself. In company, also, he often milked a joke arid. As his old friend Théophile Gautier said of him, he would have chopped down a whole forest to make a box of matches. He flogs dead horses unmercifully. As Sartre stresses, in his *Dictionnaire des idées reçues* Flaubert fails to distinguish (and putting them in alphabetical order is an admission of defeat) between clichés, idioms, puns and howlers. It is 'un fourre-tout' (a hold-all, or, perhaps more fittingly, a stuff-everything). 'Plus d'un millier d'articles et qui se sent visé? Personne' (More than a thousand articles and who feels got at? Nobody). All Flaubert can

manage to do is to set clichés side by side or face to face, and hope they
will appear self-evidently ridiculous, and somehow destroy each other: a
truly passive activity.[39] Sartre's chief complaint is that Flaubert does not
analyse his sampling, indeed that he allowed 'the constant leakage of
thought or, to be more precise, the flight from thinking itself'.[40] Flaubert
does not give the context (place, time, class-affiliation): as a result we
never know who is thinking or failing to. It is as though Flaubert had
vapourized the speaker, and himself in the process. An arrogant elitism
and a self-lacerating modesty warred within him. His destructive urges
did not rule out a 'bump of veneration' for the great writers of the past.
He crouched in the foothills of the Himalayas; he was not even a dwarf
standing on the shoulders of giants. If indeed 'tout est dit', one way out
was to hammer on the repetitiveness of human discourse.

His notorious horror of repeating words or sounds, yet his general use
of reiteration as a fact of life; his predilection for the imperfect tense (the
tense of habit, of clichés: 'Tous les perroquets s'appelaient Jacquou' – all
parrots had to be called Polly); the insistence of *Bouvard et Pécuchet*, so
akin to Ravel's 'Bolero'; the equation of marriage and adultery in
Madame Bovary (one apes the other): life for Flaubert was an everlasting
radish, coming back on him. As Marx was arguing contemporaneously,
all repetition is farce. Flaubert's work is a mournful riot: he galumphs on
the grave wherein lies the corpus of human pronouncements. The use of
the imperfect tense (the very name suggests failure) turns even nonce-
situations into cliché. Proust noted the *trottoir roulant*, the horizontal
escalator, of Flaubert's style: its non-stop stasis.[41] Flaubert once wrote of
parrots as winged apes, and in 'Un Coeur simple' mingles together the
prayers of the servant Félicité and the squawks of her pet parrot, the
bird's litany. Religion as mindless harping. In this tale, as Felman
observes, repetition is even squared, the screws are tightened, for the
parrot reproduces also sounds which are already repetitive: a spit clicking
round, a carpenter's saw (and a *scie* is a cliché in French as 'saw' is in
English).[42] Flaubert's *sottisier*, his compilation of clichés, aimed to
silence the bourgeois for good: 'clouer le bec' (to nail the beak), as the
French idiom has it. The hotchpotch Sartre complained of was designed
hopelessly (Flaubert would never have penned 'hopefully'), not to
evacuate clichés (Flaubert was closer to Sisyphus than to Hercules), but
to saturate people with them, to give everybody a bellyful. After all, if you
try out silence, elective or enforced mutism, against platitude, the latter
still has the upper hand, for silence gives consent. Flaubert the path-
finder and Sartre draw closest together, to use one of Sartre's pet
expressions, always more plausible for writers than for sportsmen or

warriors: 'Qui perd gagne' (Loser takes all). In Flaubert, loss is gain. Simplicity is the goal which most human beings seem doomed to forgo. You really have to be born into it, with a tin spoon in your mouth. Though generally poor at discriminating (and this is the nice Henry James's chief reservation about his master), Flaubert does distinguish between active and passive *bêtise*. Charles Bovary, Félicité are dumb but (in intention at least) innocuous. The rampant variety is most blatant in Homais.

'The diffusion of ideas in the innocent countryside is the plot of *Madame Bovary*', argues Mary McCarthy.[43] Charles's dumbness (in both senses) saves him from the fate of his semi-educated fellows: Emma, Léon, Rodolphe, Homais. Bouvard and Pécuchet, who eventually learn to unlearn, streamline their over-cluttered existence, heaped with alien goods and evils; their genuine friendship outlasts the ruination of their enterprise: we leave them side by side forever at their two-seater copying-desk. It is well to remember such things, in case Flaubert ends up seeming only a monster, even *un monstre sacré*. He was a monster, as he knew and as we can all be in our little ways, but he could also laugh at himself in the mirror while performing the absurd ritual of shaving. I for one would like to grin with Flaubert's shaving grace. Was he relenting, or speaking the simple truth, when he wrote to his good friend, Louis Bouilhet: 'Il n'y a que les lieux communs et les pays connus qui soient d'une intarissable beauté?' (Only commonplaces and familiar countries have inexhaustible beauty).[44] Would the idea he long caressed of a book 'about nothing' be the only way to escape cliché? There, too, the urge to escape and to twist settles into its own pattern, becomes a counter-cliché, an elite talisman.

Flaubert is, as Felman states, our commonplace.[45] Our true Penelope is Flaubert. It is probably stupid of me to dwell on Flaubert's obsession with *bêtise*: a professional reflex or deformation, a Masonic signal, and thus a form of unthinking. It is so easy, it so tickles the meninx, to speculate on Flaubert's illustriously lacklustre *sottisier*. Like a good Party hatchet-man, of whatever ideology, the anti-ideologist Flaubert practises the unsparing *amalgame*, putting all eggheads in the same basket. Sartre, entranced, describes Flaubert leaning vertiginously over the bottomless pit of human *bêtise*, but a less glamorous image would be that of an unending plain, the steppes of boredom, the pampas of pomposity, the veldt of *Weltlangweile*. Platitude is flatness, dead level. Flaubert, inescapably reactionary, saw the democratic extension of suffrage and literacy as dangerous and productive of ever more cliché. Listen to Hugh Kenner: 'Art tending toward the general and human behaviour tending toward the cliché, we are back again to the fact that the supreme artist is the cliché expert and cannot do better than to imitate, as closely as he can, the procedures of the hack.' [46] Flaubert gives rise to, but cannot be held responsible for, such unthinking cleverness, or clever unthinking. The 'fact' has not been established. Even if it had been, such logic works only if the artist is merely a mimetic one, reproducing what he finds. Despite his passivity, Flaubert is more, and other, than that. A great deal of contemporary doubt about the possibility or validity of creating literature at all stems, for good or ill, from the example of Flaubert. When it comes to clichés (and for Flaubert it always does), we are all the family idiot. If clichés are ersatzes, they are also our daily bread. Some part of Flaubert's levelling was democratic.

Apart from the area of sex, many languages have more words, posh, factual or coarse, for mad/drunk/stupid than for any other area of life.[47] Is stupidity a choice, an imposition, or a fact of life? What a stupid question. Can we understand intelligence without trying to grasp stupidity? A Norwegian proverb states: 'If there were no fools how could one recognise the wise?'[48] We do resemble original computers if only in this, that we need a binary choice, though we do more interesting things with it.

Poised on the jet of their Cartesian wells, the French offload stupidity on to thought-less animals (*bêtise – bête*). English makes more use of the link between stupor and stupidity, even if we also lumber select animals with this burden. All students of stupidity run the risk of being taken either for snobs or for idiots. What indeed is apparently more idiotic than to spend years of your life swotting up often bad books? The real 'Enfer' of the Bibliothèque Nationale, as of any other library, is not in the basement but scattered over all the shelves. But why should we expose ourselves only to the masterpieces of previous ages? As Bechtel and Carrière claim in their *Dictionnaire de la bêtise*, studying stupidity does not mean advocating rubbish; it is a means of resituating survivors, the great, in the ocean of mediocrity which surrounded them.[49] Though they specify that theirs is not 'un dictionnaire des idées reçues' but 'des idées rejetées' (not received but rejected ideas), they cite many successful writers as well as forgotten men, and the link with clichés, pet ideas or unthinkingness, is fairly constant. The specimens are more over-heated, or half-baked, than in the work of their great predecessor, Flaubert. Many are anodyne, for instance, the strained theory that the language of Eden was Breton: *a-tam*! (what a bite!) and *ev*! (drink up!) (p. 23). More dangerously inane things are proclaimed by those in a position of power: politicians, the military or the police, the churches, bosses, the media, teachers, parents. But people kill each other over quibbles. Does the lexicologist Pierre Larousse's view that the members of pederasts are spiral because of the infundibuliform anus give us a merely quaint or a potentially harmful slant on screwing (p. 374)?

As fanaticism is the great seed-bed of stupidity, unsurprisingly a fair number of anti-semites figure in this chrestomathy (Drumont: 'Every Protestant is half-Jewish') (p. 401), though sometimes by reason of their loony notions on other matters, as in Toussenel's hatred of felines because they are, he believes, fascinated by asparagus (p. 54). The tenacious French myth of the prodigious amount of excrement released by German troops crops or craps up in Auguste Blanqui's assertion that Teutonic intestines are a metre longer than French ones (p. 33). True stupidity cannot be argued with; unlike some evidence it is incontrovertible. There is no room for dialogue with a closed mind. See the monumental quality of Brunetière's response to Darwinism in 1890: 'These ideas must be wrong because they are dangerous' (p. 137). The same man, the leading critic of his day, positively pleads for obscurantism ('The heretic is the man who has an opinion') (p. 227). But most people blunder into sense at some point. As a Dr Auvard commented: 'The only truly imbecilic things are vegetable and, even more so, mineral' (p. 240). What this dictionary demonstrates is humankind's genius for extrapolating, and our glaring failure to be modestly ignorant. The only consolation, in the face of such accumulated *bêtise*, is to view it as a kind of living death, therefore needing no further liquidation, as in those literally immortal (and deathless) words of Marshal MacMahon: 'Typhoid is a terrible disease; it can kill you or damage your brain. I know what I'm talking about, I've had typhoid' (p. 504). True stupidity is of course boring; it empties or stalls the receiver's mind. A hint of enigma and it can provoke thoughts, or at least seem interestingly eccentric, as when a Zola heroine is described as drinking her soup tight-lipped (p. 359). Ogden Nash, as so often, strikes the just note, snobbery merged with humility:

> So away with you, all you parrot-like repeaters of high sounding
> phrases that you never stop to consider what they actually mean,
> I wouldn't allow you to stay in any college of which I was the Dean.
> I can never listen to you without thinking Oh my!
> Thee but for the grace of God speak I.[50]

Or, as George Eliot put it, more soberly: 'The quickest of us walk about well wadded with stupidity.'[51] And as all of us got something wrong at school, we all enjoy howlers, or in the nice blend 'nitwitticisms'.[52] As well as common-or-sea pearls there are also the cultivated variety.

We rejoin the literary tradition with another 'grand exaspéré', Léon Bloy, who takes cliché on to an other-worldly, metaphysical level, while keeping his feet in the mire of this earth. He is a striking example of a writer who, though most of his values are retrospective (an idealized Middle Ages), is so incensed by the harm clichés produce that he coins neologisms, the new to combat the established. The urgency of what he hungers to communicate, and repeat, pushes him in the same direction. Writing is for him what Flaubert finally yielded to when working on *Bouvard et Pécuchet*, an escape-valve: 'Je vais enfin dire ma manière de penser, exhaler mon ressentiment, vomir ma haine, expectorer mon fiel, éjaculer ma colère, déterger mon indignation' (I am at last going to speak my mind, vent my grievances, spew out my hatred, spit out my bile, ejaculate my anger, purge my indignation).[53] Theme and minimal variations, the hiccuping of the great anti-repeater.

Commonplaces are *crucial* to Bloy. For many people who fret over them, they approximate to a bad smell. Bloy is obsessed with the rotting soul giving off this stink. The conjoined meanings in French of *lieux* (*topoi* and latrines) suit his scatological temperament. The epigraph to the second series of his *Exégèse des lieux communs* is from Philippians: 'Omnia arbitror ut stercora, ut Christum lucrifaciam' (I count all things as dung, that I may win Christ). For Bloy everything was a sign needing decipherment, and he proposes in this text the founding of a chair for the art of reading between the lines.[54] In his *Journal*, he wrote: 'Telle parole banale, éternellement ressassée par les imbéciles, est une affirmation prodigieuse de leur néant et ... par conséquent, elle est *divine*' (any banal utterance harped on nonstop by imbeciles is a prodigious confirmation of their nothingness and is therefore *divine*).[55] Truly, God moves in a mysterious way his wonders to perform, for the mouthing of common-places is thus self-revelation and self-punishment. It is as if Bloy were saying: 'Damn them, Lord, for they know not what they say.' (Damn, because Bloy was vindictive, and gloated over the fire at the Bazar de la Charité in 1897, where over one hundred members of Parisian high society, mainly ladies, died.) Clichés therefore have unsuspected depths. As the complacent Bourgeois is a relativist, a middle-of-the-roader, Bloy has to be an extremist: 'On ne voit bien le mal de ce monde qu'à la condition de l'exagérer' (We can get a clear sight of the evil of this world only by exaggerating it).[56] Pushing the logic of unwitting self-revelation still further, Bloy finds in it unconscious irony: the set formulae of the mindless mean the opposite of what they seem to say. Despite many periods of immense lassitude over the twenty-six years that he nursed his exegesis, Bloy with sublime perverseness thought this was his most original work. He had to whip himself up, quite literally, for he was given to metaphysical algolagnia, in the best tradition of the Romantic Agony, and was prone to speak of 'the paradise of pain'. He saw himself as engaged in an ethical linguistics, claiming that, where others have tried to disclose the underside of behaviour, at ground-level, he wanted to reveal the underside of language, which had to be pursued to frightful depths.[57]

The text is dedicated to St Jerome, the patron saint of translators and, as Bloy says, the cataloguer of divine commonplaces (p. 33). There are good clichés. In a would-be cleansing operation he compares to that of Jerome rooting out heretics, Bloy takes up Flaubert's savage dream of silencing the cliché-mongers (p. 33). Verbicide as a substitute for genocide, though silencing the enemy would lead to a severe fuel-shortage for his invective. The lexis of the Bourgeois is a kind of pidgin, or Basic French, of the mind; a small stock shifted *ad nauseam*. Clichés are thus paradoxically rich (a fourscore of them have generated his fat book, after all), full of meaning in their inanity. Bloy leaves it to the reader to work out that the proverbial wisdom of Solomon and that of the French middle classes are not of the same kind; the phrase undergoes a sea-change of meaning as it passes from one to the other. For God 'a toujours dit la même chose de mille manières!' (has always said the selfsame thing in a thousand different ways!), although divine clichés are full of thunder and lightning (p. 35). Iconically, it is true, angels harp. All this is another world away from the mean-spirited and hypocritical foundation of bourgeois 'good sense' maxims with their fundamental anti-Christian bent. The link I have already noted between platitude and flatness finds its expression here: 'Toute sa lignée, depuis les siècles, garde l'horizontalité absolue dans la platitude géométrique du lieu le plus bas' (The whole line of the bourgeoisie, for centuries, has kept to absolute horizontality in the geometrical flatness of the lowest place) (p. 153).

In keeping with his stance as the unloved, unpaid, unsupported exegete of unwelcome truths, Bloy claims, in a nice cross-section of his target-class, that he is misunderstood equally by the public notary, the sanctimonious lady and the suppository manufacturer (p. 269). He perseveres in his ritual undertaking as the mortician ('employé des Pompes funèbres') of commonplaces (p. 274). At times, commonplaces, under his pen, seem to be the true universal language, invincible stupidity: hence his periodic weariness in combating them. They are *infaillibles* (p. 419), like God, or his Vicar on earth. As Donat O'Donnell puts it, Bloy's thought is 'consistently "amphibological" – a favourite word of his, referring to his perception of the multiple supernatural symbolism of actual events and the supernatural repercussions of human language'.[58] Bloy, in short, keeps punning between divine and human-all-too-human commonplaces. Perhaps the simple truth is that all who desire infallibility are catholics, whether closet, emergent or professed. That is one of *my* clichés.

An anti-extremist son of Flaubert was Raymond Queneau, as unlike Bloy as could be imagined. Encyclopaedic in interests yet sceptical in all things, more often tickled than disgusted by man's insanities, Queneau wrote of Bouvard and Pécuchet as 'cultivating the pearl-oysters of human stupidity with well-tempered enthusiasm'.[59] Like those of his admitted master, Queneau's characters sometimes achieve with clichés a sort of low-grade but touching lyricism. It is Queneau's sharp ear for the parrot-talk of the human race that makes him dream up heroes, like the eponymous one of *Pierrot mon ami*, who think 'of nothing a great deal'.[60] Here, 'nothing' receives the strangely positive quality lent the word in *Alice in Wonderland*, by that other literary mathematician. Perhaps the most unarguable statement made in Queneau's whole fictional output occurs in *Pierrot mon ami*: 'Du temps eut lieu' (Time took place).[61] The observer in *Le Chiendent* notices bitterly that the banalities of café-chatter 'correspond exactly with reality'.[62] In *Zazie dans le Métro*, however, Queneau uses a sombre and antisocial parrot to mock human speech by his sarcastic refrain: 'Rabbiting on, rabbiting on, that's all you can do.' Queneau's own comment on the bird's role was that, as soon as people start clearing their throats, he tells them to wrap up.[63] On occasion, as if by contamination (and psittacosis is a communicable disease), some of the humans take up Laverdure's slogan, and they frequently repeat each other mechanically. At one point, four men have a long debate as to whether any of us can talk nonsense unless we have first contracted it from someone else: a perfectly circular argument. As the controversy lurches along, the word *connerie* (Queneau's down-market version of Flaubert's *bêtise*) acquires a kind of plus-value, as if talking rubbish were a social accomplishment. Finally, Laverdure and his own master, surrealistically, swap places – the bird carrying the cage with the squawking man in it, for they have exchanged languages as well as roles.

Queneau, now dead, is a living proof that the ludic does not exclude but rather illuminates the serious. His 'classical' preference for craft and graft over effusion is patently blatant. One of the figures in his ambitiously philosophical, enigmatic and comical *Saint Glinglin* realizes that, as a result of meditation, he has come up with a commonplace, but, because it is his discovery, the banality takes on vertiginous proportions.[64] Queneau, who was as fascinated by neologisms as by clichés, then proceeds to breed variants on the root *vertige: vertigénial* (a kind of prize idiocy), *vertiginosité*.[65] As Flaubert and Bloy had already focused on this metaphor, vertigo itself becomes a commonplace, the abyss a stamping-ground. We cannot, however, go further than the extreme limit, and so we have to accept at face-value such formulations as 'La connerie, c'est parfois insondable' (balls is sometimes un-fathomable),[66] where the posh and the colloquial bang against each other. Though he extracted much urine from the inflated bladder of human speech, Queneau was fully conscious of how fundamental clichés are. He offered no escape. Having declared that repetition is one of the most sweet-smelling flowers of rhetoric,[67] he illustrates, under the heading 'Maladroit' in his *Exercices de style* the whole Ouroboric (tail-biting) phenomenon:

> Coucher par écrit ne me paraît pas bien fameux. Ça doit être une de ces expressions toutes faites qui rebutent les lecteurs qui lisent pour les éditeurs qui recherchent l'originalité qui leur paraît nécessaire dans les manuscrits que les éditeurs publient lorsqu'ils ont été lus par les lecteurs que rebutent les expressions toutes faites dans le genre de coucher par écrit. ('Set down in writing' doesn't seem much cop to me. It must be one of those ready-made expressions that put off readers who read manu-scripts for publishers in search of the originality they think necessary in the manuscripts which the publishers publish when they've been read by readers repelled by ready-made expressions such as 'set down in writing'.)[68]

A circular structure like that of many of Queneau's novels. No wonder Queneau spoke of Flaubert's rhetoric as 'fending off repetition in horror and pursuing it methodically'. [69]

James Joyce was, like Queneau who admired him greatly, a meeting-point of many traditions and a great eclectic. I will now vamp for a while, and lazily, but economically and above all appropriately, merely marshal a get-together of critics' views on Joyce's liaison with clichés.[70] First, a no doubt shop-worn but still vigorous outburst from D. H. Lawrence: 'My God, what a clumsy *olla putrida* James Joyce is! Nothing but old fags and cabbage-stumps of quotations ... what old and hard-worked staleness, masquerading as the all-new!'[71] After citing *Finnegans Wake* (pp. 181–2): 'Who can say how many pseudostylic shamiana, how few or how many of the most venerated public impostures, how very many piously forged palimpsests slipped in the first place ... from his pelagiarist pen', Levine points out the double image: 'Sham is both sham and shaman, plagiarist and Pelagian, common and holy man', and expatiates on the long tradition of scribal transcription:

> pious copies of the signature of God. He was the first cause and as such the only significant point of origins for language. Transcription was not theft: it was, rather, a recognition of our dependent and subordinate status ... The old view of the writer as copier, always referring back to an earlier and more authoritative source, has been replaced by that of the writer as an original, whose ultimate value depends on a liberation from sources. And yet, as the lines from *Finnegans Wake* suggest, we may see writing as pious transcription or as deception and theft: total originality, given the shared nature of language, is impossible.[72]

Levine goes on to argue that, in Joyce's hands, cliché is subverted through recycling, a familiar proposition from pro-Joyceans, which sounds only just above the tawdry in Sabin's reformulation, when she talks of 'the Joycean comic art of stringing multicoloured verbal clichés from different orders of discourse along a loose sentence thread so that they sparkle and jingle in collision'.[73] Levine's more charitable version, defending *Ulysses* against the charge of being built of clichés, runs like this: 'Somewhere along the way the "familiar tracks" have been sabotaged, and we find ourselves derailed, bumping along on a jolting series of prearranged disappointments'.[74] Switching to a different image, or stereotype, McLuhan declares that 'the need of the poet for ever-new means of probing and exploration of experience sends him again and again to the rag-and-bone shop of abandoned cliché.'[75] Quoting Yeats, 'The Circus Animals' Desertion', 'What can I do but enumerate old themes', McLuhan might have gone the whole hog and cited Shakespeare's Sonnet LXXVI ('All my best is dressing old words new'), which is possibly counterbalanced by the later line: 'For as the sun is daily old and new'. I will cease here aping Joyce's strategy of interpolation, the thickening of the (Irish) stew, for I have said elsewhere how irredeemably corny I find much of Joyce.[76] I would add only that, on the other side of the paper-thin medal, Joyce works to wake in us the slumbering stereotyped paraphernalia, the trite detritus, of our semi-conscious minds.

Another area of modernism that underwhelms me is Surrealism. Genette, impeccably up-to-date, still objects to Breton's *style gendarme*:

> Breton chaussait le cothurne, ou le brodequin, pour le moindre pet de travers (la pratique de l'écriture automatique, tissu de clichés, y était peut-être pour quelque chose), et ce pompiérisme d'avant-garde a fait école

(Breton would put on the buskin, or the sock of the Ancients: he could get steamed up over a trifle (the practice of automatic writing, riddled with clichés, would perhaps explain this, and this with-it conventionalism has set a fashion).[77]

Julien Gracq, who being a creative writer as well as a pungent critic, is, even more than Genette, his own man, describes with telling intricacy how this intended revolution so often ended up in the banal:

> Une langue, et surtout une langue qui a beaucoup servi (il s'agit ici de son usage littéraire) tend à ressembler de plus en plus à un système compliqué d'aiguillages entrecroisés – où le mécanicien aux yeux bandés, beaucoup plus souvent que de provoquer quelques-unes de ces magnifiques catastrophes de locomotive renversée dans la forêt vierge dont rêve Breton, risque, plus banalement encore que d'autres, d'aboutir au cul de sac ensommeillé d'une voie de garage. (A language, especially one which has been well used (I am speaking here of literary use) tends to grow ever closer to a complicated network of criss-crossing points – where the blindfolded engine-driver [i.e. the 'automatic writer'] instead of derailing his locomotive in the virgin forest, in a stupendous disaster such as is dreamed of by Breton, runs the risk, even more probably than lesser mortals, of ending up in a sleepy blind siding.)[78]

No wonder the younger Queneau beat a retreat from the Surrealists and went it alone, that is, in better company. When the Surrealists proclaimed that 'literature must be made by all and not by one',[79] they were of course conning their readers, for by 'all' they meant principally the rest of their coterie, not the great unwashed. Their taste for ready-mades, for bad taste tastefuly plucked out, for popular posters and idiotic jokes, their fixation on madness (the deprived who are both 'automatic' and 'autonomous' or inimitable), their attempts to discover the marvellous in the quotidian, all of these became the decreed commonplace of Surrealism. In our present-day world, where it might be thought that 'the surreal becomes banal',[80] in pop videos for example, I am more taken by the reverse. Things as tough and long-lived as commonplaces must have something to teach us about the artifice of self-preservation.

The resolutely individualistic work of Nathalie Sarraute lays the stress not on the team-effort of writers but rather on those of man-in-society. As Sartre commented on her *Portrait d'un inconnu* (Portrait of a Stranger), in addition to the meaning of worn-through ideas, commonplace indicates the crossroads of the community, where we can all find ourselves and each other. It is common property; 'il est la présence de tout le monde en moi' (the presence of everybody in me).[81] Speaking for herself, and while denying that she is merely a formalist, Sarraute defines her own literary target in this way: 'Movements in an embryonic state, which cannot as yet be named, which have not yet surfaced in consciousness where they will congeal into commonplaces, are the substance of all my books.'[82] Already, in Gide's *Les Caves du Vatican*, the stiff-brained scientist, Anthime Armand-Dubois, had discovered in such 'tropisms' purely automatic behaviour. What Sarraute evokes is not a free movement which then becomes a prison, but a chaos which coagulates, and not a very fertile chaos at that. As a result, even those of her figures who have inklings of the spurious nature of social discourse, and even of soliloquy, have to resort to banality in order to express this awareness. She reveals a fidelity to chaos, a mimeticism not vastly different from a Naturalist writer's fidelity to observable fact. Reputedly Sarraute leaves politics outside the door of her study; she does not date or explicate her characters' 'loss of language', and it is hardly astounding that Simone de Beauvoir mutes her admiration for a writer over-engrossed by a kind of discreet, socially acceptable schizophrenia, which reverberates within a self-entranced class.[83] Nevertheless, Sarraute communicates a strong sense of a secondhand culture, especially among the supposedly educated.

Ionesco provides more variety, though he possesses his own monotone. The life-preserving (or life-boosting, at least) clichés of his little-men heroes fight a battle, which they lose, against the more crushing stereotypes of their more numerous enemies (for example, the herd, cuckolded by indoctrination, in *Le Rhinocéros*). A linguistic exile, a stowaway in French culture, a guest-worker, Ionesco tries to keep his distance from the more mechanical absurdities of his host-language. Yet the doubt persists whether he is really so much attacking clichés as exploiting them. Like Catholic novelists and sin, where would he be without them? In his prejudiced view the mass of mankind are stupid and engage in rhubarb-talk. He illustrates, and hopes to prove, this preconception, by making his puppet-like figures speak in far more concentrated clichés than anyone ever would or could in practice. Then, through repetition, and the ambient glamour of the theatre and its traditions, and of course his own dramatic nous, Ionesco begets an inane sonorous poetry, reminiscent of jingles or nonsense verse and rhythmically achieving paroxysm. The antagonists on his stage use Humpty-Dumpty words and pseudo-arguments, hectoring, brooking no dissension. The linguistic bully-boys and girls of *Alice in Wonderland* at least literalize or otherwise twist their set expressions (e.g. 'Take care of the sense and the sounds will take care of themselves')[84] and thus use them in surprising ways; Alice is always being nonplussed. Ionesco wants us to believe that, in his plays, we are listening to the animated corpses of our own speech. Behind the effort lies the fundamental cliché of despondency. As Susan Sontag pungently expresses it, Ionesco's early and startling plays are 'not "about" meaninglessness. They are attempts to use meaninglessness theatrically.' When he settled into his comfortable rut, his morbid farces became 'the boulevard comedies of the avant-garde sensibility'.[85] Among younger writers, Denis Potter's plays forcefully embody his belief that even, or especially, fantasies can be pure corn (*Pennies from Heaven, The Singing Detective*). In France the recent mode of *rétro* resurrects old corn. In a riotously bookish, that is, French way, the novels of Patrick Modiano update the cliché-life of Emma Bovary by breeding lookalike protagonists (or agonists). One of these, the wilfully-named Raphaël Schlemilovitch, not only pastiches umpteen writers' styles, but steals Kafka's TB and is tempted to purloin Nerval's suicide. It is a near-perfect illustration of what kitsch can mean: the twisting of clichés to non-productive ends.[86] Flaubert's agony over clichés and what they suggest about the poverty of existence seems more genuine than that of writers like Ionesco and Modiano apparently living off the unearned income of despair. That, no doubt, is my chosen prejudice.

It is hard for any honest person to disagree with Pope's lines:

> Like buoys, that never sink into the flood,
> On Learning's surface we but lie and nod.[87]

Buoys, of course, are useful markers of dangerous depths; and all of us could periodically benefit from what Barfield called 'the gentle art of unthinking', that is, escaping from the mental moulds of our dominant culture.[88] This does not entail the mystical flight into the cloud of unknowing, nor the retreat into 'absinthe-minded' evasion, but simply refusing on occasion to kowtow, to let received ideas through on the nod. Admission of ignorance and a regular effort at cleaning out the blocked passages of the brain might help us to avoid some of the perils of semi-education, of half-baked thinking. I do not plead the virtues of going native, of harking back to some mythical lost simplicity. The untutored and unread do not thereby evade the tug of clichés, for they have ears to hear, and, besides, many clichés, as we have seen, appear to spring spontaneously from our own depths. Clichés are both common ignorance (which we display when the answer jumps the gun on the question) and common knowledge. One of the several French terms for cliché is *passe-partout*: the all-purpose, fit-anything response. The servant

Passepartout, in Jules Verne's *Around the World in Eighty Days*, has the menial task of touristic sight-seeing (the bee-to-the-honeypot syndrome), taking mental snaps (*cliché* also has a photographic dimension), whereas his master Fogg unmistily sets his mind on higher things: the challenge of mathematical patterns and timetables.

Voltaire said that the multitude of books is making us ignorant, a proposition that *Bouvard et Pécuchet* set out to demonstrate at length. In that text Flaubert conveys the non-scientific mind's part-dismayed and part-jubilant discovery that scientific experts produce collectively a mishmash of facts, fallacies, controversies, fakes and fictions not so dissimilar from that of art. There is a lovely French term, *un pense-bête* (memory-jogger) which coalesces the two false opposites of thought and stupidity. Just as 'oxymoron' (sharp/stupid) is itself an oxymoron, and sophomore a wise fool, so wizards and dunces wear the same coned cap. An even more healthy chastener is to dwell on the phenomenon of 'idiots savants', those rare people with one amazing talent, who burst the stays of categories. One such, in Tournier's novel *Les Météores*, has total control, via his prodigious memory and lightning mental calculations, over the regular world of calendars, but none whatsoever over the incalculable elements (*le temps*: time/weather). Franz dies drowned in a storm, though he is even more significantly liquidated in order to fulfil his author's final solution of signs and reversals. Jacques Audiberti, who knew what he was talking about, coined the nice neologism, *onanité* (*onanisme* + *inanité*) to describe sterile intellectual masturbation.[89]

Is the consciousness of clichés such an onanity? Clichés propose themselves as ready-made answers, recipe solutions (or consolations), and surely people have always been aware of and frequently hostile to such posturing, for the multiple forms of parody and satire, common to all cultures, feed off it. This does not mean, of course, that the same clichés are familiar to everyone at the same time, which is the politician's chief excuse for resorting to them: the tiredest idea may still be news to someone. Historical allusions are lost on many people, and parts of any language are forever slipping away into oblivion or at least hibernation. It may well be that most people do not have the time, energy or yen to be watchful to the extent of fastidiousness ('chercher la petite bête') about language, the expression of ideas or feelings, and would regard such activity as spoilsport or wet blanket. We are all, nevertheless, alive to tone and implication. After all, where we live most of the time is the common place, and why make such a song-and-dance about ordinariness? If we think of cliché as typifying the unexamined life, that is what most students wish they could, and most adults are glad they do, have. Though we may like nit-picking in private, we feign that in public it makes us squirm. Cliché reminds us, and needs to remind us, of what we share, whereas so much tells what separates, indeed atomizes, us. Consciousness of cliché separates us out again. In a characteristically neat and telling turnaround, Jean Paulhan points out that it is not the author but the receiver of commonplaces who gets obsessed with them.[90] Flann O'Brien's 'Catechism of Clichés' is a splendid Catholic joke, based on the pattern of question-and-response (and they are often in Latin, as in the old-style Mass): conditioned reflexes: 'And what is comment? Superfluous.'[91] Indeed it is, very often. But such consciousness of cliché leads logically only to silence (the dry dream of Flaubert and Bloy). Once we become hyperaware of them, clichés become the unspeakable. Yet they will slip out or explode like curses, lapsus and other broken taboos. The boundary-line between conscious and unconscious cliché meanders.

As for the signalling of consciousness, for we want to spread the word here too, there are *italics*, which can underline the oddity or reprehensibility of an utterance. There are quotation marks, suddenly inserted in an otherwise unmarked typography, which also act to put something beyond the pale.[92] There is free indirect speech, which Flaubert brought to a high level of ambiguity, in that two voices, the director author's and the directed speaker's or thinker's are fused, and the tone plays uncomfortably between sympathy and irony. It is in effect an authorial double-talk, and a product of the less sure, or less blatantly dogmatic, modern mind hedging its bets. Or phrases can be interpolated: 'comme on dit' (as they say), 'selon la formule' (in the set formula), 'so to speak', and so on. These and the markers already mentioned stand in for the tell-tale tone of the speaking voice we can only imagine on the printed page; they are the tongs or barge-pole. They all add up to what Haig calls 'a graphic *cordon sanitaire*'.[93]. As Culler says of Flaubert, by use of such distancing devices as ('as M. Prudhomme, or the grocer, would say'), he 'protects himself from the stupidity which contaminates any speech'.[94] This is, of course, to forget the numerous occasions on which Flaubert encloses himself with the stupid, embraces himself (in both senses, for self-belittling can also be self-boosting). In his story, 'L'Enfance d'un chef', Sartre adroitly extends the lessons of Flaubert. By quoting without comment the potentially lethal clichés of those around the anti-hero, Lucien Fleurier, Sartre has them condemn themselves apparently out of their own mouths, though he is of course the director of operations, the hidden God – despite his famous rudeness towards Mauriac for playing such a role in his fiction. Amossy and Rosen comment on this ploy: 'In this way the thesis-narrative escapes the trap of having itself to portray the authentic by its own clichés ... The authentic is thus left in suspense'[95] rather, I would add, like Laclos's putative humaneness in his *Liaisons dangereuses*. By a comparable twist, Lucien graduates in this story from a juvenile fog (interspersed with a few inklings as to where authentic behaviour might be) to adult certainty (the fascist option). Sartre thus stigmatizes the Enemy without openly saying a word against him. Simultaneously, he probably enjoys mocking *the* great French, Cartesian, cliché: *la clarté*.

The largely post-Romantic anathema against cliché is governed by the soon consecrated polarities: Individual versus Society, the New versus the Old, Spontaneity versus Calculation. For all, writers or the citizen in the street, cliché is a supremely relative phenomenon.

6

Plumbing the Depths: Plagiarism

After, when they disentwine
You from me and yours from mine,
Neither can be certain who
Was that I whose mine was you.
To the act again they go,
More completely not to know.

Theft is theft and raid is raid
Though reciprocally made.
Lovers, the conclusion is
Doubled sighs and jealousies
In a single heart that grieves
For lost honour among thieves.

Robert Graves

In another book (*Georges Darien: Robbery and Private Enterprise*), I studied thieving as a social and literary complex. Clichés (purloining others' thoughts) and neologisms (blending existing fragments to forge anew) seem to fit roughly into the same scheme. Of the numerous varieties of plagiarism, I find the educational version, which vaults some colleagues on to high horses, tedious. Students necessarily are parasitic, which does not prevent their being simultaneously or subsequently creative. Imposed plagiarism, however – dictatorial pedagogy – is, as we saw earlier, fascinating. Legal attempts to pin down plagiarism are usually hilarious, as whenever the law tries to cope with the legally unmanageable. Plagiarism in culture, in everyday life, and as a psychological inescapability with attendant anxieties, these will be my focus in this chapter.

Mythology begot great thieves: Hermes, Prometheus, Robin Hood, the gentlemen-burglars of the turn of the century; the Trickster who wriggles his multifaceted way through most cultures. Proverbial wisdom chips in: 'Lo mío mío, y lo tuyo de entrambos' (What's mine is mine, and what's yours belongs to both of us); or, more sadly, 'Omne meum, nihil meum' (Macrobius): it's all mine and nothing is mine.[1] Stuart Gilbert borrows from a divine context to make a nice point: 'The conception of a poet cannot be wholly immaculate.'[2] 'Nothing can come out of nothing' was hardly news when Lucretius formulated it two millennia ago.[3] More recently, the anarchist Luis Buñuel quotes Eugenio d'Ors: 'What doesn't grow out of tradition is plagiarism'.[4] Within my own scheme of things in this book, the leitmotif of overlap (epicycles, trick-cycling) touches also on plagiarism. This in turn links with clichés, for these are mass plagiarism, the short-cut for our laziness or cowardice, but also our umbilical cord.

I discussed earlier some aspects of the classical concept of imitation. Montaigne proves that it can take as much genius to be a fruitful imitator as to be an out-and-out original. The classical attitude housed both feudal and democratic impulses. As we are all indebted to our illustrious predecessors, let us openly acknowledge this. But, ideas are common property, therefore what is someone else's is also mine for the taking. By general consent, slavish imitation was worthless: something else (further ideas, a changed expression) needed to be added. In Antiquity, some of the favourite figures for this process included bees gathering honey, digestion, and 'the blending of diverse voices in a choir, instruments in an orchestra, or essences in a perfume'.[5] White goes on to cite indications that, while the culture of Antiquity did secrete the idea of plagiarism, the main motives for accusations on this score were: the jealousy of rival authors; the pedantry of non-creative critics; or the propaganda of racial or religious apologists (for example, Clement of Alexandria, pro-Jewish and anti-Greek).[6] We have seen how 'invention' in the regeneration of Antiquity during the Renaissance meant something like our 'information-retrieval' today. The growing number of charges concerning plagiarism in the England of the seventeenth century, and the vigorous self-defence against them, indicated no doubt a growing sense of literary property-rights, but, perhaps more significantly, it betokened a ferment of ideas, a vital intellectual culture. Today, we engineer brainstorming sessions, where the term hopes to describe floods of ideas and assaults on the ramparts of a problem, but cannot avoid the suggestion of temporary lunacy.

There are degrees of (and indeed in) plagiarism: winnowing at one extreme, looting at the other. Some, said Colton, 'give us the mere carcase of another man's thoughts, but deprived of all their life and spirit, and this is to add murder to robbery'.[7] Some do away with themselves so totally that they need a ghost-writer, or devil (that is, from beyond the usual dimensions); in France or Italy they employ a negro (which is either cynical realism or residual imperialism). This practice, and politicians' use of speech-writers to provide their ventriloquial material, is a different, though related, kettle of fishiness. About 1950, the American University in Washington announced a new course in ghost-writing. The *Washington Post* (which years later was to publish the spectral leaks of 'Deep Throat' in the Watergate scandal) ran an advertisement reading 'The Ghost Artists – We Paint It – You Sign It – Why Not Give an Exhibition?'[8] There can be umpteenth-degree plagiarism (as in the incessant reworkings of the Mona Lisa). When you know that many of your precursors have stolen, why feel any guilt at adding to the company of thieves ('Everybody's doing it')? The range can go from selected words to verbatim.

The word 'plagiarism' has the root meaning of 'kidnap', but is also connected with the Greek word for 'oblique'. The *idea* of plagiarism has attracted a large array of metaphors: the clichés of 'plagiarism'. In his incomparable study of the whole phenomenon, Schneider lists some of these: tree/graft; dwarf on giant's shoulders; mosaic, patchwork; the fallen woman rescued; journey to bring back treasures; digestion; plucking flowers; hatching stolen eggs; rebuilding ruins; monkey/parrot/jackdaw.[9] Plagiarists are so inventive in self-defence that you wonder why they need to filch the creativity of others. Obviously, the main imagery centres on the main feature: the taking of what is not yours. Hence the whole range of terms for stealing, annexing or scavenging. The word 'hackney', over the years, has linked carriage-horses, prostitutes and triteness. The great euphemism is, of course, 'borrowing'. Above all, like most things, plagiarism cuts both ways: vampire, and leech; extraction, and cleansing. Often the plagiarist transfuses new blood into a decrepit body. And, unlike the thieving magpie, the cuckoo offloads its own elsewhere, as when Sartre relocates his own neuroses in Baudelaire, Genet or Flaubert.

The search by commentators on literature for influences or precursors is often a petty-minded attempt to tame the new, or, as Schneider says, to find it a family, to make it like everybody else.[10] For Schneider, great writers, on the contrary create, or to put it less paradoxically reactivate, their forerunners. Such tracking down of sources which are, as Gide said of the mainsprings of human motivation, as varied and hidden as those of the Nile,[11] is still a concern for many Stanleys of the literary-historical enterprise. Yet writers, in their spasmodic moments of honesty, seem to sponsor such research. Barthes, for one, says that 'une rémanence obstinée, venue de toutes les écritures précédentes, et du passé même de ma propre écriture, couvre la voix présente de mes mots' (An obstinate residue of all previous writing, and from my own past writing, muffles the present voice of my words).[12] Acoustic memory: the head of Barthes buzzes with others' sounds. 'I am no pick-purse of another's wit', claimed Sir Philip Sidney, translating Petrarch's words to back up his boast.[13] One making rather than resisting the charge, like Martial, says:'Dicitque tibi tua pagina fur es' (And your very page tells you: you are a thief).[14] The whole business is so intricate that Schneider in describing it uses convoluted imagery: the plagiarist is like blotting-paper, soaking up but giving nothing back, registering the traces but burying them in an inverted transfer or a criss-cross of illegible marks.[15]

'Innocent', or involuntary, plagiarism always stems, in Gourmont's view, from a mental slackening; and he cites the case of Macaulay in old age, writing down in the morning, convinced that they were his own, ideas he had culled from books the evening before. Equally clearly we may remember what we have read but, as if sleepwalking, forget where we read it.[16] The fear of forgetting passing thoughts makes many of us note down everything, though the sources are sometimes omitted. The phenomenon of *déjà vu* further blurs the matter of sources. Our memories, like lumber-rooms, ragbags or dustbins, are places of disorderly storage, dumping. As well as burdening us with junk, this fact of life also helps to save us, for conscience depends on memory. The cynically realist Rev. Colton states: 'Memory is the friend of wit, but the treacherous ally of invention; and there are many books that owe their success to two things, the good memory of those who write them, and the bad memory of those who read them.'[17]

It is because of the bad memory common to all that training-schemes have proliferated since Antiquity. In classical theory, subjects were schooled to associate memories with places (*topoi, loci*). Proust resurrects this ancient tradition by ensuring that all remembering in his vast novel dedicated to this pursuit has a frame, a local habitation and a name, as focus. Bloody-minded as it is, memory often opts to recall uncommon places, for it is that which sticks out which sticks. The mnemotechnic devices eruditely analysed by Frances Yates are also connected to the habit of viewing the outer world as a book.[18] The would-be memorizer imprints on the man-made world (the room or house) the set ideas he wants to use in speeches; the world is transformed into a storehouse of orderly meaning to replace the chaotic space that the French call *capharnaüm* (after the town in Judea where Jesus attracted an outsize crowd before his door).[19] The mind was frequently compared to a wax tablet, re-usable, where meanings could gather as in palimpsests. As we all know if we stop to think, all arts of memory posit an already exceptional memory, for we have to master and retain the method as well as the target topics. Puns were suggested as memory-aids, for they are a kind of mental stenography, and phonic resemblances can be cultivated. Instructors tried to systematize our often chance association of ideas, though they insisted that apprentices should form their own examples; they reacted primly, however, if these turned out to be scabrous.[20] The section of Flaubert's *Bouvard et Pécuchet* given over to the pair's attempt at orderly recall of historical dates makes idiotic mincemeat of the rhetorical tradition studied by Yates. They transform their property into a repository (the apple-trees stand for genealogies, the bushes battles): 'The world turned into a symbol. They looked for all sorts of things on the walls, finally found them there, but had forgotten the dates they represented.'[21] As with mementoes, we make a fetish of memory itself.

At a different level, we all suffer at some time from cryptomnesia: 'the submerged or sublimated memory of events forgotten by the supraliminal self', as the dictionary informs me. We are familiar with the sporadic difficulty of putting out of our minds (and this includes the subconscious) something once read or heard. Before he acknowledged his debts to Börne, Freud evidently had to wrestle with his own preference for being unbeholden. The paper where Freud ruefully admitted the inspiration by Börne was unsigned.[22] Thomas de Quincey poetically evokes the whole twilight zone:

> A thousand accidents may, and will interpose a veil between our present consciousness and the secret inscriptions on the mind; accidents of the same sort will also rend away this veil; but alike, whether veiled or unveiled, the inscription remains for ever; just as the stars seem to withdraw before the common light of day, whereas, in fact, we all know that it is the light which is drawn over them as a veil – and that they are waiting to be revealed, when the obscuring daylight shall have withdrawn.[23]

There is, outside actual amnesia, no total forgetting. Yet we need the twin arts of memory and forgetfulness, in order to survive. We can even forget clichés, as we do the names to go with faces or vice versa.[24]

It would be in the spirit of Schneider's book, which has helped me to avoid waxing moralistic about plagiarism, if I did not acknowledge how very much I got from it. He works on the premiss that we live in each other's pockets, get into each other's pants, infiltrate and are permeated by alien minds. Ecumenical towards other psychoanalysts, who are adduced if not reverently at least accommodatingly, he has written a truly humanist book which stresses in umpteen persuasive ways the communality of mankind. My only reservation (while murmuring 'Doctor, heal thyself' to myself), is that his study is at times too clever-dick, playing self-indulgent variations on a given, or taken, theme. His freely admitted gurus are: Borges, Montaigne, Burton, Proust and Nodier ('a great plagiarist and subtle theoretician of this swindle', and a hinge-figure in the evolving view of plagiarism as something heinous and thus, for some, glamorous).[25] Schneider's practice exonerates him of any stickable charge of plagiarism, for, with all his 'citationism', he is so passionately caught up in his subject that he is clearly taking no facile short-cuts; his repetitions, and the general obsessiveness, show that he is not creaming off the question. His humour proves his seriousness. At times he does seem to virtually disappear into his elegant antitheses and cross-overs ('When I think I'm writing, I am quoting, and when I try to copy, I speak for myself') (p. 85) but even this reflects the shuttle-movement of plagiarism. He keeps his sanity in its vicious circles.

Essentially, Schneider sees plagiarism, whether inflicted or suffered, as an identity-crisis (p. 124). It is yet another in our copious supply of defence-mechanisms, our artifices of self-preservation. Schneider compares it with melancholia which, like plagiarism, rehashes even when claiming that everything has already been said: 'Cette stérilité féconde' (p. 335), which I would vary to 'cette stérile faconde' (this sterile gabbing). 'Everything is therefore not yet said since it is necessary to repeat that it has all been said. Melancholics are great optimists. Behind a constant depreciation of the present and an exasperated rejection of the past, they entertain the secret hope of a truly new future' (p. 336). Stretching his enquiry, Schneider draws on the analogy between plagiarism and copying at school or in higher education (the area where many people fume over this practice). The person I copy from (to underline that no man is an island, Schneider regularly uses the first person) must know more or better than I, simply because he/she is other, not-me (p. 121). He shows compassion for this 'hell of the plagiarist', and notes that such a one is often an idolator, to the extent of wanting to immerse himself in the person copied, so as to become what that one is (p. 121). Similarly, I myself imagine show-business impressionists must often wonder whether they possess a face or a voice to call their own. 'Plagiarists are enviers. They seek to take over the creativity of the plagiarized author rather than any actual creation, they take his powers of taking, and steal his robber's essence' (p. 351). This is reminiscent of the cannibals as reported by Montaigne, who gain borrowed strength from eating their enemies.

It seems as though the plagiarist has decided too soon that he cannot go it alone. As in a premature ejaculation, he jumps the gun, goes off at half-cock. (*Coitus interruptus* is known, around Sydney, as 'getting off at Redfern', the last stop before the terminus.) Whether coming too soon or arriving too late on a scene which seems not to need him, the plagiarist oscillates in a no-man's-land. 'To be first: to be only an imitator. Anyone can be pushed to extremes. The former ends up in a kind of megalomania about origins; the latter, not excluding the mania for belonging to a group, typically takes the form of a docile silence' (p. 92). But what about the victim of expropriation?

> Extreme vulnerability about plagiarism is a symptom veering between the ludicrous 'This is my idea, don't steal it!' and the tragic sense of being dispossessed, robbed, raped of one's thought by another. It can even intersect with the unbearable experience of many psychotics, especially schizophrenics. To hold on to one's ideas is something that commands respect. You hang on to them as on to a thread connecting you to an identity, as on to a skin which if torn off would expose you to an uninhabitable environment. It's not like hanging on to something you possess, contain or retain, but rather something that holds you, holds you together, keeps you alive. The victim of plagiarism is, literally, beside himself. (p. 239.)[26]

Of course, the perpetrator can feel victimized. Like the child who thinks you have left him when he leaves you, or the lover feeling abandoned when he parts, the plagiarist believes himself plagiarized when he plagiarizes (p. 239).

Not only patients but analysts can undergo similar anxieties. Jean Cau relates a marvellously malicious anecdote about Lacan working himself into psychic disarray, an insane rage, because his little daughter had dared to put her tiny feet into his clodhoppers. The humourless analyst read this innocent spatial experiment as a symbolic murder of the genitor: stepping into dead men's shoes.[27] This was, incidentally, the only good, pointed pun of the many Lacan concocted, or rather suffered. He could not stand common reality punning back at him (the child was 'following in the old man's footsteps'). Lacan once said 'Moi, je pense avec mes pieds'.[28] For Schneider, psychoanalysts are often little in themselves and seek substance from their patients. A frontiersman, neither scientist nor creative writer, but a bit of both, the analyst traffics between the source and the outside world, a shuttling smuggler. Schneider reminds that the words 'douane' and 'divan' appear to have the same origins (p. 250). If anyone should feel guilty over this sequestration of alien goods, he has only to let himself be ruled by the rod of iron

wielded by a guru, and to repeat the master's word (pp. 249–50).
Schneider obviously relishes relating the case of a patient obsessed with
plagiarism, and who habitually ate fresh brains in a restaurant. Schneider
comments that his action signified a response to his analyst: 'brain for
brain, I prefer those in the café next door to your plagiarizing taste for
sucking out the brains of your patients' (p.224). A welcome turning of the
tables and an invitation to the doctor to heal himself. Schneider
frequently stresses the oral determinisms of the general phenomenon:
'The plagiarist is a cannibal, as the inhibited person is an anorexic and
the compulsive quoter a bulimic' (p. 300). Yet it never works: 'A
nauseous bulimic, ready to throw up, and with an ever-increasing
emptiness in the pit of his being which he tries to stuff with words'
(p. 124).

Although he calls it 'intellectual kleptomania' (p. 317), Schneider is
fully aware that such larcenies can sometimes be committed (though too
frequently explained away by the accused as having occurred) in a
somnabulistic trance. Indeed, as he says, plagiarism is sleep-walking,
neither the just sleep of non-writers nor the insomnia of real writers
(p. 124). The plagiarist is a 'writer without work, without a body of work,
an out-of-work writer' (p. 123). He suffers from reading difficulties. He
reads too much and badly. He suffers from a strange malady: unlike the
émigrés of the French Revolution, 'he has learnt everything and forgotten
nothing. He has too much memory and not enough thought' (p. 120). We
have already heard Barthes complaining gently of his buzzing, saturated
head. Barthes takes in general a far sunnier view of the question than
Schneider's, which is more desperate, urgent and central. For Barthes,
the 'pleasure-text' cannot be talked about: 'You can only talk "in" it, on
its terms, yield to a delectable plagiarism.'[29] A manic sympathy.

I make no apology for having spent several pages playing (second
fiddle) at being an amateur psychologist, for all who utter clichés play at
being amateur sages (the type that Sartre dismissively labels 'l'homme
d'expérience'). Much of what Schneider says would seem to be restricted
to writers, but he is really talking about parasitism, which affects us all.
Plagiarism is unearned income, the attempt to profit from the labours of
others. When he describes imitation as the desire to get one's name on a
lineage, are we not all in this respect bastards, greedy and snobbish,
wanting to be grafted on to a better family-tree? Plagiarism is, like
quoting, tightly connected to both vanity and humility. Desire, claims
Schneider after René Girard, works like metonymy, by a kind of
ricochet. 'A thing appears desirable or beautiful only when evoked by
someone else.' Yet, Schneider adds in a crucial if unspecific *distinguo*:

'There are plagiarists and there are writers' (p. 291). So as not to end this section on too comforting a note, I must state that the bleakest part of Schneider's enquiry finds at the heart of plagiarism, 'the desire to be nothing. Nothing but the shadow of the other, his trace, his footstep. Not even his copy, but rather the empty wake he leaves behind. Flight from ourselves is our primary concern' (p. 247). To fill lexical gaps, I myself have found it necessary to coin *neminity* or *nihility* to describe this recognizable urge, and for the wish, which is not necessarily a death-wish, to be nowhere: *nusquamity*. Why should the positive, why should ubiquity, rule the roost? We will come back to nothing, later, indeed we will.

While they can wreak their own kind of havoc, borrowed ideas are probably not as dangerous as borrowed emotions (faking it; rent-a-crowd). One of the main reasons for concern about clichés is that the sentiments expressed in such reach-me-down garb are not genuine. As if pain or joy had to be verbally creative, whereas we are probably closer to our fellows (and therefore least original) at the extremes of experience, and furthest from them in the huge and variable middle ground. We fear then that clichés do not mean what they say. (The other possibility, that they might not say what they mean, is still relevant, but less urgent.) A working definition of cliché might be: a conventional expression of something that is not truly felt. As well as borrowed, there are distanced emotions, which are the stamping-ground of George Steiner:

> The capacity for imaginative reflex, for moral risk in any human being is not limitless, on the contrary, it can be rapidly absorbed by fictions, and thus the cry in the poem may come to sound louder, more urgent, more real than the cry in the street outside ... Thus there may be a covert, betraying link between the cultivation of aesthetic response and the potential of personal inhumanity. What then are we doing when we study and teach literature?[30]

A truly crucial question, which I only just stop myself evading by adducing the figure of Françoise in Proust, who sympathizes with far-off catastrophes and callously ill-treats the pregnant servant-girl at hand. Here, the literary figment jabs at the reader's conscience, though to what practical avail? I do not believe that literature should offer us a programme of behaviour, though the best (and worst) provides models and warnings to set us thinking.

For Schneider, writers are probably too obsessed with their own morality to set themselves up as role-models. Citing Malcolm Lowry, terrified over being rumbled about his liftings from Conrad Aiken in

Ultramarine, Schneider comments: 'Every writer trembles at being called a plagiarist, because every one knows full well he is one' (p. 93). I am unable to decide which of the two following breast-beatings really hurts. Mark Twain: 'We are nothing but echoes. We have no thoughts of our own, no opinions of our own, we are but a compost heap made up of the decayed heredities, moral and physical.'[31] Or Vladimir Jankélévitch, who writes later in the same book very intelligently about verbal escalation:

> I cannot open my mouth without imitating someone or faking something. No matter how hard I work to be the first, to think originally, tradition or fashion always tug at my strings; my sentences, my ideas ... my feelings themselves, I regret to say, are more or less pastiches; we think we're in love and we recite a lesson! ... My whole person is a mere plagiarism, the sum total of my performances. Isn't it enough to make you give up love or sincerity at all?[32]

We have already mentioned the ancient tradition of fawning to previous writers, which no doubt fulfils the realistic need for sponsorship, as well as the psychological need for precedents and guarantors. 'Quote your authorities', students are told.

Recitation is re-citing: quotation is copying out. While quotation can be parasitic, self-boosting, anxious or pedantic, strangely those writers who make a heavy practice of it (Montaigne, Burton) seem to have immediately recognizable voices. It may be that the choice of quotations (like the choice of companions, for Ignazio Silone) tells us a great deal about the chooser. In conformity with their cultural, theological and no doubt temperamental distaste for ego-centred writing (Pascal: 'Le moi est haïssable' – the self is abominable),[33] the grammarian Jansenists of Port-Royal, Arnauld and Nicole, castigated Montaigne's habit of self-quoting, that is, adducing oneself as a source of examples. They equated this practice with 'violent self-love', though did not criticize the subterfuge of their protégé Pascal for speaking of himself from behind a disguise, a pseudonym-cum-anagram.[34] It seems to me that the real grievance of these critics of Montaigne was that he was not piously didactic. The key words in the Christian tradition for so long were authority (*auctoritas*) and obedience. The also-rans dutifully quoted from the Bible, and from the Fathers of the Church. While such authorities could be interpreted, they could not without heresy be contested. As Compagnon says, such *auctoritas* is at heart an initiation-rite; by quoting the authorities you hope to accede ultimately to their status, to become an *auctor*.[35]

In a more mixed, part-pagan tradition, Montaigne did become, by dint of copious citing, his own man. He is one of the very best examples of the receptive mind untroubled, despite his heavy import-bill, by any balance-of-payments. No doubt Montaigne nursed the always frustrated desire of being unbeholden, for his aim was self-knowledge, and incrustation might impede that goal. In terms I warm to, Compagnon describes the resultant tension, or mess: 'But everything gets mixed up, everything is overlap. Exact repetition is no more possible than pure originality.'[36] To counterattack, Montaigne opts for the strategically ludic. He occasionally buries quotations from illustrious predecessors, and gloats when commentators insult Plutarch or Seneca, under the illusion that the ideas are Montaigne's.[37] In two senses, Montaigne seeks to disarm critics. He complicates for the reader's understanding his own efforts at self-understanding. Montaigne, as any reasonably sensitive reader soon spots, is 'diverse, heterogeneous, plural, he is as many separate people as there are sentences in the book' (p. 305). I have often felt that Montaigne is the truest French novelist of them all; no one better affords the sense of life lived in its complexity; no one moralizes more nor is less judgemental. He flees, says Compagnon, on the spot; we cannot pin him down (p. 305). Quotation, too, is repetition: running on the spot.

Compagnon plausibly argues that there are three gradations in the practice of quoting: possession (as if by some alien influence), appropriation (the midway state), and ownership (total, assimilated take-over of material) (pp. 354–5). For myself, I would recall that 'to cite' covers the act of magnetizing the attention of the bull (quotation as provocation); designating someone for a medal (and citations are often thus paraded); or to summon to court (as a quotation is called upon to provide evidence). The latter sense, quotations as proofs (or at least a browbeating hint) that we are qualified to speak on a certain topic, joins up with the ambivalence of the other two. In quoting are we being humble or vain, bowing to authority or curtseying to applause? Droppings of names always smell sweet to the launcher. But why calling on somebody else to speak for you guarantees anything remains puzzling. If the quotation is in a foreign language, this can be a way of avoiding taboos, as well as a kind of vanity-publishing of your knowledge. In a rhetorical manual which stereotypically gives each rhetorical figure the name of a flower in a typically tailored French garden, quotation is the narcissus.[38] As with all things, the quotation of context – how a quotation is *set* – is crucial. A quotation is not only a crutch but also a springboard. Indeed, confident use of it can often betoken a person who has thrown his crutches away to walk unaided. For Compagnon, it is a conjunction of opposites – like the oxymoron: disjunction and conjunction, mutilation and grafting on, export and import, cut-up and collage (p. 29). I am reminded of the word 'cleave': to split, and to join together.

For Compagnon, quotation gets everywhere, like plagiarism for Schneider, or puns for your disobedient servant, the breath of literary or literate life. Self-evidently, stereotypes and clichés are quotations, levied or lifted from others. Even paraphrase is a kind of annexation, the act of putting another's text into your own words, though of course you are still wearing the blinkers of the original writer. (Yet another instance of the dubiousness of this term, for it can mean merely 'first', with no guarantee of quality and indeed a strong suspicion of incompetence, primitivism.) Equally, of course, paraphrasing can be a critical exercise, since it acts as a cross-check on the sense or nonsense of the text to be resumed; it can ask the valuable question: 'What is behind the smokescreen of words?' According to Kellett, the first alluder 'was an original by virtue of his very scorn of originality ... to have seen that he could give an added pleasure to his hearers by stirring their memories in this fashion, by making them recognise the old in the new, required insight of a high order'.[39] Of course, the alluder, to be successful, has to pick material familiar to his audience, and so cannot venture too far from the trite. Allusion is a word to the wised-up: *verbum sapientibus* (often shortened unflatteringly to *verb sap*); tipping the wink instead of blowing the gaff. While it is often more economical, it can also be more coy, than direct quotation; it resembles in this fishing for compliments. On the other hand, as Genette has noted, an ill-judged allusion functions as a gaffe, as when M. Verdurin in Proust, intending to intimate that he knew Charlus belonged to the intellectual elite, uses a phrase usually signifying homosexual affiliation ('que vous *en étiez*'); or when his wife, irritated by Charlus's loquacity, exclaims 'Ah, quelle tapette!' (gasbag/poof).[40]

People can of course misquote deliberately, woundingly, as well as forgetfully or uncomprehendingly. The Spanish moralist Gracián recommended taking liberties with quotations (quotation by antithesis, displacement of the sacred to the profane or vice versa, and so on).[41] Gracián was a subtle analyst of wit, and would have relished Montaigne's twists of borrowed material, 'like horse-thieves who paint the mane or the tail, or sometimes put out one eye'.[42] We can quote to pillory others, forcing them to condemn themselves out of their own mouths, as well as to celebrate them or congratulate ourselves on the company we keep and court. Selective quotation (but all quotation is necessarily selective) can kill off an opponent. Less lethally, in more oral cultures, quotation-jousts enact a formalized one-upmanship; competitors score quotation as well as debating points.[43] Belittling quotation can naturally also occur when we trivialize famous sayings, or, as Merton puts it, 'millions of repetitions by those of us who insist on converting the language of giants into the clichés of dwarfs'.[44] Sabin contrasts the set phrases of idioms with such endangered speeches: 'In idiomatic language, fixed phrases, released from original or specific contexts, carry the authority of common experience and wisdom. In literary quotation it is *uncommon* wisdom that seems to become magically manifest through a set combination of words, even through the mere tag of a phrase, "to be or not to be".'[45]

We can also trivialize by self-quotation. Overdone, this sets the reader or hearer humming: 'It seems to me I've heard that song before/on some far, far distant shore.' It can of course be self-mocking. Queneau, for one, is fond of such intratextuality, a kind of in-joke for retentive readers. All the same, while ready to enrich his own texts by prestigious imports, he often gently guys these cultural monuments; like Rabelais he inflates and cuts down to size. In *Zazie dans le Métro*, his fiction suggests that human heads are junk-rooms of miscellaneous material, but also that from this chaos we can salvage grains of meaning. 'In a sense', says Kellett, 'all, or practically all, our writing is quotation. A thousand years of writing have given us a set of vocabularies, each appropriated to particular uses.'[46] From an opposite angle, of course, every book, and almost every sentence within it, is a total neologism. Yet the very champion of originality, Emerson, admits: 'The originals are not original. There is imitation, model and suggestion, to the very archangels, if we knew their history.' If we replace 'Chinese' with 'Japanese', we can echo his question: 'Is all literature eavesdropping and all art Chinese imitation?' But the unregenerate originalist re-emerges when he concludes: 'We cannot overstate our debt to the Past, but the [present] moment has the supreme claim ... This vast memory is only raw material.'[47] And the latecomers, presumably, are the manufacturers.

Swift advised poets in 1733 'to quote quotation on quotation'. He might well have been addressing critics and scholars, though he probably had in mind the still safe bet of classical tags. Not all such looting is used to boost one's own text or ego; it is often indispensable, for, if you want to comment, you need a text to work on. Yet no even spasmodically sane or honest person would deny that it is easy to abuse – in both senses – quotation. Think of the way that some of the most progressive, and the most traditional, critics lick each other's bumptiousness by devising scripts that are very largely quotes from fellow-critics. Perhaps, in the case of the former variety, it is a kind of proof *per absurdum* of their hobby-horse: intertextuality. Most jobbing critics acknowledge the tools of the trade: the bibliography which orders the sources of quotations; the epigraph, which is a sort of star-spangled quote, 'la quintessence de la citation', as Compagnon says, 'a throat-clearing before starting to speak, a prelude or a profession of faith' (p. 337). Footnotes (or, more usually today, end-notes) are buttresses, necessary because 'the text is a bridge suspended over the void which terrifies it; it is afraid of falling' (p. 339). These are fetishes we are scared not to revere. Scientists (soft or hard) have another fetish – the citation-index, which is a breeding-ground for the dangerous clichés of contemporary Academe, imposed on it by its managers but with some fifth-column support from insiders: the belief that intellectual value can be computed, like the sales of records behind the hit-parade.

'To con' means to peruse, and to dupe. Much literary detective-work no doubt entails plants, cooking the books, framing (*passe-partout*, turning up here again like a bad sou, is a frame as well as a master-key and a ready-make thought). A plagiarist, like a parodist, is often erudite. As documentation is inescapable, plagiarism then becomes an occupational hazard and a cause of professional deformation. Lindey cannot decide who originated the idea that 'copying one book is plagiarism; copying several is research'. Possibly Charles Reade, who theorized elaborately about the matter under the labels of homogeneous and heterogeneous borrowing. Or the unlikely contender Wilson Mizner, gold prospector, brawler, fight-manager and coiner of mordant sayings. Lindey makes the obvious but essential point that many charges of plagiarism can be defeated by stressing the commonplace nature of much literary material (the limited number of basic plots), coincidence (the great and some-times true let-out), joint use of the same material, both authors' robbery from the same predecessor, 'the impact of influence, the imperatives of orthodoxy and convention'.[48] Despite this, he talks of the 'abduction of brain-children' (p. 59), though he must have known that none of us has any more ultimate control over the conjoined product of our loins and wombs than over our bright ideas.[49]

Just as vicarious living is living by proxy, at a second remove, so commentary sponges off the text under discussion. Critics have been defined as the stowaways on other writers' flights of imagination. At times the critic feels not only obligated but more or less physically bound to his subject, like the Catenists (the theological chain-gang) who from the fifth century onwards relayed Biblical commentaries via strings of passages from previous exegetes: the 'Catana patrum'. Scholia on glosses on commentaries. Thomas Aquinas contributed a *Catena Aurea* on the Gospels. In earlier paragraphs I wrote at third hand (with a modicum of firsthand knowledge) of Compagnon's *La Seconde Main*. This is par for the critical course, where we take in each other's washing, trying to get it whiter than white; to write virginally when we are practised in inter-course. Others adopt a more practical attitude. The novelist and television presenter Melvyn Bragg, defending his cultural programme *The South Bank Show* against David Nokes's charge of 'easy formulas' (the particular formula was the statement that V. S. Naipaul's career had been 'a voyage of self-discovery'), responded that his job was also to inform viewers with little or no knowledge of the subject: 'Clichés are adopted precisely because of their helpful familiarity.' He went on to maintain that such a conscious policy was 'of course, at the centre of any discussion about television and books'.[50] That is, critics as reassurers: take my hand and you won't get lost. This may be sensible but it sounds condescending.

Montaigne should round off, or at least put an end to, this section on plagiarism in its broadest aspects. 'It is harder to interpret the interpreta-tions than to interpret the questions themselves, and there are more books about books than about any other subject; all we do is gloss each other ... Everything seethes with commentaries; but authors, there's a great dearth of those.'[51] Thus Montaigne on metawriters. Finally, Michael Edwards adroitly reworks Marianne Moore's well-known lines to remind us, in respect of poetry criticism, especially the latter-day kind where the critic chooses to lord it over the poet, that 'there are things important beyond all this second fiddle'.[52] Maybe we critics are plagiar-ists, like the psychoanalysts. Not counterfeiters but impostors:[53] that is, not just passing forged notes, but taking over another's personality, assuming an alias, a second identity, a borrowed name. And this Other can be a topic as well as a person.

I want now to treat sources or stocks and attitudes towards them. Most sources, especially in the age of universal pollution, could be more aptly described as sewers, where everyone has done a job (crapped/burgled). Stock characters are the most imitated, stock comparisons the com-monest kind, and stock emotions the most inescapable. Humankind, to survive, always stockpiles, though food-mountains and nuclear build-ups (unnaturally) threaten, or do nothing to ensure, such survival.

The advent of print-culture encouraged the collecting, classification and indexing of data and, as technology advanced, multiplication and diffusion.[54] Increasingly, since the printing revolution, human memory has grown to rely on books, either for reading or writing: we minute everything. The futuristic film *Fahrenheit 451* posits a world where, after the burning of the books, small groups of determined souls labour to memorize what they have read, to become walking storehouses, muttering the great works of the past. Alain Resnais's documentary on the Bibliothèque Nationale is entitled *Toute la mémoire du monde*. It is as if we are afraid of over-burdening our heads. If knowledge were there, we might control it better, having, as a current cliché has it, taken it on board. While it lies in books (and lies, and lies …), it possesses an authority of an often spurious kind. The modern phenomenon of reproducibility (photocopiers, video recorders, cameras, cassette-players) clearly lessens the concept of authenticity. What was copyright is now so often taken as public property. Pirate editions (not a new phenomenon) give a commercial slant to plagiarism. Art is increasingly (if often in vulgarized or miniaturized artificial form) available to almost all. Yet the change of context alters perspective: think of studying a photo of a cathedral on your home settee. Widespread availability promotes rapid obsolescence or blaséness. The conversation of the global village becomes parochial on a universal scale.

Earlier ages, of course, had ways of popularizing the creativity of the few. The commonplace book recorded noteworthy sayings. 'What tho' his *Head* be empty,' exclaimed Swift, 'provided his Common-place-Book be full.'[55] Such collections were also called copybooks ('books assuring *copia*, or the free flow of discourse essential for oratory'),[56] or, because of their condensed usefulness, epitomes. In case we might be tempted to dismiss such practices as passive or parasitic, Ong roundly declares that 'where modern literature is at its peak it retains a living connection of some sort with the commonplace tradition, and when it is poor its poverty is due to its failure to establish this connection – which is to say to its ignorance of itself, of how it comes to be where it is. The older we get, the more mature our literature deserves to be'.[57] In short, Ong pleads for continuity and thus updates and seeks to resolve the Ancients versus Moderns polarity. *Florilegium*, the Latin calque of the Greek *anthologia*, means 'flower-collection'; the rather pansy English equivalent is 'posies'. There were collections of gnomic quotations, or of *exempla* – illustrative stories, either historical or imaginary. The whole set of mental habits crystallized into the following stylized picture: 'The busy rhetorical "bee" goes through the garden (or at times the forest) of invention to visit the "places" (*loci, topoi*) from which "arguments" are to be extracted. From the garden he gathers nectar to make honey (orations or poems).'[58] The greatest of such bees was Erasmus, whose *Praise of Folly* nevertheless shows how wittily he knew how to distance himself from passive consensus. I relish also the idea of Textor's *Cornucopia* (1518), mainly a catalogue of things to be found in great abundance in specified places. It ends, however, with its own opposite: 'There are no swine in

Arabia, *especially* in the country of the Scaenites.'[59] This upping of an absolute denial seemingly defies logic: there are none at all, above all in this place! Textor's *Epitheta* (1524) 'provides an assortment of options for giving the presumably bare or "naked" thought of the rhetorically untrained weaver of words a richer, more attractive – which is to say more commonplace! – texture ... One could find here the accoutrements and often the substance of thousands of poems of Western Europe through the Renaissance and indefinitely later'.[60] This view of the human mind as a patchwork quilt (a *cento* was a coat made of scraps) or mosaic finds its most beguiling expression in Burton's *Anatomy of Melancholia*, the omnium-gatherum of them all. The frying-up of leftovers often makes for a tastier dish than the original. Human beings have always been adept at do-it-yourself which so often involves the recycling of the materials to hand.[61] And we all have to learn in all walks of life to use a *chrestomathy* – a collection of passages with explanatory notes. From the debris of others' labours rise our own constructions.

Of all linguistic manuals the dictionary is the most frequently used. Lexicographers are the greatest of all plagiarists, as they compile from and add to other reference-works. In intention a hold-all, a dictionary is necessarily the great reservoir of clichés – language in its most normal and normative aspects. The very definitions which constitute dictionaries, like maxims or proverbs or clichés, seek fixity, conclusiveness, all-embracingness. Dictionaries have to behave like authorities (and many want to police, as well as to keep only descriptive tabs on, the language in its current state). We defer as we refer. It is easy to confuse the authors of such weighty tomes and the authors of our days (whether parents or gods). But the fact of print-culture and progressive liberalization in society and attitudes have led many to a hostility towards such authority and its enforced commonplaces. In our own time we have witnessed a counter-movement towards the anonymization of the written word, and it sometimes seems as if texts should bear tattooed numbers as in extermination-camps. The *locus classicus* for this reversal, this 'death of the author', is due to Barthes, whose *Le Plaisir du texte*, however, confesses that, though the institution of authorship is dead, he still 'desires' an author:[62]

We now know that a text is not made up of lines of words releasing one definite meaning that we might call 'theological' (that is, the message from the Author-God), but a space with many dimensions, where various writings, none of them original, wed or fight together: the text is a web of quotations coming from countless cultural sources... The writer's only resource is to mix these writings together, to play them off against each other, and never settle for any one of them. If he wishes to 'express himself', he should realize that the 'inner' matter he claims to 'translate' is itself only a ready-made dictionary whose words can only be defined by other words and so *ad infinitum*.[63]

'Playing off', or perhaps *bugging*: that is, interfering aggressively, and tapping, a highly parasitical practice. The dismissal of this absent (classical) author leads to a correspondingly greater presence of the (modern) reader. I am reminded of John the Baptist's sacrifice: for the Messiah to grow, the precursor has to diminish. Barthes beheads the text. As Schneider remarks cuttingly, it is an age with a lot of dying: after God, Man, the individual subject, it's the author's turn; but phantoms die hard, and history and the subjective have resuscitated after the structuralist interlude.[64] He focuses the central paradox: an author is needed to sign the book proclaiming that authors do not exist, that all texts are a web of unassignable, anonymous citations without quotation-marks (p. 36). Besides, I would add, Barthes himself spent his life being different, elusive; despite his affection for the Marxist Brecht, anything but common property.

Decades before, moreover, Jean Paulhan had countered the 'terror-ism' of the vanishing author. That is, the author who refuses to be accountable for clichés or indeed for anything else. Such a 'terrorist' claims to be only a medium, in either the spiritualist or the mass-media sense, and such abdication can be found in both realists and surrealists, who are lodged at the same inn. 'Both of them erect a curious system of alibis. On one side the writer disappears behind the human document, on the other behind the superhuman document. The slice of life or the wedge of dreams enable both groups to say: "I wasn't there".' To which Paulhan responds with the simple, tough reminder: 'You do write all the same, whether you like it or not, and are fully conscious of it.'[65] He resolutely resists the contemporary cliché: 'Language speaks us', so widespread in certain critical, linguistic and psychiatric circles. His argument resembles that of Sartre against Flaubert: you ignore the speaker/writer and fix on the spoken/written; you thus sidestep motive, responsibility, particularity and context – the specificity of clichés.

'Although the logos is shared', declared Heraclitus in one of his less riddling fragments, 'most men live as though thinking were a private possession.'[66] This is the other end of the scale from plagiarism: the drive to protect what you think yours. In *The Gutenberg Galaxy*, McLuhan argues that the concept of the private ownership of ideas and words could have evolved only with the printed text. Commenting on this, Steiner says: '[McLuhan's] own use of a cluster or mosaic of long quotations is meant to illustrate an earlier attitude, a "collectivity" of truth.'[67] Presumably this is the catholic in McLuhan. The conundrum, or Gordian knot, has forever been: if language belongs to us all, how can some phrases be deemed an exclusive property? But all property is theft, claimed Proudhon, after others. Besides, in the unconscious, Freud believed, there is no originality: 'Originality relies on forgetfulness of borrowing, just as the manifest content of a dream is only the result of the latent content.' Schneider draws an analogy with a psychoanalytic 'cure', at the end of which the original (in both senses) phantasm results in common misery: the patient sees he is no longer unique, but sick like so many others.[68] We have seen earlier Freud's painful generosity in admitting his debts to forerunners, especially creative writers (and 'debts' joins other financial terms in psychology, like 'psychic economy' or 'balance'). After a visit from Jung in 1907, Freud started mooting the notion of 'communism of ideas', pooling of resources, a kind of tit-for-tat plagiarism. This project of teamwork, intended to economize on effort and to evade the anxiety either of giving or of taking, could hardly escape economic images, for somebody in the chain would be bound to capitalize on the ideas of others. It could not resemble a chain-letter, where nobody wins. Schneider sees in the experiment a pre-capitalist motif, based on primitive bartering.[69] Or, as the earthy French say, 'pass me the rhubarb and I'll pass you the senna'. Clichés are the communism of language, the common property, the commonwealth.

The law is no doubt more interested in property than in propriety. Legal arguments about plagiarism have often been violent, even though as early as 1768 the English Judge Yates ruled: 'Ideas cannot be the object of property: they are not visible, tangible, or corporeal.'[70] Whereas 'pre-empting subjects by copyright would progressively narrow the field of thought', the Canadian novelist James Oliver Curwood did not flinch from laying claim to the entire, huge North-West as his territory, not to be transgressed or appropriated by any rival writer.[71] Subject-matter is often literal-mindedly seen in this way in spatial terms: domain, field, coverage, scope. Such possessiveness is petty-minded, and 'de minimis non curat lex' (the law does not concern itself with trifles): petty larcenies, adjudication about which would clutter up the courts. The law, though often lacking common sense itself, often appeals to it in such conflicts. And what should happen when books fall out of copyright and into the public domain? Perhaps, and feminists would no doubt agree, we should talk less of the *paternity* of an idea. If we said maternity, we would place more stress on creativity, and on generous sharing. Despite the undeniable possessiveness of mothers, it is fathers who, if only by their example, encourage thinking in terms of property: house, job, etc. In France authors' rights date from the French Revolution. In an excellent pun, Schneider comments: 'At the same time as it abolished gleaning rights for peasants, the Revolution put a stop to centuries of intellectual cropping.'[72] On the same page, he remarks that, because 'renown is less protected than an author's name', pastiche and parody, the comic and critical dimensions of plagiarism, are not legal concepts. Provided we do not libel, we can get away, so to speak, with murder.

7

The Modes of Plagiarism

We are, in truth, more than half what we are by imitation.

Lord Chesterfield

The modes or moods of plagiarism embrace imitation, pastiche, parody, forgery and related activities, and complicate the issue of parasitism still further. I am tempted to quote Schneider citing Nerval imitating Nodier on the theme of imitation throughout history. Schneider stresses how very much Sterne, a great plagiarist, was plagiarized.[1] A plagiarist is, in everyday parlance, a copycat, as are the high artistic goal of mimesis and one of its larger sub-divisions, realism. 'The most important characteristic of a stereotype is its truth; it is recognizable as a copy of something, it is true to an original.'[2] But what about misplaced fidelity? 'Original' is polysemic, and so is 'copy': we have mixed feelings and confused ideas about the whole business. A 'fair copy', *une copie conforme* (certified true copy) on documents – and 'certified' covers norms and insanity. For printers copy = the original. A copy can give currency, publicity, renown to an underestimated original. The praise-word 'inimitable', like 'unique', is, we know, a pious hope. And yet anyone, infant or grown-up, has experience of the difficulty of copying flawlessly; now we have machines so that we do not have to try it for ourselves. An echo is never identical to the sound it rebounds from. A ringer means both a double and a substitute, a fraud. Impersonators on the stage, and con-men off it, make honest or dishonest livings from imitation. As Genette suggests, unlike in music or literature, copying in the plastic arts is a truly artistic act; on the technical level at least the copier is up to the master.[3] On a more cosmic scale, 'Man, as he is, is not a genuine article. He is an imitation of something, and a very bad imitation'.[4] Ouspensky probably has God in mind, or on the brain. The comparison is unfair and, besides, as Lindey recalls: 'Not even God could avoid a prototype. When he created man he could not or dared not invent him. He made him after his own image.'[5] God, the original self-plagiarist.

Obviously, there is much good imitation. Sympathy and empathy demand it: putting yourself in the shoes or skin of somebody else. Diderot spoke of 'la singerie des organes' (the body's mimicry),[6] and Flaubert notoriously, when imaginatively rehearsing Emma Bovary's suicide, vomited at the taste of arsenic in his own mouth. In some cultures husbands labour to simulate the pains of their wives as they give birth. This is creative, or at least compassionate, imitation. It can happen in speech too: the deliberate use of the vocabulary or register of another to avoid his/her feeling embarrassed or stupid. In high culture, 'immature poets imitate; mature poets steal; bad poets deface what they take and good poets make it into something better, or at least something different. The good poet welds his theft into a whole of feeling which is unique, utterly different from that from which it was torn; the bad poet throws it into something which has no cohesion'.[7] The rather undistinguished language here would place banker Eliot on the debit side of the account book. Schneider puts it more succinctly: 'great writers are thieves, bad ones fences.'[8] Writers not only talk shop, they lift it. They launder their larcenies. They recognize, more lucidly than the rest of us, that we are all mortgaged up to the hilt, not only in the West to our local bank and in the Third World to the World Bank, but to each other. If, like good poets, we put our thefts to art, we avoid passivity and achieve the combinatorial. For Rousseau, impersonation (in stage-acting but also in everyday life) corrupts and reduces us. For Diderot, it *also* enlarges and enriches us, or at least thickens the social stew. I doubt, however, that he would have applauded the spectacle of a fellow-intellectual, Umberto Eco, in our own age, going over the top, like the scene he analyses, Disneyland: 'The pleasure of imitation, as the ancients knew, is one of the most innate in the human spirit; but here we not only see a perfect imitation, we also enjoy the conviction that imitation has reached its apex and afterwards reality will always be inferior to it.'[9] Inferior, but better, I would amend.

'When people are free to do as they please, they usually imitate each other. Originality is deliberate and forced, and partakes of the nature of a protest.'[10] And, of course: 'Imitation is the sincerest of flattery' (usually quoted with the addition of 'form', which stresses the ritual nature of such imitation).[11] We are reminded constantly today of terrorist or psychotic duplication of violent acts, as well as the usually non-lethal aping by groupies, in dress or behaviour, of their idols. Sociologists can make it sound like a no-win situation, as in Gabriel Tarde's sewn-up formulation: 'A society is a group of people who display many resemblances produced either by imitation or by counter-imitation' (that is 'doing or saying the exact opposite of what they observe being done or said').[12] This would imply that rhinoceritis or maverickhood was the self-same herd-instinct; rogue elephants would be assimilated. When, however, the Communist novelist Paul Nizan cites the traditional view that Nature is the home of mimicry, this *mimétisme* also covers self-protective colouring, operating (as Mao advised) like a fish in water.[13] In this perspective, camouflage secretes subversion; the secret is to imitate imitation. In thus copying Nature in general, the revolutionary does not copy animals in particular. If animals do communicate, it must be by clichés, set if adaptable responses. If they think, they do not do so seditiously: they do not pun, or otherwise twist.

Now a short section defending animal rights. Diderot shared the belief of Nietzsche and Thomas Mann that the basic feature of the artist is apishness: greed, sensuality, amoralism, mimicry. I doubt whether any of the three was being orthodoxly moralistic. Indeed Diderot once declared 'that the genius and the beast overlap' (or, in another reading, exchange caresses: 'se touchent'). The dubious hero of Diderot's *Le Neveu de Rameau* is, in the social menagerie of his time, something of a chimp, something of a parrot, whereas the self-righteous MOI-figure tries to act the wise owl. We people like to offload on to selected animals the human-all-too-human propensity to mimicry. Perhaps the mocking-bird should remind us that repetition can also be ridicule; it is at the root of sarcasm. We all know about having someone or something 'off to a T'. Despite the pejorative value attached to 'aping', monkeys are thought of as clever; and there is an ancient phrase from venery: 'a shrewdness of apes'. The ancient Egyptian god of writing was often represented as an ape. Even parrots have been defined as the only creatures with the power of speech that are content to repeat what they hear without trying to exaggerate it.[14] The well-named Henry Parrot (*fl.* 1600–26) was much skitted for echoing other writers. 'Speaking without knowing is called "psittacism" but it is a practice not confined to human beings.'[15] We anthropomorphize animals in more ways than one. In folk-tales the world over, parrots talk, very much to the point; they speak frankly, rudely, even obscenely. The implication is usually that the bird has mulled over a situation and is commenting freely on it. In such tales parrots stand in for obstreperous children, and just think of their comparable dirty habits.[16] Even scientists practise the take-over: attempts to teach monkeys to talk mean that people train them to ape people, rather like God creating his own image. There is voluntary and induced mimicry.

We owe the phrasing, if not the practice, of '[playing] the sedulous ape' to Robert Louis Stevenson, who honestly listed his masters (Hazlitt,

Lamb, Sir Thomas Browne, Hawthorne, Montaigne amongst them), so as to show 'by what arts of impersonation, and in what purely ventriloquial efforts I first saw my words on paper'.[17] This was self-chosen imitation and not the kind enforced in schools over centuries. This is pastiche as a writer's learning-method.[18] 'Taking off' is both dependent (you need a model) and a step towards independence, taking off from – thrust or impetus. Taking off is, however, also subtraction, stripping: discounting your own pride, for example. A blatant pastiche, a naked plagiarism, can be a form of homage, in which the Cretan liar is happy to blow the whistle on his own shifty doings. Proust is explicit about the exorcising and therapeutic effect of pastiche: 'Do wilful pastiche to find your own voice after that and thus avoid doing involuntary pastiches all your life.'[19] In social gatherings, too, Proust was an excellent mimic; there he sang for his supper. He stresses the *sine qua non* of intuition and empathy: the pasticheur has to sing the same song, sing along with the pastiched. Proust said he set his inner metronome to the cadence of Renan's prose.[20] The same 'démon de l'analogie' which produced his constant comparisons, his urge to abridge chasms (metaphor = to bear across) helped him in this. As, in his view, all great artists repeat themselves – as if they had consumed an everlasting radish – apprentices should seek to reiterate masters. This is the creative use of plagiarism. At the end of his novel, Proust uses a pastiche, of the Goncourt brothers, as a means of self-definition and self-affirmation: he invents his difference, sets his own benchmark. For the novice to become an expert, he has to cast off the cast-offs of his precursors: repetition as mastery. Proust used as a basis for his pastiches of Balzac, Flaubert and so on, the contemporary case of a confidence-trickster, 'L'Affaire Lemoine'.[21] For André Malraux, too, every artist begins with pastiche, but each then, if he has true talent, goes on to destroy the copy and to forge his own style.[22] Malraux was much more of a swashbuckling, piratical operator than Proust, though Proust did enjoy a hard head as well as limp wrists. It is this reaction against antecedent artists, rather than against society or themselves, that creates the constant metamorphoses which fascinate Malraux, and which occur in the 'museum without walls' of artistic traditions. These form an invisible buffer-state between artists and the outer world.

For W. H. Auden, man is 'the only creature ever made who fakes'.[23] A neat example is the invention of the codpiece, which simultaneously houses, conceals and exaggerates. Much writing is, in a different sense, a codpiece, seeking to have readers on, passing itself off as something it is not. Forgeries aim to fool the supposed experts, whether of museum, publishing-house or treasury; the biters bit. Genette provides a subtle analysis of the affair of *La Chasse spirituelle*, purportedly by Rimbaud: 'Its authors had written it to prove that they were capable of writing like Rimbaud', but, by an ironic backlash, 'it was eventually decided that they must indeed have written it, as it was quite unworthy of Rimbaud.' Hoist by their own petard, then. Genette concludes that such, and perhaps all, pastiches go over the top and are inevitably vulgar, because it is always vulgar to overdo things.[24]

Parody gladly takes on this danger and the related one of corniness, for as Dwight Macdonald points out: 'A peculiar combination of sophistication and provinciality is needed for a good parody, the former for obvious reasons, the latter because the audience must be homogeneous enough to get the point.' While most written parody is necessarily bookish (an 'upper-class folk art', as Macdonald puts it, or 'literary shop talk'),[25] the urge to mock is universal. Everybody, of whatever level of literacy, understands the parodic spirit, even if they would more readily call it 'piss-take' or (more genteelly) 'leg-pull'. It varies in fondness or vicious-ness. It makes use of clichés, the most obvious marks of the targeted writer, generally as a means of hostile comment. In this way clichés may be brandished as weapons. It is a *double* genre: conforming and transgressing, resembling and distancing.[26] For Bouché, who talks of Lautréamont's parodies in these terms, the effective reader of parody is in a constant state of oscillation between these poles: a dizzying per-spective. To twist an advertising term, parody is knocking copy. It is also, like pastiche, the dodgy homage vice pays to virtue, successors to fore-runners, youngers to elders.[27] It is all very incestuous, of course: art imitating art to raise a laugh or make a point; and, while exploiting clichés, it can easily become one itself, that is, facile and automatic. On the whole, only famous or infamous texts attract parody; and, as it is in many ways a conservative genre, a calling to order, avant-garde writers are often picked as targets. In their *Roland Barthes sans peine* (without tears), which sports a cover-design replicating the most traditional French school-manual, Burnier and Rambaud make hay with what they term Barthes's two kinds of truism: the clothed and the stark naked. The authors want to strip the emperor of the clothes they deck him in, for they write texts in his name and approximately in his style.[28] This illustrates the trap of all parody. You have to be hooked, and saturated in the subject, in order to qualify as a parodist; you need to be thoroughly contaminated. That is why Robert Desnos attempts to work a cure of intellectual disintoxication on language.[29]

Parody is blatant plagiarism, begging to be rumbled. Although every speaker dislikes being quoted out of context, we enjoy parody which frequently does exactly this, and, in so doing redraws the boundaries, reframes the picture. Such perverse quotation, such embezzling, is the reverse of metaphor, for it does not seek out similarities: it provokes separation; it does not build bridges: it sabotages them. While nobody can demoralize language itself, as Aragon boasted of doing,[30] a living writer can certainly be thrown off his stroke by such misappropriation of his funds. Like all good things, parody can be overdone, and then risks seeming to flog a dead horse. You probably cannot successfully parody a comic writer, for he would be quite likely to applaud your deviation. Seeing parody, on top form, as literary criticism makes it less parasitic (unless all criticism is deemed superfluous). Leeches, after all, though sucking blood, help to clear the system of impurities. Parodists can also extend the life of parodees, by creating sequels to famous works. Defending its practitioners, Kellett fancifully claims that 'Parody must be a sort of corollary to the original, deducing from the theorem conclusions latent in it all the while, but not perceived till the geometer has drawn them out'.[31] More down-to-earth, I would say that parody can serve to blow the gaff, to expose the innards or workings of a text.

The fact that great writers like Cervantes used parody suggests that it need not be a small-minded activity. As Genette says of the 'hypertext', the text taking off from a preceding one or several: 'At its best it is an undefinable and unforeseeable mixture of seriousness and play (lucidity and ludicity), of intellectual accomplishment and entertainment.'[32] (This *apologia pro arte sua* is a perfect model of Genettique engineering, swivelling adroitly between distinguos and blurrings in a way I find worryingly congenial.) Parody has given rise to the coinage 'play-giarism'.[33] It has the versatility of all ludic genres. It can be used 'as much to resacralize as to desacralize'.[34] Yet the ludic can still teach a lesson, that of the usefulness of 'co-opting the art of the past by textual incorporation and ironic commentary'.[35] Like blends a parody is a hybrid, and like puns it speaks with a forked tongue. For many, parody is a sign of decadence, of an over-ripe culture abusing its sophisticated talents; for others, and more charitably, it becomes 'a major mode of expression for a civilization in a state of transition and flux'.[36] As such it is surely a way of keeping in touch with the best, as well as the worst, of more settled ages. 'It is in this sense that parody is the custodian of the artistic legacy, defining not only where art is, but where it has come from.'[37] Finally, it is wise not to respond to parody. Wordsworth's feeble reply to his many mockers (Byron amongst them) was itself an imitation of Milton's *Tetrachordon*.[38] Which rather proved their point: a more self-critical poet would have been more self-reliant both in writing and in defending himself.

Genette defines 'hypertextuality' as one of the names for 'that incessant circulation between texts without which literature would not be worth a second glance'.[39] This is the *perpetuum mobile* of writing, towards which he is acutely sensitive, though he sometimes mars his flexibility by recourse to neologisms of the most tongue-twisting variety and most classical stamp, as if, having let it all hang out like a hyper-civilized hippy of Academe, he must at times chastise the flesh with pseudo-scientific taxonomies. While very recognizable as a writer himself, Genette is clearly the product of a long and dense tradition highly aware of itself. He is himself, like the authors he loves to analyse, a 'palincestuous' writer.[40] This is Anthony Burgess's coinage for Joyce, who rhetorically asks in *Finnegans Wake*: 'Who can say ... how very many piously forged palimpsests slipped .. from his pelagiarist pen?'[41] The palimpsest, that is, the re-use of paper, parchment, canvas after a summary cleaning, was obviously an economy measure, but also resulted from a different attitude: art was not yet sacred. It has been taken over as a metaphor containing the notion of overlap, the persistence of the past into the present (the traces of the original text). Etymology, archaeology, psychoanalysis all represent differing efforts to return to sources. Schneider suggests that we are all, as creatures, palimpsests, and reminds that Freud compared the ego to a copyist offering successive versions of the same text, altering, interpolating, censoring: 'no version is original or true.'[42]

Intertextuality, the presence of other texts in any given text (a kind of sedimentation) often seems to be used as a neutral, 'value-free' or euphemistic alternative to plagiarism. Kristeva attributes to Bakhtin the primacy of the discovery that 'every text is constructed as a mosaic of quotations, every text absorbs and transforms other texts. In lieu of the idea of *intersubjectivity* takes root that of *intertextuality*, and poetic language is to be as double at least'.[43] A ghostly view: *doppelgänger*, or even *vielgänger* – texts whispering to or eavesdropping on each other across the unpopulated spaces of libraries and studies. Yet the aim of supporters of intertextuality has been to deculpabilize plagiarism, by making it so commonplace. Something so universal could hardly be an aberration or a sin. Describing the ideal intertextual critic, Laurent Jenny declares dispiritingly that a long apprenticeship in decoding is necessary with only jadedness in store at the end. He also suggests that swapping around of critical modes is principally a change of metaphor or rather *poncif* (conventionalism): a cathedral for Joyce but for Raymond Roussel the folly assembled by the *facteur* Cheval: the aquatic metaphors of 'influence' or 'sources' yielding to the textile ones of *imbrication, web* or *texture*.[44]

One text above all has mesmerized recent critics, Jorge Luis Borges's 'Pierre Menard, autor del Quijote'.[45] Menard's 'merely astounding' project (an oxymoron leads into a highly paradoxical text) is to continue being himself yet to compose *Don Quixote* (pp. 52–3). He admits the impossibility of the enterprise, for all he needs is eternity (p. 53). Note that there is nothing inevitable in the choice of *Don Quixote*; like Huysmans, Borges loves going against the grain, and Menard's other works often promulgated ideas the exact opposite of those he actually held. *His* Quixote is defined negatively: *not* a reduplication, copy, anachronism or coincidence (it is wilful). The two texts (admittedly Menard's is considerably shorter, as he has managed only a chapter or so) are verbally identical, but Pierre Menard's, it is claimed, is infinitely richer; it is also written in what is a foreign language for Menard (pp. 56–7). The narrator of this tale has in vain tried to reconstitute Menard's drafts. This would be a third remove from Cervantes's novel, which thus becomes, as it was already no doubt, a palimpsest. Menard's lesson for us is that we misattribute great works. Céline or Joyce are the authors of *The Imitation of Christ* (p. 59).

As Borges said of Henley's English rendering of Beckford's French novel *Vathek*: the original is unfaithful to the translation[46] – which is a joke reversing 'traduttore traditore' and a further indication of Borges's love of paradox, as evinced by his cult of Chesterton. For all its efforts to boggle the mind ludically, the story of Pierre Menard does tell the fundamental truth that nothing ever is totally the same as another thing. Copies, replicas can be told apart. Texts can be twins but not clones. If plagiarists literally take a page out of another's book, Borges's hero wants to take the whole book, but it is then a different book. In order to recreate *Don Quixote*, Menard needs to forget it ever existed. If this were even remotely possible, cliché would vanish, as every restatement would be neologistic. Of course we cannot switch off, unlearn, disremember in this way – wipe the palimpsest totally clean.[47] Maybe the reason why so many recent critics have gone overboard in admiration for this text of Borges is that they too would like to be unwitting geniuses, prolific virgins, ultra-sophisticated savages.

On the local occasion of his hero's writing the same sort of letters to Albertine as he had previously to Gilberte, Proust comments: 'The human plagiarism which is hardest to avoid, for individuals (and even for whole peoples who persevere in their faults and even add to them) is the plagiarism of oneself.'[48] How can we rely on ourselves without aping ourselves and becoming, if only at times, self-parodies? 'Life', said Ortega y Gasset grandly, 'is a poetical task, and man is the novelist of his own life, either original or, mostly, a plagiarist.'[49] Foreigners often remark on the English flair for self-parody (either conscious or unconscious). It is indeed pronounced. But this is surely also the common reaction anywhere to the foreign, the strange. I remember entering a bar in Marseilles. As soon as the quietly conversing locals realized they had a foreign audience, they all started to behave like extras from a Pagnol film. They lived the stereotype up to the hilt. In a discourse to students, Sir Joshua Reynolds declared: 'He who resolves never to ransack any mind but his own, will be soon reduced, from mere barrenness, to the poorest of all imitation: he will be obliged to imitate himself, and to repeat what he has before often repeated.'[50] Diderot said the sixty-year-old Voltaire was the parrot of the thirty-year-old one. Resignedly, Joseph Roux murmured: 'When young we imitate others; when old, ourselves.'[51]

A way of shaking off the anxiety (if felt) of plagiarism is to turn the temporal tables. Aelius Donatus (tutor of St Jerome), who flourished in the 4th century, put it beautifully: 'Pereant illi qui, ante nos, nostra dixerunt' (A pox on those who got in first with our lines).[52] It comforts to think that we are the victims of anticipatory plagiarism, of unscrupulous forebears who scooped us. In a more foreshortened perspective, Eco says: 'the media learn; and thus the spaceships of *Star Wars*, shamelessly descended from Kubrick's [in *2001: A Space Odyssey*] are more complex and plausible than their ancestor, and now the ancestor seems to be their imitator.'[53] Such plagiarism by anticipation, to thoroughly mix up time-scales, forges behind. This is all a splendid joke (and much loved by Pataphysicians), but is it any more? Even the least mystical of people sometimes experience the strange sense of *déjà vu*. Schneider adduces the word *Ahnung*, a favourite of the German Romantics, in his investigations into the theft of ideas, and glosses: '*Ahnung*, a premonition which is a memory, a reminiscence looking forward, a retrospective anticipation, the future in the past.'[54] He describes the plagiarist thus: everything he reads seems to him to be an earlier book written by himself (p. 91). All writers, he suggests, have similar anxieties and confusions:

> Writing is amnesiac, and doesn't know where it comes from. Who is speaking. It's not that it has no memories, but they don't tell it what it is, whose it is. Literary space is ruled by an essential vertigo. Each book is the echo of those which antedated it or the presage of those which will repeat it.... Literary time is this dimension where the future has already happened. It parts company with ordinary, ordered time-sequences, and chronology gives way to chronophagy. (p. 81.)

Just as a parasite can eat the host out of house and home, so latecomers can efface predecessors; or vice versa. On a more comic level, but still troubling in its own way, is the thought that John Hamilton Reynolds published a parody of Wordsworth's 'Peter Bell' before the latter was written; in the preface, he states: 'It has been my aim and my achievement to deduce moral thunder from buttercups, daisies, celandines.'[55] This is parody *avant la lettre*.

Here are two opposing views from writers, presumably those most concerned by plagiarism. One indignant: 'They will not let my play run, and yet they steal my thunder!' – spoken by John Dennis at a performance of *Macbeth*, which used his new process of thunder simulation which he had not been allowed to feature in his own play *Appius and Virginia* (1709). And another, slap-happy:

> When 'Omer smote 'is bloomin' lyre,
> He'd 'eard men sing by land and sea;
> An' what 'e thought 'e might require,
> 'E went an' took – the same as me![56]

More proudly Montaigne claimed to quote others so much only so as to boost himself.[57] More blasé, Giraudoux explained that plagiarism was the basis of all literatures, except the first one, which is totally unknown to us.[58] Lautréamont, who relied heavily on borrowings, said plagiarism was inevitable; progress demanded it; it hugs an author's text tightly, uses its expressions, corrects a wrong idea and replaces it with a correct one.[59] It is indeed true that much plagiarism is corrective; it twists, adapts, rescores. What looks parasitic can, like the leech, be life-giving. 'Vamping' can mean refurbishing, harping, improvising, sucking dry.

Much writing is derivative, but so are rivers, so are genes. And those rivers need to be dredged to open up the silted channels of communication. Young addressed the problem nobly: 'It is by a sort of noble contagion, from a general familiarity with their writings, and not by any particular sordid theft, that we can be the better for those who went before us.'[60] Are there more sneak-thieves than grand larceners among writers? Should we emulate the stereotypical Japanese:

> He grins, and bows a friendly bow;
> 'So sorry, this my garden now'?[61]

Plagiarism proper is forgery, concealed theft, but even here the range can go from the light-fingered (the gentleman-burglar) to the heavy-handed. Many would differentiate stealing ideas from stealing expression of ideas, the latter regarded even more as private property; raw materials are for the taking, but the manufactured product should be protected from piracy or industrial espionage. Plagiarism continues to confuse us. As well as standing on the shoulders of giants, we peek over each other's shoulders, and the cheat, in Walter de la Mare's phrase, can be sweet.[62] 'God helps those who help themselves', but 'God help those found helping themselves.' Enright talks, in a good blend, of 'genuine fakesimiles'.[63] Like Rameau's Nephew who, in miming musical performance, includes miscues, Victor Hugo, pilfering from Guizot, took over his source's mistakes as well.[64]

Poe swung, as might be expected, pendulum-fashion on cribbage (which as well as plagiarism or a card-game means the internal lining of a shaft to prevent cave-ins. Plagiarism can shore up a tottering text): often violently censorious, but then understanding. In a more balanced moment he wrote: 'The poetic sentiment implies an abnormally keen appreciation of poetic excellence, with an unconscious assimilation of it into the poetic entity, so that an admired passage, being forgotten and afterwards reviving through an exceedingly shadowy train of association, is supposed by the plagiarizing poet to be really the coinage of his own brain.' [65] In contrast with this heavy-breathing approach, the gravity-free La Fontaine switches easily from describing the jay borrowing the peacock's plumage to the ubiquitous practice of epidermic thievery: 'Loin d'épuiser une matière, On n'en doit prendre que la fleur' (far from exhausting a subject, you must take only the cream).[66] Unless you aristocratically dismiss the whole question, as Voltaire does, when he says plagiarism is the least socially dangerous of all thefts,[67] you need to justify the practice. One tactic is to claim to be carrying out a weeding job on works of the past, freeing the essential from the dross. Another is to play the nationalist card: 'To take from one's compatriots is theft; to take from foreigners, conquest.'[68] The plea of the need to recycle, valid in itself, can in the wrong hands help to make a commonplace of an original, just as tourists can spoil a lonely paradise and remakes of classic films often obscure the founding work. Though it hurts me to admit this, twists can be unproductive. Eco reminds us of the political dimension of falsification, the 'non-bloody guerrilla warfare' of computer break-ins (hacking): 'electronic dissent' and disinformation.[69] Hence the growth of nightmare scenarios about computers being hijacked to trigger off a nuclear holocaust, or, an even more frightening prospect for the haves, the collapse of the stock-market. On a quieter level there is surely often a gloating element in plagiarism: 'Look what I can get away with!'

Then there is mutual plagiarism, two-way dependence: the drawn-out controversy, for instance, between Camus and Sartre, where a work of one yodels to a work of the other (*La Chute: Saint Genet; Les Justes: Les Mains sales*) across the yawning gap of their disagreement. They relied on and fed off each other in order to define themselves by contrast. In so doing, they were illustrating the essential fact of literary life, as Schneider says: 'écrire à la dérobée',[70] which suggests both stealing and stealth (as in 'stealing away' or 'stealing a glance'). But the true writer legitimizes his robbery, to the extent, as Hazard found, that many of the ideas in Stendhal's *Vies de Haydn, Mozart et Métastase* (notorious for its wholesale liftings) that seem most 'Stendhalian' are not his at all.[71] There can be no last word on an activity so complex, so prevalent and so rich, except the wise reminder of the Sotho proverb to plagiarists, pasticheurs, parodists, and myself their student: '"I and my rhinoceros", said the tick-bird.'[72]

I cannot resist glossing, having the last word in this chapter. The tick-bird (also called the oxpecker, a word that might set some drooling) is a hard-working hanger-on, feeding itself while cleaning the body of the host. Crime does pay.

8

Letdowns

That Sotho proverb which ended the previous chapter, with its mixture of bathos and disproportion, provides a handy if part-spurious link to this chapter. Clichés avoid the climax, and indeed often seem like excessive onanism, rubbing unproductively on the same spot. But who spoke of 'the fruitful bathos of experience'?[1] It may be significant that French lacks a common single word for climax (except, of course, in its sexual sense), or anticlimax; and elitist French culture certainly has little time for such English concepts as 'good bad poetry', or (in sport) the 'plucky loser' with his 'moral victory'. *The Art of Sinking in Poetry*, chiefly by Pope, referred by contrast to Longinus' *On the Sublime* (*Peri Bathous* to *Peri Hupsous*), just as the Latin words *altus* and *altitudo* covered both depth and height. Although much of what Pope satirized can be found in his own poetry, he was on permanent guard against solemn nonsense. As Kenner remarks: 'Pope used the bad verse of others as Flaubert was to use his *Dictionary of Received Ideas*, as a huge commonplace book on which his own creative enterprise could draw.'[2] A twentieth-century successor, D. B. Wyndham Lewis, in his anthology *The Stuffed Owl*, recorded the strange ways in which poetry could fail, 'so that failure becomes a kind of positive quality. This is transcendental: it is as if someone could invent a new sin'.[3] The introduction to the collection itself defines bathos as 'that sudden slip and swoop and slither as down a well-buttered slide, from the peaks into the abyss'. Other ingredients include: 'poverty of the imagination, sentimentality, banality, the prosaic, the *style pompier*, and what Mr Polly called "rockcockyo"; anaemia, obstipation or constipation of the poetic faculty; inability to hold the key of inspiration; insufficiency of emotional content for metrical form.'[4]

In addition to ups and downs between extremes, banality takes the form of an even level of mediocrity: the 'duck-billed' platitude.[5] French lacks a word for flatness to accompany the adjective *plat*, but writers have impressed the word *platitude* to this end, as we saw earlier with Bloy. Ponge, for example, describing a meadow, says: 'La platitude est une perfection.'[6] Don Marquis, with something similar in mind, recommends that the platitude be honed or fine-tuned: 'Stroke a platitude until it purrs like an epigram.'[7] What else, with his aim of 'bien écrire le médiocre' (giving a style to mediocrity), was Flaubert attempting? 'Emma retrouvait dans l'adultère toutes les platitudes du mariage': banality is a vicious circle.[8] Charles's conversation is 'flat as a street-pavement, and the ideas of the man-in-the-street trooped by there in their unremarkable clothes'.[9] *His* actual clothes, and the bovine body they encase, enrage Emma, and she sees, displayed all over his coat, 'toute la platitude du personnage'.[10] His poor defenceless back is vulnerable to such ocular attack. For Flaubert's successor, Queneau, it may well be that the only realm any of us is capable of inhabiting, apart from the special few who can cope with higher mathematics, is that of platitude. It was this bleak possibility surfacing here and there in Queneau's generally ludic universe that incited Gaston Bachelard to describe his work as 'dynamite disguised as candy-floss'.[11]

Euphemism camouflages; exaggeration blurs; cliché is often smoke-screen, concealing either vacuity, or unavowable motive. Just as a speak-easy was a clandestine bar, so euphemism promotes secrecy and is a bar to plain talk.[12] In order to cloak, doctors' prescriptions use Latin, or scholars its nearest relative, Italian, to cover up dirty bits from Latin when translated into other languages. Wishing to take the heat out of situations, diplomatic speech uses international tokens like *détente, modus vivendi*, often couching criticism in terms which suggest the impact of being struck by a wet lettuce. A Jules Feiffer cartoon of 1965 captures the clichéic nature of double-talk, well-meaning jargon, perfectly: 'I used to think I was poor. Then they told me I wasn't poor, I was needy. They told me it was self-defeating to think of myself as needy, I was deprived. Then they told me underprivileged was overused. I was disadvantaged. I still don't have a dime. But I have a great vocabulary.'[13] The apparent search for the *mot juste* can in fact lead away from straight talk. Such efforts produce the 'weasel words' Theodore Roosevelt attacked in 1916:

> One of our chief defects as a nation is a tendency to use what have been called weasel words ... You can have universal [military] training, or you can have voluntary training, but when you use the word voluntary to qualify the word universal, you are using a weasel word; it has sucked all the meaning out of *voluntary*. The words flatly contradict one another.[14]

Nineteen Eighty-Four indicates how even plain words, however, can be euphemistic, and mystificatory. '"Goodsex" is not the simultaneous orgasm of the marriage manuals but its opposite, sex deprived of pleasure and dedicated only to procreation.'[15] The reality is whitewashed.

No doubt we need euphemism, 'Society's basic *lingua non franca*'.[16] It is a prime source of clichés, for it shrinks from thought, it finds so much unmentionable and to a large extent, therefore, unthinkable. One of the umpteen nineteenth-century stand-ins for 'trousers' – 'ineffables' – curiously spiritualized these down-to-earth objects, so much so that Dickens jokingly referred to them as 'ethereals'. Lawrence stresses the frequent humour of Victorian verbal fig-leaves, and their usefulness in enlarging the register of the national lexis.[17] We have our own present-day equivalents, especially in job descriptions, for example: 'creative accountancy' for cooking the books. Euphemism swivels between evading unpleasant suggestions and enhancing the humdrum ('casket' for 'coffin'). It is a major means of reality-control. Some matters, varying with time and culture, will no doubt always remain taboo, and the 1968 slogan 'Forbidding is forbidden' was a short-lived dream. As well as reflecting the human genius for complicating matters, euphemism also stems from the urge to ward off, to propitiate, and it does recognize the magical strength of words. The inexplicit works against the counter-urge to let it all come out. But the whole effort backfires: a replacement-word becomes smeared with the same suggestive associations as the word it displaced. Conversely, one of the coarsest of Yiddish words for the sexual act was originally a euphemism: *yentz*, from German *jenes* (the other; cf. 'a bit of the other'). The trouble with euphemism, as with all codes, is that you want to unscramble, to translate back. 'Intestinal fortitude' sounds like a crossword-clue or pun (and the two are often one), and so focuses our attention, making it home in on the (once) forbidden 'guts'. And yet we go on, as Lawrence prettily puts it, 'turning up our noses at "snot-rag"'.[18]

Disguise seeks to hide something vetoed, or lethal; but the disguise can itself become lethal, as in the CIA jargon 'to terminate with maximum prejudice', which sounds like a call for a nuclear bomb to crack a nut. This is language dressed to kill. The verbicide in US discourse concerning Vietnam extended the strategy of herbicide.[19] Euphemism entails not coining new words but using existing ones in a new and deceitful way. Are they the same words after this cosmetic surgery? Can words, like erring young ladies, be saved from a life of sin? Can there be good censorship, when 'censorship involves the arraignment of language itself. It is the homage power pays to words. It is language judging language'?[20] If censorship takes the form of blanks – dashes, dots, asterisks or bleeps – again it is counter-productive. Dots are also used for suspense, and asterisks beg for our attention in *romans à clef*. As so often, Queneau provides a thoughtfully comic insight into the prurience built into euphemism. His falsely naïve Irish heroine Sally Mara, a tyro in the French language, uses the learned zoological term *périprocte* (the anal area of sea-urchins). With her motto 'tiens bon la rampe!' (hold tight), even though in terms of language she often gets hold of the wrong end of the stick, she instinctively knows how to grasp the rod.[21] Coyness gives rise to lasciviousness, which smuggles the contraband. In the hide-and-seek guessing games we all play with words, euphemism can be a way not only of preserving, but also of circumventing taboo.

Litotes also enables us to be jesuitical, to have mental reservations beneath our words. Like irony, punning, conundrum or circumlocution, it expresses by specifying least. (Strangely, 'emphasis' meant originally a kind of under-statement or evasive statement intended to encourage the listener to seek out the true import of what was said.) As Robert Browning suggested, 'Less is more.'[22] Yet this de-escalation, the apparent opposite of hyperbole, is just as much a rhetorical device, an agent of persuasion, in its own quiet way. Remember the muted rhetoric – which can become quite deafening via repetition – of Hemingway or Camus. It relies on allusiveness. Circumlocution invites, like conundrum, guesswork. What is being got at? As such it cannot always control responses, though in another function, that of spelling out more fully, it can generate definition. It suits those who emphasize the circumambient – environment, upbringing, circumstances – and underplay choice and personal responsibility. Like euphemism it aims to avoid embarrassment. For a very long time it was central to poetry, and probably still is in new guises (disjointed presentation of scene or mood, reluctance to name what it is addressing), for poetry puts things differently, evokes a thing by naming another or several, suggesting, and avoiding prosaic brass tasks. This can produce ludicrous periphrasis, a worthless riddle, as in Roucher's avoidance of the word 'hippopotamus': 'Des rivages du Nil le cheval amphibie' (the amphibious horse from the banks of the Nile).[23] Of course, it is Dickens who makes comic sociological capital out of this mode, in his Circumlocution Office, in *Little Dorrit*. In his own typically circumambling prose, he satirizes the practice of postponement, inaction, the endless bureaucratic circling with no result: officialdom defined as empty rhetoric. His means are reiteration, drawn-out hyperbole and general grotesquerie, perhaps not always intentional, as in: 'Its finger was in the largest public pie, and in the smallest public tart.'[24] Mr Barnacle, one of these clinging to the ship of state, speaks '"at the Circumlocution" – giving it the air of a word of about five-and-twenty syllables – "Office"'.[25]

Rhyming slang is another form of circumlocution (with a leer or a wink), a way of beating about the bush noisily. It is a gesture towards innovation, and indeed the permutations look very extensive, if not endless. For instance, 'wank' breeds Jodrell (Bank), Sherman (Tank), J. Arthur (Rank). Even so, as with all allusiveness, to rhyme in slang effectively, you have, as above, to refer to something or someone famous: that is, consecrated, corny.

If euphemisms are akin to white lies, exaggeration tells whoppers. If euphemism chooses the soft pedal, exaggeration (like slogans) employs the hard peddle. If litotes underwhelms, hyperbole overkills. Starting off by standing out, it can easily, through repetition, become a boring norm, bombast, hot air. An author (*auctor*) is by definition an augmenter. He who writes piles it on thick; and, if he seeks to edify, he builds up. When Poulou, the boy Sartre chastises throughout his partial autobiography, *Les Mots*, answers, with only rhetorical veracity, a questionnaire during the First World War by claiming that his dearest wish is to become a front-line soldier and to avenge the French dead, the reader and the adult Sartre see easily that it is only in words that he goes over the top. He supplies to the captivated bourgeois consumers of his *comédie* all that, and even more than, they demand. Language constantly escalates. People commonly talk of 'punching the buttons' of a television set or car radio, when the more accurate term would be 'prodding' or 'poking'. If we indeed tried to punch the close-set controls, we would give the machine simultaneously contradictory instructions. We picked it up because it sounded decisive; we fell for the over-statement. No wonder advertisers entertain such high hopes of bending us to their will. No less than litotes, exaggeration is a cover-up job. Only the full frontal assault of dysphemism plays no tricks, goes straight to the point, refuses to mince words. Luckily, language survives our misuse: 'Any euphemism ceases to be euphemistic after a time and the true meaning begins to show through. It's a losing game, but we keep on trying.'[26] As happens when fake coins wear thin, reality penetrates the crust of convention.

'Threadbare' is a metaphor often applied to metaphors. Why is our speech so metaphorical? Why this itch to move crabwise instead of head-on? It might be an assertion of our relative freedom, the small room for manoeuvre we really have, just as neologizing is also a form of self-assertiveness training. On a less daily level, 'truly creative and non-mythic thought in the arts, the sciences, religion, or metaphysics, must be invariably and irreducibly metaphorical.'[27] Metaphor pleads: 'Do not take me literally, read between my lines.' Its opposite, literal-mindedness, is habitual in young children, schizophrenics, people speaking a foreign language less than masterfully, and all of us when we do not make the effort to jump gaps. Yet language has to become decolourized for the sake of speed and efficiency. If we were constantly distracted by the images called up by our own or others' words, we could never get anywhere, except into diverting sidetracks. Just as we need to forget that much language is ambiguous when taking in sentences, so we need to practise wilful ignorance of the imaged nature of much speech. Swift's pointed joke about the Academy members of Lagado carrying round objects in lieu of the words designating them satirized the project of Thomas Spratt and the Royal Academy to strip language of its figurative contents. When we talk of the arm of a chair, this is so familiar and natural that we no longer think of it as a metaphor at all, a borrowing. Much of our everyday thinking, or discourse (for thinking is often conspicuous by its absence), requires such linguistic cardboard cut-outs, such templates, in order to function unjerkily. Many, however, react differently. 'When a phrase like "the lap of luxury" catches the eye, the mind relaxes but is not rested; for we are wearied, without exercise, by commonplace.'[28] Still others, whom I would join, believe that no metaphor is ever truly dead. It is playing possum, or is in the suspended animation of hibernation.

If clichés, dead metaphors, can be reactivated, they are not dead but dormant; if dead they can be born again. We can all practise linguistic voodoo. 'A cliché is not a half-dead metaphor, it is one that refuses to die.'[29] Empson expands on this view: 'All languages are composed of dead metaphors as the soil of corpses, but English is perhaps uniquely full of metaphors of this sort, which are not dead but sleeping.'[30] Marx was fond of a metaphor concerning the dead. In the Preface to *Capital*, he states: 'We suffer not only from the living but from the dead. *Le mort saisit le vif!*' (the dead seizes the living).[31] Auguste Comte had earlier written in his *Catéchisme positiviste* (1850): 'Les morts gouvernent les vivants' (p. 29). And of course we have the ancient command: 'Nil de mortuis nisi bonum'. 'Le mort saisit le vif' is an old French law axiom which states that at the moment of someone's decease, his inheritor becomes proprietor of his wealth without any need of legal formalities. Thus in this legal concept the old benefits the new and does not stifle it. So Marx takes this formula back to front (either through ignorance, or punningly), and thus reanimates an old metaphor about the living and the dead.

Intentionally or not, Marx mixed a metaphor. Journalists are especially prone to this verbal scouse, because of the notorious haste with which they have to work (deadlines, *Fleet* Street, The *Express*). Perhaps writing half a sentence each, two reporters coined a hotchpotch which, self-referentially, comments on itself: 'Round-the-world trading threatened to turn itself into a self-fulfilling downward spiral.'[32] Clichés intermarry happily. I have heard accidental blends like: 'There's more ways than one to swing a cat'; or 'That's no grist to my mill', where 'that's no skin off my nose' was clearly intended by the context. There is in the second example not even a phonic connexion between the two phrases, unlike the first where the cat doubles up; just a metrical or symmetrical reminiscence, a pattern. The doctor giving evidence in court who declared 'The whole chain of events consists entirely of missing links' was offering an accurate description of human bitty-mindedness.[33] Irish Bulls depend entirely on clichés merging. Lest anyone feel superior, I would say we are all mixed metaphors (oxymorons), glories and jests, angels and beasts, and that is a very ancient commonplace indeed. Such a realization does not stop us relishing the spectacle of any citizen dropping unconscious *double entendres*. Howlers, malapropisms or spoonerisms; or politicians, for example, slipping on banana skins they have themselves let fall in public speeches. Orwell claims that 'the sole aim of a metaphor is to call up a visual image. When these images clash – as in *The Fascist octopus has sung its swan song, the jackboot is thrown into the melting-pot* – it can be taken as certain that the writer is not seeing a mental image of the objects he is naming: in other words he is not really thinking.'[34] Metaphors do not in fact always call up pictures; we twig the point of the comparison usually by something other than a visual cross-check; and the examples quoted are, in their pell-mellery, comic and surrealistic in an obvious way which Orwell, humourless here, ignores. However, Orwell is surely right to put us on our guard against the verbal flannel of the powerful and their apologists, by scrutinizing their habitual, would-be mind-bending metaphors.

The huge area of poetic licence, which extends also to prose, depends often on such elision of thoughts, rapid telescoping; and a local slip-up may end up justified when viewed in the total context of the work. From the reader's or listener's end, rapid scanning, inattentive ears or inefficient short-term memory alike skate over many blemishes, which only slow-motion action-replays throw into relief. Besides, the anxiety about avoiding mixed metaphor often leads to extended metaphor, (*métaphore filée* in French, which can display its own pearls): an even likelier source of the ludicrous, because it seems produced by inertia, the dictates of mechanical euphony, over-literal decorum. It might be felt that mixed metaphors, Irish Bulls and the like subvert, albeit unknowingly, stock ideas via zany juxtaposition. Sir John Pentland Mahaffy, a famous Irish classical scholar, once asked for the difference between Irish and English varieties, replied: 'The Irish bull is pregnant, whereas the English bull is sterile.'[35] Another celebrated practitioner, Sir Boyle Roche, drilled his bulls; his impromptu ragouts were carefully cooked up in advance.[36]

We constantly seesaw between the literal and the figurative, as if we needed to play between them, to play them off against each other. Reseeing the literal in the figurative, especially when it is consecrated, is a prime source of comedy and rethinking. We resort to body-metaphors to express non-bodily phenomena: this is our existential *esprit de corps*.

Unmixed metaphors, stock epithets (Homer, Virgil), kennings in Anglo-Saxon poetry, depend, in the view of Lerner, 'on there being no fear, because no danger, of cliché'.[37] I am unconvinced. The fact that such set forms coexisted with striking words, unusual adjectives, surely indicates some awareness of the need for renewal and variation. Homer may have wished to re-sing old songs, but not the same old song. Poets know how to exploit set forms; educators over-literalize. Ong points that 'an epithet is generally one word, a least common denominator, an atom, in commonplace composition. This is doubtless why Ravisius Textor's collection and others like it were useful for relative neophytes in the art of rhetoric. These collections provided the elemental particles of discourse.'[38] This was adjective-use heavily controlled and channelled, no doubt because, like another disease, conjunctivitis, which interferes with clear sight, adjectivitis has always been regarded with suspicion, and targeted when critics smell affectation. Camus's little hero, Joseph Grand, having sweated throughout the novel over the opening sentence, pure commonplace, of a novel he will never complete, announces at the end, when the epidemic has subsided: 'J'ai supprimé tous les adjectifs' (I have deleted all the adjectives).[39] Adjectives carry more clichéic potential than nouns or verbs. They are more peripheral, the show-off fancy bits, tacked on to the essentials. As such they are more subject to modes, obsolescence and pretentiousness. They are also more moralizing, judgemental (guilty, not guilty, not proven). They are often a lazy short-cut. Above all, they can merely repeat the permanent quality of the object qualified. What the French neatly call *une épithète de nature* ('le dur caillou', the hard stone) is an adjectival truism, a pleonastic hiccup, like the corpse described, with no apparent intention of punning, as 'rigorously immobile'.[40]

> I have lived through a visit from a lady who is best described as overflowing;
> She is full of truisms but she is not like a truism, because a truism goes
> without saying, but she says without going.
>
> 　　　　　　　　　　　　　　　　　　　　　　　(Ogden Nash)[41]

It goes without saying that 'it goes without saying' or 'needless to say' are tautologous. Spanish has the more scientific idiom: 'Eso cae de su peso' (that falls by its own weight, which lends the phenomenon a certain Castilian gravity). The self-evident should be taken for granted or as read, although to presume can often be an evasion of thought. 'It goes without saying' often really means 'it goes through without thinking'. Admittedly, there are many occasions when any of us may want to take such evasive action. Hyperawareness, analysing every statement as if it were the small print of a legal document, can destroy all spontaneity, or at least reduce the lubrication of discourse. In addition, about common superfluities like 'dead and gone', Rogers comments: 'Tautology has almost as much appeal to the human mind as alliteration.'[42] We superadd, a word which is itself a prime pleonasm, like James Joyce's 'tautautologically'. Classical wisdom, represented by Horace, instructs us that 'Bis repetita non placent' (things repeated twice are not pleasing). But they are: children demanding to be reread favourite stories, adults replunging into Jane Austen for the tenth time (and Horace actually wrote 'Haec decies repetita placebit' – This will please even if repeated tenfold),[43] the universal taste for catchphrases. Theoretically, I myself dislike repetition, I hate reiteration, I loathe harping, in short, I detest duplication.

A truism labours, or belabours, the obvious, and remains a truism, even in translation. A foreign one is just alien corn, among which not a few feel at home. The Spanish term is *perogrullada* or *verdad de Pero Grullo*, a fictitious personage who said only blindingly obvious things. The French counterpart is *vérité de La Palice* (or Palisse), or *lapalissade*: a patently self-evident or fatuous remark. The French noun *évidence* should but does not derive from *évider*: to hollow out. General de Gaulle's many pleonastic public utterances (often amounting in effect to: 'I am here, you are here') are termed by Revel 'l'annonce de la présence réelle, de l'eucharistie'.[44] Revel does not discount the fact that such non-statements state an ideology, project an image, institute a hierarchical power-relationship, and elicit stock responses as in a Mass. De Gaulle's monopolizing tendencies, described by Sontag as pure camp,[45] in which, like a thrusting reporter, he claimed exclusive rights over all he surveyed, produced what Revel calls 'le truisme hyperbolique', to which de Gaulle's habit of referring to himself as *on* sought to add universal status. I heard him addressing students at the Ecole Normale Supérieure in 1959 in these terms: 'Que vous êtes nombreux, que vous êtes jeunes, que vous êtes gentils!' (how many, young and charming you are). The first two adjectives merely stated an unremarkable fact; the last was a base attempt to flatter an audience preponderantly hostile to him. A more complex truism of his was: 'Les chagrins sont les chagrins, les difficultés sont les difficultés. Mais la France est la France.' There is a kind of off-glide on the third component here. In the first two the repeated word means the same. In the third, France is different; it can rise above woes and problems, by its eternal virtues. Thus he simultaneously appeals to a fixed essence and yet suggests that it evolves. God's sublime tautology, in response to Moses' question what to call him – 'I AM THAT I AM' (*Exodus*, 3, 14) – is echoed by the multiperson Trouscaillon in Queneau's *Zazie dans le Métro*, who thus mocks the idea of the fixed identity to which God laid claim. In a more everyday dimension, phrases of the type 'un sou est un sou', or 'boys will be boys' are only apparent tautologies. The second mention underlines the importance of the assertion, and extends the meaning. 'Boys will be boys' equals 'these specific boys naturally behave in the manner of archetypal boys the world over'. There is a slide from the literal to the figurative, and context again tells us when to decode a seemingly absurd formula.

True truism or tautology is like the cognate object, that is, when an intransitive verb is made transitive, as in Trollope's 'She smiled a little smile and bowed a little bow'.[46] This is a regular rhetorical tactic in order to emphasize, and is a common idiomatic form in French ('pour de la chance c'est de la chance' – you are lucky, and no mistake, or 'pour un été chaud c'est un été chaud' – this is a hot summer, right enough).[47] In intention, no doubt, truisms strive to be the golden mean between exaggeration and understatement; they say (so they think) what is, and so achieve spot-onness. It is true that we mainly overreach or under-perform, and often lack such *adéquation*. Perhaps the only real clichés are truisms – things that it was never worth thinking or saying in the first place. Yet Biblical wisdom loves playing with 'first' and 'last' ('the last shall be first', and so on). Pascal noted that the last thing you find out in writing a book is how you should start it.[48] Many writers do write the introduction after all else, and thus endow it with a kind of posthumous foresight. Camus declared that first truths are those we take longest to reach.[49] This is the area in which we post-empt (as when we say 'I'll buy that').

As well as truisms, there are of course fallacies, which take similar root. Or mere decorativeness, as in much architecture.[50] Much of what we say is strictly pointless, talking to say nothing, and repetition fills empty spaces. For those of more critical inclination, an incontestable truth is no truth at all, or at least one unworthy of little respect. 'Familiar things happen, and mankind does not bother about them. It requires a very unusual mind to undertake the analysis of the obvious.'[51] One way, though often facile, is to invert a truism or tamper with it, as in Wilde or Cocteau's dandy tricks, which sometimes only simulate paradoxicality. Colie reminds us that: 'In tautology, what is, is; in paradox, what is, is and is not.'[52] Though a truism is, oxymoronically, an open secret, it can be converted to paradox only through hard labour, as in Barthes's struggle to valorize the 'obtuse' over the 'obvious'. Talking of a frame from an Eisenstein film, Barthes contrasts 'l'obvie' (normally used in French only in theological discourse: 'what comes naturally to mind') with 'l'obtus', the slippery area of signification (at least for Barthes). Recalling that *obtusus* means blunted, Barthes obviously favours such toning down of clarity (cf. Mallarmé: 'Too precise a meaning mars your vague literature'). Proteus does not like to be pinned down. Just as an obtuse angle exceeds a right angle, so an 'obtuse' meaning opens up 'the field of meaning'. While acknowledging the common pejorative connotation ('defective'), Barthes asserts that, beyond restricting moral or aesthetic categories, the 'obtuse' is kin to carnival. Making a big song and dance about how hard it is for him to be specific, Barthes analogizes himself to Saussure's buried anagrams and to *haiku*. Finally he equates 'obtuse' meaning with 'le filmique' – that which, in a film, is not reducible to critical discourse; presumably a platonic idea of filmicity, which he admits is a very rare phenomenon.[53] Barthes ends up asseverating that film is film, and whether the second occurrence of the words adds anything to the first is anyone's guess.

'The truths of the past are the clichés of the present' is a metacliché, a commonplace about clichés, and thus a truism: unnecessary.[54] Some truisms, however, are timely reminders, and need at least periodic reissue, like Vallès's 'Youth is a time of life, and not a talent nor a virtue'.[55] (We could substitute for 'youth' various insufficiently questioned values like 'the good old days', 'modernity', etc.) The framers of the American Declaration of Independence found it natural to declare certain truths to be self-evident, and no doubt prayed that such truisms would be a self-fulfilling prophecy. Clichés can come true, in the world of fiction: 'the wind was warm breath, as poets often say, but that day the cliché was true: the breathing of a living being'.[56] Or in society, at least for an optimist like Wells: 'Certain phrases – parroted phrases empty of belief – are already to be found in the newspapers and speeches – the abolition of war, the abolition of distance, the abolition of competition and social inequality. But after people have repeated a phrase a great number of times, they begin to realize it has meaning and may even be true. And then it comes true.'[57] This equates certain clichés with magical chants, and grants them for once an instigatory, creative function. Haig asks the unanswerable but compelling question: 'At what point, we might ask, does something said become a saying and a saying a saw? Are clichés distortions – or distillations of the truth?'[58] Looking in the mirror, am I in this book, as the French idiom has it, kicking down open doors; flogging a dead horse; using a steam-hammer to crack a nut? Am I employed in redundancy? Do I sufficiently realize that bathos is not a *pièce de résistance* but a *pièce de reddition*, a surrendering to the facile? Like truism and tautology, am I running on the spot, occasionally stalling, otherwise idling, and at best juddering?

9

A Few Well-Chosen Words

PUBLISH AND BE DAMNED
Duke of Wellington

It hardly becomes us to sneer at primitive societies, when we still live in a drum culture ourselves, and, as long as we have pulses and heartbeats, perhaps always will. We are rocked into repetition and thoughtlessness by the rhythms of received phrases. Are we so unlike the decrepit conundrummer in O. W. Holmes's story who in old age is satisfied by the mere beat of his riddles – the actual contents he leaves blank?[1] With limericks we mentally start tapping our feet as soon as one starts. The familiar is catchy. But, as we beat out cadences, the stamping-ground produces the well-trodden, the trite. Papist bulls instruct the faithful to use the rhythm method. Despite the sceptical nickname of Vatican roulette, this still offers safety in numbers. The rhythm method of clichés likewise numbs the mind, silences the questioning. The care for euphony can carry the words along undeviating tramlines, and creativity degenerates into a production-line. To shift from a mobile to a stationary image, clichés fall into the wide area of the pre-cast: slots, moulds, stencils (possibly deriving, ironically, from the French *étinceler*, to sparkle), patterns, recipes, formulae. Thinking simplified, programmed on a plate. Slogans loom.

'Man is a creature who lives not upon bread alone, but principally by catchwords.'[2] Our minds can be caught by catchphrases, mottoes, and these often surface when the speaker lacks a logical retort, is at a loss for words. 'The cliché is a convenient conversational password which dispenses you from emotion.'[3] The borrowed, ready-made phrase economizes on effort. Like Masonic signals and other forms of tribal affiliation or clubbability, the password is a shibboleth, sorting the goats from the sheep. Slogans aim wider and need a closer look.

Like proverbs, slogans use ellipsis and concision, in their pursuit of memorizability. Like jargon, the propaganda served by slogans relies on what Humpty Dumpty in *Through the Looking-Glass* called 'knock-down arguments'.[4] The early form of the current word (like the German *Schlagwort*), 'slug-horn', captures more sharply the idea of impact. A slogan is an offer purporting to be a guarantee, and taking the form of an oath of loyalty: all of these are in the optative mood. Coteries, cabales, schools of thought command a mandatory style and lexis. They want to condense their philosophy to manageable proportions, put it in a nut-shell. Yet, as Reboul in his excellent study remarks, though we tend to think of slogans as blatant, hitting us smack in the eye or the guts, there are many more about than we ever notice and the more virulent ones are perhaps those we notice least.[5] They can be insidious, hidden persuaders and subliminal seducers, but, whatever their tactic, their goal is to pressurize, and they use many rhetorical devices to this end. Reboul issues a chastening reminder that intellectuals, too, need slogans, because trying to think for yourself is a lonely and often anguishing activity.[6] Clichés are rallying- points, but so was Nuremberg, and slogans help to produce that glassy-eyed look of people bombarded with prepacked material. Today, every group has them, as protest organizes itself. The need to 'get the message across' to employers, to the government, to possible but distant sympathizers within the nation, means that every demonstration comes equipped with placards and banners, all inscribed with punchy, insulting and sometimes witty slogans. Their bearers line up before the press or television cameras, as if on a beauty-parade or march on the spot. They cannot each be interviewed: their separate chants produce a cacophonous Babel. Their slogans speak, briefly and pungently, for them. The danger, of course, is of predictability and a blasé response from onlookers. Some persevering sloganeers, however, do not expect immediate effects, and think of their messages more like delayed-action bombs, or as something to be repeated *ad nauseam*. It is always ambiguous, when a crowd moves into action and storms a position chanting slogans, whether these are the impetus or the accompaniment, the linguistic bandwaggon rather than the vanguard.

Just as a proverb can mean opposite things, so many slogans can serve opposing camps. Their very concision entails this possibility of rent-an-idea, to go with rent-a-crowd. Just as causes vary in honourability, so slogans can vary from 'The Rights of Man' to 'You've Never Had It So Good'. Both of these have designs on us. 'Strength Through Joy' is an admirable sentiment, if Hitler had not poisoned it forever. As always, we need to know the context: who issued the slogan, where, when, to what end? Within themselves, slogans can reconcile contrary needs, for example by stoking up hatred and exorcizing fear as in Mao's 'Imperialists are paper tigers'.[7] As well as blowing the gaff (exposing) or blowing the trumpet (self-boosting), slogans, like those of *Nineteen Eighty-Four*, can produce disinformation, seek to hoodwink the receivers. Very frequently, slogans inspire pity, for they represent a frustrated banging of the head or tongue against the wall of indifference or incomprehension. A sense of political impotence can lead to verbal over-compensation, the brandishing of unacted threats, the inertia of phrase-making. Dilation of language or eyeball begets exorbitance. If there are metaphors we live by, there are slogans people die for, or from. Slogans can be genocidal in intention, as in the early Ku Klux Klan: 'Kill the Kikes, Koons and Katholics.'[8] In a cosier tradition, Disraeli could respond in these words to phrases like 'fancy franchises': 'Alliteration tickles the ear and is a very popular form of language among savages ... but it is not an argument in legislation.'[9] Tell that to lynchers. Montaigne, who worked hard for sanity in a very violent epoch, personalized the business of slogans by painting fifty-seven maxims on his ceiling-beams. Impersonating Montaigne as he periodically does, Compagnon (as we now say) takes these on board: 'The slogan is a sign keeping an eye on me, a guardian angel that I try to live up to ... My emblem represents me: it sticks to my skin like a tattoo.'[10] Most slogans widen on to more public ideologies.

In Sartre's novella, 'L'Enfance d'un chef' (The Making of a Boss), that exuberant massacre of self-justifying clichés, the wobbly protagonist Lucien, as he grows increasingly authoritarian in aspiration, convinces himself that the Action Française-type slogan 'Trouver sa voie' (Seek your path) exceeds in dynamism the 'Freudian' watchword 'Suivre sa pente' (Follow your inclination). In so doing he flees individuality, abdicates in favour of the gang ethos. Even the founders of ideologies become disciples or slaves of their own doctrine. 'All official institutions of language are harping machines: school, sport, advertising, mass media, song, news all repeat the same structures, the same meaning, often the same words: the stereotype is a political fact and the major embodiment of ideology.'[12] Barthes recognizes that such dunning can be as seductive as newness, but makes his excuses for not joining in: 'As soon as a thing *stands to reason*, I desert.'[13]

Barthes's 'mythologies' are in fact stereotypes themselves: fixed forms (e.g. 'Nature' = the unchanging). Despite his splendid mockery of those who try to defuse argument and tame discomfiting truths, he runs the danger himself of turning his uniform condemnation into a totalitarian frame: of becoming an essentialist, a refrigerator, himself. He focuses on end-products and never shows us the genesis of a 'mythology'. Perhaps he sees himself as coming late in the line of pro-Marxist, anti-bourgeois critique. Later in his career he became more deviously subjective and re-founded the old French school, baptized by *Le Canard enchaîné*, of *nombrilisme* (umbilicism) – the Gidean narcissism *redivivus*. As with Gide, you feel that the sudden abolition of the enemy – orthodoxy – would leave him with precious little to write about.

Convinced of the 'granite stupidity' of the masses, Hitler practised what he preached: 'The masses are slow-moving, and they always require a certain time before they are even ready to notice a thing, and only after the simplest ideas are repeated thousands of times will the masses finally remember them.'[14] A dictator commands that people copy what he says. As dialogue vanishes, the likeliness of bombast, the urge to impress oneself, increases. Discourse becomes all style. 'It is the gap between the pretension to style and the absence of the stylist which creates absurdity. Cliché is style without the man himself.' [15] All purple patches: would-be emperor language. Propaganda seeks to take our mind off.

It is often held that all political discourse is clichéic, and unavoidably so. In evading truthfulness, politicians necessarily take refuge in obfuscation; endless repetition of statements lacking in precise content is their stock-in-trade. Overexposure, as Mrs Thatcher for once admits honestly, partially explains this: 'The trouble with politicians is we have to speak more often than we have something to say.'[16] In a characteristically pleonastic passage, Carlyle wrote: 'Parliaments travel so naturally in their deep-rutted routine, commonplace worn into ruts ankle-deep.'[17] As politics entails hanging on to or attaining power, it is inherently conservative and could not afford, even if it were capable of, originality. It must appeal to the most uncritical part of people, while appearing to set them a challenge. Clichés are democratic, egalitarian: everyone has access to them, a right to them; they are non-exclusive and non-arcane. In an age when multinational firms often seem to dominate governments, the same kind of behaviour tends to predominate in both areas. 'Party Man and Company Man are expected to accept the principle of Total Immersion in Work. Both protect themselves by means of a thick coat of clichés and formulae.'[18] Pondering the case of Edward Heath (when he was Prime Minister), Hudson goes on: 'Here ... is the ultimate, totally formed *homo politicus*, a person with no private life to conceal, a Lenin. The clichés are the man, his blood and bones as well as his skin.'[19] This, surely, is even more true of the mulish *mulier politica* Thatcher. Fónagy actually claims to detect a kind of music in the parroting of party-lines, which he writes out in staves.[20]

'Claptrap' means also a device, linguistic or otherwise, to catch applause. Churches knew, long before Pavlov, all about induced acquiescence, stimulus and response. Political oratory no doubt has to simplify because of the large (and since the coming of television, disparate) audiences it targets. Every so often the worms turn, and large numbers of individual voters give parties or governments a shocking reminder that their pet dogmas need revising or ditching. Electoral behaviour is often called 'volatile' when it is behaving as it should: freely. Social change is brought about by the challenging of clichés (the status quo), and the result is not inevitably just another cliché, as the cynical would have it, but a positive improvement. A favourite cliché of reactionaries is to hark back to a mythical past towards which all are urged to strive. Orwell stressed the archaizing tendencies of 1930s fascism (Roman architecture, Greek athleticism, medieval knights). 'Victorian' values in 1980s Britain or the 'frontier spirit' in contemporary America perform a similar function, though the language has changed. '*Propaganda*, another of those tired expressions one seldom hears nowadays because *public relations* has taken its place (or *education*, or *consciousness-raising*): the propagandist does not coax, wheedle, in-doctrinate, or inveigle the public into accepting his point of view, but *educates* it or *raises* its consciousness.'[21]

Orwell tried to raise his readers' consciousness in more honourable ways. In his influential 'Politics and the English language', he claims that 'prose consists less and less of *words* chosen for the sake of their meaning, and more of *phrases* tacked together like the sections of a prefabricated hen-house'.[22] He is hostile to the prolix phrase-making which he terms 'verbal false limbs'; it accompanies a flight from the concreteness which he himself practises ('An accumulation of stale phrases chokes the writer like tea-leaves blocking a sink' (p. 164)). The crucial connexion is that such lazy writing goes in tandem with party-mindedness (p. 166). While honest enough, as always, to admit that his essay sins in the very areas he is protesting about (p. 167), he ends on a note of some optimism: 'One can at least change one's own habits, and from time to time one can even, if one jeers loudly enough, send some worn-out and useless phrase – some *jackboot, Achilles' heel, hotbed, melting pot, acid test, veritable inferno* or other lump of verbal refuse – into the dustbin where it belongs' (p. 170). This is the passage Christopher Ricks picks out in order to perform an act of ecological recycling on the garbage of cliché. Ricks maintains that Orwell creates 'a bizarre vitality of poetry' out of the italicized items:

> The *jackboot* has, hard on its heels, *Achilles' heel*; then the hotbed at once melts in the heat, into *melting-pot*, and then again (a different melting) into *acid test* – with perhaps some memory of Achilles, held by the heel while he was dipped into the Styx; and then finally the *veritable inferno*, which not only consumes *hotbed* and *melting pot* but also, because of *veritable*, confronts the truth-testing *acid test*. Orwell may have set his face against those clichés, but his mind, including his cooperative subconscious, was another matter.[23]

In my fourth remove from the original clichés (to coin an oxymoron), I would say this gloss impresses flashily by its pertness, its punning (mind-matter); I know comparable temptations. I value Ricks's perception of a critical mind such as Orwell's *collaborating* with clichés even while attacking them. Ricks later exemplifies, or destroys (it's a free country), his case for the serviceability of junk by pleading specially for the lyrics of Bob Dylan.

In Orwell's own fiction, Winston Smith tries to shore up his crumbling morale by reminding himself that 'the obvious, the silly and the true had got to be defended. Truisms are true, hold on to that!'[24] He clings to common sense, or in the special world of *Nineteen Eighty-Four*, uncommon sense, as the only resistance to the big lie. Sentimentally and irrelevantly, he likes to think that the proles are immune to propaganda; double-think, besides, is too hard for them, but so is single-think. The system of double-think aims at maintaining cliché, freezing language and thus aborting what can be thought in it. Smith's vestigial form of semi-private double-think is all he can oppose to the official system seeking to control and liquidate such subversion. Both Big Brother and Goldstein are maintained fictions, a necessary polarity (the Hero who embodies the collective mind, and the Enemy who symbolizes solo thinking). Of course, as some are more equal than others, the two poles are of unequal force. Goldstein is an evacuated power, whereas Big Brother has pumped-up omnipotence. As Anthony Burgess argues, 'Orwell recognized his own doubleness very sharply. He was both Eric Blair and George Orwell, a product of the fringe of the ruling class who tried to identify himself with the workers, an intellectual who distrusted intellectuals, a word-user who distrusted words ... Our own attitude to double-think is inevitably doublethinkful.'[25] No wonder that Orwell makes a kind of common cause with clichés. ' Double-think is also a grim joke',[26] concludes Burgess, though whom the joke is on is unclear, or nuclear, perhaps. Equally frightening is the idea of official writing 'about nothing', probably borrowed from Aldous Huxley, 'the expunging of meaning by language, from language, and in language'.[27] Winston Smith is not only the 'last man in Europe'; he is the last to speak a meaningful, sane English.

Sloganeers, to sell their image, need to advertise their wares, or at least their promises. Profiting, as they live to, advertisers employ slogans. They promote, amidst great dynamic flurry, congealing agents, fixatives, adhesives: clichés that consumers must not be allowed to forget, mnemonics. Virtually the only poetry most Western people ever hear or read after infant school is the lyrics of pop-songs and advertising jingles. They invade our minds and may re-emerge still jangling on our lips, though whether they actually cause us to spend money on the product is a question not even the producers have resolved. Like political slogans, those of publicity ('pufflicity' in Walter Winchell's timely blend) exploit four of the many functions of cliché: they seek repetition, and hope to have a mesmeric, sedative, or galvanizing influence. At their most blatant, they resemble the act of knocking a nail, with repeated blows, into wooden heads. Analysing the markedly less innovative French tradition, Duisit underscores the unavoidability of such hammering on the same spot: 'It's a cheap way of restating the obvious, of valorizing banality, or of pushing home something already known. The semantic investment in each slogan is almost non-existent ('C'est Shell que j'aime'), but to make up for this fact advertising images are scattered everywhere to reduce fading in the transmission of words.'[28] Also in the French tradition, one of the words for advertising, *réclame*, like 'slogan' and like the intentions behind argot and jargon, meant originally a rallying-call, the signal by which a group recognizes its members. The present-day equivalent is 'corporate identity', for employees' loyalty is as precious as consumers'. Slogans are household words at both ends of the chain.

Given the plagiaristic nature of much contemporary culture, however, and the rapid turn-round built into commerce, variation and surprise relay the old emphasis on sheer refrain. Bandwaggoning on the success of rival slogans can both amuse customers, and put down competitors without resorting to sullen knocking-copy. Such thumbing of rides has become so acceptable that comedians, at a further remove, have only to cite well-known slogans to trigger the laughter of recognition; allusiveness exists at all levels of culture. Suggestiveness, however, still appears to be confined more to images than to text, just as broadcasting companies receive more complaints about 'bad' language than about violent or erotic scenes. In the iconic age, words still count for much. Though Bolinger talks of the 'din of euphemism in advertising', he stresses that it is a mock toning-down, aimed really at visibility.[29] Litotes, as we have seen, can go over the top.

As can some student of slogans. Jaubert, for example, because slogans condense different images and often display fabulous heroes, twins them with other manifestations of the unconscious. They are 'made of the same fluid matter as our dreams and hence will always make us dream'.[30] Or rave. Reboul sums up the nature and functions of the slogan more pointedly:

> It is not only a short formula, for that is a pleonasm ('formula' implies brevity), but a formula that is too short for what it wants to say. And it is by what it leaves out that the slogan comes into its own. It rallies people but by not being too specific about the goal. It incites, but keeps quiet about the implications or promises. It asserts but in a cursory fashion. It grabs, but by appealing to the unconscious more than the conscious mind. It obeys the language code, but plays on its ambiguities. It can seduce, like a witticism or a poem, without the bewitched mind noticing. In all of its functions, it is a ready-made thought, which thinks for us in our absence.[31]

In this view, like clichés, slogans are more akin to Trojan horses than to battering-rams. Jingling formulae cannot be dismissed as merely a twentieth-century aberration. Pope's attack on eighteenth-century poetasters beautifully enacts their unthinking refrains:

> While they ring round the same unvary'd chimes,
> With sure returns of still expected rhymes.
> Where e'er you find 'the cooling western breeze',
> In the next line, it 'whispers thro' the trees;'
> If crystal streams 'with pleasing murmurs creep,'
> The reader's threatend (not in vain) with 'sleep'.
> Then, at the last and only couplet fraught
> With some unmeaning thing they call a thought,
> A needless Alexandrine ends the song,
> That, like a wounded snake, drags its slow length along.[32]

Thus every doggerel will have its day, and cannot easily be laughed away.

Advertising language also resorts to proverbs and idioms, towards which I am heading. The Mieders argue that 'this process of innovation on the basis of tradition becomes the proof of the continuity of the traditional forms'.[33] The logic here is piously hopeful, for such recycling could be seen more undeceivedly as the rape of the past, as they admit in a footnote defining such commercial re-use of folklore as 'folk-lure'.[34] It may be their concentration on the cracker-barrel aspects of American culture which makes them see such folksiness as paying off. Some proverbs are admittedly cited straight, and Spitzer has warned that it would be 'wrong to see a sermon in all advertising'.[35] Perhaps it is their German-American origins that lead them to make the statement, dubious in a god-forsaken age: 'There probably is no better way to stress authority and trustworthiness in an advertising headline than to use a biblical proverb' (p. 313). Yet the link between protestantism and the rise of capitalism, and the American practice of selling religion capitalistically, suggest that even untampered-with quoting does not imply respect for the wisdom of the past. The Mieders note also the reverse procedure, whereby slogans become so familiar (Coca-Cola's 'It's The Real Thing', now almost fifty years old) that they operate as proverbs (p. 311). I would modify this: as catchphrases, for such slogans hardly aspire to the status of general wisdom. That slogan, plastered across the world in many languages, aims only at warning consumers against competing colas. When it comes to altered sayings, the Mieders aptly select the Volkswagen slogan when the 'Beetle' range was extended: 'Different Volks for different folks' (p. 312). This matches the structure and rhyme of the original formula, and puts across the message pithily. A reconditioned idiom hits the target even more pointedly; the Committee for Hand-Gun Control asked for donations to its campaign to ban the sale of ammunition with: 'We need bullets like we need a hole in the head' – the message driven home by the picture of a pretty girl's cranium with entry-points (p. 314). In purely commercial terms, a clothing firm very simply exploited the idiomatic reverberations of its own name: 'JONES NEW YORK. No wonder everyone is trying to keep up with us' (p. 315).

Proverbs are often used as if they were catchphrases. Part of one is quoted, as a trigger (cf. reading poetry to young children), setting off a conditioned response: 'A stitch in time ...' A Swiss-German proverb states: 'A proverb places the words in one's mouth',[36] by a kind of collective ventriloquism. Ponge – as a poet he has more invested – asserts that 'C'est toujours au proverbe que tout langage tend'.[37] If we transfer this to everyday discourse, we could claim that, except when we regret having said something, we do generally wish to inscribe our words in other people's memories. The fact that we seldom can gives us, as compensation, the welcome chance of second thoughts.

In *Deuteronomy* (28, 37), Moses warns the Israelites of the penalties for disobeying the Law: 'And thou shalt become an astonishment, a proverb

'*God does exist*', from *Creative Review*, August 1986, reproduced by kind permission of Saatchi and Saatchi

and a byword among all nations.' The word 'proverb', like the thing itself, is polyvalent. The terms for proverb in various languages straddle this wide range of meanings: old sayings, by-play (twisting of words), analogy, parable, maxim, example, repetition, elegant speech or writing.[38] Like clichés, one reason why proverbs enjoy durability is that they can be all things to all men, women and children. For many, this is precisely what is wrong with them. As well as the often noted fact that many proverbs within a tradition contradict each other, it happens that the same proverb reoccurs in various languages with a totally opposite or different application. Noting this, Champion, who has collected them worldwide, stresses that it is a lesser aspect: proverbs as a totality show remarkable clang-effects from one culture and language to another (p. xxii). He lists four of the common characteristics as opportunism, fatalism, diplomacy and charity (p. xviii). The first two already indicate a polarity. Perhaps foreseeing such objections, it is significantly an Irish example which declares: 'Proverbs cannot be contradicted' (p. 58). Another catch is that 'wise men make proverbs but fools repeat them' (p. 38). It seems to me that proverbs provide an authoritative shield, which protects the speaker from having to make a personal statement; they save effort, as they are ready-mades; and they obviate the demands of precision, for they generalize. Such pithy statements appeal to the laconic, since how much of human breath or ink is normally wasted. Isaac Disraeli relished their 'parsimony of words prodigal of sense', and recalls that 'proverbs existed before books'.[39]

Proverbs try to be wise before the event, to foresee dangers ('tristis *ante* coitum'), or to console when things go wrong. They adopt the pose of the worldly-wise; their domain is 'wiseacreage'.[40] No doubt the wisdom of proverbs is *sometimes* usable (every dog has his day), just as I use clichés to talk of clichés. For Reboul, proverbs do not even claim to be fixed truths; they are situational and refer to general but not universal cases; so they shift their ground in the event of a new situation.[41] In this perspective, proverbs are like so many fingers plugging the multiple leaks sprung by the dyke of existence. Kenneth Burke sees them as social medicine, witchdoctors who tell us what we already know, but authenticated, ritualized, made special. Often, they simply name a situation: 'We need a word for it.' Keen to break down barriers which narrowly compartmentalize life, Burke argues for literature, defined very catholically, as 'equipment for living'. Within that overall strategy, proverbs persuade us to 'keep our weather eye open'.[42] As a matter of fact, most proverbs, if quoted at all, are probably called upon after the event, and, as such, are more by way of a gloss on conduct – ironic, pedantic, or consolatory ('Patch grief with proverbs', as Shakespeare exactly phrases it).[43]

Proverbs seek to teach economy: of expression, effort, suffering, expense, and do so economically. Terseness is all ('A proverb is shorter than a bird's beak'),[44] and that is why long-winded proverbs easily sound comic. Maxims and epigrams (and the many related figures) also generalize and do not seriously offer precise guides to conduct. They are dedicated to the pursuit of snappiness, and are an area in which the Anglo-Saxons often concede advantage to the French, although the compliment is often typically back-handed. In Flaubert's *Dictionary of Received Ideas*, writes Sabin, 'an implicit standard of aphorism and maxim governs the entire satiric attack on *idées reçues*. He leads us to understand cliché as failed aphorism, and it is perhaps only in the light of French pride in its brilliant tradition of aphorism that the demand on language made by this implicit standard does not seem more arbitrary and limited than it does.'[45] The dictatorial French tradition positively invites contradiction from all but totally passive consumers. In what seems to me a facile, piously hopeful and spurious distinction, Barthes opposes the bourgeois maxim – which he views as static and tautological, and implying that nothing new is to be discovered, declared or done – with the popular proverb, pointed, so he claims, towards a world still in the making.[46]

Taking the long-term view, proverbs act like time-capsules, though the pill they offer is sometimes bitter. They are often silencers, of complaint or of opposition; the last word on the subject. They are frequently associated with mystery or mystification, like other forms of roundabout or veiled discourse (allegory, irony, paradox). 'Proverbs are little gospels.'[47] They are preponderantly metaphorical. As a German example admits, with marvellous sophistry: 'A proverb never lies, it is only its meaning which deceives' (p. 178). An international rash of jokes erupted after the publicizing of Khrushchev's quoting of baffling and possibly invented Russian proverbs. These often aped the common proverbial trick of animal analogies, as a way of underlining the unchanging, eternal presence of Nature in Man. Animal rights supporters today would term this 'animalism' – offloading on to innocent beasts the sins of humans, scapegoating them. ('Chacun a son chien', as Diderot said). Whether a cowardly or a distancing device, such recourse to animal fables obviously aims at picturesqueness, a time-honoured way to lodge any message in others' minds. The archaizing form of many proverbs is not only traditional, it is wellnigh indispensable, as even fake proverbs (Californian Chinese 'he say') recognize. As advertising slogans can resuscitate proverbs to gain authority, so proverbs hark back to some mythical time when people are imagined as talking differently and better. Similarly, the presence of rhyme, assonance, alliteration or wordplay in many proverbs also refers back to the most traditional forms of communication, and indicate that it is the shape, the clinchingness, that matters even more than the content. The repeatability of the proverb would be neatly caught by the Spanish word for it, *refrán*, if it ever meant 'refrain'. Much of the point of proverbs lies in the phraseology: we relish recipes, short messages (telegrams also alarm, of course). And playing with words hints at some kind of mastery over them: 'Praemonitus, praemunitus' (forwarned is forearmed).

The one incontrovertible proverb I know is the American 'Life is just one damned thing after another'. Some are extremely parochial, as in the Peruvian 'Avoid living in Quive', which remains opaque until you know this was a village cursed by an archbishop (p. 636). The obscure can still surprise, as in the English 'Mad men and lame men copulate best' (p. 24). (Flattish-footed and provisionally sane I cannot compete.) George Herbert's collection is called *Outlandish Proverbs* (nobody seems sure why); many proverbs certainly strike as bizarre. The majority, however, like idioms sound tory; their appeal is usually: 'You know it makes sense.' They tend to appeal to our more selfish, grasping, statusquoing side, while appearing to offer us choices. Denis Saurat voices this view: 'Proverbs are the greatest help to mankind in that they present clearly both sides of any question, thus putting the choice on man himself.' Where it was to begin with, so why bother? In this optic, proverbs return the ball to our lonely courts. He goes on: 'Perhaps in the case of French proverbs we can see merely that general tendency which is so visible in French literature to reach after universal statements, statements which can be regarded as valid for the whole world.'[48] France's universal mission: an exploded umbilicism. This 'sagesse des nations' is less ecumenical than it sounds from this term, and *sagesse* covers both conformist behaviour (as in *enfant sage* or *prix de sagesse*) and wisdom. Non-conformism is spread as thinly in France as liberalism in the United States, or plain dealing in England. Despite or because of their highly contentious history, French speech and writing places a high premium on conformism: the rules for drama, however elastically obeyed; the rules of social conduct, however cynically circumvented.

Three left-wing critics of conventional wisdom, eternal verities, speak their piece against the lesson of proverbs, Claude Roy argues that, hostile to the present or to any open future, they play safe by referring habitually to the past, to experience, generally sorry experience. The only door they leave ajar is the one that never will open – the day that hens have teeth, quails fall ready-roasted (or, as we say in English, pigs fly). They resemble the cautious gambler who bets on both black and red, and its amazed at always getting his stake-money back. The famous brevity of proverbs is in league with the petty economizing tendencies of popular wisdom – the fear of risk and expenditure.[49] Sartre finds the wisdom of nations a melancholy thing ('Charity begins at home'). The metaphysics or subtext of proverbs is realist, fatalist, conservative. 'We must not struggle against the authorities ... do not reach out above your station ... Experience shows that human beings always head for the worst, and so need strong restraints around them, to keep anarchy at bay.'[50] His partner, Simone de Beauvoir, is in unison: wisdom means protecting yourself at every turn from misfortune, which leads to an ethics of mediocrity: 'To live happily, let us live in hiding.'[51] In effect, she argues that Existentialism is the polar opposite of proverbs and fable-wisdom, none of which says: 'You are free, but you are responsible for your actions.' In this view, 'la sagesse des nations' involves alibis, abdication of responsibility, psychological tax evasion. In short, it is codified bad faith.

The neutering tendencies of proverbial wisdom can be countered in less solemn ways: by play, which can even sharpen the teeth of those old saws. The Wellerism (or Yankeeism, for Americans like to think of this twister as peculiar to them) can attempt to torpedo a cliché saying. 'As the priest on the *Titanic* said: "the family that prays together stays together".'[52] Here a formula applied pat to reassure, or to browbeat, is subverted, or diverted to a black joke, an unsettling reminder that prayers cannot reverse shipwrecks. The Wellerism ploy puts the set phrase in a different context, and shows it up for what it is: unreliable, a weather-vane, an idea for all seasons, and thus not specifically true for any. Or set expressions can be slightly altered, set askew: '*When* is the younger generation coming to?'[53] Rejuvenated paroemiography – the twisting of congealed forms such as proverbs – is an act of semantic and linguistic ecology, very useful when natural resources are being rapidly exhausted. As an Esthonian example has it: 'With the old one must serve the new' (p. 127). Proverbs into proverbs. Sayings for a long time inert can be reactivated and, like trampolines, give bounce to ideas and speech. It is precisely because proverbs are a highly conventionalized formulation that they lend themselves to distortion. The desacralizing urge empties the container and refills it with new meaning. In addition, as many formulae now seem passably meaningless to us, we feel free to appropriate them to our own purposes. Of course twisting a proverb, like parody, can still work to preserve the old form; and it is sometimes argued that such mocking re-use at least helps to stop the ancient stock (cf. museums and 'heritage-trails') falling into oblivion. That would be a side-effect; the main component is the need for retaliation, minor victories, morale boosts. Being playful, it can easily become skittish. It is very easy to bifurcate a proverb, for instance by throwing particles of two separate ones together heterogeneously: 'You can't make an omelette without skinning cats.' The French surrealists were fond of this sport, which has been termed, pleonastically, 'bricollage' (for collage is already *bricolage*).[54] It would indeed seem to be a case of opposite poles attracting. Eternal verities and precast forms are the diametrical opposite of surrealism, and so make ideal starting-blocks for surrealist flight. But they were sometimes trapped by their wily adversary, and then they deviated into sense: 'Quand la raison n'est pas là les souris dansent' (When the mind's astray, the mice will play).[55]

Just as what's bred in the bone will come out in the flesh, so, when 'the new drives out the old', the old returns at the gallop, and nowhere more than in oral cultures, from which, in print-cultures, we are cut off mainly by prejudice rather than for any better reason. In the sophisticated West, we vestigially believe in the power of words; we still have a sense of word-magic, just as much of our present knowledge really has pre-scientific foundations.[56] In more traditional societies, set forms like proverbs act as an accepted bondage, but also provide materials for competitiveness: they remind of the rules of the social game but allow room for manoeuvre within those limits. Proverbs *are* literature to many peoples: special language, memorability, wit, wisdom. Unlike Western literature (except in the more genuinely freewheeling psychodramas of the 1960s), tribal cultures permit and encourage interchange between all present, star performers and audience. It is natural and logical that non-print (or less-print) cultures should invest so much effort, artistry and value in oratory, in palavers of all kinds. In parts of Africa, there are even drum-proverbs, stylized messages beaten out in regular metrical form.[57]

The grey eminence of French letters, Jean Paulhan, studied before the 1914–18 War the Hain-Tenys of Madagascar: unanswerable traditional proverbs used in public jousts as a form of aggressive self-defence. Many he found gnomic and suspected of being Nonsense, but beneath all the chiaroscuro of the words he detected a 'persuasion-machine'.[58] The participants were engaged in a capping competition, one-upmanship. Formally, nothing new was introduced into the bouts: there was a common stock, with variants, and the champions were the best selectors. Half a century later, Keenan studied the verbal tournaments. She found that the code of oratory involved 'the winding of words', that is, speaking in an allusive manner. 'They made circles around the thought', a phrase which nicely captures the mastery and the indirection involved. As time had moved on, Keenan observed that part of the oratorical stock now came from how-to pamphlets sold in local markets. The tradition was thus a mixed bag: brochures, memories of listening as a child to other performances, family oral transmission, plus individual variation. Of course, even in oral societies memory is still selective, still a matter of eliding inconvenient facts, still tied to power-play situations. Concentrating on ritualized marriage-proposals (*kabary*) Keenan noticed the rigged nature of the contest, the ground-rules agreed in advance by both parties to the transaction. The whole practice was highly self-aware: 'a metalanguage that refers to the structure of the discourse in process'. Total humiliation is out-of-court: the punches are pulled (as, sometimes, in Jewish cursing). Proverbs are used heavily to emphasize the ties between the families, vital in a marriage proposal. Lest this sound like an empty ceremonial, Keenan stresses that the partial unpredictability of the oratory makes all the difference between a heated and an insipid performance. It is, she maintains, the most developed art-form in the culture.[59] Comparably, Finnegan, studying types of trials in African tribal culture, finds that, more frankly than in our own law-courts, trials in oral communities recognize that litigation is above all a verbal struggle and a verbal game conjoined.[60] (Presumably, lawyers, like mathematicians, relish their proofs and would similarly talk, if only indirectly, of the beauty of their case.) In such cultures, proverbs can often clinch a case (just as legal precedents are cited in Western courts). They further add embellishment, flourish, and thus give vent to artistic pride. I am reminded of our (highly dangerous) concept of a limited war. In all, proverbs are seen in such cultures as so special that they are sometimes monopolized by a power-elite, as their secret language.

Some of these attitudes and practices were those of Europeans in the gradual evolution from oral to manuscript to print culture. As we have earlier seen, 'oral culture had generated the commonplaces as part of its formulary apparatus for accumulating and retrieving knowledge'.[61] Such communities are sometimes called by anthropologists 'shame cultures', which institutionalize 'public pressures in individuals to ensure conformity to tribal modes of behaviour'.[62] Yet, like the African societies described above, oral cultures, and their successors, also gave rise to continual polemic, disputation, which provides much of the drama in the plays of Shakespeare. For centuries the educational system was based on that highly sententious and forensic language, Latin. 'Even after print, storage processes proper to the original oral culture or manuscript culture, with the latter's very heavy oral residue, persisted through many generations: that is to say, the drive to consider what had been said as demanding perpetual reiteration continued strong.'[63] Logic, but not events, supports Ong when he deduces that the advent of print made 'the cultivation of proverbs outmoded or even counter-productive'.[64] People are not as neat as theories, and proverbs have gone on patchily living, presumably because they derive from some deep-rooted need of the mind for formulaic expression, in catchy form – a kind of mental, dogged doggerel. If we today rarely quote them without irony, if we quote them in shorthand form, if our anxiety about cliché makes us overlay them ('like the proverbial water off the duck's back') self-consciously, we are still paying a kind of homage to the incantatory mode, which despite its authoritarianism, has never abolished the personalizing of commonplaces.

Idiom is perhaps the most magic, the least rational part of normal language, and overlaps very considerably with proverb: 'A kind of topsy-turvydom of poetry, full of blue moons and white elephants, of men losing their heads, and men whose tongues run away with them – a whole chaos of fairy tales.'[65] I have rhetorically asked before why we are so metaphorical, so reluctant to call a spade a spade. Like irony, punning, allegory, periphrasis and other oblique modes, idiom is non-literal. Like proverb, but often less comfortingly, idiom implicitly, and often explicitly, asserts that 'we are ... all in the same boat'.[66] Beyond such daily, observable reality, of which we need occasional reminders, idioms go into hypothetical, hyperbolic, far-fetched realms. Nobody, for instance, can literally run with the hare and hunt with the hounds. We can only lay a false trail or whoop in joint pursuit. It could be that some people use idioms because they do not understand their meaning, but wish to borrow glamour or authority from their support.

Idiom, and even more so the French term *idiotismes*, despite deriving from the relatively value-free Greek word for 'private', cannot wholly escape the connection with lunacy, or at least idiosyncrasy. It is strange how these counters, these very basic forms of linguistic currency, should so often seem illogical and happy to transgress rules. Logan Pearsall Smith (writing in 1925: his tone is sometimes quaint but his heart is approximately in the right place) wonders whether 'there is a certain irrelevance in the human mind, a certain love for the illogical and the absurd ... We like our words to have a meaning, for we like them to be vivid; but we sometimes seem almost to prefer inappropriate meanings'.[67] He is very receptive to the cussedness, waywardness, elasticity of popular speech, and pleads against elitism:

> Our figurative and idiomatic phrases are of popular origin, are drawn from the interests and occupations of humble life. The phrase-making, like the word-making, faculty belongs preeminently to the unlettered classes, and our best idioms, like our most vivid and living words, come to us, not from the library or the drawing-room or the 'gay parterre', but from the workshop, the kitchen and the farm-yard (p. 212).

He adduces plenty of examples to back up this claim, though no one can ever locate precisely coiners of language. His main theme is that 'quotations from the poets weary us if too often repeated, flowers from the garden of speech soon wither, learned figures become trite and hackneyed, but the pot and the frying-pan, the wet-blanket and the spilt milk ... never lose their moral application' (p. 269). When on the same page he talks of 'the radio-active quality of popular idiom', we need to remember that in the 1920s this phenomenon was associated only with the treatment of cancer with x-ray photography. Having analysed the recurring motifs of English idioms, he confidently proclaims that the great body of them are expressions of 'determination, of exasperation, and vituperation' (p. 262).

Idioms are the hardest part of a language for a foreigner to use or understand appositely. As their root suggests they are the most autarkic area of speech and writing. The segments that make them up frequently create something different as a totality. Anybody requested or feeling the need to explain an idiom is in a not dissimilar position to that of the schizophrenic patient tested in this way. Asked what he understood by 'No use crying over spilt milk', he replied: 'Don't get upset; you can buy some more at the shop.' Some idioms remain obstinately incomprehensible (and were perhaps invented for that reason): 'As drunk as a wheelbarrow'. No doubt the private idioms of any family or pair of people, like in-jokes, constitute a code not easily penetrated by outsiders. Idioms, then, can be impenetrable, misreadable or ambiguous. Congealed sequences (*syntagmes figés*) can behave in a quicksilvery way. Like clichés, they have hidden depths, or at least can suck in the mind as if they had. A truly safe-bet truism from a linguistician runs like this: 'Some clichés are idioms and some idioms are clichés, but neither group includes the other fully.'[68] I imagine that a transformed, twisted idiom no longer is one, unless it is widely accepted as a replacement or addition. (One of the Spanish words for idiom is *modismo*, which seems to link the form with fashion.)

In his study of French idioms, Guiraud, like Smith, places the origins of many locutions in the trades, in dialect and in slang.[69] Most idioms, like proverbs, are marked by archaism. Guiraud is clearly fascinated by the creative mess (or in linguistic jargon, *motivation*) people make of such received material. Idioms here overlap with lapsus, 'folk-etymology' and the whole area of linguistic 'contamination' – all of which adds to the gaiety of nations. As he says, sayings throw light, but often it is more of an optical illusion. 'You cannot stop *croquer le marmot* from evoking the idea of "eating a little child", whereas it actually means 'to wait impatiently"' (p. 10). *Dur à la détente* is taken from a weapon difficult to fire, but signifies a hard-hearted skinflint. This is a pun, though subliminal for most users (p. 57). A complex set of puns links lawmen, traditionally associated in French with cats, with scratching, scribbling (*griffer, griffonner*), *un chat fourré* (a magistrate), the female pudenda, the eye of a needle (*chas*) and furriness (p. 95). *Jolie à croquer*, pretty as a picture, but most people surely think of the alimentary suggestion: good enough to eat, a sweetie (p. 10). But we can, however, devour with our eyes.

Many idioms wilfully exaggerate: 'Il est léger comme un éléphant (dans un magasin de porcelaine)' – (He is as gentle as an elephant (in a china shop), where the extension extends the hyperbole). Of course such extensions then become fixed also (p. 56). Stock types recur: Guillaume, a yokel, and Gautier (Walter), a prankster and joke-cracker (p. 87). Few sayings, he points out, refer to historical landmarks (p. 35). History may not be bunk, but for many people it is eminently forgettable. A lover of putting the cart before the horse, Guiraud finds many instances of language inventing, rather than reflecting, reality (p. 101). In a captivating finale, he declares: 'In the beginning was the Word; then came poets who gave things to names [Note the inversion]; and last came linguists who messed everything up' (p. 104).

He believes that French idioms tend to be more abstract and generalized than English, and cultivated Anglophones are readier to use racy speech than their French counterparts (the provincial and the vernacular have always been marginalized in France): 'Rags are not stored with towels'; most hunting idioms come from the noble variety, venery (pp. 18–21). I feel he overstates his case, for French is often perfectly earthy. For instance, 'it's a mutual admiration society' is matched by 'ce sont deux ânes qui se frottent' (two donkeys scratching each other). Because ears are likened in shape to oysters (*portuguaises*), to be a deaf-lugs is to have your oysters silted up (*ensablées*). *Prendre un billet de parterre* (to buy a stalls ticket) means to come a cropper via a joke on *par terre* (on the ground). The fact remains that few dispute the high degree of metaphoricity in English, which might be another source of our reputation as hypocrites, perfidious double-dealers. Perhaps the most inimitable feature of English idiom, as of the language in general, is that so much hangs on prepositions – the humblest fragments of speech dictate the total meaning. A slight change; 'to kick one's heels', 'to kick up one's heels', and we move from bored waiting to spirited movement.

Repetition in idioms (and jargon, especially legal), as in 'let or hindrance' is an attempt to nail down precise meaning by emphasis. Sometimes such structures seem inevitable: I myself actually think in bits and pieces, by fits and starts. These are known as 'irreversible binomials': nip and tuck, spit and polish, sink or swim. These double-barrelled phrases, pairs for a single meaning ('rags and tatters') are frequent in both legal jargon and mumbo-jumbo; prayer-books also feature this divine redundancy. Undoubtedly these pairings can be useful – opposites conjoined as in 'to and fro' – or for linking associated but distinguishable things: flotsam and jetsam. The danger, as Fowler saw clearly, is that one of those 'Siamese twins' might be 'one of those clichés that are always lying in wait to fill a vacuum in the brain'.[70] These inseparables (as in the song, 'Love and marriage, love and marriage / Go another like a horse and carriage') are the Mutt and Jeffs of language, the habitual, mutual hangers-on. Words of a feather flock together. 'Most wonderful of all are words, and how they make friends one with another, being oft asscociated, until not even obituary notices them do part.'[71] It is as if there were magnetic forces in language, pulling words together inexorably. We want words to cluster, to socialize.

As in proverbs, rhyme, alliteration, emphatic rhythms play a large part in idioms: 'faire du'un boeuf un boeuf' (to make a mountain out of a molehill). Ionesco often makes scenic capital out of intensifying this linguistic trait, reducing it to absurdity and building up aggressive paroxysms of sound, though he once had the grace to admit: 'I have to forget my own clichés.'[72] Literature in general, and across the world, both underlines and makes more supple its reliance on set forms by all these varied forms of repetition, which give lilt to static words. While the more blatant and pounding uses of alliteration have long since become comic (typified by the master of ceremonies in 'Old Time Music-Hall' or in circuses), briefer forms can still be as potent as ever. The great repeater is of course rhyme. It can rule the roost, for some: 'When you write in prose you say what you mean. When you write in rhyme you say what you must.'[73] For others a curiously liberating constraint: 'Rhyme, together with other conventional ground-rules, has the magic knack of giving you crowds of ideas ... you think thoughts different from your thinking.'[74] Many cannot escape clichéic rhyme: June-moon, *amour/ toujours*, and so on. Banville orders poets to avoid like the plague degenerate rhymes like *gloire* and *victoire, lauriers* (laurels) and *guerriers* (warriors). 'Just thinking about them makes me want to vomit.'[75] All languages, however, are short of rhymes for some combinations of sounds. In French *célèbre* and *funèbre* have only for partners *vertèbre* and *zèbre*.[76] As well as setting up an inertia which drags similar-sounding words along, rhyme frustrated or fantasticized can subvert such expectations, as in Queneau's 'Un jeu simple / que j'invimple / dans la nuimple'.[77] Such fluidity of language makes 'Quenaquatique' the aptest epithet from his name. Likewise verses which sidestep anticipated obscenity by substituting harmless words – which, like euphemism, can suggest the removed meaning forcefully. Far more significant sources of banal thinking and expression, in fact, are rhythm, obsession with euphony and rhetorical balance. Cliché phrases often have a gait, a rhyme, assonance or alliteration which matters more than the meaning of the words involved. Thinking gets caught in its own patterns.

10

Habits of Mind/Odious Comparisons

Ortega y Gasset once wrote that 'commonplaces are the tramways of intellectual transportation'.[1] Can we detect here some ecstasy (transport) clashing with the idea of rails (and the common fear of going off the rails)? As it happens, the writer was imaging our proneness to automatism. 'Trains of thought' embraces expresses, milk-trains, *tortillards* (wagtails), but always suggests running on well-worn tracks, in grooves or furrows. Clichés are ruts; they guide progress and inhibit sideways movement. For most part the channels of communication must be well dredged and straightforward. The form often dictates the comment, as is shown by the Frenchman who composed in his sleep verses which, while not saying much, were in impeccable Alexandrines:

> Perçant l'ennui des boeufs, la blanche solitude
> Réveille, au lieu des morts, les épouvantements
> (Piercing the boredom of oxen, the white solitude
> awakens, instead of corpses, terrors).[2]

If cliché is the cement of discourse, not only does it hold it together, it also sets it hard. Words come all too easily in prepacked gobbets. 'It is likely that many people think mainly in phrases, as we all do in all but strenuous conversations.'[3] Analogy, which should open the eyes, often curls back on itself: Captain Cook found the Maoris strangely like the highlanders of Rob Roy. Truly home thoughts from abroad, when he should have been enjoying a foreign experience; and a further instance of *déjà vu*. Yet the least sophisticated can escape this kind of mental tic. 'Imaginative metaphors are highly in evidence in the tools that ordinary people invent and use, because old terms are constantly pressed into use by analogy.'[4] Even if, strictly, there is no such thing as 'free-association', for the subconscious has been got at, Bolinger is surely right to be heartened by hearing people try to free-associate, when 'you have a clue to the ganglionic ramifications of metaphors and themes'.[5] We can be encouraged to be ourselves.

Whereas Freudian slips, spoonerisms and howlers may trip often painfully off the tongue, like sticking-plaster off flesh, clichés plop out. *Pat* phrases, phrases on *tap*, are often *apt* phrases; they fall pat into place. When Ernest Bevin was asked his opinion of Anthony Eden's speeches, he is supposed to have responded: 'Clitch, clitch, clitch!' – an unwitting nonce-word which suggests an automatic falling into place (as with cameras clicking, doors clicking to, realizations suddenly clicking, or a boy clicking with a girl). We do, of course, all have to pass through the same clicking turnstiles, into the same colosseum of the commonplace. In speeches, especially, the best-intentioned orator may be carried along mechanically by prolixity, amplification, orotundity. We need stock responses to survive as creatures, and our linguistic behaviour must obey a similar survival-instinct. But the reminder 'think before you speak', or the apology 'I said it without thinking' imply that, whether or not (the ancient conundrum) we can have thought without words, it seems that we can have words before thought, reflexes instead of reflexions. The mentally deranged exaggerate a common tendency in their sometime proneness to palilalia, the chronic repetition of the same word or phrase; but supposedly sane minds can stall and yammer.

On a cosier level, 'familiarity breeds contentment'.[6] As George Crabbe wrote: 'Habit with him was all the test of truth, / "It must be right: I've done it from my youth".'[7] The psychologist William James stated that habit was 'the enormous flywheel of society, its most precious conservative agent. It alone is what keeps us all within the bounds of ordinance'.[8] There is no arguing with such claims, but it is intellectual comfort that interests me, in Marcel Aymé's two-edged use of that term: mindless bandwaggoning, smug ensconcement, *and* the very necessary reluctance to gambol on the wilder shores of whatever: the virtues of the honest peaceful mind. While inertia in physics sounds respectable – the property of matter by which it continues in its existing state, whether of rest or of uniform motion in a straight line, unless that state is altered by an external force – and while the 'inert' gases (also called 'noble' gases), colourless, odourless, tasteless and virtually inert chemically, have their uses in balloons and incandescent lamps – it is hard to speak passionlessly of inertia in human affairs. 'The inertial mass of language is like the inertial mass of society... We drag a vast obsolescence behind us even as we have rejected much of it intellectually, and it slows us down. Language is a stage built over a graveyard from which fossils rise and dance at night.'[9] If clichés reflect human inertia, this does not stop them moving ever onwards and, as Bolinger picturesquely suggests, coming back to ghostly life.

Bergson exemplifies the physician-heal-thyself syndrome. Studying in *Le Rire* the notoriously mercurial subject of comedy, he seeks to 'determine the manufacturing processes of the comic'.[10] He loves such pseudo-scientific terminology. Laughter, for Bergson, is always hard-hearted; it breaks the circuit connecting us to other people as human beings, 'a momentary anaesthesia of the heart' (p. 3). Laughter thus hurls others beyond the pale; this Jew, aesthetically speaking, favours ghettoes. What interests him mainly is mental distraction, inelasticity, automatism of behaviour or attitudes (including professional deformation) (p. 7). In theory the mocker of such conduct is supple, though in fact Bergson is hogtied by his own schemata. Anyone out of step, eccentric, anachronistic, is fair game for criticism (p. 8). At times it appears Bergson is happy to consider people as puppets on a string (p. 59). His appeal is always to constituted authority, even if this is disguised as the dynamic Life-Force: it is in fact the ancient criterion of decorum, *les bienséances*, rephrased but not truly updated or rethought.

Diderot is something else. It was probably the ceaseless activity of contemporary *automates*, burning up energy like humming-birds, which fascinated him more than any take-over bids they could be envisaged as making over a consenting humanity. One of his multiple paradoxes was that this man of often frantic energy (the best coinage would be Diderotic) should be so taken by the large area of automatism in human behaviour. 'O combien l'homme qui pense le plus est encore automate!' (How robot-like still is even the man who most uses his mind.)[11] His best work, where he is most himself of his competing selves – *Le Rêve de d'Alembert*, *Jacques le fataliste*, *Le Neveu de Rameau* – dramatizes what looks like (if we feel optimistic) the free play of the imagination contesting and often outdoing the constrictions set upon it by the body, human and social. Rameau's Nephew's passionate, entranced and entrancing mimes help him to escape for a spell from his social conditioning and his actual status as a failure and parasite. Gestures, in him, seem more honest than speech or writing, though Diderot knew full well that acting, like art in general, is a concerted lie. Miming, of course, is second-hand; Rameau has a genius for the second-rate, and, when he imitates a musical performance, he is operating at a third remove (creation/performance/mime). This 'walking madhouse' entertains and alarms his spectators, the more thoughtful of whom register the fact that he is revenging himself for his menial position by enacting a universal pantomine, the choreographed round-dance of social compulsions. To imitation he adds frenzy, though, realistic even in his fantasies, he mimes miscues on his imaginary violin. He is a Proteus, a quick-change artist of the psyche and the body. I should add that, without a responsive audience, he barely exists: he depends on those he apes and ridicules. And sycophancy, which keeps him alive, is a heavily dependent activity. It still remains that Rameau could boast, like Diderot himself: 'Je sais aussi m'aliéner, talent sans lequel on ne fait rien qui vaille' (I know also how to split myself in two/go mad, a gift without which nothing worthwhile is ever achieved).[12] Diderot at times felt that people are all monsters; everyone is an exceptional being. His masterpiece about a unique failure, an 'impossible man', shows that being a 'creature of habit' can have its dynamic aspects.

One of the several French terms for a trite, parroted phrase is *une tarte à la crème*, which serves a dramatic function in Molière's *Les Femmes savantes*. Arnolphe is talking of his ideal wife (he is trying to programme his own): extremely ignorant, indeed stupid (and thus, he hopes, immune from infidel temptations) – so much so that she cannot even participate, except with total naïveté, in party games. He wants a literal-minded wife who would make a prosaic and innocent reply to the ritual question ('Qu'y met-on?' – What do you put in it?) in the game of *corbillon* (literally, pastry-basket).[13] As the whole drama play teeters on the edge of prurience (the husband's obscurantism perversely opens the wife's eyes), as the player is supposed to answer with a word ending in *on*, and as the basket is a common stand-in for the female pudenda, Arnolphe wants his wife, educated into mindlessness, to respond with 'une tarte à la crème'. This echo-word is repeated. In the 'critique' of this play by Molière himself, a carper comments that this *tarte à la crème* made him feel nauseous, and a reference is made to the practice of throwing cooked apples (cf. custard-pies) at the actors.[14] The stupid husband fails in his campaign to induce stupidity, his *idée fixe* of installing the woman in childlike housewifeliness.

Diderot did not specialize in *idées fixes*. Though he periodically reverted to favourites, he generally kept on the move. Most of us are less elastic. Our fixed ideas tend to be undefined, unshakeable and (in intention) transferable to others. Pet ideas: the frequency of the phrase 'I always think'. We ride hobby-horses to death; old chestnuts can also be old warhorses. The French equivalent *dada* is: a child's word for horse, a favourite stamping-ground, and the word chosen (at random, it was claimed by its founders) as the title, and manifesto, of the pre-Surrealist art movement. A related word, *marotte*, used to mean a doll or puppet (cf. marionnette), later became linked with the fool's cap and bells, and finally settled into its present dominant meaning, as in Flaubert's admission: 'Life is tolerable only when you've got a bee in your bonnet (une marotte), some kind of fixed task. As soon as you leave the land of fancy, you die of boredom.'[15]

Paul Valéry, one of whose fictional figures boasts calmly, 'Stupidity is not my forte',[16] and who was himself quicker on his mental pins than most, denied that there was such a thing as an *idée fixe*. In an essay with that title, he argues that, if we could register the processes of our psychic activity, we would witness a 'perfect disorder'.[17] Life is 'something like an accident which has taken root' (p. 231). 'An idea cannot be fixed... An idea is a change, or rather a process of change... Nothing stays still in the mind. I defy you to bring anything to a halt there. Everything there is transitive ... and nearly everything is renewable... Nothing is more walkabout (*ambulatoire*) than an *idée fixe*' (p. 205). The essay, with its set-up of two thinking and competing men clambering about peripatetically over seaside rocks and exchanging machine-gun sprays of thought, often paradoxical, enacts and backs up these ideas about ideas. Or does it? As someone said of an American pundit: 'He writes like a revolving door.' That is: always on the move, but getting nowhere. No wonder Valéry was so addicted to the Ouroboros motif. The cult of mental agility is Valéry's hobby-horse. I am reminded of André Maurois's description of Jean Cocteau on his reception into the *Académie Française*: 'Un Paganini du violon d'Ingres' (roughly: a Gordon Richards of the hobby-horse).[18]

Set ideas can have terrible consequences, all the same. Prejudice in law-courts against non-conformists of any type; teacher-expectation in schools; the unwritten rules any of us can unknowingly transgress; people judged by their appearance or skin colour – the list of areas where people suffer from the fixed ideas of others can be extended at will. Like conventional metaphor, set comparisons can stiffen the mental joints; sloth can be harmful, even lethal.

I'll begin doomily. The Viennese satirist Karl Kraus once wrote: 'I am convinced that happenings no longer happen; instead the clichés operate spontaneously.' Perhaps this is what people mean, vaguely, when they talk of 'the system'. Social life seems to have become a self-regulating machine (which occasionally goes haywire), with no one in control, either for good or for evil. Modern cultural life in particular often appears a large-scale, collective experience of the *déjà vu* and *déjà entendu* – despite the emphasis on the new: neophilia (only a couple of letters from necrophilia).

Such a gloomy generalization would be a stereotype, and reek of prejudice and the desire to label (libel) and to classify. (In Michel Tournier's *Le Roi des Aulnes*, the Nazi scientists and the dubious hero are alike drawn to such compartmentalization of the human race.) Stereotypes are yet another labour-saving device, of the malignant kind (like clichés) rather than the fertile (puns). In questionnaires stereotyped questions elicit stock responses; you know the blank extra space sometimes offered for further comments, if filled in, will not be accommodated by the computer. And yet, just as proverbs contradict each other, so stereotypes clash between themselves. How can Scotsmen be simultaneously penny-pinching and expensively drunk? How can the French welcome you into their boudoirs but not into their country? How can the fair-playing English be double-dealers? Such chastening comparisons occur more rarely than chastising ones.

In a witty relocation of the word 'ideal', Walter Lippmann writes: 'Our repertoire of fixed impressions ... contains ideal swindlers, ideal Tammany politicians, ideal jingoes, ideal agitators, ideal enemies.'[19] When we idealize we misrepresent, to ourselves or to others, for stereotyping preaches to the converted and aims at increasing their numbers. Lippmann continues: 'We do not like qualifying adverbs. They clutter up sentences, they interfere with irresistible feeling. We prefer most to more, least to less ... In our free moments everything tends to behave absolutely – one hundred percent, everywhere, forever.'[20] In a footnote, he refers to Freud's *Interpretation of Dreams*. '"No" seems not to exist, so far as dreams are concerned' (in fact, Freud later modifies this assertion several times).[21] Lippman sees such categorization as a sedative, an over-the-top comforter: 'Without standardization, without stereotypes, without routine judgments, without a fairly ruthless disregard of subtlety, the editor [of a newspaper] would soon die of excitement.'[22] It is a kind of end-stopped, self-censoring opinionating. For Barthes, the stereotype is

> the word repeated, outside any magic ritual, any enthusiasm, as if it were perfectly natural, as if by some miracle these recurring words were just what was needed each time for different reasons, as if imitation could be experienced as non-imitative. The stereotype is a cool customer which lays claim to being consistent and cannot see how insistent it is.[23]

Even less mindless thinking, such as various forms of edification, in setting up *exempla*, provide the unusual as a model to be copied or emulated. The mentally deranged could teach us, as they often do, that 'stereotypy' in medical language refers to actions or gestures repeated involuntarily, but not quite so convulsively as tics or spasms; it is also used of the harped-on attitudes and words or automatized gestures of schizophrenics. As we have seen before, clichés have touches of the insane, as well as the safely, cosily sane.

Filing, I should know, can become a mania, however rough-and-ready it might be. Racial stereotypes are potentially and actively murderous: people kill for a received idea, which freezes the brain, imagination and sympathy. Why do our pet aversions have to be black beasts? We are now moving clear out of the realm of *péchés mignons*, sinlets, peccadilloes. What can be venial about thinking other human beings less than human? In this area blood images, as Hitler understood so well, predominate: purity of racial stock, blood-brothers, bad blood, letting blood: a consanguinity of lethal imagery. Fear of the new and the different, by a crude process of stimulus and response, promotes hatred and fear of colour, or the lack of it (albinos). The unknown is lent fearful and poisonous gifts, like twins credited with extra powers. Etiemble, in an essay on racism, has a telling anecdote about his native village in the Beauce, where the local peasants liked to drink together every evening. A neighbour who chose not to join in was imagined as drinking 'en juif' (like a Jew). This a Freudian slip-cum-folk etymology on *boire en suisse* (to drink on the sly).[24] Etiemble offers samples of mutually warring fixed ideas in this domain: 'The Jews are sensual, and that's why all of them are impotent... Each Jew is thus a squared circle, the bodily and metaphysical locus of contradictions and excess.'[25] Clearly, a no-win situation, which might help to explain why so many jokes told by Jews apotropaically bite themselves in the rear. Etiemble corroborates Norman Cohn's claim that anti-semitism has been most virulent in those parts of France where hardly any live. The Jew's absence is the perfect excuse for his excessive presence in the anti-semitic mentality: 'Les absents ont toujours tort.'

A good example of a whole book devoted to analysing and protesting the stereotype of a total outlook (and many feminist works would serve equally well) is Edward Said's *Orientalism*. It attacks the racialist, ideological, intellectual, fixed essence summed up in that term. It wishes to act as a warning 'that systems of thought like Orientalism [fatalism, exoticism, irrationalism, etc.], discourses of power, ideological fictions – mind-forg'd manacles – are all too easily made, applied and guarded'.[26] Like Barthes and his study of the representation of the *Other*, Said asks: 'How do such ideas acquire authority, "normality", and even the status of "natural" truth?'[27] Racialist stereotyping of this overarching variety spawns cliché on a vast scale: the fossils of ancient beliefs embedded in language. No doubt such an umbrella attitude is applied in particular circumstances, but most people notice the latter more than the former. The Polish word for a Jew also means a boil, and the Jew is felt as a pain in the neck. Phonic and semantic associations count for much in slurs (Jew–Judas).[28] Like present-day burglars befouling the rooms they ransack, bad-mouthers add insult to injury, or preface the injury with insults. Suffering at the hands of one member of another race can lead to generalized disparagement of that entire race, a process which Roback likens to synecdoche, where the part is similarly taken for the whole.[29] Rhetoric may be highly artificial but it mimes some of our deepest instincts.

Name-calling, nicknames (obviously destined, through heavy use, to become clichés) can hurt badly, and often serve to distance another from the self or the group. But what of a 'Mohican: a very heavy man who rides a long way in an omnibus for sixpence'?[30] Would he who used to be called a Redskin feel threatened by this poetic, or at least circuitous, title which is probably more of a congratulation than an aspersion? Ethnic ticketing and jokes, like caricature, solidify, inflate, and proliferate. They are a collective reinforcement of interpersonal chauvinism (I versus the Other, We versus Them), and there is much disagreement as to how harmful or harmless they are. Finding others, of different cultures, odd perhaps embodies a fear. Yet, oddly, this making strange, this defamiliar-ization, becomes, through endless repetition, extremely familiar: we can see the joke coming, we have, or think we have, 'heard it before'. As well as foreigners and immigrants, resident aliens are also dragged in. Christie Davies argues that, just as most murders and other violence occur within the family, so most insults are directed against those who, though speaking the same language as the mockers, are thought of as stupid butts. The criterion, he stresses, is often linguistic: the assumed dumbos are considered as speaking the language badly, slowly, old-fashionedly (as in English jokes about 'archaic' Indian English).[31] This frozen antithesis of quick and slow, light and heavy, needs the corrective of Nietzsche's remark about rumination – a talent which cows possess and modern man lacks. Shaggy-dog stories, on the other hand, are metajokes, where the teller feigns slow-wittedness, the better to shock with punch-line wit at the delayed end.

At a more innocent stage of its career downhill, 'wog' could be offered as 'an attached foreign body, an ornament'.[32] By a comparable leap, the reverse of sexism (I will come back to sexist language in the *Neologisms* section) might be the praise of women, typified by the many *blasons du corps*, all the thousands of comparisons of select parts of the female anatomy to jewellery, plants, and so on. But this really is to turn women into sex objects: it congeals them, estranges them, *sets* them, either in a bezel or concrete. Being obliged by feminists (who have struck back against the age-old reservation of hysteria to women by the merited coinage 'testeria') to mind ps and qs, to dot the is, to watch the tongue, helps men willy-nilly to stay alert, to think more clearly about what they say and think. Some writers in the West complain that the absence of overt state censorship undervalues literature: we can say anything, get away with murder, but such impunity is crippling. Feminists and anti-racists provide this indispensable form of censorship, which clarifies context and choice. The more thoughtful of such attacking defenders must surely agree, however, that the greatest prejudice of all is against thinking itself: mindism. 'Mentality' is generally employed with a restrictive and pejorative connotation, as if only 'primitives' possessed it (or children, often amalgamed with them). Commonly it alludes to irrational or extravagant behaviour or beliefs.[33]

I will next risk some forays into comparative mentalities myself, and may well turn out guilty of some 'ethnophaulisms'.[34] Comparisons can illuminate or, of course, install inanition where once there was independent life. If they are indeed always odious, *odi et amo*.

We learn foreign languages, at least if our learning is scholastic rather than by total immersion, parrot-fashion, as cliché systems of set expressions. In this process, for a long time it is hard to be inventive, to feel free, to take liberties, even though the very fact of being an outsider does help to see more sharply than most insiders the mechanical tics, the unexamined idiocies, to which any given language is prone. This should give comic perspective and a readiness to experiment. Whorf theorized that all of us are prisoners of our native languages, and that to this extent our minds are made up for us. One of the several arguments against this view is that great creeds, political or religious, straddle supposed language barriers. Another relativizes his generalization: 'Whorf overemphasized one point (that languages differ in what *can* be said in them) at the expense of a greater truth (that they differ as to what is *relatively easy* to express in them).'[35] Translation sets us astride two languages. It is well known that many translations read very flatly. Perhaps this is the worst 'betrayal' perpetrated by rendering one language into another; the translator often plays safe (or knows no better), using the triter resources of his/her own tongue. Conversely, a Russian expert once told me that some of the more baroque similes (for instance, explosions likened to pancakes) in the English version of *Doctor Zhivago* were the result of mistranslation. In an essay on translation, Valery Larbaud says of one of the great classical exponents of this activity that, though highly conscious of the whole issue of plagiarism, to the extent of translating sources to prove where plagiarists had pillaged, St Jerome himself often left his pages littered with unattributed quotations, like the merest novice.[36] This charge prepares the ground for Larbaud's coming admission that translation (and he was a fine one himself) is plagiarism:

> Translating a book which has appealed to us is to delve deeper into it than mere reading could take us, to possess it more completely, in a way to annex it for ourselves. Yes, that is where we're always heading, plagiarists that we all are, from the outset... We've all begun with imitation and even with plagiarism, conscious or unconscious.[37]

The first of my possible slurs is to wonder whether plagiarism and other forms of parasitism may be commoner in a heavily incestuous culture like that of France, whereas the protestant work ethic puts a premium on individual sweat and self-help. French has had in fact to take over many *self*-compounds this century from English (except for *autocritique*, which comes via the French Communists from Soviet Russia). The two cultures have always squared up to each other: *les anglais* = menses (because of Redcoat soldiers), and 'French gout' = syphilis; and by now even governments want us to know about French letters and *capotes anglaises*. Freud reports a joke in which an Englishman says to a Frenchman (and it has to be in French): 'Du sublime au ridicule il n'y a qu'un pas (from the sublime to the ridiculous is just a short step), to which the Frenchman responds: 'Oui, le Pas de Calais.'[38] Either national can make his side win in this verbal exchange, by inverting the speakers, imagining one party as a masochist, or simply interpreting the sequence as ascending or descending. Similarly there are no outright winners in such comparisons. I find a lovely example of an intelligent man's cliché in Pierre Guiraud's study of dirty language: 'Combien pâle et exsangue est le *shit* anglo-saxon en face de notre *merde* omniprésent et triomphant!' (How pale and bloodless is the Anglo-Saxon *shit* compared with our ubiquitous and all-conquering *merde*).[39] Guiraud seems to me to be poking his nose where he shouldn't; but I forgive easily, since we say 'Pardon my French' after letting off a curse.

I plug on all the same. Alienation (I am thinking of the noticeable difference between French and English Absurdist writers) seems always to have exerted a stronger spell over the French. They appear readier to leave common ground behind, take off, and are aided in this flight by the greater divorce between the elitist language used by most writers and common speech.[40] Sabin speaks very persuasively of the 'characteristically English distinction between the contemptible and the possibly valuable, even in commonplaces. The French nouns *stéréotype* and *cliché*

more sweepingly dismiss in a stroke all fixed forms of expression'.
Indeed, her general theme is that, in English,

> a continuing ambivalent attachment to the old and familiar – in language
> as in sex and politics – has kept even the most notably defiant of
> modernists from enlisting in the French avant-garde. The French slogan
> of *le Nouveau*, repeated (paradoxically) from Baudelaire to Barthes,
> becomes complicated, if not compromised, in the English modern tradi-
> tion by deeply rooted yearnings towards the common, and by anxious
> intimations that to repudiate old language is to risk repudiating the life of
> language itself.[41]

The French do make a sharp distinction between cliché, which they
often limit to high style, and idiom. In their more polarized perspective,
only the pretentious elements of the upper social and writing classes sin
in this way; the great unwashed are seen as relatively spotless. Two
external defendants of French vision, Amossy and Rosen, declare,
however, that: 'If "cliché" slides from the meaning of "typographical
plate" to that of "worn-out expression", commonplace turns into
"topos", public space, meeting-place of the crowd, that is to say, the
plebs.'[42] From mechanical reproduction to stamping-ground – there
seems to me little real difference of connotation here; it is as broad as it's
long.

Despite continual sabotage from within the community, the great
operative (and optative) French cliché, *la clarté française* ('ce qui n'est pas
clair n'est pas français'),[43] breeds clichés, since it entails unimpeded
discourse, the most heavily used components of the language. Not
content with accessibility, an admirable goal in itself, the predominantly
cerebralist tradition there logically opts for the Anti-Physis. The idealist
wing because its supporters want to elevate the mind above or away from
the body, and the pro-Marxist wing because it wants to de-emphasize
how much a prey to the concrete human will is. Outsiders or deviants like
the pro-Italian Stendhal and the pro-Dickens Vallès face up, in their
differing ways, to the fact of fiasco – all that the best-laid plans of mind
cannot control. Clichés are also negatives, and may be more easily
developed in French; as with negatives you get the drift, but the spectral
presence lacks reality. In French, an unmarked police car is *une voiture
banalisée*. The English phrase is concretely descriptive: it removes the
distinctive markers from the car. The French one generalizes, relates
this particular car to a general class of vehicles; it states in fact that the
car is marked by an absence of markedness. From his Swiss eyrie,
Charles Bally said of his own language: 'French is a language in which it

is extremely easy to speak and write by stringing clichés together. This same need for fixed associations has helped to give the French the taste for definitive formulas, maxims struck like medals; no nation has had a larger intake of "famous last words".'[44] In contrast, English prose is characteristically loose-limbed, often paratactic (trailing, tack-on, like this sentence). Tighter French syntax corrals words into more ready-made combinations. Corsets make figures stand out more than does letting it all hang loose. French single-mindedness, which gives acuity to their thinking and writing at its best, and which does not preclude the use of ambiguity, for example in irony, as a polemical arm, also tends to the creation of cliché. The pedagogic instruction: 'Une idée par paragraphe et un paragraphe par idée' – a golden and a tautological rule – militates against plural viewpoints. Yet, other kinds of mixing interfere. The reciprocal contamination of literature and life, which makes *Madame Bovary* in many ways the key French cultural text, the criss-cross of literature and politics which struck Tocqueville, heighten the awareness of, and perhaps the propensity towards, cliché.

Let me add some others' prejudices to my own. Robert Graves and Alan Hodges, in the course of attacking some varieties of verbal misuse in their own culture, take some time off for a side-swipe across the Channel: 'English does not run on its own rails, as French does, with a simply managed mechanism of knobs and levers, so that any army officer or provincial mayor can always, at a minute's notice, glide into a graceful speech in celebration of any local or national event, however unexpected.'[45] This sounds like the fruits of a short-stay, war-service experience, and is a good example of how English metaphoricity does not produce of its own accord generous or liberated thinking. A full-time Gallophile, Richard Cobb, vents similar-sounding, but more essentially sympathetic, critic-ism in these words on 'the sort of moralizing *lapalissades* that one associates with *Messieurs décorés, pères de famille* and *inspecteurs d'acad-émie*, as if every affluent parent, every citizen of girth and means had adopted, as his form of everyday communication, the rumbling periods of a Speech Day discourse'.[46] Though such use often hints at snobbery, the preservation of French terms here seems to guarantee a general love which houses this particular grievance. After nearly forty years immersed in things and abstractions French, I have aired above some of my grievances. It is in the name of fairness and not of lily-livered making up that I add this: of all the books I have read deliberately or accidentally for this book, the most truly stimulating were all French: Schneider (on plagiarism and secondhand living in general), Paulhan (who helped me to give clichés a chance), Reboul (on slogans), Guiraud on many different linguistic issues, and, of course, Flaubert, who was the first to make me see cliché as central rather than peripheral to life. If only by reaction, the French make you think. I can never forgive the chief English (not Irish, Scots or Welsh) knee-jerk: anti-intellectualism, which leads even intelligent people at times into what students of speech term the 'mucker-pose'. Finally, what Finnegan says of Ashanti professional orators ('Linguists') no doubt transfers, with suitable modifications, to speech-makers in all cultures:

> When the Linguist rises up to speak in public, he leans upon the King's gold cane ... He is going to make a speech now, and it is sure to be a happy effort. It will sparkle with wit and humour. He will make use freely of parables to illustrate points in his speech. He will indulge in epigrams, and all the while he will seem not to possess any nerves – so cool, so collected, so self-complacent! He comes of a stock used to public speaking and public functions.[47]

From his Spanish vantage-point, Gerald Brenan needles our smugness. 'The cliché is dead poetry. English, being the language of an imaginative race, abounds in clichés, so that English literature is always in danger of being poisoned by its own secretions.'[48] George Santayana, part-Spanish, American-educated and Anglophile, in a contrast between the clear-cut Mediterranean landscape and mind and their foggier North Atlantic counterparts, seems to favour the latter:

> But where the Atlantic mists envelop everything, though we must re-peatedly use the same names for new-born things, as we continue to christen children John and Mary, yet we feel that the facts, like the persons, are never really alike; everything is so fused, merged, and continuous, that whatever element we may choose to say is repeated seems but a mental abstraction and a creature of language.

I do not find this woolly claim by a self-proclaimed philosophical materialist convincing. The theme of his sermon is: 'Repetition is the only form of permanence that nature can achieve.'[49] More off-handedly, the American James Thurber, a humourist here being perhaps simply joky, said: 'The English treat the commonplace as if it were remarkable and the Americans treat the remarkable as if it were commonplace.'[50] Not all Americans, though.

Harold Rosenberg, in *The Tradition of the New*, takes as a premiss that 'the best French poetry since Baudelaire has been enlisted in a siege against the cliché'.[51] I would add: 'and has felt besieged by the cliché'. Like other observers quoted earlier, he believes that

> any educated Frenchman can make up a poem, just as any American can improvise a new 'popular tune'. The French language is heavy with old literature, as the American air is loaded with ta ta ta tá tá ... A word over there, as soon as it enters the mind, begins rolling down into a fine ready-made phrase ... The Frenchman has so much tradition he can easily say anything except what he wants to say. To be conscious of his own feelings, to see with his own eyes, he must restore freshness to his language (p. 87)

Referring to a French poet's description of the 'fragility of the common-place', he concurs, for the commonplace is 'the effect of a perspective to which the observer is held by a web of vocabulary' (p. 88). Perceptively, after remarking on the obsessive theme of silence in French poetry, he sees the rationale of this in the need 'to turn off the belt-line of rhetoric that keeps automatically pounding away in his brain twenty-four hours a day. Before any poetic event can happen, the cultural chatter must be stopped' (p. 89). Suddenly leaping back into American space, he baro-quely contrasts the French poet and the Kansas farmhand, whose silence is a simple fact of topographical life. 'The Frenchman has to will his silence ... make himself ready for a new word ... which will open to him a continent of things' (p. 89). (Rosenberg was the chief apologist of Action Painting, which he baptised – paintings as things; he is hostile to extractable messages, à la Claudel (p. 89).) He distinguishes between the efforts of a Mallarmé or Valéry to 'restore words to innocence' and the Dadaist/Surrealist efforts to 'find innocent words ... to pick up in the streets a word that had never been in a poem before', yet both campaigns attempted to silence the old rhetoric by an act of verbal alchemy (p. 90). Rosenberg then starts pulling the French and American strands together in what he hopes is a productive *rapprochement*. About 1935, René Taupin pointed out that poets in America were 'lucky in having a lingo that hadn't yet settled into a literary language' (p. 91). The American equivalent of a literary tradition is Hollywood, with 'its treasury of poetic platitudes' (p. 92). Rosenberg's theme is that American poets would learn more and better from radical French models than from English ones, too cosy and safe. The great modernist mediator between tradition and the new, T. S. Eliot, is lumped with all those Rosenberg urges the aspirant poet to reject. 'Precisely the fact that it gives them something to do and keeps them out of trouble is perhaps what makes the filing cabinets of tradition so desirable to the morally insecure' (pp. 94–5). Comparisons, as well as being fixatives, can also be cautionary tales, and a dose of salts.

11

Pop Eyes

Presuming the listening child to want repetition, and the child reading for itself to be in search of novelty, Auden erects this antithesis: 'The ear tends to be lazy, craves the familiar and is shocked by the unexpected: the eye, on the other hand [a shocking idea], tends to be impatient, craves the novel and is bored by repetition.'[1] It does not take a Pataphysician to respond: 'The opposite is also true.' Otherwise, listening to great and adventurous poetry would not be pleasurable; and much art, lofty or petty, would have no public. The eye is every bit as prone to favour the conventional and the reiterated as the ear or mind. Blessed with poorish sight and unimpressive powers of visual discrimination, I feel less confident in tackling this area, but am sustained by the helpful cliché: 'I don't know much about art, but I know what I like.'

We all know, for a start, that there are gestural as well as verbal clichés: hand-movements, body-postures at rest or in motion. Still photography merely underlines the fact that even the kinetic can be frozen, as indeed it has to be in sculpture, painting and drawing. Some linguisticians exclaim at human skills like responding instantly to the request, which has probably not been formulated before, 'to do a Napoleon'.[2] What the guinea-pigs produce, of course, is the conventional parody (hand inside coat), the cartoon version, of the prodigious historical figure. A new phrase elicits a stock response. Invitations to 'do a Frederick the Great' would probably produce nothing at all. The actual test seems to me as rigged and inconclusive as that administered on himself by Sartre's Lucien Fleurier in 'L'Enfance d'un chef', when, in order to decide whether he is indeed homosexual, as he fears, he gazes at a French *flic* to see whether he fancies him. Cartoons are visual nicknames; they typecast people by congealing and distorting their features; they are clichés. Custard-pies are a cinematic *tarte à la crème*. That democratic and public form of the cartoon, graffiti, is the home from home of the derivative, whether in the 'original' graffito (usually a variation on a well-known theme or proposition) or in the later deletions and accretions, as in the counter-revolutionary slogan: 'America – love it or leave it.' Graffiti protest, proselytize and, given space-restrictions, unavoidably simplify. Before graffiti began to proliferate, *images d'Epinal* in France, and equivalents in other countries, were visual clichés, naïvely celebrating heroic and edifying events in schematized form.

Baudelaire, an acute critic of art as well as of literature, in his 'Salon de 1846' studied *le chic* and *le poncif*.[3] He found that *le chic* is more of a hand than a brain memory, and illustrates his meaning by reference to those who have the knack of drawing, with closed eyes, a faithful reproduction of some object. *Le poncif* is related, but concerns the postures chosen for depiction, so often hammy in their stylization (as I find the gestural language of ballet). For Baudelaire, everything traditional and conventional stems from *le chic* and *le poncif*. (Another term is *pompiérisme*. *Pompier* has slang connections with fellatio. An American might say: 'This kind of empty formalism sucks'.) Baudelaire found particularly offensive the commercial, sentimentalizing exploiters of genuine religious art, and called them 'The apes of emotion'.[4] An artist of his day, Frémiet, inauguarated the long-living pictorial cliché of the gorilla abducting the beautiful girl, which resurrects in different places like the film *King Kong* and the song of Georges Brassens 'Gare au gorille!' (Gorilla on the loose). *Le poncif* also meant a habitual quoter of others.[5] *Poncer* means 'to pounce', like a predator on a brass-rubbing, a calque, a copy. *Chic* bifurcates, one way to the dandy area: the one-off, the smart original, and the other to the modish and repetitive. 'Radical chic' captures this ambivalence.

Cliché in art has been defended. 'Its overuse is its greatest virtue', argues Thompson, 'for then we can assume a wider area of common acceptance. Without it there is little communication.'[6] It is true that the allusiveness of posters, book-jackets, record-sleeves and so on has to veer to the corny, to be instantly or very rapidly recognizable, like jingles of all kinds. Though pop videos are often structured surrealistically now, such surrealism is generally banal, a kind of mobile décor, neither more nor less significant than furnishings or fashionable clothes. Chaos or fragmentation do surprise, but to what end? Springing 'boo' on someone does not enlarge him/her; it rather makes the surprised one contract. As well as shock, these defence counsels stress the wilful, programmatic role of much contemporary art. 'It is axiomatic that if something is good it is worth repeating. The psychological effect of a repeated element as in a sheet of postage stamps or an Andy Warhol painting of Coke bottles is strong. One's eye rapidly scans the surface as though to spot a discrepancy.'[7] This sounds like desperation to me, the desperation of the

The Gorilla by Frémiet (photograph © Roger-Viollet)

teacher planting deliberate mistakes in order to arouse sleepy students. Would-be subtler rhetorical ploys like euphemism (and the air-brush has been described as 'a visual euphemizer'),[8] or litotes, are also pressed into service. Thompson/Davenport speak of the 'arrogant understatement' of advertisements which feature only the name of the product, with no puffing copy.[9] Carrying this even further: the product itself, unnamed. As we saw earlier, just as euphemism can excite, litotes can boast.

Obviously, words and pictures are separate, even if there is continuum or chiasmus (the whole shuttle-service between the plastic arts and literature). There is a gap between an uttered cliché ('sick as a parrot') and an iconic one (The Mona Lisa). The verbal one has been on millions of lips. The iconic one may have been seen by millions of eyes (in the original or, more probably, in reproduction), but it has not been taken over by them. Only a few (talented) artists have actually repainted, generally with variations, the Mona Lisa. Perhaps this painting could never become a full (that is, empty) cliché, no more than 'To be or not to be, that is the question'. It can only be misrepresented, diverted, and then it is the remade Giacondas, which have only vicarious existence, that become, with repetition, trite. Or the unkillable three ducks above countless fireplaces or sideboards.

Collage and ready-mades admit (in both senses) cliché, in fact feed off it. Louis Aragon, predictably, is both shifty and dogmatic about this reliance: 'Collage is the recognition by the painter of the inimitable, and the departure-point for a pictorial organization of what the painter refuses to imitate.'[10] I take this to mean that piecemeal lifting creates original art, just as for Aragon the poetry of Lautréamont is 'an immense monument erected with collages'.[11] The even less energetic practice of offering *objets trouvés* as art-objects is illustrated by this quotation, which manages to sound both interesting and incomprehensible: 'Like an *objets trouvés* sculptor, [the French film-director] Claude Chabrol (*La Femme infidèle*) likes to give commonplaces a classic aspect. Is coincidence a cliché?'[12] Marcel Duchamp is much more frankly ludic, for instance in his 'ready-made' bird-cage, which is in fact a *trompe l'oeil*, as the 'sugar-cubes' are chunks of marble, thus making the 'cage' surprisingly heavy to lift.[13] He denies that his aim was to confect beautiful objects, and indeed claims his art is uncaring, unconcerned by questions of good or bad taste, in fact completely anaesthetic (p. 191) (here art and the operating table come together). The 'assisted' or 'rectified' ready-made involves more input, although, of course, the element of choice (picking the *objet trouvé*) already implies some effort. More fancifully, the notion of a 'reciprocal ready-made' ('chiasmic' might be more accurate) proposes a Rembrandt

Magritte Lisa, 1974 by Terry Pastor, reproduced by courtesy of the Nicholas Treadwell Gallery, Bradford

used as an ironing-board (pp. 191–2). Duchamp deliberately curtailed the number of ready-mades, so as not to drug the public into a dependent habit. He makes no claim to uniqueness, for the replica of a ready-made conveys the same message (p. 192). Turning the whole issue round, he reminds that paint itself is manufactured, so that all artists' canvases in the world are 'assisted ready-mades and assemblages' (ibid.).

Behind his whole joking programme hides a statment on cliché; ready-
mades are metaclichés, clichés conscious of themselves and mocking
people for taking them as gospel.

Collages and ready-mades have affinities, at least in my mind, with
linguistic borrowings: imports brought in to strengthen or to glamorize
the home area. As any infant classroom demonstrates, anybody can do a
collage, whereas musical or literary pot-pourris require higher skills and
knowledge. Children's puzzles (*têtes folles* in French – crazy faces), where
different sections of anatomy can be juxtaposed to give baroque results,
or fairground photo-stalls where you stick your head through a hole in a
predesigned screen, are all forms of *bricolage*, combinatorial art. Serious
artists engaged in such forms presumably feel that 'everything has
already been said', and that only reshuffling is left. Just as pastiche or
parody are often homage, so reference is often reverence, yet it has its
own sources of pride. Though collage uses snippets of 'reality', it is anti-
mimetic, in that it never pretends to be 'natural' or 'transparent'. It draws
attention to itself, makes its presence felt, and makes the act of selecting,
juxtaposing or simply plonking, palpable. Writing can be collage, too, and
the typewriter has been likened to the sewing-machine, stitching
together a text.[14] And in the sphere of general living, the acronymic
coinage 'rejasing' (re-using junk as something else), putting discarded
items to useful purpose, is central to our jumble and car-boot-sale world,
as well as to some varieties of contemporary sculpture. It solves, or at
least postpones, the problem of disposal, and adds to the stock of human
contentment. The makeshift cannot aspire to immortality, but can have
new leases of life.

Much of popular culture is deathless. Many listeners, viewers or
readers do not want truth-to-life, argues Bagnall, but fidelity to an ideal
(that is, a preconceived idea).[15] They want foregone conclusions,
confirmation. This is true also of the consumers of high culture. We, in
the main, want to listen to the high-flown laments of King Lear, not the
moans of the abandoned old wretch who lives next door. If there are fans
of Cole Porter's lyrics who look down on those of 1960s–1980s pop
music, it may well be because of the admixture, as in mock-heroic or
burlesque, of the vernacular and titbits of high culture that they contain.
Arguing on these lines, Baldick quotes the words sung by Gene Kelly in
The Pirate:

> But since I've seen ya,
> Niña, Niña, Niña,
> I'll be having neurasthenia
> Till I make you mine.

Baldick comments that 'the appeal of Hollywood's sublime doggerel is still unexplored territory'.[16] Great annexers, the Americans, even more than the Japanese in Nash's poem, make everything theirs. The verses are self-aware, self-ribbing (but not self-critical); they have their cake and scoff it. They have a hard-boiled sentimentality. A very large area of cliché is the sentimental, the melodramatic, the trivializing, the cheaply pathetic. As Coleridge said, to estimate a play solely by its power to draw tears is to measure it by a virtue it possesses in common with the onion.

Mass-produced and mass-consumed fiction, whether on the printed page or in television soap-operas, stockpiles and exploits cliché in huge quantitites. Padding out the telling of the same old plot, the demand for on-tap emotions, so that patience and duration are undervalued, heroines much obsessed with their image, all these produce and feed off stereotypes. Characters rarely hang together, they are a bundling, often a bungling, of contradictory impulses (fleeing and being attracted), drifting oxymorons. Such fiction, while apparently (as with Emma Bovary) stoking the fires of high expectations, in fact lowers emotional intensity by simplifying and conventionalizing it. This is formula or recipe writing (which not everyone has the skill to conform to; these are cliché experts). To what extent, however, is it addictive, if people can switch off from such enchantment and go back to ordinary living and working? Do they carry over from one realm to another? What particularly appals militant feminists, who deeply resent the male imperialism of much popular fiction, is that the frequently pliant heroines are vibrators in the hands and arms of men. Such literature of wish-fulfilment is neither conventional in the sense of adjusting people to real-world demands nor rebelliously unconventional. So much of it seems like a prophylactic against real emotions (anger, for one).

An even more blatant example of the phoney is kitsch, which Zijderveld unproblematically defines as unproblematic consumption, appeal to cheap or facile emotions, and anti-intellectual.[17] It often fascinates intellectuals, perhaps because it offers a melting-pot which they can try to purify, the mingling of the three traditional cultures: high, middlebrow and popular. Like cliché, kitsch is hard to judge without thereby involving your own taste in the verdict, for it infiltrates everywhere. Many furnish their rooms, and their minds, with ready-made junk – other sobriquets include crapola and schlock – out of the fear of emptiness, unadornment, silence. Those who can afford the choice reject subsistence living, and conspicious consumption, in varying degrees of blatancy, the collecting of trophies of all varieties, is common to most people. Conspicuous recycling, the urge to put to new and generally decorative uses what once had a practical purpose, is a major feature. Curtis Brown talks of the 'muddle-headedness' of kitsch, and cites the example of coffee-cups designed to simulate embroidery.[18] This product probably derives from Surrealist make-overs in the same vein (fur cups). If it is argued that the predecessor was a sophisticated joke, an anti-commercial comment, it has to be recognized that kitsch too is often anti-utilitarian. And so describing 'high' kitsch, as 'the arbitrary joining of disparate elements' (p. 66) does not demarcate it from Surrealism. Both are fired by 'aesthetic chutzpah', triumphant gall, which tastes bitter to their critics. Both are conditioned by the culture of advertisement, by the 'sensory neon signs' (p. 105) flashing out stereotyped messages. Brown speaks of the 'bug-eyed youngsters' (p. 106) (and no doubt hears also 'monsters') of kitsch paintings. Ever since they adopted as national emblem the bald eagle, Americans search everywhere for hair-restorers, replacements, palliatives; it is a mania for tampering, in which they lead the world, but much of the world is only too happy to tag along. Brown selects as the perfect 'do-it-yourself cliché' the offer to paint the Mona Lisa by numbers. The cheek, the frankness of such parasitism, the oxymoronic shop-window displaying 'New Antiques', I find resistible but not morally reprehensible, perhaps because of my own proneness to bad taste and fascination with twisting.

'Camp' is often thought of as self-aware and self-mocking kitsch, meta-kitsch, exploiting the bad taste which is already a commercial exploitation. Hyperbolic, affected, theatrical, effeminately homosexual, such epithets seek to lasso a very slippery customer. Camp, for many, is a drag routine (as in 'it's a drag', or 'c'est rasoir', the object dragged over protesting flesh). There seems often to be an absurd and prejudicial assumption that the nineteenth and twentieth centuries invented bad taste (in conservative eyes, a slatternly handmaiden of democracy). Such gripers forget that generally it is high art which has survived from the past, as kitsch rarely employs durable materials. Every society has had its 'false' pleasures. Anything can be made into kitsch by the reception and use given it. Dorfles, though he spends much of his time high-mindedly belittling it for not being high art, says that kitsch can be 'good, bad or even original'.[19] To a large extent, and its more thoughtful writers have always been deeply conscious of this, the United States has had, because of the shortness of its history as an independent state, to borrow cultures. Hence the large part played by replicas. Eco writes understandingly of the American taste for hyper-realism (wax-works, reconstructed rooms of great figures): 'the "completely real" becomes identified with the "completely fake". Absolute unreality is offered as real presence... Not the image of the thing, but its plastercast. Its double, in other words.'[20] It is this double, the alter ego aspect, which troubles. The Strong Museum of Fascination in Rochester, United States – a nineteenth- and twentieth-century collection of many thousands of gewgaws, rarely assembled by other people and certainly nowhere else on this scale – produces this mystifying comment from a visitor: 'Making the exclusive commonplace is one of the great social phenomena of the modern age.'[21] This could mean, either: making what was exclusive into a commonplace, or making the commonplace into an exclusivity. Of course, ashtrays in the shape of lavatory-bowls may be a prosaic hint not to squash the wrong sort of butts on the former.

Much of the press is a cess-pit, which is not to be sniffed at. It is normal but unjust to say that it is 'the last refuge of clichés'.[22] It was, however, a journalist, saying farewell to Fleet Street in a speech, who said: 'To make a cliché is to make a classic.'[23] Competition for news-delivery puts the stress on attention-grabbing. It is this aspect of cliché which most preoccupies Lerner: 'It is best, then, to regard cliché as an attitude to one's language, rather than the use of individual objection-able phrases: to speak of cliché, and not clichés. And we may define it as the use of commonplaces with sensational intent' – what he terms the 'purple cliché'.[24] This is, on the face of it, puzzling, for it would seem hard to captivate with worn-out devices. Do not greedy and blasé publics shout: Surprise Us? Lerner's notion presupposes that much sensational-ist discourse carries a still potent mesmeric charge. The fact that journalists avoid abstraction and seek to use metaphors in every other unit of phrase promotes the myth of colourful writing as against cooler forms of language. Reporters' hectic conditions of work, the determinism of deadlines, beget headlines. The famous 'Hicks Nix Sticks Pix' (country filmgoers disrelish pictures with rustic settings) has got every-thing: rhyme, pattern, concision, tongue-twisting. Nobody talks like that, but then nobody talks like Hamlet. Journalistic prose and advertising slogans here overlap. Such forms save breath, tone, eye-strain and brain-fag (except that the brevity of wit is notoriously fatiguing in any but smallish doses). More run-of-the-mill headlines in fact compact clichés, because shortage of space limits vocabulary and the complexity of what can be expressed. Journalist hacks are a major subdivision of the hackneyed, together with nags and strumpets. The need to comply with a 'house-style' tends to iron out individual texts; rewriting produces anonymous copy. 'The standard treatment of staple topics ... the rules at issue are never spelled out but are understood and internalized, and the system becomes self-regulating, through anticipatory self-censorship.

Whatever comes in to the press office will be processed and reprocessed by a succession of people till it conforms to these underlying principles.'[25] The miracle is that the best journalists, whether working on quality or popular papers, can buck this system and function as successful Winston Smiths.

Some journalists (like S.J. Perelman or Flann O'Brien) and certain serious popular novelists (like P.G. Wodehouse) made careers out of being cliché-experts. Bagnall speaks of Wodehouse's 'invisible quotation marks' which subtly but unmistakably set off a word or phrase as banal.[26] In addition to affording humour opportunities for twisting, clichés are central to humour. Jokes rely on the stereotypes (mothers-in-law, nagging wives, Scots, Jews, Polacks, drunken husbands, misbehaved children), even on the fantastic cliché of talking animals. Repeated jokes, circling the world, become themselves humorous clichés, and correspond to the same theft of the ready-made we have witnessed in so many other areas. Like clichés, jokes aim at social lubrication, easement, and cover-up (the state of being at a loss for words).

An American journalistic term for cliché, bromide, in Britain traditionally suggests a means of keeping a soldier's pecker down: clichés as anti-climaxes. The inventor of the term, the humorist Gelett Burgess, intended it to cover both persons and ways of thinking, and in an essay treats it as an extended serious joke.[27] 'The Bromide does his thinking by syndicate' (p.17). Indeed, any traveller across the United States cannot fail to notice the enormous quantity of syndicated material in newspapers. Bromides speak bromidioms, totally predictable remarks (pp.21–2). The contrary term is Sulphites, which hardly improves the smell, for bromide means 'stench'. The wholy essay is a running contest between the dull Bromides and the bright Sulphites, though rather self-destructively Burgess claims that 'Sulphites are agreed upon most of the basic facts of life, and this common understanding makes it possible for them to eliminate the obvious from their conversation' (p.33). I would have thought that consensus was half-way to cliché. For Burgess, Bromides are self-entranced, talk without listening and so 'escape all chance of education' (p.35). A certain wobble, or chiasmus, sets in when he talks of a calm Sulphite (elsewhere described as explosive) and an excitable Bromide (p.35). Children are the leading Bromides: 'What boy of ten will wear a collar different from what his school-mates are all wearing. He must conform to the rule and custom of the majority or he suffers horribly' (p.37). Alice in Wonderland is 'the modern type, a Bromide amidst Sulphites' (p.38). Burgess admits that the latter are not necessarily agreeable: 'All cranks, all reformers, and most artists are sulphitic. The insane asylums are full of Sulphites' (p. 40). Maybe it is the fear of going over the top and round the bend that lands Burgess finally in a middling, mugwump posture, finding Bromides essential after all, 'the veriest staff of life' (p. 62). The real distinction between the two apparent opposites is the question of independence of mind rather than actual differences of behaviour. 'A man may be a devoted supporter of Mrs Grundy and yet be a Sulphite, if he has, in his own mind, reached an original conclusion that society needs her safeguards' (p. 44). Unrelenting Sulphites and pedantic eccentrics can turn into Bromides (p. 50). Presumably Burgess quakes somewhat at the prospect of Sulphites as aliens from another world, who 'see things separated from their environment, tradition, precedent' (p. 57). Like many jobbing humorists, he shrinks back from the full implications of his founding idea, and settles for and on the comforting bosom of orthodoxy.

12

A Dead-and-Alive Hole

A much repeated metaphor for commonplaces is the 'meeting-place of the mob, the haunt of public eloquence'.[1] We will later see Baudelaire in his dandy posture, but here he is being less thinkingly elitist. A mood aped by Louis Aragon at his most would-be dandaically bolshy:

> Mankind loves to speak proverbially ... to rely on a set expression for its anxieties. It thinks by proxy. Words which have impressed it come back, and it uses them as one hums a tune that has seeped into one's subconscious. Its poets and thinkers thus contribute to its cretinization. The influence and power of a mind can be measured by the quantity of nonsense it gives rise to.[2]

A common belief – but how inevitable is it? – seems to be that, whenever anything new is generalized, it grows stale, rather like drugs becoming ineffective against disease. But many durable clichés resemble, rather, nits that resist all scalp treatments. The sentence before last offers the mandarin, anti-egalitarian view, for which Remy de Gourmont makes an eloquent spokesman. He starts with an unconvincing attempt to differentiate between cliché and commonplace: the one a matter of solidified expression (he was probably recalling the genealogy of 'cliché', from printing), and the other more the banality of a thought.[3] He hardly stays within his own guide-lines, and switches quickly into an attack on 'anonymous brains and complete intellectual slavishness' (p. 305). He slips into the standard nineteenth-century commonplace: clichés as whores. The cliché writer would never 'sleep with an idea that had not prostituted itself to several generations of scribblers' (p. 312). With much justification he blames traditionalist French education for the production of such minds, especially the pedagogical weight placed on parrot-learning of ready-made phrases (p. 315). After distinguishing between visual memory, which retains the thinginess of objects, and abstract, recipe-like, verbal memory, he argues that pupils are not taught to look but rather to listen (p. 315). He might have added: and to listen to themselves, for there is something highly narcissistic about the whole tradition. It seems, he says, that children's eyes are required only for reading books, like 'false eyes they could put away in their pockets when they have learned their lessons as the teacher puts away his glasses' (p. 315). Above all, Gourmont despises celebrated authors who drag behind them a suspect train of followers repeating their words and doings (p. 319): the curse of modishness.

Paulhan, as I have shown on several occasions, has a much more complex and rich attitude to cliché. Disgust over clichés, he believes, is kept up out of hatred of ordinary life and everyday feelings.[4] He favours the term 'misology', though I think 'sceptology' would be apter, for it is more mistrust than hatred of language that he diagnoses. Poets get so nervous about the stock images – moon, stars – that they grow afraid of mentioning such objects at all (p. 32). By 'Terror', Paulhan means the attempt by *misologues* to persuade that words have some uncontrollable, mystical power over us; it refers no doubt to the political and rhetorical discourse of the French Revolution at its most virulent. Paulhan accuses such writers of a cult of *difference*, 'any old' will do (p. 154). Such modernists (for example, Apollinaire, Eluard) try to go one better than language ('valoir mieux que lui'), to outwit it (p. 60). This tactic would still presuppose that language is alien and hostile, but, as it can be combatted only with language, the whole struggle seems schizophrenic. Paulhan notes drily that it is always the effects of this linguistic incursion on others that the Terrorists bemoan, not that on themselves (p. 76). They see the mote in their brother's eye, but not the beam, the leer of smugness, in their own. How many of us would honestly admit: 'I am a sucker for the word "caring", or "human", or "deconstruction"'? All in all, Paulhan wishes to put language in its sufficiently honourable place. Words and things are separate. 'Like sirens or the Minotaur, the power-of-words is formed, by a strange telescoping, of the junction of two alien and incompatible bodies' (p. 94). Words are at our command; they are not in charge. Indeed, I imagine, to think that they are would be to indulge in a kind of demonology, as in Cold War rhetoric. Paulhan offers some excellent cutting analogies for the language-sniffers: a tennis-player bungling his stroke and then glaring at his racquet, or the poor workman blaming his tools (p. 107). This is too often the received attitude towards language: to see it as something distinct from ourselves, out of our area of responsibility. The clichés clogging up language have been put there by each of us, actively or consentingly. Without wishing to sit on the barbed-wire fence between the contending forces here, I feel sure that we are neither as dominant as Paulhan maintains, nor as servile as the

Terrorists chant. I also am convinced that elitist views on language need to be resisted, without thereby abandoning a belief that some kinds of language are better than others: more apposite, more colourful, more honest.

Lanson declared that La Bruyère tried to avoid all clichés: those of vocabulary, construction or movement; and the man himself claimed that he had taken care to distance himself from commonplaces and long-serving proverbial phrases.[5] The heroically sane Fowler stated: 'Avoidance of the obvious is very well, provided that it is not itself obvious; but, if it is, all is spoilt.'[6] I remember an adolescent poem describing a 'plumbic sky', where the avoiding action itself is leaden. French has a telling term, *cache-misère*, for a decent coat that conceals the shabbiness beneath. How much writing goes about like mutton dressed as lamb? Where would my style be without recourse to numerous dictionaries and Roget's *Thesaurus*? Where is it with them? Tax avoidance is legal if not universally loved, whereas tax evasion is sanctionable. Can we distinguish between avoiding and evading clichés? I imagine that the polar opposite of a cliché text would be one starting a new hare each sentence. Joyce's *Stephen Hero* flees the obvious ('the hell of hells') like the plague. Hemingway and the Camus of *L'Etranger* aim for what Barthes calls 'white writing'; an a-literary, anti-rhetorical, non-lyrical style; they seek to evacuate their language. In the case of Camus, any deviation from the truly flat, like an official telegram with its euphemisms, the prison chaplain's hell-fire propaganda or the lawyers with their metaphorical pathos, immediately stands out as abnormal, comic and lethal. Yet, as with euphemism and litotes, such an anti-rhetoric ushers in another rhetoric, deafening in its own quiet way. As Bagnall reminds: 'There can be no such thing as plain English.'[7] Straight talking from the shoulder or the hip is as liable to slip into commonplace as any other form of speech.

When we mouth clichés we are often, naturally enough, only paying lip-service to them. Many ritual commonplaces apparently putting our hearts on our sleeves are in reality lodging our tongues in our cheeks. On a wider scale, a tough audience (like the archetypal wet Monday night at the Glasgow Empire) will greet unconvincing talk with horse-laughs. We can have a heckler, for similar purposes, at the back of our minds, or indeed in the front row, if need be; we can keep our wit about us, like armour. As with torture, along with passivity, human beings have the power to resist saturation, to refuse the sponge. (We saw earlier how clichés, as well as saturating, can fill the gap when we are caught short.) Often, as a result of efforts to emphasize, to persuade, to hide nervousness, to animate silence, or (paradoxically) out of a desperate searching for *le mot juste*, we emit a whole string of clichés: a hiccuping redundancy, which can turn the would-be grave into comedy.

Do we need brain-sized condoms to protect us against clichés, foreign aids? No doubt the ideal prophylactic against cliché would be simplicity, if we could achieve it rather than simplism, but, like virginity, it cannot be regained. 'Simplicity cannot be studied', as Nerval said.[8] Sophisticates cannot easily go native, and would anyway find there a different sophistication. Cliché is part of our complication as creatures. When we seem limpid, it is a surface quality as in the polluted Mediterranean. As Geoffrey Strickland points out, the 'sancta simplicitas' of a Blake or indeed a Balzac derives from a sublime unawareness of their own frequent pomposity and naïvety.[9] Silence would seem to be another panacea, but, as I said concerning Flaubert's and Bloy's ambition of muzzling the chief bayers of platitudes, the Bourgeois, mutism is no real answer, for 'silence gives consent'. At times, all the same, it is to be wondered why we break silence (cf. breaking wind), that holy vessel. It is strange how the proverb is truncated in all its European versions: '[Speech is silvern], silence is golden.' The availability of words, through no actively evil intent on their part, allows us to think we are being more precise about naming our feelings, which are surely often confused and self-contradictory, than is justifiable. 'No comment' should be an acceptable comment, but it has been ruined by spokespersons everywhere. We are thus sometimes forced into cliché by having to speak when we would rather not, and what might have been a dead letter comes back again into circulation. We do, of course, also take refuge in silence, which need not be brave or honest.

There is a fair amount of death's-head prose devoted to cliché; opening up black holes beneath our feet. Pietra maintains that commonplaces are unobtrusive, but as inexorable as determinism or fate. 'Often they have only expletive value, but they are rarely bullying. Mostly we give into them not as to an inspiration but rather an expiration.'[10] While it is true that a heavy dose of clichés can numb the brain and kill off a conversation, I do not want to believe that this is because, as Pietra argues, their deadliness reminds us of emptiness and death: 'le lieu commun ne dit pas rien: il dit le Rien' (the commonplace does not say nothing: it conveys Nothingness).[11] Riffaterre takes an opposite stance, in glossing Louis Aragon's haughty view of cliché: 'Banality is loquacious – this is Aragon's perception of the verbal panic of these "human maybugs" driven by an urge to get out. "They think they're in a cul de sac and look for what they call a way out. A way out from what, one might ask. They are the possessed of the word 'way out'."'[12] Still contrary to Pietra is

Riffaterre's own view that 'we should not confuse banality and thread-bareness. If it was worn out, the cliché would lose its clientèle and its enemies, which is not the case. It does not pass unnoticed; quite the opposite, it always stands out'.[13] Whether discreet or blatant, this area of language I am considering has been described as 'cet ineffable qu'est le cliché'.[14] Yet, of all people, Samuel Beckett laughs at (while reiterating, but the long-winded repetition is surely ironic) the topos of the in-expressible: 'And perhaps also because what we know partakes in no small measure of the nature of what has so happily been called the unutterable or ineffable, so that any attempt to utter or eff it is doomed to fail, doomed, doomed to fail.'[15]

Xerox never comes up with anything original.[16]

The conscious opponent to cliché is self-evidently originality, though the cynical would say with Dean Inge: 'Originality, I fear, is too often only undetected and frequently unconscious plagiarism.'[17] A softer version comes from Aldrich:

> No bird has ever uttered note
> That was not in some first bird's throat;
> Since Eden's freshness and man's fall
> No rose has been original.[18]

That penetrating analyst of plagiarism, Schneider, clinging to what has been called the 'personal hallmark view', declares that despite the excellencies of much pastiche, style is unplagiarizable: 'Le style est ce qui ne se viole ni ne se vole' (style is what cannot be ravished nor robbed).[19] We say 'in his own inimitable style', and this must be a reality, over a total output, even if sections can be mimicked perfectly. Would-be originals (and an earlier meaning is lunatic) go in a range from rogues and mavericks at one end to apostates at the other, with non-conformists perhaps in the middle. Emerson would, pantheistically, place himself at every point of the gamut. In the essay 'Self-Reliance' he acts as the spokesman for the drive towards originality.

He starts with a very American encouragement to practise scooping. 'In every work of genius we recognize our own rejected thoughts: they come back to us with a certain alienated majesty.'[20] The lesson, then, is: get in first. Thus he places us on our honour and best behaviour, and some might find the prospect more depressing than stirring: 'Who can thus avoid all pledges, and having observed, observe again from the same unaffected, unbiased, unbribable, unaffrighted innocence, must always be formidable' (p. 20). Attacking conformity he moves Rousseau's rhetorical excitement up several notches. 'Nothing is at last sacred but the integrity of your own mind' (p. 20). This recalls Rousseau's claim of uniqueness at the start of his *Confessions*: 'Voici le seul portrait d'homme, peint exactement d'après nature et dans toute sa vérité, qui existe et qui probablement existera jamais' (Here is the only portrait of a man, painted exactly and honestly true to life, which exists and will probably ever exist). As Sabin comments: 'Rousseau's obsession with his uniqueness in the *Confessions* seems oddly inconsistent with his other philosophic positions. Rousseau frankly assumes that the idiosyncrasies of others are more conventionally accountable than his own ... He differs from other people more than they differ from each other.'[21]

Emerson underlines the predictability of much discourse. 'If I know your sect, I anticipate your argument' (p. 22). In reaction he eulogizes what Sartre would later call 'la fuite en avant' (keeping ahead of definition): 'A foolish consistency is the hobgoblin of little minds' (p. 24). There is, of course, an inner consistency. 'A character is like an acrostic or Alexandrian stanza; – read it forward, backward, or across, it still spells the same thing' (p. 24). This suggests that the constant flight in fact runs on the spot. He accepts, nay welcomes, misunderstanding (for it proves the cretinism of inferiors), but urges us not to pule if it should happen to us. Instead of helping us to be self-reliant, 'our reading is mendicant and sycophantic' (p. 26). The stress, rather, should fall on the intuition of our 'aboriginal self', and not on tuition (p. 27). Making notes impairs memory and libraries 'overload [our] wit' (p. 36). The rousing call is to put off all foreign aid and stand alone; a plea for the home-grown virtues of Americanness. The thrilling vision of his protégé, Thoreau: 'If a man does not keep pace with his companions, perhaps it is because he hears a different drummer'[22] has one drawback: it might encourage you to think that you alone are in step.

In the same period, Baudelaire was elaborating a more decadent kind of originality. Many have noted the troubling coexistence in his poetry of corniness and 'modernity' (that automatic back-slap), as in 'La Muse vénale':

> Sentant ta bourse à sec autant que ton palais,
> Récolteras-tu l'or des voûtes azurées?
> (Feeling your purse as skint as your throat,
> will you gather in the gold of the heavenly vaults?)

The word-play helps here to distance the cliché, while preserving the quintessential Baudelairian oscillation between squalor and dreams.[23]

Elsewhere, Baudelaire stated that prosodies and rhetorical treatises have never impeded the production of originality; indeed the opposite is truer – they have positively aided originality to blossom.[24] It was his glorification of the dandy which most focused his thinking on his variety of originality. A 'lawless institution', wilfully non-utilitarian, dedicated to cultivating style above all, and welcoming the 'aristocratic enjoyment of being unpopular': the Dandy lives in constant proximity to a mirror.[25] Time and money (preferably in the form of indefinite credit) are indispensable to the programme (p. 483). As he proceeds, he switches the emphasis from fancy dress to absolute simplicity of apparel, 'the best way to stand out' (p. 483). 'The burning desire to create originality for oneself' (ibid.) leads to the pleasure of startling others, coupled with the proud satisfaction of never being taken aback onself (p. 483). Dandyism can on occasion reach spiritual or stoical heights, and always keeps its gravity in the midst of levity (p. 484). In fact, it imposes a discipline as strict as that of the Jesuits. Baudelaire sees the link himself between such aspirations and decadence: 'Dandyism is a setting sun; like the sinking star it is magnificent, lacking in warmth and full of melancholy' (p. 485). This pathos keeps the dandy just this side of the insufferable, as he bends over backwards to displease. Like Flaubert, Baudelaire felt threatened by 'the rising tide of democracy, which invades and levels out everything' (p. 485). In this perspective, cliché results from universal suffrage. Sixty years later, at the outset of the Great War, Gide's Lafcadio, a spiritual son of Baudelaire, and so keen to be nonpareil that he conceives the monstrous idea of a totally motiveless murder, cannot help parodying his forerunner, who was already blackly comic. Whereas Pascal (an original mind trying to punish himself for his presumption) had jabbed a sharp pin into himself for each sinful thought he entertained, Lafcadio sticks a pen-knife, meticulously sterilized first, into his thigh, in delectable self-chastisement for every commonplace idea that occurs to him.

Originality is proving as ambivalent as banality. For Bagnall, one of the many consequences of its cult is that 'in our efforts to be different, to cast off the dead paraphernalia of the past – to stand, as it were, in our own shoes – we find ourselves strangely naked. We have congratulated ourselves on our freedom, and have ended up tongue-tied'.[26] Especially, he adds, in the matter of condolences. That is, not the healthy silence which stonewalls against cliché, but the embarrassed muttering in a limbo between speech and chosen mutism. Ionesco, whom I showed earlier hovering between exploiting cliché dramatically and succumbing to it in his discursive writings, invents in *Le Rhinocéros* a hero, Bérenger, who laments that he cannot follow the herd of rampant conformists: 'Wretched is he who wants to preserve his originality.'[27] It is a sheepish uniqueness, not unlike Camus's shamefaced Romanticism when compared with Stendhal's franker variety.

Originality and the desire to neologize are related. From a purely quantitative viewpoint, most speech can be thought original. Farb declares: 'If conventional remarks – such as greetings, farewell, stock phrases like *Thank you*, proverbs, clichés and so forth – are disregarded, in theory all of a person's speech consists of sentences never before uttered.'[28] This overstates, as a moment's recall would show ('I've cut my finger', 'Is it time for the TV News yet?' etc.). We spend much of each day's speaking-time making such unoriginal but not 'conventional' statements. Stylistically unremarkable phrases can still be arresting; they pull us up short and make us think or re-think. And we can of course originate a false idea. In a test of observational powers, it was found unsurprisingly that 'the eye-witness brings something to the scene which later he takes away from it; oftener than not what he imagines to be the account of an event is really a transfiguration of it'. Reporting this, Lippmann comments, coinciding with Guiraud's perception about our back-to-front ways with language: 'For the most part, we do not first see, and then define, we define first and then see.'[29] Nature may make no leaps, but Man is a bounder, relying on preconditioned first impressions. As Gide exclaimed: 'What a mistake it is to think that it is by letting oneself go that one becomes most oneself! What comes straight off and naturally to mind is commonplace, clichés.'[30] That is from the official champion of spontaneity. For Gide, truly great writers like Goethe achieve a state above mere originality: 'il devient banal, supérieurement.'[31] Camus tries very hard to make Meursault in *L'Etranger* into a nondescript nonpareil. Valéry is more frankly voracious: 'The desire for originality is the source of all borrowing... There is nothing more original, more truly one's own, than to feed off others – but we have to digest them. The lion is made of assimilated lamb.'[32] As he so often does, Barthes rejoins modern classics such as Valéry and Gide when he points out that 'the avant-garde is never anything but the progressive, emancipated form of past culture: today is born of yesterday, Robbe-Grillet is already present in Flaubert'.[33] A student of literary cliché across the ages, Naffakh-Perrin, echoes the Gidean reminder of the conformism which quickly settles on non-conformity, when she speaks of 'the two poles of required conformism and imperative originality'.[34] We are between the frying-pan and the deep blue sea. What she does not consider is the dominant present-day French cliché about neologisms and their attempt to make new: their valorization via such terms as *l'écart* (infraction), *le monstre, l'hybride, le fou, le désir, la pulsion*.

I have mentioned some of the criticisms levelled at the pursuit of originality, but it remains a persistent dream. 'In every writer resides this old dream of being original, that is, ultimately, of being without origins, of being one's own originator.'[35] It is the desire 'to be the son of nobody, to be a truly self-made man'.[36] Such hankering for self-creation propels Laclos's splendidly evil Mme de Merteuil, who boasts she is her own work of art. It is a kind of impacted, centripetal Frankenstein-syndrome, where the monster that you create is yourself, 'this incomparable monster ... that each of us is in our own eyes'.[37] Joyce's version is 'He Whom Himself begot ... sitteth on the right hand of His Own Self'.[38] This parody of the Credo also mocks those who would be onlie self-begetters. Clearly, we cannot create ourselves, though we can create, or helplessly watch the birth of, second or even multiple selves. After extolling Outsider Artists in these words: 'The Outsiders create their works in a spirit of indifference towards, if not plain ignorance of, the public world of art', Cardinal later qualifies this statement. 'Yet no artist is ever graced with complete immunity to culture ... Any creative work which achieved absolute independence of a context would simply lie beyond all hope of recognition, and be invisible to us.'[39] Several of the artists presented in Cardinal's survey are mentally disturbed to varying degrees. When you have lost your grip on your self, you may assert it excessively. Originality begins to disappear in that puff of blue smoke which accompanies the auto-sodomistic, palindromic eroticism of many pictures by mentally ill artists.

Originality is an ancient dream. An Egyptian scribe of 2000 BC, Khakheperresenb, lamented already: 'Would I had phrases that are not known, utterances that are strange, in new language that has not been used, free from repetition, not an utterance which has grown stale, which men of old have spoken.'[40] Bate, after quoting such complaints, comments that scientists are less affected by these longings, since science is cumulative in ways that art is not (p. 7). He wonders whether the real weight on human beings is not determinism, but the 'burden of choice' (p. 67). Weighing the rival claims of Ancients and Moderns, he stresses the unequal balance of the equation, for the present is a few decades whereas the past embraces millennia (p. 71). In this long view, which so few take, he asks the crucial question: who wants 'general amnesia, a brutal excision from our consciousness of all that has been so precariously won' (p. 90).

The impossibility of total originality is recognized not only by plagiarists, parodists and pasticheurs, but also by adhocists. The authors of the splendid *Adhocism*, Jencks and Silver, discover all kinds of connections between juggling with words, divergent thinking and the recycling of the old, whether in science, the arts or daily life. Other branches of this vital activity include improvised jazz, serendipity, retrieval-systems and hybridization. Remaking new can apply equally to things and to thoughts and words: we can be verbal or semantic handymen. 'Cliché, or a standardized subsystem, is the necessary element for creation, since all inventions consist of the association of previous material.'[41] They marvel at Buster Keaton's 'Yankee ingenuity and fascination with gadgetry': 'he is always trying to find a new use for old objects.'[42] Though a ready-made (*phrase toute faite* in French, *frase trillada* – a 'threshed' phrase – in Spanish), a cliché can thus be a springboard, and adhocism a more creative form of plagiarism. Ready-made can obviously also be a limiting term: off-the-peg, automatic, as in ready-made solutions. The term 'cannibalization' covers a major aspect of adhocism. It is something of a misnomer, apart from the extreme case of the street-artist who literally ingurgitates whole bicycles, reduced to swallowable fragments. Yet the word has a metaphorical use: the absorption of others' materials, the means to hand. True cannibalization presumably does feed the eater.

The eminent geneticist, François Jacob, follows a similar line of argument in applying to evolution the concept of tinkering. Like a cook, 'the tinkerer has to enrich his stock with left-overs'.[43] This has a similarity – which he admits is ludic, but then treats as totally serious – with the processes of natural selection: 'Evolution does not produce novelties from scratch.'[44] This conclusion is that living organisms are historical structures, 'literally creations of history. They represent, not a perfect product of engineering but a patchwork of odd sets pieced together when and where opportunities arose'.[45] Just as in biology, a perfectibilist would argue that, since we are descended from lower forms of life, we must continuously improve, so linguistic meliorists might claim that, even though we largely derive our words and ideas from earlier sources, we make capital of them. As with mutation, such changes can be fortuitous or engineered. Not only do we come from monkeys, we can also make monkeys of ourselves, as in howlers, another windfall tasty to some palates. 'Existentialists believe that we must try and prolong death for as long as possible' – 'Carmen counts the number of times she has slept with members of the opposite sex on her fingers.'[46] This regurgitation of received material has clearly involved the intake going down the wrong way. Lévi-Strauss's term for adhocism, *bricolage*,[47] likewise embraces a large range of natural activity from games to mythological thinking: all human life is there.

It has been apparent throughout that my particular fondness goes to the act of twisting for re-use. Cack-handed at domestic do-it-yourself, I want to be dexterous in the mental version, and not simply perpetuate the English amateur tradition of messing about.

First, a mental health warning from the Orient:

> and i should never whip the commonplace
> for the meaning of its opposite.[48]

The Americans certainly did not invent, but they have boosted, the desire to do something useful with stock material. 'Familiarity breeds contempt – and children', said Mark Twain, putting many marriages in a nutshell.[49] The set phrase is here given a new lease of life, the familiar made somewhat strange. The Russian Formalist critic, Shlovsky, has habituated readers to the technique of defamiliarization, which he sees as central to all true art. 'The tecnique of art is to make objects "unfamiliar", to make forms difficult, to increase the difficulty and length of perception, because the process of perception is an aesthetic end in itself and must be prolonged. Art is a way of experiencing the artfulness of an object; the object is not important.' He offers as an embodiment of this practice Tolstoy, who 'describes an object as if seeing it for the first time, an event as if it were happening for the first time'.[50] It is easy to see the appeal of such a theory for artists, critics and sophisticated readers, for it demands slow-motion reading or viewing, and effectively removes the creation and certainly the reception of art out of the common orbit: hence, the Martian-eye view. Such refusal to name also invites periphrasis and the concoction of riddles and enigmas. It is potentially schizophrenic. It starts by arguing, like realism, that art exists 'to make the stone stony', and swivels, as quoted above, to forgetting the stone altogether. Yet the general tactic of 'seeing things out of their normal context'[51] is an exercise everyone could benefit from, as long as the foregrounding involved serves to make us see things differently and not just hyper-conscious of the artistic technique on display. Such writing is re-writing at its best, and not in the corrupt sense of Stalinist, or *1984*, or editorial, re-writes.

We talk about *turns* of speech (*tours* in French). Language, with our active support, lifts itself on its balls, takes off, as the word 'trope' itself invites. Human beings had been practising lateral, or upended, thinking millennia before de Bono codified the knack. (I could add: 'De Bono nil nisi mortuum', but there would not be much point.) Even subconsciously, in dreams, we can evade, renew, complicate the given. A pursued animal twists and turns in order to survive. In general life, of course, twisting often grates or anguishes (ankle, knee, neck); we do not like to have our arm twisted. A fractious child, in some regions, is 'twisty'. The two sexes can, respectively, get their knickers, or their tassel, in a twist. By all of us the twist can be gone round. 'I a twister love what I abhor.'[52] A twist is, etymologically, a length of rope; give a twister enough of it and he will hang himself. Joys and dangers surround the whole phenomenon of twisting. Above all it is necessary, for psychic and social health. Sacred cows, unexamined taboos, Holy Writ, and other such fixtures, need to be scanned, altered or disloged. Present-day fundamentalists in the United States or Islam take their highly figurative scriptures too literally.

Clichés, like puns, can be put or made to work, like so many layabouts. Twisting clichés by the tail may help to rehabilitate them, restore them to full employment in new contexts; open a second career. It need not be destructive; it can be a revivifying tonic. Such massage can be the medium of retoning. Manipulation need not be only crooked; it can set straight the crooked. After a particularly trite protestation by a woman, Cabrera Infante's narrator adds: 'From such corn mighty oaths grow'; the rapid pivot on *acorns – oaks* debunks the preceding cliché.[53] The stale spiel is made productive. Though we often forget this, clichés often began as figurative phrases, and literalizing them gives them back a strength they formerly possessed. In one of Flaubert's sketches, a father catches his son boozing in a bar and exclaims: 'tu n'es qu'un pilier d'estaminet' (you're holding up the walls of this pub), whereupon the lad changes into a doorpost. Flesh is turned into thing in this transmogrified cliché, and it is ambiguous whether the censorious father has wrought this chastisement, or whether the boy's response guys the paternal discourse. Vallès reanimates the proverb 'manager son pain à la fumée du rôt' (to be only a looker-on) by having his starving young hero Jacques Vingtras wave his stale crust in the smell of fish frying downstairs. In so doing he enacts, pictorializes, dramatizes the proverb. This is an existential twist, necessary for survival, summed up in the idiom 'tromper sa faim' (to stave off one's hunger). Vallès's hero here puns for his dear life.[54] A related variant of literalization is the tactic of dumb insolence, as practised by the oppressed peasants in Silone's *Fontamara* and *Bread and Wine*: they take official obfuscations at face value and thus engage a return to basics. Wilful misreading or wilful mishearing can have the virtue of at least passive resistance to the tyranny of words.

Some French writers, of the type termed 'révolutionnaires de salon', often seem incapable of distinguishing between verbal questioning or ridicule and storming the Bastille. They take concepts like 'subversion' literally, and are thus victims of their own metaphorization. It is generally impossible to quantify the social impact of mockery, and it generally seems hard today to laugh anyone out of office, as politicans in democracies learn the formerly aristocratic or totalitarian art of brazenness. Still, politicans go on twisting. Churchill's (inaccurate) description of Attlee as 'a sheep in sheep's clothing'[55] is a would-be lethal tautology, in which Churchill was essentially saying: 'There's nothing more to Attlee than what meets the unimpressed eye. He is what he looks like.' A militant feminist might say: 'One man's meat is another woman's poison.' A telling recast with minimal adjustment is: 'An atheist is a man with no invisible means of support.'[56] Black humour, one of the few areas of common language (apart from bank accounts) where black is beautiful, also rings changes to score points. Much twisting, whether of words, ideas, handkerchiefs or attitudes, no doubt springs from desperation and panic – like that of deadlined journalists having to come up with something eye-catching. We have all seen amended posters and graffiti. For Jencks and Silver, who see this reworking as a variety of adhocism, 'suddenly the poster presents a dialectic instead of merely an assertion, which is typical when fresh elements are added *ad hoc*'.[57] Such reforming play produces a mock edict: 'Register all puns', with the scrawled corrigendum underneath: 'Puns don't kill people, people kill people.'[58] This exchange mingles views on the pointedness of wit and the controversy over gun-ownership. The phrase 'détournement d'affiches' (poster-abduction or embezzlement) was a slogan of the *Situationnistes*. Within the advertising trade itself, an incursion into the entertainments industry produces countless punning twists, which, because of the built-in obsolescence of the whole programme, require constant renewal. Dragged out, like the long-running but singularly unpointed 'Black' advertisements for John Player's cigarettes, and like a juggler protracting his act, such wordplaying copy can impress only as virtuosity, not as signification, or even entertainment. As we saw earlier, one advertiser can feed, with inventive parasitism, off another, as with Carlsberg claiming that '9 out of 10 cats say that their owners prefer it to other lagers'. In a stolid Swiss view, 'this Anglo-Saxon attitude towards language as a piece of clay or a toy and the enjoyment derived from double-meanings, ambiguities and plays on words, is a centuries old tradition quite distinct from that found on the Continent'.[59] This might be one of the root causes of the myth of perfidious Albion. The urge to twist (invert, reverse, criss-cross) is very often ironic, as well as ludic, in intent; and the poker-face of irony also serves to separate the English not only from Continentals but from many Americans. As with punning, ironic diversion demands the complicity and intelligence of a partner, who has to know what the ironist is getting at (attacking/referring to).

As for the various types of twisting, Milner has listed some of the major ones: phonological ('Diplomacy: the noble art of lying for one's country'), morphological, syntactical, lexical ('Hang-over: the wrath of grapes'), situational.[60] They can work by opposites, as in Robert Desnos's 'langage cuit' (cooked language) which he opposed to 'langage cru' (crude/raw language). Revamping proverbs or idioms can be, like homeopathy, a treating of like with like, taking a hair of the dog that bit you. In addition, the very rigidity of structure in maxims, proverbs, slogans and other set forms seems positively to invite reversals, permutations, substitutions. A collaborator of the OULIPO regime, Benabou, paradoxically urges the mass-production of such regenerated aphorisms. He sees this as instructional rather than dogmatic, the aim being to encourage many others to spawn their personalized aphorisms, though he does sound a snobbish or realistic warning about the need for artisanal care. He proposes as an example this twist on Clausewitz: 'L'art est la continuation du hasard par d'autres moyens.' This example is significant, for Oulipiens, blending Surrealism and Classicism, favour constrictions and loathe randomness, except in so far as such generation of new material from old is potentially infinite (cf. Queneau's *Cent Mille Milliards de poèmes*). It is all based on the paradox of mechanical creativity.[61] Classical as well as modernist writers have worked to resuscitate clichés. In his *Polite Conversation*, Swift's characters 'know what their word-hoard tells them'.[62] Yet the effect is strangely full of life: 'The demented farce has something to do with the inexhaustible flow of stale expressions; the rhyming jingles and folk wisdom; the regular rhythms that bespeak gusto and energy among the participants' (p. 208). Rogers differentiates between Swift's use of such aggressive testing of familiar phrases in poetry and in prose: 'Swift is able to "foreground" the clichés in verse, while in the prose conversation they follow with an inevitable sequentiality – no individual phrase is made salient' (p. 219). Also a great punner and ironist, Swift in this area 'is constantly burrowing beneath the surface of humdrum conversational language, so as to bring up amusing or damaging implications unsuspected in normal usage' (p. 222).

It does not go without saying that tropes can stall into tropisms (automatic reactions), that twists can be forced and futile (like the vast majority of puns). This happens especially when the originating metaphor has virtually sunk without trace and is beyond raising. It is unprofitable to joke about the *wing* of a building ('the castle was wounded in the left wing') or the *arm* or a chair ('the carpenter had to put the chair's broken arm in a sling'). Similarly, happy turns of phrase are mini-utopias and likewise static, for if you achieve perfection, you stand still. Much twisting, like much play, is half-hearted or lazy, imitative; we talk of 'idle pursuits'. Milking clichés can turn sour. While the twister does not echo words or ideas passively, he *bandies* them. 'Bandy' also suggests askew; 'bent' also connotes deviant and criminal. Even reactivated clichés have to be spaced out, like puns, or they may grow wearisome and slow down the helter-skelter pace of usual reading or talking. No doubt all writers, unless they have something to hide, beg to be read in slow-motion, but this is baying for the moon, or pissing against the wind. Such rejigged formulae have their best effect if the total work of which they are the high spots is also dedicated, like Queneau's *Le Chiendent* or *Madame Bovary*, to undermining habitual modes of thinking, feeling or expressing. Otherwise many twists have long since become mechanical new clichés of the 'man bites dog' type.

We all like to spend what Cabrera Infante calls, after and a bit away from Henry Miller, 'quiet days in cliché'.[63] Even or especially twists lean on the cliché they transmute; they allude to it in the process of reacting against it. The permissive society, even with its repressive tolerance, cries 'Anything goes' and feels nothing is sacred: four clichés in succession, but they have a point. A man of great learning and fine sense of humour like Gershon Legman can still criticize the 'dubious merriment of the "perverted proverb"'.[64] In the business of literalizing idioms, people have come to expect the twisting, to feel secure if it appears and frustrated if it does not. Of such routinization of the transformative, Zijderveld comments: 'The manipulation of clichés in mirth has itself become a cliché, not in the [*sic*] least for commercial reasons.' He does modify this in a measured fashion: 'Nevertheless, in our mirthful playing with traditional and routinized meanings ... we have a chance to subdue clichés to our ingenuity and wit, and thus to relativize their power.'[65] Cunliffe mounts a more spirited attack. Naturally accepting as a thinking being that reversals 'commonly entail repudiation, a challenge, a *versus*', he finds a troubling coincidence between capitalist practices and those of much intellectual enquiry and humour. 'The demand for "turnover" in the economic order causes a craving for "turnover", or rather "over-turn", in the realm of imagination and the intellect.' He is frankly hostile to 'this relentless formulaic inversion, with its unearned, knowing "novelty"'.[66] In his study of American humour, Jesse Bier dates the phenomenon to the literary comedians of the native tradition. He sees the instinct for reversal as basically healthy in the context. 'Since much of the American mentality itself battens on simplifications – on clichés, on shibboleths, on proverbs, on slogans, on formulas – an equal amount of our humour is in the service of unholy complication.' He cannot, however, accept so readily the commercialization of this urge: fun-cards, bumper-stickers. 'In these ways, we are relieved of the burden of origination.'[67] That burden, of course, has been too heavy for most people since the beginnings of social existence.

Innovation is not always so methodical. There are happy accidents, windfall-proneness, as in serendipity. Perhaps it takes skill as well as luck to come across the interesting *objet trouvé*. Not all twists are perverted; some simply remind of hidden depths and resources. Clichés can contain plural meanings. We can, in more senses than one, pull chestnuts out of the fire, at the risk, naturally, of burnt fingers. 'Loose connections', for instance, yields: approximate association of ideas; a hint of madness; raffish acquaintances; a malfunctioning mechanism; distant contacts; to cast off moorings; and hit-or-miss coition. 'Different strokes for different folks' suggests varying ways of swimming; administering corporal punishment; caressing; calligraphing; making friends with oarsmen; having a thrombosis; and making love. In both cases, not double but septuple entendre. Now, it is quite true that the specific context would indicate the proper meaning, but the realization of other, improper meanings, once gained, colours all later responses to the phrase. Finally, my own twist on a current twist. The series 'X do it – (for instance 'Surfers do it standing up') relies on double entendre: one literal and one figurative ('suggestive') meaning. My proffering is: 'Dons do it in their sleep', a quadruple entendre that squares the original twist. On the literal/idiomatic level, it contains: dons teach in a comatose fashion; or, dons teach with no sweat (it comes naturally). On the figurative/ suggestive level: dons make love without concentrating (the distrait professor syndrome); or, dons make love as easy as falling off a log. If clichés did not exist, we at-a-removers, metamongerers, would have to invent them.

It is blatantly obvious that my personal cliché is an urge to see or put puns everywhere. They are my salvation, my US Cavalry. I never suffer, however, from that other cliché or reflex: the rush to apologize for puns.[68] Punning involves montage: the stacking or juxtaposing of meanings. While I find obvious and pointless puns an especially excruciating form of automatism, a turn which has stalled, as if tetanus had set in, I reject the French twist on 'jeux de mains, jeux de vilains' (roughly, no mucking about; literally, rogues are dextrous) – 'jeux de mots, jeux de vilains' (wordplay is rogues' play). I relish the way good, effective puns can tip the wink, which is as good as a nod, and prevent nodding off:

sous-entrendre as well as double entendre. I value the seriousness of proper language-play. Think of the gambling connotation of play, wager, stake (a bet, a place of execution for schismatics, a weapon to kill vampires); *jeu, être en jeu* (to be at stake). As Pierre Reverdy said: 'On joue à qui perd gagne sur les mots' (What we play on words is loser takes all).[69] Like puns, clichés are the downtrodden of the world of words, and excite the only missionary zeal I possess. Since writing *Puns*, I have become conscious of a gathering movement to 'recuperate' this mode, indeed to make it modish. This fits in, I imagine, with the navel-reviews, and general self-referentiality of much contemporary literature and critical practice. I prefer mainly to think of puns in terms of an alienation effect, a socio-intellectual BO, which reminds us that the mind is not top dog. For me, as for Thomas Hood, 'a double meaning shows double sense'[70] – a way of packing the slack, of offering a bargain, two meanings for the price of one sound. I trust I genuinely believe that everyone can have admission to the 'pungentry'.[71] Punning is playing language at its own game, for while human beings have collectively built up language, no individual being can master it totally, and to that extent it escapes us and has a kind of autonomous existence. Of Milton's punning Satan, Pope wonders whether he wrote thus 'to suggest . . . that the Father of Lies was also the Father of Puns . . . It must be own'd a Christian practice, used in the primitive times by some of the Fathers, and in later by most of the Sons of the Church'.[72] There are even punning clichés. 'See Naples and die' ('e poi mori') is one such, for Mori is next to Naples, and itself the scene of more than one lethal plague. And the Land of Nod, where some readers may be at this very moment.

Harriet Weaver said to James Joyce: 'I am made in such a way that I do not care much for the output of your Wholesale Safety Pun Factory.'[73] One of my favourite, telling clichés is 'Many a true word is spoken in jest', and it is indeed the case that the apparently audacious Joyce finds safety in numbers, and can shelter behind the vast super- and infra-structure of punning in *Finnegans Wake*. Macdonald himself speaks of 'coincidences and other manifestations of the chance symmetry of life, including puns'.[74] A reviewer complains of a punning author: 'It is as if he feels a continual urge to prove himself to be some sort of top-flight, whip-cracking ringmaster of the performing word . . . Out-and-out linguistic spivvery.'[75] Many undoubtedly do feel that punners are shysters, con-men, who play dirty tricks on others with words. Puns, the agents of central intelligence, are spat upon, marginalized. Even con-firmed punners like Christopher Ricks occasionally ask themselves: 'Or am I imagining all this?'[76] as they tuck into a Barmecide Feast of language. Punning is double exposure, and often blurred vision, as after or during concussion.

Are we in control of verbal associations? Our minds are mini-Rogets. We were all Rogeting words long before Barthes egged us to roger them. Freud judged that, as with coincidences in action, language too can meet us half-way, through what he called 'linguistic compliance'.[77] Of course it takes two opposite and wilful motions to complete a true encounter; it takes two to tango. Language is not our boss; we bend it to our ends, make it go along with us. We do not have to be on rails set down before us. This view grants us more dynamic choice than Lacan's influential decree that 'to the unconscious things are what they sound like. Paronomasia is one of the tropes that reveal the unconscious'.[78] In a talk on Joyce, Lacan used the coinage 'sonne comme' (sounds like), whereas French usually expresses this idea by words denoting appearance, consonance, even smelling ('That sounds like heresy': 'Cela *sent* l'hérésie'). Crossword clues are fond of 'sounds like'. The clang or rhyming effect can take its toll. 'That rings a bell', we say, in tune with Pavlov's pooch. Lacan, it seems, tended to insinuate that he *was* the unconscious of his neophytes.

Good puns are true laxatives, and loosen up costive speech and thought, keep it on the run. I like the mixture of randomness and rigour in paronyms, approximate puns. I hope I am sketching a 'speaking likeness'[79] to a kind of truth about language. One of the truths I hold to be self-evident, in my declaration of relative independence, is the pursuit of snappiness. I believe purposeful punning to be a sign of life.

For pessimists much within language leans in the opposite direction, towards death. Schopenhauer: 'The actual life of a thought lasts only until it reaches the point of speech: there it petrifies and is henceforth dead but indestructible, like the petrified plants and animals of prehistory. As soon as our thinking has found words it ceases to be sincere or at bottom serious. When it begins to exist for others it ceases to live in us, just as the child severs itself from its mother when it enters into its own existence.'[80] I find this idea curious. It gives a different slant on the notion of intellectual property from those we saw earlier, for it claims that others are needed to give the kiss of life to our stillborn thoughts, in a kind of relay race in which the guttering torch is rekindled by the next carrier. The idea is gloomy for the individual, if promising for the species. Both Emerson and Max Müller thought of words as a kind of 'fossil poetry'.[81] Fossils may be durable but they can hardly be brought back to life. Education for centuries, and some of its practitioners still today, have treated living languages in terms of the 'dead' ones, which were considered the role-models. Clichés are not really fossils; they are more the living dead. Like bodies threatened with hypothermia, they can be warmed up. Are twisted clichés alive only in the sense that selected bits of our cadavers may still be useful to other livers? Is it the same cliché if it has been tampered with (you can make out some rejased objects; others are unrecognizable)?

We bank often on financial metaphors, like devaluation; ideas, like money, may not be worth the paper they are printed on. Lakoff and Johnson thoroughly document how pervasive and how systematic are our daily clichés. 'Time is money' proliferates into 'I don't have *enough* time to *spare* for that', 'you're *running out* of time', 'Is it *worth* your while?' and so on.[82] This habit shows also how alive clichés, proverbs, set sayings of all kinds, can be: they spread and go on acting in multiple guises. 'They are "alive" in the most fundamental sense; they are metaphors we live by. The fact that they are conventionally fixed within the lexicon of English makes them no less alive.'[83] The authors' own discourse is clichéic, perhaps of necessity, and extremely redundant (I have rarely read a more reiterative text). Once they have tipped us the wink, we could open our eyes fully and carry on for ourselves, *ad nauseam*. (Strange how many academic works spell things out as if for patronized infants.) Lakoff and Johnson are taken with systems, networks of metaphors. This might suggest that we are trapped within our habitual utterances, or it would, if we were not also able to modify and renew these moulds. Honestly, they confess that other, non-Western, cultures might well see and put things differently.

Bagnall offers a nicely judged analogy between the career of office talk and Black Beauty's downward spiral: 'Phrases like this began their careers in respectable company and have gradually gone downhill; like Black Beauty, born a thoroughbred, finding himself in livery stables and eventually working as a broken-down cabhorse, they hobnob with the great writers, get tired, do a long spell in national newspapers, are relegated to the provinces, and end up, working as hard as ever, as poor old camp clichés in the offices of London export firms. Unlike Black Beauty, they will not be rescued, but there is life in them yet.'[84] Overall, Bagnall is less censorious than many about clichés and often argues for their usefulness, indeed their unavoidability. As McLuhan asks: 'May it not be that the staying-power of clichés, like that of old songs and nursery rhymes, derives from the involvement they demand?'[85] Even an academic attempt to say a good word for commonplaces proposes that 'the banality of conventional components in no way prevents them from being expressive'.[86] Against unimaginative sociologists like Zijderveld,

Ricks stresses more the two-way process, cooperation, between clichés and (selected) human beings, as we saw in his analysis of Orwell. Ricks calls, in an exceedingly fine distinction, for 'a vigilant – not beady-eyed – engagement with clichés'. He sounds circular, as though preaching to the converted, when he says: 'Clichés invite you not to think – but you may always decline the invitation, and what could better invite a thinking man to think?' He declares that clichés are not 'to be truckled', though I would add, as he would agree, that they are to have truck with, for 'truck' is exchange.[87] In an essay on the poetry of Geoffrey Hill, Ricks applauds the 'argumentativeness of the clichés'. Describing John Gower's account of the wrestling bout between Hercules and Achelous, Ricks describes himself in the process: 'The gliding Protean elider'. All the time, as in his study of Gower, he asks the key question: 'Are clichés and verbal formulae passive within his poetry, or active?'[88] I feel myself that many clichés which maybe should have caught their death long since, lead a charmed life, can be given a new lease of life, can indeed be socially the life and soul of the party. Clichés are as large as life, and a fact of life. Do we always even understand them? They may be dated, used in a private sense or context; we may well have less than perfect command of our own language. Like proverbs, clichés can on occasion be enigmatic. I do not entirely share McLuhan's sanguine faith that 'to release energy in the cliché needs the encounter of another cliché'.[89] But I know from a long marriage of two minds (and our sweet old etcetera) that my wife's writing style, cornucopiously strewn with clichés but propelled by her passionate educational beliefs, has an energizing effect on most who read it. I am less impressed when the dauntingly well-read Eco relaxes, becomes a big softy, a Little Sir Echo, as when he admits of the film *Casablanca*:

> When all the archetypes burst out shamelessly, we plumb Homeric profundity. Two clichés make us laugh but a hundred clichés move us because we sense dimly that the clichés are talking among themselves, celebrating a reunion... Just as the extreme of pain meets sensual pleasure and the extreme of perversion borders on mystical energy so too the extreme of banality allows us to catch a glimpse of the Sublime.[90]

We have heard this song before (play it again, Umb) from consenting and relenting aesthetes. It is a perfect instance of High Camp.

There are less strident ways to defend, and indeed celebrate, clichés. They have their day, like any dog. Where would we be without such instantly applicable codes, such memory-joggers (*pense-bête*), such professed solidarity? And think of the opposite: the desire to be original at whatever cost can produce the most godawful tripe. The fact that clichés are memorized and repeated, as well as indicating laziness, proves that the original formulation had something, was not bland. Middleton Murry seeks to exculpate literary commonplace on these grounds: 'Suppose we take a familiar metaphor, as that the fiery spirit of Emily Brontë burned up her body. It cannot fairly be called cliché; it is rather a familiar and necessary idiom... This obvious necessity of the metaphor, this absence of genuine alternatives.' He dates the figure back to the moment 'when the existence of the soul was first surmised; for only by such an image could the nature of the soul's existence be at all apprehended'.[91] The argument is that of inevitability, just as we talk of the inevitability of high art. Michael Frayn defends not a leading writer but the stock of phrases itself:

> The more one thinks about our common kit of metaphors for mental states and events, the less inclined one is to take it for granted, or dismiss it as banal. 'At the back of one's mind', 'to run over the alternatives', 'to reach a decision', 'something stirred in her memory', 'he groped for words' – they're brilliant! A whole literature, really, trodden down into the soil like last year's leaves, fertilizing, unrecognized and forgotten, whatever pushes above the ground now.[92]

Montherlant presses the point: 'The energy of despair. It is a commonplace. But it is true. It is so important to say something which expresses what really is the case that we must respect commonplaces, for eight or nine times out of ten they express reality. It is all well and good to be original but only by speaking the truth.'[93]

'The poet measures out his clichés [if he is T. S. Eliot, with coffee-spoons]: he cannot do without them or he will be incomprehensible.'[94] This view combines the ideas of spacing out and of padding, two necessary parts of any sustained discourse. Where *would* we be without clichés? Much of our complaining, our illusions of mental superiority, our joking, our creativity (especially in its recycling aspect) would have no material to work on or to kick against. Of course, much the same could be said of governments, schools, families and workplaces. We can take off only from a solid foundation, from what is there – the common place. 'We reach agreements only on commonplaces. Without common ground society is no longer possible.'[95] Paulhan wonders why clichés are singled out for opprobrium, when rhythm, rhyme, literary genres and fixed social forms like the family have many of the same supposed characteristics. His simple answer is: they are shorter, easier to focus.[96] His study of the formulaic, competitive, but sociable and productive *hain-tenys* of Madagascar helps him to think well of clichés, against the elitists who decry them. He finds the whole area of cliché a polysemous phenomenon, and a baggy monster. In my own way, I concur.

FAMOUS LAST WORDS

There is little point in collecting and analysing clichés.
Kenneth Hudson[97]
It was an uphill climb. A cliché novitiate is no bed of roses.
Frank Sullivan ('The Cliché Expert')[98]

How eagerly we try to live up to the clichés we have inherited or devised, and how perverse it seems to go, however mildly, against their grain. So few, if any, of us dwell among the untrodden ways. We are all expert at clichés. No doubt in broadcasting my pearls on clichés before you, expensive readers, I am carrying coals to Newcastle. Embroidering on clichés is possibly like decorating an elephant. Is it dignified? Is there any point? What was wrong with the original wrinkled grey? 'On va maquiller le cadavre!' (They're out to put make-up on the corpse), Camus's Clamence warns.[99] Am I, after a good flogging, tarting up a dead horse? Just as, according to Woody Allen, when you masturbate you are at least making love with someone you like, so when you utter and talk about clichés, you are sure (or are you?) of an understanding audience. I have a dream: a marathon, involving millions of people, from every place and age, combined with a relay-race. The batons, those dry old sticks, would frequently get lost, or end up in the wrong hands, but the total movement would be, stumblingly, onwards. Is it impossible, as a contribution to the question of race-relations, to combine my favourite French cliché ('vive la différence!') and the melting-pot technique?

It has proved hard to disentangle clichés from idioms. Like puns and fleas, clichés get everywhere; hence my sidesteps into plagiarism, proverbs, and so on. *Passe-partout*, as we have seen, embraces several meanings. Generalization spreads like the plague. 'Spread' itself (middle-aged or sandwich) may be distasteful, or impressive (wing-span, large ranch, big feast). Language is multifarious; words can be loaded, like weapons, dice, or seamen on shore-leave (by definition, a tight ship is run by drunken sailors). 'What we say about [language] is momentarily the case.'[100] Yet we must, as George Moore urged, 'try to distinguish between the quick and the dead'.[101] I have tried on the whole to evade such polarities, and to concentrate on overlap, interchange; my wide approach is an umbrella for all seasons. A conclusion normally makes out that some proof of a proposition has been attained. I doubt that I have proved anything, as I did not have one central augument. No doubt some will say I have been having my cake and eating it. A natural enough thing to do, after all. Clichés have been presented here as bad, indispensable, sometimes good, things. Why don't I conclude, come down on one side, abandon the poise of mugwumpery? I do not because I honestly cannot. Whether this failure is mine or caused by the polymorphous nature of the topic, only readers can decide. My ideal would be a book composed of islands of insights, roughly linked, if at all, by flimsy rattan bridges. Rightly, few would buy this 'doctrine of scattered occasions'.[102] In my own bitty way I have tried to rethink the obvious, the unthinking, to plumb the depths of the trite. It has been at times rather like attempting to think about death, notoriously unthinkable, though not unimaginable or uninventable. The danger is of triggering off a kind of mental implosion, a black hole, for the author and the reader. More calmly, as Bolinger encourages, 'stopping to think is just stopping to ask what the words mean'.[103] It would be arrogant to feel flattered by this over-neat opposition: 'Little minds are interested in the extraordinary; great minds in the commonplace'[104] – a cross-over is more plausible.

Clichés are highly contagious, and there is no known immunity, except possibly silence, oral or graphic, and even that only conceals the infection. If there is any original sin, cliché is it: the desire, not to know, but to be knowing. A hyper-awareness of cliché might fulfil the dream of Bloy and Flaubert: silencing the parrot-talk of humanity; people might become elective mutes. More moderately, can a greater awareness of what we do and fail to do with our minds be all that harmful and even beneficial? How easily we are tempted not to think, to think less than we ought, to think only and uncritically what others have already thought. I wanted to investigate our common laziness, our settling for the less, our short measures, our (false) economy of effort. It is true of course, as Schneider reminds, that 'ultimately, each of us has little to say. One or two things. How can we avoid saying them over and over again?'[105] We give endless repeat performances, comebacks; at best these are reprises rather than mere reiterations. There is a lot of smattering about, not least in this book: compulsory and extended education, the mass media, the phenomenon of reproducibility, saturation, passive consumerdom. But the fact that we not only use, or are used by, clichés, but also re-use them and exploit them suggests that they are curiously inexhaustible – a bottomless pit; a suitably ambivalent image – hell, and a mine that will not run out. In some ways, though not much of a talker, I would have liked to speak this book. 'In speech, intonation, pauses, emphasis, these and other means can invest a cliché-ridden sentence, or set of sentences, with humour and wit, and with realism and trenchancy. In writing, we lack these dramatic, these extraneous aids: we *stand or fall alone*.'[106]

Some quarters will view this whole book as a tissue of clichés. At the same time, as a complete text, it is neography: this has not been said before and statistically (apart from the quotations), the majority of the constituent sentences are brand-new. That, of course, does not mean that the ideas carried by each sentence are mint-fresh. I will not boast, though I would love to, like John Bunyan: 'The whole and every whit is mine.'[107] We all have it both ways. We ape, and we strike out for ourselves. We steal, and we make up with interest.

We cannot escape rhetoric; we just switch to a different key. Rhetoric, simply (or, rather, complexly), codifies what we say and how we say it. It is difficult to codify cliché, however. 'There is indeed no canonical reading of the cliché that could be contained within the reassuring limits of a norm.'[108] Personally, I rejoice. Amossy and Rosen speak of the 'bad conscience about cliché, imposed by modern Western culture'.[109] I hope I have shown that, while the awareness of cliché has spread in the last two centuries, like the increased reporting of crime or disease, it cannot be thought of as narrowly age- or place- or culture-specific. Everybody knows about it; it is not a discovery of recent critics. Being dedicatedly against censorship, I have no desire to prohibit clichés, and have been amused by those who, learning I was writing on clichés, became temporarily self-conscious and watched their tongues. I do not want to be censorious, for clichés are the very air we breathe, often stale and polluted, but our systems have their own defences. If they are not the whole world, neither are clichés the end of the world. I want merely to put them in their place, which is not the dung-heap of human discourse. Have I made a meal of it – a dog's dinner, a pig's ear? If we cannot escape them altogether, perhaps we can briefly give them the slip, slip the leash. To pick up on my opening motif, *à cheval*, we are astride clichés (and the colour of this particular nag is of course chestnut). They bear us, transport us (in both the utilitarian and the exalted senses). They can run away with us. But we have reins and knees and voices, to change their course. We can mix clichés, like metaphors, and end up in that challenging position: between the frying-pan and the deep blue sea.

At the outset I spoke of my proto-Existentialist wish for self-creation *ex nihilo*. I have learned better. 'Quisque suos patimur manes.'[110] I have seen five, and there are no doubt other possible, translations of this quotation. We all have to pay for the sullying of our moral envelope; we are guiltily aware of the imperfections of our souls, stained and blotched with earthly sins; we bear each one of us his own ghostly doom; we pass through our several purgatorial experiences; each of us finds the world of death fitted to himself.

All is not lost. If the theory proves correct that the universe is heading for a state when everything will be thrown into reverse gear, and time will run backwards, then somebody will have to reinvent all our clichés, or coin some new ones...

13

Change of Gear in the Melting-Pot

To grasp the meaning of the world of today we use a language created to express the world of yesterday. The life of the past seems to us nearer our true natures, but only because it is nearer our language.

Saint-Exupéry[1]

We are indeed slow on the uptake. Even at midnight on New Year's Eve, when we ring out the old and ring in the new, we sing 'Auld Lang Syne'; we first-foot into the novel, carrying the traditional coal, bread and coin. At the year's pivot, we look both ways. As well as being interested in both cliché and neologism, and avoiding wherever possible facile moralizing about the commonplace, I wanted to study something more clearly positive and creative: coinage. There is obviously an imbalance in the two sections. As with sin there is more to say about cliché. Creativity is less easily analysable, if more marvellous, than copying. Language snobs and conservatives claim that it is for poets and, at a push, critics to invent, and not the common people; by extension thinking is also deemed a privilege of the few. For many people change implies decay, as in the reprehending exclamation or silent thought on remeeting someone after many years: 'Oh! how you've changed!' Many are irritated when stores or newspapers change their format, or timetables are altered, so that they have to refind their way about them. The resistance to coinages, or to borrowings from other languages, is part of the defence system of stereotyped thinking. Hostility to the new is naturally a clone of clinging to the old. Making up words, unless you are a child or a comedian, has often been regarded as tantamount to making up stories, so as to hoodwink or to show off.

I have scattered some coinages and blends among my discussions about clichés. The word 'melting-pot' figures in the mixed metaphor heading this hinge-chapter, because it suggests the softening of frozen polarities (if not the abolition of differences), the spawning of hybrids and occasionally monsters, and the interplay between languages – all of which will figure much in the remaining chapters. Although Nietzsche says, with accurate sarcasm, that 'as soon as we are shown the existence of something old in a new thing, we are pacified',[2] we can hardly do without some balance or overlap between maintenance and innovation, keeping old and making new. 'New lamps for old', is the cry in the *Arabian Nights*, 'old lamps for new!' The phrase 'to coin a phrase' is used only ironically, by way of introduction to a hoary saying. Neologisms and clichés cannot, of course, be talked about in the same breath. That would produce only gibberish, suffocation or a rebarbative portmanteau-word, 'neologismiché', which sounds like an exotic form of sexual appliance. Yet there are connexions. Both clichés and neologisms, in differing degrees, rely on the existent, and thus cast doubt on the possibility of anything being born from nothing. The gamut, or rather the shuttle, goes from the *tour heureux* to the happy hapax; as in the British Rail logo and network, the connecting lines run back and forth. Many coiners no doubt want their neologisms to become clichés, common coinage: that is, accepted into the mainstream of language and memorized. A new word may be an adjusted older word, just as a commonplace may be rephrased. Neither coins or notes, nor ideas and expressions, stay in mint condition. Just as lies create new truths, so we can talk of minting clichés afresh, as in verbal seduction: 'One mustn't coin new phrases but rather mint counterfeit clichés',[3] argues Cabrera Infante's hero, in a criss-cross, for coin can suggest forgery and mint freshness. As semantic calques are often misleadingly called 'faux amis', so clichés are our staunchest false friends.

In addition to borrowing words or expressions from foreign languages, we can transfer them from one specialized field to another (computers to linguistics, for example), or they may leak or filter from esoteric use to common parlance. There is indeed much needless importing of vocabulary, and frequently excessive knee-jerk resistance, especially to Americanization, 'cocacolonization'. Loan-words and borrowed ideas must have some links; and 'cliché' itself is a borrowing (within French from printing terminology, and between many languages and French). What is surprising to the host community is often old hat to the lender. Borrowings, like archaisms, are ready-mades, and often look ill at ease in their new surroundings. Borrowing, as we will see, is just as unreliable a term in linguistic study as in the history of ideas.

To balance what I said earlier about clichés in crisis situations, I would add that, under stress, we are as likely to come out with something startling (spoonerism, malapropism, blend, coinage) as with something familiar and automatic. In more deliberate moods, neology is akin to the twisting of clichés – the attempt to get a new slant on affairs. Nietzsche believed that 'the worst coinage is still better than the best cliché'.[4] In the section on jargon, I quoted or originated several blends and proposed them as weapons of criticism, or at least retaliation. Though some coiners want to become popular, others aim at shock effects, a one-off impact. On a wider scale, Simone de Beauvoir's *Le Deuxième Sexe* not only cites and dismantles many commonplaces about women; it presents Woman as a cliché that individual women partly consent to and partly suffer from as victims. Woman, she demands, needs to be rephrased, to become a vast neologism. It is equally obvious that new words can grow trite through overuse or misuse. Even that put-up job of Chomsky, designed to embody the fact that a sentence can be syntactically well formed but semantically self-cancelling (* 'colorless green ideas sleep furiously') is by now grubby from use in other linguisticians' hands.[5]

While clichés can be, as I have tried to show, productive, they are inevitably less creative in themselves than new words expressing interesting new or revised thoughts. My metaphors must change. 'Perhaps when thought is like a mummy its most befitting garb is verbal cerements; but when it is alive, let us look elsewhere than to our wardrobes for comparisons.'[6] Yet Flaubert's shadow looms up. Where but in his 'Dictionary of Received Ideas' would we find a more perfect cliché about coinages than: 'Néologisme: la perte de la langue française' (Neologism: the ruination of the French language).[7] As anxiety about new words is deeper-seated in French than in Anglo-American culture, in the pages that follow I will more often refer to French theory and practice. All the same, the more embattled French neologists will prove as inventive as their looser-limbed counterparts in Britain and America.

14

First Words

It is easier to define a neologism than a cliché, but the definition is only the start of the story. The *New English Dictionary* states that the word was taken over from French in the eighteenth century. It is not surprising if the French needed the term earlier than us, as their Establishment has consistently been more hostile to new words. In theology, 'neologism' signifies the tendency to adopt novel, rationalistic views. Neologisms cause dissent wherever they appear. In psychiatric terminology, the word denotes the invention of incomprehensible words or phrases, often interpolated in otherwise correct sentences. A variant in the same area is: 'A compound word coined by a psychotic and meaningless to the hearer.'[1] As for the inventor, Mencken attributes to Dr Charles E. Funk the term 'neotrist', but there are earlier English occurrences of 'neoter-ist', and 'neoteric' goes back to 1596: both cover a wider area of innovation.[2]

Where do new words come from? Some seem, like Topsy, to have just growed. Neologizing is part of ad-libbing and making things up, though, like much improvisation, it is quite often as rehearsed as jokes, anecdotes or dying words. Adam was clearly the first originator, after God; he started the endless selection of names for things and creatures. God's 'fiat lux', as all Merseysiders should know, led to the construction of Port Sunlight. The *neologos* and the *logos* (whether Jehovan or Heraclitan) were in on the start. Sanskrit, a 'dead' language, but how influential beyond the grave, was thought of as perfect, definitive, whereas the more popular spoken form Prakrit, was allowed to evolve naturally and freely. Horace and Varro called neologisms 'ficta verba' (fabricated words). The parallel and competing ideas of spontaneous generation and artificial production have framed the history of new word-making.

We borrowed the term *le mot juste* from the French, because we had nothing like it. Yes we did. The right word, the exact word, the apt word, and so on: we were well-off already. Why then, add to the stock? Presumably, it was felt that the borrowing carried a nuance that the home-grown words could not quite match. Perhaps it was a matter of the ancient snobbery about exotic imports. Whether urgent, luxurious or frivolous, the need engendered the action. There is a continuous need for fresh synonyms as a kind of reserve force, for variety or increased precision. What individual languages lack is a fascinating subject of speculation. 'If a people have no word for something, either it does not matter to them, or it matters too much to talk about.'[3] Why has English kept *atopy* to a restricted area; and not thought of inventing 'nusquamity' (the opposite of ubiquity), or 'neminity' (the urge to be no one)? Both might dwell darkly in many minds, but not surface to be talked about. It remains true, however, that neology usually springs from lacks and gaps. Spinoza remarked that, although we have the word *commiseratio* for pain arising from another's hurt, he knew of no word for the feeling of pleasure arising from another's good.[4] Congratulation is more distanced. Despite his nostalgia in most areas of life, including language, Orwell did entertain the possibility that new words might be needed, not only for new objects, but so as to communicate better what all human beings share. What we talk least well of, he felt sure, is the inner life.[5]

Brunot and Bruneau offer a corrective to the stock idea that new practices create new words at once. Favouritism, they point out, was established in government long before the word was coined. 'The word *favoritisme* is not the acknowledgement of a system but a way of criticizing it. It was born when public opinion started to disapprove of a procedure which had seemed natural to it before.'[6] They see the whole process as spiral or cyclical: the backlash of purism following experimentation, and revolutions succeeding arterio-sclerosis. In this historical perspective, a neologism is often a Johnny-come-lately. Lacks can sometimes be best spotted by an outsider, as when the Polish poet Mickiewicz said: 'La Pologne a mouru trois fois, mais elle n'est pas morte' (Poland has died three times, but she is not dead).[7] Many neologisms attempt only a small-scale modification of an existing word, adding a nuance, as when Hervé Bazin, on the basis of *institutionnel*, coins *adaptionnel*. As the whole novel in which this figures, *Le Matrimoine* (itself an adaptation from *patrimoine*, and suggesting the lioness's share of the married state), deals with adaptation, learning to live with matrimony, the addition is, so to speak, organic.[8] Neology is not invariably triggered by new concepts or products; it can spring from the desire to review or extend old ones. As puns constantly remind us, semantic neologism involves polysemy, in that it locates new meanings in an existing word or phrase.

Who neologizes? Nyrop summarizes usefully: 'Whether it is a question of a scientific discovery, an industrial development, a change in social life, a new idea, a new mode of feeling or understanding, an enrichment of moral awareness, neologism is called for imperiously, and everybody creates new words, the educated person and the unschooled, the worker and the idler, the theoretician and the practician.'[9] Guilbert narrows the field: regular word creation is the work of a small number of writers and speakers, though he admits that anyone, however uncultured, possesses a sufficient awareness of the mechanisms of language to produce new items, as is shown by popular speech and slang.[10] We are all no doubt guessing in this area, and Algeo's charitable bet seems to me fair: 'It is not possible for the average speaker to invent new sounds or new grammatical structures; but if we ask whether many men can invent new words, the answer is a Johnsonian response: "Yes sir, many men, many women and many children".'[11] Justifiably anxious to avoid making neology a preserve of the academic, Brander Matthews claims: '*hunch* and *grouch*, *pussy-footed* and *high-brow* were grown in the open air of out doors, and not in the hot-house of the learned.'[12] In a longer perspective, Spitzer points out that the conditions of knowledge in a democracy give us 'no easier access to the arcanum of authorship than the civilization that coined the names of the months *Julius* and *Augustus*'.[13] In contrast with elitists like Gourmont or Migliorini (to be discussed later), when Spitzer talks of 'that generous artistic mood that admits more than one world as possible' (p. 83), he excludes no one from membership. He relates a telling and poignant anecdote of Italian prisoners-of-war, who wriggled to escape censorship of their letters home begging for food parcels by referring to hunger in extemporized, sometimes roundabout, and often poetic, terms. This neologizing, in desperate circumstances, was both practical and artistic (p. 86). Even here, nevertheless, Spitzer remains fully aware that the innovating individual 'carries in himself the mind of the people to whom he addresses the innovation: he knows their linguistic habits and anticipates their (favourable) reaction to his innovation' (p. 76). Several commentators have stressed how new words spread out from a clan to wider usage. Spitzer talks of the need for 'fixing factors' to follow the 'creative moment' (p. 77).

The whole statistical and micro-analytical side of neology I will gladly leave to those who have more training, talent and patience than I. Those who, favouring pseudo-scientific computations, sneer at intuitive and impressionistic approaches forget that we all have computers in our heads, not only for mental arithmetic, but also for the quick information-retrieval which operates in our mental lexicons. Most of my examples of coinages, borrowings and blends are nouns. I imagine there are more new things than actions or qualities that would need coined verbs or adjectives to denote them. I will look at both passive (accidental) and intentional neologisms. On the whole, I have no room for purely functional, naming neologisms, except when they contain other elements of interest. As with puns, I prefer pointed neologism, often but not necessarily humorous. I am very aware of, but do not realistically hope to avoid, the snobbish privileging of the written over the spoken language. Overall, I am still looking at and for the possibility or impossibility of originality. Is Widal correct in declaring that 'the neologism devaluates the cliché'?[14] Can this area of human experience, any more than any other, escape the commonplace?

15

Illustration of Defence

In words, as fashions, the same rule will hold;
Alike fantastic, if too new, or old;
Be not the first by whom the new are tried,
Nor yet the last to lay the old aside.

Pope[1]

It is not to be wondered if few pronouncers on language have obeyed the cool sanity, the Golden Meanness, of Pope's lines. I want to start with negation, spoiling tactics, on the part of various rearguards or vanguards. In what ways might it be reasonable to resist new words? First: we have enough already, provided we use them properly. Second: much innovation is mere faddishness. Third: we have not exhausted the potential of the existing stock. Fourth: who could be entrusted with the creation of more words? Five (and the swivel starts towards neology): why not reanimate archaic words, dialect words or borrow ready-made foreign words? Neophobes sometimes allow that, when a new word has survived the test of time, it is then acceptable, rather like the process by which stiff shoes mould themselves to the feet and become comfortable. Furthermore, many hostile to neologisms mind less if they are unsigned, anonymous, as this would seem to guarantee general consent to the word; whereas a singular inventor might be judged as overweening. Neologarithm is a strategy for preventing their birth, practised by those of certain persuasions.[2]

Neologisms have for centuries been much more of an issue, a mooter point, in France than anywhere else. It is hard to believe that French pride is touchier than that of other peoples. Rather, I would guess that the French urge to keep connexions, when making neologisms – principally by using methods of derivation from existing words – which moderates a common distaste for the creation of any neologisms – stems from a culture where hostile incest (as compared with the club atmosphere of English culture) predominates. In addition, the French want to keep things tidily compartmentalized, so that perhaps they can more comfortably play off the opposing factions against each other.

I will now put my skates on. Any historical survey of word-coining serves to recall that, like lemmings, neologisms have a high mortality-rate. In sixteenth-century France, those many who bred new words on the basis of the classical tongue were called, by Geoffroy Tory, 'escumeurs de latin' – Latin-scourers, or lifters, and were clearly regarded as behaving parasitically. Though, in the preface to his epic *La Franciade*, Ronsard encouraged 'the wise boldness of creating new words', in his own practice he tended to blow hot and cold. He dosed neologisms according to the person addressed, the period of his career, or the genre he was using; he often suppressed them in collected editions.[3] As a court poet, Desportes had to be careful not to offend the sensibilities of his consumers.[4] Thus, the upper classes were as much an inhibiting factor as the common folk who, as was argued by some Protestant writers hostile in particular to foreign borrowings, needed to be protected from incomprehensibility and intimidation.[5] Even Montaigne complained about the coining mania of the Pléiade school of poets. Though ever ready to invent on occasion himself, he preferred extracting the maximum juice from the existing language. Guiraud sees the whole situation levelly: 'This verbal superabundance in Rabelais or Ronsard goes way beyond the immediate needs of expression to reach that fecundity, that exuberant generosity which is the true mark of the rebirth of humanism.' Guiraud loves this overspill, 'This poetic function of neologism' (where 'poetic' takes on its full sense of creating).[6]

In seventeenth-century France, the struggle between those for and those against neology became heavily overweighted to the latter's side. Even that workhorse conjunction *car* (for) was widely considered an unwelcome addition. I must confess an interest (that is, a prejudice). I have to work hard on myself to accept any of the premises of the French classical outlook; I am unlikely to be post-modern, but I am certainly post-Romantic. I have precious little sympathy for willed cultural immobility and its standing injunction to let sleeping dogs lie. Vaugelas tried to out-herod Herod in his massacre or contraception of the French language. He liked to boast that the French were choosier about rules than the Latin models even, an arrogant way of implying that the pupils outstripped the masters. In his highly influential *Remarques*, he asserted, reluctantly, that only the King, or one of his favourites, or a prominent minister, had the right to create new words, for such models would be copied and the words themselves gain rapid currency; even then such inventions had to be derived from current words and fill a semantic gap.

He totally disapproved of borrowings from dialect or from technical languages.[7] The stress falls on rapid assimilation; sore thumbs could not be accommodated by classical decorum. A common belief among pundits was that neologisms should be as rare as comets.[8] And a common feeling among the elite was that the French language had reached its acme and could only be spoilt by further development. The age of the 'Roi-Soleil' seemed to want to stop the earth moving round the sun, or the sun roaming the heavens; it was time to mark time. The American Brander Matthews misreads naïvely when he claims that Vaugelas's edicts signified that 'language is not a monarchy or an aristocracy; it is a democracy with universal suffrage.'[9] It would be truer to say that a sizeable proportion of Frenchmen in that century rehearsed the great collaboration, not with an invader, but with the system imposed on them from within and above. Writers habitually submitted their texts for checking by authorities, thus signing away their own rights. Why were they not braver? As Versailles sucked in political, administrative, cultural and grammatical/lexical powers, it is not hard to see why a writer like Guez de Balzac could write in 1636 (the year the French Academy was founded) that 'everything outside the Court is called barbarous'.[10] The *désert* began at the gates of Paris. Absolute power seeks to purify absolutely. Bouhours, nicknamed 'the ape of Vaugelas', ventured the opinion that 'the safest bet was to innovate nothing, for there was a great risk in making a new word'. If one was absolutely unavoidable, the introducer should apologize ('if I may be so bold as to put it this way').[11]

A greatly reduced vocabulary overloaded each word of the permitted stock. Aiming for universality (at an elevated level) and for *clarté*, the seventeenth century in France often veered paradoxically into indetermination, in which words were waved as magical counters. Expectably, proverbs were deprecated, as smacking too much of the common people. The preference for general, non-specific words ended up in abdications like 'un je ne sais quoi' (which, admittedly, has been borrowed by foreigners for their own mystifying purposes). Fear of the mixing of genres, idiolects or registers led to a kind of linguistic racism, even though it has always been known that mongrels tend to be tougher than thoroughbreds. Some of the *distinguos* and wriggles were jesuitical. 'Vomir des flammes' or 'vomir des injures' (insults) were acceptable, but not plain puking.[12] The genteel purism of the Précieuses and their horror of 'dirty syllables' gave rise to a chastity of language not always matched by that of conduct. Luckily, censorship is often self-defeating, and what is banned gets more healthy attention than what is authorized. (Rousseau felt that French, in which so much is submerged, is the most obscene of tongues.)[13] This purism existed in a social vacuum, or hothouse, as the legislators under Louis XIV were increasingly severed from the people. Litotes, however, had an oblique power that I must acknowledge. Laclos puts it beautifully, talking of a négligé 'which reveals nothing and suggests everything'.[14] The smaller stock, at least in the best hands, demanded a correspondingly greater finesse in the manipulation of the words available.

La Bruyère was one of the first to kick, politely, the habit of misoneism. Purism began, for some, to be a dirty word. The Protestant thinker, Pierre Bayle, complained: 'Our language is dearthful' (*disetteuse*).[15] Fénelon believed it needed enrichment for it had been constricted and impoverished for a good hundred years by those who wished to purify it.[16] He proposed that, when a lack was felt, a word should be created, pleasant-sounding, unambiguous, in keeping with the genius of the language and enabling economy of discourse. Try it out on good society, repeat it until it is accepted: 'That is how a path opened up across a field soon becomes a beaten track.'[17] This seems to suggest that the quicker the novel becomes trite, the better. Naturally, comic writers in the seventeenth century took greater liberties, and, as Brunot stresses, the purists had no control over trade-words and artisans' terms within those distant worlds, which grew apace.[18] By a kind of schizophrenia, such words, if thought of at all, were deemed by the law-givers as not belonging to the French language, as if they were foreign enclaves. Perhaps the aptest image for the ideal language of the French classical period is that of 'clipped box-trees in Le Nôtre gardens'.[19] Leaving the seventeenth century, Brunot murmurs in audible relief: 'No discipline ever shuts off a language completely from life as it is made by events, fashions and accidents, day by day.'[20]

At the same time that writers in France were clinging on to the given language and braking development, scientists (trail-blazers of necessity) in England were demanding not only a purer, but a new, language (though the slogan of 'mathematical plainness' in speech or writing is a joke, when mathematics is Hebrew to the majority). Members of the Royal Society, irritated by pulpit wit, excessive metaphor and rhetorical festoonings, caressed the fond delusion that a self-explanatory language could be found (that is, the names of things should indicate their natures).[21] In fact, being British, scientific writers of the age did not eschew metaphor or the rhetorical arts; and, as some of their opponents joyfully noted, certain of these writers were themselves prone to clumsy Latinate neologisms, and to jargon. This was particularly ironic seeing that the growth of modern scientific thinking at that time often went with a mistrust of language, for in the Ancients v. Moderns controversy, Antiquity was frequently characterized as verbose and logic-chopping.

Another essential difference from the French classical tradition was that most champions of the English language at that time, whether progressive or conservative, made a virtue of its massive borrowing from other languages. There was, nevertheless, a movement to curb and regularize such allegedly chaotic activity. Defoe proposed an English Academy to match the French, and gave it a policing function: 'Twou'd be as Criminal then to Coin Words as Money.'[22] A little later, Addison spoke up for such an institution 'to settle all Controversies between Grammar and Idiom'.[23] Lord Chesterfield said: 'We must choose a dictator.'[24] Swift also, but 'Swift was pleading for the establishment of a standard, not a fossilized, English'.[25] The title of Swift's piece – *A Proposal for Correcting, Improving and Ascertaining the English Tongue* – does suggest a non-refrigerating intention. Seventeenth-century, as well as eighteenth-century Britain, and the United States in the following century, made varying inconclusive attempts to parallel the sixteenth-century Italian, the French and the eighteenth-century Spanish Academies. In case this list tempts anyone to a Nordic/Latin, Protestant/Catholic, liberal/authoritarian divide, I should add that the eighteenth-century Swedish Academy still functions. Such academies, besides, tend to be so ponderous in movement that they have little effect on the evolution of the language. Bengtsson offers a telling instance of the French Academy's atomized *modus operandi*. The words *démailloter* and *emmaillotter* for some time had different endings, though based on the same form, because they were discussed at different sessions and secured differing majorities. He also describes the vicious circle: the *Académie* claims only to register usage, but many users have referred to it as a prescriptive agency.[26] *Défaitisme* (which begat our 'defeatism') was vetoed in the early 1920s by Marshal Foch on the grounds that it was an un-French concept.[27] When England eventually got a language monitor, the Society for Pure English, it was lucky in its founding members: Robert Bridges, Logan Pearsall Smith and H. W. Fowler, men of broad-minded sanity who entertained no ambition of stopping the language in its tracks, and coolly studied slang, Americanisms, borrowings and neologisms, among many other topics. As J. Y. T. Greig exclaims somewhat melodramatically: 'In wrong hands it would have long ago become a dreadful curse, a veritable Inquisition and Congregation of the Propaganda rolled into one.' Later, he gives a paean to word-making or word-adopting: 'We have the richest language in Europe now, and all because our forefathers paid no heed to the flyblown Priscians of their day, but, when they needed a word, made it, or stole it, little caring if its synonym was lying ready by. Enough can never be as good as a feast, when the feast is of vivid and expressive words.'[28]

We left France and La Bruyère starting to speak up for new words. The opposition to them persisted strongly, and the early years of the century saw a purging even of Classical writers like Corneille and Racine, despite the unaudacious nature of their syntax and vocabulary. The chief purist was Desfontaines, whose *Dictionnaire néologique* was reprinted for fifty years. In the early eighteenth century the word *néologisme* most commonly indicated turns of phrase and preciosity (periphrasis, euphemism, guessing-games), for example, 'le suisse du jardin' (the Swiss guard of the garden: the hedge), or *anti-vestales* for prostitutes,[29] whereas a good reason for neologizing is the desire to avoid circumlocution, to be more economical of wordage. *Néologie*, on the other hand, stood more neutrally for the art of making new words. In the age of budding Enlightenment, the elite still held that coinage was best left to the experts: mandarinnovation. The *philosophes* in general were as unrevolutionary in their word renewal as they were in their political views: revision, not upheaval, was the lesson. Voltaire, a flexible conservative, commented in a letter to Frederick II, that 'our language is a haughty beggar; alms have to be pressed on to her'.[30] Though Rousseau promoted the passing of authority from usage to the writer himself, he invented few new words. Even proponents of neology spoke mainly of extending the family-tree of words, and were far less keen on unrelated new words.[31] Derivation from Latin (and to a much lesser extent from Greek) was still the norm. The development of French away from Latin (generally more marked than in Italian or Spanish) means that derived neologisms seemed almost inevitably to have to be based on the original Latin word rather than the evolved French one: *noeud* (difficult to add to) gives *nodosité*, and *jeu* gives *ludique*. The further the language breaks away, the more it is tugged back by its possessive mother. As François points out, the well-worn precepts: necessity, euphony (as if all existing words uniformly pleased the ear!) and analogy, trotted out so often by seventeenth-century purists, were accommodating enough to be recycled by neologists in order to promote expansion of vocabulary.[32] Yet a flood of technical words built up, encouraged by the *Encyclopédie* of Diderot and D'Alembert; Diderot was especially captivated by so many *mots propres*. A good many reborn archaisms were welcomed, for even purists of the day tended to lament the loss of old French words, by which they usually meant sixteenth-century language, specifically that of Montaigne. Borrowings increased with the growth of cultural cosmopolitanism.

In 1760, Charles Bordes, an Academician from Lyons, imagined a comparative dictionary (the French section featuring gaps) in order to inspire French writers to enrich their stock: 'Every thinking man would long to create some happy terms.'[33] The neologizing movement was most often tied up with the will to classify, to systematize, to rationalize in new fields of enquiry and practice (arts and crafts, sciences, political philosophy, industry). Already many felt that the progress in knowledge and speculation, coupled with the gradual transfer of arbitration from the Court to Parisian high society, demanded an expanded language. Thus Restif de la Bretonne proposed to replace *hasard* by *fortuité* (to link up with *fortuit*) and *puérilement* by *enfantinement*.[34] It seems that the previous century's fear of heterogeneity was taking a long time dying; and the move towards *vulgarisation* still kept many technical terms at bay. By the late eighteenth century, it had become commonplace to claim that words grow tired and need replacing; a fondness for mechanical and biological metaphors encouraged this thinking. In this perspective, neology is not just a matter of invention, but also of pruning and spring-cleaning. It faces both ways, like Janus, and often involves the recouping of words fallen into disuse.

Louis Sébastien Mercier (1740–1814) overturned many clichés in his blissfully unsystematic approach to linguistic reform. A plagiarist obsessed with novelty, he praised actual speech over academic discourse, since the latter provoked endless dispute and pedantry. 'Who would have thought that forty men [the Académie française] would pool their minds, thus reducing them to zero, in the centuries-long labour of a voluminous ABC: a sterile production.' Consequently, 'only a nation without an Academy can have a strong, new, daring and great language. The common people scoff at language dictators.' He thought it more likely that a language would die of inanition than of abundance. Unusually, he emphasized the value of single new words, for sentences and circumlocutions promise much and deliver very little, whereas a new word 'wakes you up more than a loud noise does and makes a secret fibre vibrate inside you'. He boasted that he had resurrected several entombed words, by saying: pick up thy bed and walk.[35] Compared with other partisans of neology of his day, Mercier typically went off at a tangent: 'I have grafted some wild stock on the trees of a vast forest, if you insist; but what I really wanted was to give people some new fruits to eat.'[36] Riffaterre overstates when he likens Mercier to those writers who 'tend to innovate out of *un esprit de système*', for his 'system' was intuitive, generous and healthy.[37] François sees Mercier more clearly as a vital hinge, by which 'the rational neology of the eighteenth century debouches into the literary imagination of the nineteenth'.[38]

In the Revolutionary period, as was inevitable, contrary impulses faced up to each other. There was a cohesive, conservative impulse to hang on to the French language as it was, a prime national asset, and indeed to extend its use at last to all French subjects. It was the Jacobins who were pledged to imposing French, and Catholics and Royalists in the provinces who sought to keep alive patois, dialects and languages. With the advent of mass power, public speakers had to change their register; new times, structures and pressures required new words. Language and politics become even more inextricably fused at such periods. The neoclassical critic La Harpe, in a speech at the Lycée Républicain in 1794, on fanaticism in revolutionary language, spoke of the new words needed to denote new crimes, which had indeed been a growth area since 1789 (cf. genocide, holocaust and the proliferating euphemisms for atrocities, in our own day). Mercier was in fact less extreme in execution than in his tub-thumping manifestos: 'Happy the man who in his work is both free and a despot', he said in the introduction to his *Néologie* – a perfect sentiment for revolutionary times. I can only say amen, however, to his dislike of thinking by committee: 'The more heads are put together, the smaller they shrink.'[39]

More daring also in manifestos than in creative texts, the French Romantics of the 1830 generation coined very few new words. Indeed Hugo declared that new words 'destroy the tissues of a language'.[40] He did borrow a few words from other European languages for local colour in his novels and plays, and his syncretistic compulsions led him to construct a small number of compound-nouns. I noted in the first part of this book the often clichéic nature of French Romantic language; it is disappointing to see how little they innovated also in lexical matters. Nodier had an almost classical distaste for neologisms, and, like the Romantics, preferred to reintroduce and give currency to obsolete words rather than create from scratch. It was the Symbolist writers, a half-century later, who really sought to revolutionize French vocabulary. As with anti-punsters, those who, like Stendhal, were hostile to neologizing, were reacting against bad and unnecessary neologisms rather than the principle of neology itself. Stendhal mocked in particular the newly prosperous bourgeois readers with pretensions to culture: 'He is most at home in the pompous mode; the *neologism* astounds him, entertains him and seems a thing of beauty.'[41] Beyond them, Stendhal attacked Chateaubriand and his ever-readiness for linguistic innovation, which Stendhal felt was a mere cloak for well-used ideas.

One of the major differences between French and English responses to neology is that, whereas the French cannot easily make a new verb from a noun except by stitching on the overworked affix *iser*,[42] English can simply use the same word for both functions: to chair a meeting, to chicken out, and is greatly helped, as in the second example, by its immensely versatile prepositions. The fact, also, that English can play between Germanic and Latin/Greek derivations helps to make it richly metaphorical, and confused. We are less conscious of the metaphoric origins of borrowings (e.g. 'eradicate' as against 'uproot'). As a result, English culture knows no real equivalent of the highly charged French concept, *franglais* (which really means Americanization). So much of our brain-drain has flowed to the west that we pay less attention to the counterflow. There is, then, much less call for linguistic trade-barriers. It would be less accurate to think of this response as fair-play than as laziness. This coolness can be perceived in Pearsall Smith's words: 'By the "purity" of an English word, its homogeneity, its anglicity, we would mean, not its Teutonic pedigree, but whatever its source, its conformity in sound and shape with the core of the language, and its complete and satisfactory assimilation.'[43] When he notes how often such lexical take-overs are managed on the basis of punning and popular etymology, I feel he might have added that there is in this an inbuilt jokiness, a kind of defence-mechanism, as in speaking foreign languages with a deliberately 'funny' accent.[44] One reason he can be so sanguine about borrowings is their well-attested habit of setting up a two-way traffic; borrowings often return to the homeland to enrich its stock, with a changed meaning from the original word (e.g. French *desporter*–'disport'–'sport', and back to France again). All in all, this English combination of metaphoricity of language, and matter-of-factness in handling it, is a great source of strength.

In America, Noah Webster foresaw in 1789 the inevitability of English and American diverging, because of distance, new modes of life that would need new names, and so on.[45] He could not foresee the 'melting-pot' phenomenon created by the mass immigration of non-English speakers. Mencken understandably mocks those many American peda-gogues who believe that 'the natural growth of the language is wild and wicked, and that it should be regulated according to rules formulated in England' (p. 51). From the start, two camps were set up: the purists who favoured standards deriving from England, and the freedom-fighters. Two unkillable clichés were born: 'polluting the pure well of English', and 'the barrier of a common language'. Despite Walt Whitman's vigorous plea for the beauty of vulgarisms and the need to incorporate colloquial speech into literature, his own brand of neologisms (with the exception of 'yawp') sound very mandarin: 'to eclaircise', 'to promulge', 'omnigenous' (pp. 74–5). Inevitably, however, superior American manu-facturing capacity spread from products to words. Until around 1885, most neologisms were called Westernisms; the West was where the newest life was happening. To an outsider, the curious fact of American linguistic life is, on the one hand, great verve (slang, raciness, colourful coinages), and, on the other, pedantry (jargonizing); short-cuts and meandering; the cult of verbal frankness, but the practice of obfuscation. This makes the common belittlement of American usage by the English even more invalid (e.g. 'The origin of "to debunk" is doubtless the same as that of American jargon in general – the inability of an ill-educated and unintelligent democracy to assimilate long words').[46] Nevertheless, the love of long words is part of talking big. Much of the warfare between the two cultures stems from contrary tastes for hyperbole and litotes. Overall, Mencken, who writes inventively himself, is more scathing than might be expected towards word-makers, whom he divides into two main groups: the promoters of new products and services, or 'sub-saline literati', that is gossip-column journalists, writers of movie and radio scripts, song writers, comic-strip artists, and theatrical, movie and radio press-agents: plus, of course, sports writers (pp. 330–1). I am only partly convinced by Kenneth Burke's comment: 'I see no reason for believing that Americans are unusually fertile in word-coinage. American slang was not developed out of some exceptional gift. It was developed out of the fact that new typical situations had arisen and people needed names for them.'[47]

If, as the stereotype would persuade, the Latin peoples gesticulate more than the British or Americans, the latter feel freer to adapt and renovate their language. Linguistic purism is essentially a Continental phenome-non. The purist wishes to leave nothing to chance or the moment's spur. Purists resemble possessive parents who cannot bear to see their children ever grow up and leave them. Such nostalgics (or nostalgolagnistics) parrot the fairy-tales they picked up when young about the good old days, when language was whipped in, under control. Many of the complaints about decay or adulteration in language echo parents' moans about offspring: the same hostility of the old to the young or the new; the same grudge that (said Beckett, eloquent for once) the whisky bears against the decanter – that is, what is being consumed against that which remains.[48] Complaints to broadcasting companies about 'bad language' surpass those about visual shocks; people tend to be more touchy and censorious about words than almost anything else. 'References to vices of style, a vicious diction: everyone refers to the corruption of language as if the corruption of youth were a similar outrage.'[49] The resistance to renovation we have tracked in our study of clichés engenders purism. Many would volunteer to run a linguistic, as well as an administrative, immigration service, to block or at least reduce the advent of new blood. Remy de Gourmont coined *misonéisme* and Valery Larbaud *néophobe* to describe such responses.[50] The very words 'preserve' or 'conserve' are ambiguous, in that they also suggest corpses, morgues or refrigeration. The much-feared impurity can come from below (the grosser parts of the body, ideally unspeakable, or of the body politic – the plebs), or from outside (foreign invasion or borrowing). Perhaps the opposite of 'purism' should be 'racyism' ... It is of course easy to mock, and I must listen to the counter-view: 'The love of our own is an elementary form of narcissism or nosism, and forms the most powerful ingredient in the love of family and country.'[51] Even so, the danger lies in the drift from linguistic purism to chauvinism, xenophobia and ethnophaulism. Ironically, foreigners themselves, especially if they have learnt another language rote-fashion, are often, like religious converts, more puristic than the natives. We will see that, just as some remedies are worse than the disease, 'the purist is more dangerous than the problem he confronts'.[52]

A good illustration of a common reflex against Yankee colonization is de Gaulle's exclamation that the French must not let themselves be phagocytized by American technology.[53] (Phagocytes are cells which encircle, digest and eliminate invading bacteria.) Defence of a language generally fastens on vocabulary much more than syntax or pronunciation, and reveals again the preference for short-term over long-term solutions to problems. Linguistic conservatives think of their mother-tongue as a long-established institution where everything and everyone have their designated place. The first puristic French letter was issued in 1757 by Fougeret de Monbron: *Préservatif contre l'anglomanie*. In itself, the urge to defend or cleanse what Mallarmé called 'the words of the tribe' is entirely praiseworthy. After all, critics operating in high culture would on · the whole resist the terminology of pop music; to them this would seem as much an alien intrusion as Americano-Anglicisms appear to French mandarins. Inversely, the gutter-press shrinks from big words in their own tongue. The widespread concern in France with the question of neologism – many newspaper columns are regularly devoted to it – reflects a real, if some think a misguided, anxiety. Habitually, the French systematize their anxieties.

The long-running French habit of control from the centre, whether in politics, culture or education, leads to the desire to impose a decided will by decrees. The Bas-Lauriol law of 1975 was the third linguistic law in French history, after the Ordonnance of Villers-Cotterêts (1539), banning the use of Latin in official documents, and that of the 2nd Thermidor, An II (1793) forbidding the publication of texts in anything other than the French language. The Bas-Lauriol law specified that French was obligatory in the advertisement and presentation of goods and services, in instructions for use, guarantees, work-contracts and other commercial documents. In 1986, Prime Minister Chirac appointed a Secretary of State for Francophone Affairs. As Joscelyne remarks, all this stemmed from 'a long-standing right-wing preoccupation with the French language. Its twin concerns were the invasion and degradation of French by borrowings and the "dwindling" of the civilizing mission of France in Africa and Asia.'[54] In addition, minority-language groups within France feel that their tongues need protection and support. As *Le Monde* commented, in a nice twist on Hugo's phrase about the Revolution placing a red cap on the dictionary, the government were trying to place 'un bonnet tricolore au dictionnaire'.[55] In the three years following the new law, thirty companies were tried for violation. For instance, the Quick chain of restaurants was fined 500 francs for using on its menus 'hamburger, big cheese, soft drink, Irish Coffee'.[56] The chairman of a furniture company, Hugues Steiner, a survivor of Auschwitz, fought back against the charge of using 'show-rooms' instead of 'hall' (equally English), by pointing out that such persecution smacked of Fascist purification campaigns. As indicated above, the fines are puny, and we must wonder what is the point of a partial purge, a half-hearted enema. It is the American Way of Life and economic imperialism, far more than Americanisms, that 'threaten' France. The lament over linguistic take-over conceals a fear of loss of dominance. It is ironic, too, how those resisting Yankee expansionism often want imperialistically to spread French not only all over her colonies, but also over her national territory, to the detriment of other native languages or dialects.

'English words which enter French usage via the media from song, film or TV show, function as linguistic equivalents to psychosocial release mechanisms for the young, in that they represent a source of freedom from the dirigiste verbal world of school, adulthood and the Law.'[57] Such dirigisme takes the form of lists of officially approved new words. The various terminological commissions themselves have to seek the blessing of the Académie Française as to 'the morphological pedigree and syntactic acceptability of their neologisms'.[58] Maurice Genevoix, Perpetual Secretary of the Académie (presumably because he services 'les Immortels') denies that his body, since its foundation, has ever sought to legislate, and tries hard for a sanely liberal stance. He admits that not only hexagonal France but also French-speaking countries

Drawing by 'La Mouche' from *L'Express*, 17–23 August 1984, reproduced by kind permission of the artist

across the world are concerned by the question as to whether or how French can innovate. Residents in the latter places, surrounded by English, would despair if their mother-tongue proved incapable of giving them the necessary updated vocabulary.[59] Genevoix sees necessity, fashion and laziness as the three main reasons for accepting foreign words into French. The key problem is how to involve the general public in the process of finding new terms. In the 1970s television-viewers were asked on several occasions to propose French equivalents for Anglo-American words (e.g. 'design'). As self-selected participants, they were frequently inventive, witty, but few if any of their proposals took root. Banning linguistic imports might have some generally marginal effect on written French, but seems to have little influence over the spoken forms. The danger to the French, some of whom recognize it, is of ghettoizing themselves, if they try to counter every possible borrowing with an existing or specially fabricated French term. One critic notes the inconsistency of the defence-system, its habit of translating run-of-the-mill foreign expressions by fancy pseudo-Greek compounds (e.g. *écographie* for 'earth resource survey', where *inventaire terrestre* would do an adequate job).[60] Word-creation after the event is largely useless. It looks like an afterthought, or Parthian shot. Some more realistic defenders of French actively look for less counter-productive ways than purism of maintaining and even extending their language. Besides, the level of foreign invasion varies with the area concerned. Statistics show that the number of Anglicisms/Americanisms is much higher in advertising, banking and computerology than in law, winemaking or aesthetics.

Isaac Disraeli had already said: 'There is no government mint of words.'[61] The sociologist Alain Touraine said of France's cultural policy in Latin America that it is pointless to build walls around 'une peau de chagrin'.[62] Some sceptics see in the whole question a replay of the theological boast that, as France is the eldest daughter of the Church, she might also be that of the Word. They laugh at the idea that French is a special case. Proust offers a timely reminder of the cock-up fact of life about language that makes automated purism such nonsense: 'The French words that we are so proud to pronounce correctly are themselves nothing but blunders made by Gaulish mouths, mispronouncing Latin and Saxon words; our language is merely the faulty rendering of other languages.'[63] Queneau was fond of quoting this passage as an anti-snobbish gesture, and himself thought that few errors are unproductive.[64] As well as diehards who resist all change, there are of course (and Proust is a superb example) true linguistic conservationists. Michel Tournier, a gifted neologist himself and a backward-turned innovator, argues provocatively that the truest patriots (no matter how suspect their political beliefs) are the guardians of the mother-tongue.[65] Punningly, Tournier devises a graded list: religious purification, political purge, maintaining racial purity, to which can be added linguistic purism.[66] Writers tend to be more interestingly balanced on the question than professional linguists, some of whom manage at best only that classical French cliché: 'le juste milieu'. Hence le Bidois plays off the 'phalanx of super-purists and the cohort of rabid laxists'.[67]

There are exceptions. From the vantage-point of an Occitan-speaker, Duneton vigorously attacks the stultifying effects of centralization, whereby an official Parisian, upper-class French lexis is imposed on the French masses, especially country-dwellers. (The French, it is true, tend to confuse the universe and high society (*le monde*).) For Duneton, French is an elaborate language which issues in a transfiguration, rather than a transcription, of reality.[68] It has been described as an 'Esperanto for intellectuals'.[69] Earlier, I picked out 'la clarté' as the great cliché about the French language and mind. Duneton mocks this ancient myth, and claims that the supposed excellence of French as a language of diplomacy fudges the fact that what it excels in is 'noyer le poisson' – the deliberate confusion of crucial issues.[70] In his view, the language is so codified that it does not know how to assimilate foreign words and is obliged to add them on top like a double-decker sandwich.[71] It certainly seems true that words in French need to acquire 'droit de bourgeoisie', the modern descendant of 'lettres de noblesse'. Protesting against foreign imports partakes of autarky, and in its more extreme forms, autism. Most borrowings are short words. French is indeed short on brevity. It may well be, as the linguistician Martinet argues, that some treat language as an end in itself (pedantic professionals or amateurs), whereas others (the majority) see it as a tool, ever ready to be adapted to new uses. While agreeing with the patrician censors that current spoken French is often impoverished and clichéic, he attributes this to the fear of being faulted and ridiculed. 'The French no longer dare to speak their own language because generations of grammarians, professional or amateur, have made it into an area strewn with traps and vetoes.' He ends with a rousing call for audacity: reclaim your own tongue against the nay-sayers. The only genuine kind of defender is Du Bellay, who championed French against its detractors, by suggesting fertilizers which would increase its spread and make its speakers feel at home in it.[72] Linguistic conservatism, in this perspective, is counter-productive, as it positively induces users to borrow indiscriminately from abroad.

I wish now to look very briefly at German, Italian and French-Canadian attitudes towards purism. Because of its potentiality for compound words, German clearly allows a great deal of lexical creativity. As a result, it may well be that borrowing is seen as far less necessary and indeed reprehensible.[73] Strangely, given its theories of racial purity, the attitude of the Nazi government to purism was flexible. 'When it suited them they preferred foreign words ... and were not going to be taken to task by petty-bourgeois zealots.'[74] There had been a continuous national-istic protectionism since the eighteenth century. In 1940 the minister for education decreed that the forced Germanization of loan-words was to discontinue. 'With this, purism or *Verdeutschung*, not to be confused with the natural process of loan translation, ceased.[75] In Italy, on the other hand, from as early as 1923 a tax was levied on foreign words used in shop signs, and at the beginning of the Second World War a law banned such words altogether. A poster appeared with 'Italiani, boicattate le parole straniere'.[76] The English-derived imperative undermined the xenophobic message. Blacklists followed the Black Shirts. One proposal, to replace 'bar' by *quisibeve* (youcandrinkhere) sounds like a crossword-puzzle clue.[77]

From the angle of French Canada, where Americanization is an even more immediate fact of life than in metropolitan France, attitudes tend to be more flexible and pragmatic. Corbeil argues that it is easier to borrow than to neologize. The foreign word is often less strange than the concocted new word in your own language. The foreign words has in addition proved itself in its home environment, and taking it over helps to form bridges to that foreign community. In addition, of course, foreign words have an aura of exoticism and appeal to snobbery, as well as to laziness. Nevertheless, Corbeil maintains that the French language is as well equipped as any other to create new words. The obstacle, for him as for Martinet, is linguistic conservatism, a certain elitist conception of language, which dates, chronologically and sociologically, from a pre-democratic era. 'It is not our language which is on trial, but we ourselves.'[78]

It has been advanced that the problem is more acute in smaller nations, where the question of catching up with the modern world leads to a greater stress on prescriptive, even 'surgical', linguistics.[79] Terms like *planification, dirigisme, interventionnisme*, even *assistance* (which makes language sound like a social pauper) crop up in the debate. Surely, however, the only properly and justifiably controlled languages are the synthetic ones like Esperanto, where intake and output can be systemized. On the basis of 'Novial' (Jespersen's contribution to the stock-pot), Ogden called the unsuccessful contenders 'Jovial', because of the hilarity they have provoked.[80]

Dictionaries prove simultaneously that language growth and change is endless, and that there is an urge to arrest this process, to take stock. The best lexicographers are conscious that their collections depend on language, and not vice versa. They have to choose 'the longer-lasting neologism'.[81] As well as being the resting-place of cliché, dictionaries are also playgrounds and battlefields, as the meanings of words over centuries contradict, interfere or mate with each other. While seeking at one level to arrest change, dictionaries also record it; they subvert their own piety. In a splendid working pun, Pat Rogers comments on the computerization of dictionaries, and the contrast between keeping your fingers in several pages at once and multiple simultaneous search: 'Manual is more dextrous than digital here.'[82] Normative approaches to language, whether they involve academies, official decree, legislating dictionaries or teachers, go on fighting a losing battle against language's natural spread. As Rogers points out, 'really live language, the sort which *OED* is uniquely equipped to describe, changes and explores experience, instead of just naming it'.[83] No doubt, as Tauli says, 'as all natural languages are imperfect, the improvement of language is indispensable'.[84] The question remains: who will do this, and how? Or does it happen largely in bits and pieces, by collective participation, and with some intervention from accident?

16

New Words Home and Abroad

We are mixed up about coinage. Think about the words 'make up'. They house at least sixteen areas of reference. Inventing, lying, cosmetics; courting (making up to someone), reconciliation (making up with or to someone after a quarrel); composition, construction, adding to or filling a deficit; to apologize or atone for; to prepare; to balance (as in account-books, 'creative' or otherwise); to decide (making up one's mind); to make do with; to catch (to make up on a ship); and delight (made up with something). Presumably Archimedes smiled when he cried 'Eureka!' Coiners are tickled by their inventions, which are the verbal counterparts to fathering or mothering. Coiners are neologenic, neologotypes.[1] Yet, amid the joy, we must remember the ambiguity of the whole phenomenon. 'Coinage' and 'forging' seem to imply that making and faking are irresistibly attracted to each other, though 'mint' keeps its association with freshness and the natural.[2] Commenting on Orwell's *Nineteen Eighty-Four*, Anthony Burgess remarks:

> Unity of thought can only be achieved by forging a deliberate technique for dealing with contradictions. (Note that when you come to the word forge you had to perform a very rapid act of double-think. You were, in a context that suggested cheating, ready to give it the meaning of falsifying a cheque or making counterfeit money. But then you had to give it the primary meaning of making, fashioning, with an aura of blacksmith honesty about it.)[3]

Playing the enemy at its own game always entails this kind of ambivalence. And, from the beginning, artists have obeyed Robert Graves's diabolic injunction 'to forge a picture that will pass for true'.[4] We cannot keep money-talk out of linguistic matters, and perhaps we should more neutrally talk of verbification or verbifacture instead of coining. Souriau literalizes the forging metaphor: 'Thought hammers freely the iron of the word.'[5] And an American wisecrack, echoing John Dennis on puns, holds that 'the man who would coin a word would coin a lead dollar'.[6] Like punning, neologisms are the linguistic equivalent of capitalism: they too capitalize on resources, fructify them. (The bad aspects of neologizing, of course, are the other side of the coin.) In numismatics, the term 'fantasy' denotes a coin of questionable origin or purpose, especially one issued by a country for sale to collectors. Many coinages are fantasy ones. But only one letter separates 'forger' from 'forager', and nothing can stop human beings exploring language.

Only God, and a handful of mortals, create *ex nihilo*. 'But only *le bon Dieu* can coin a *fraise*.'[7] (Paracelsus is believed to have added to our repertoire 'sylph', 'gnome' and 'zinc'.) Gelett Burgess was the semi-accidental inventor of the priceless term 'blurb' in 1907. This is a rare example of a 'meaningless' word (that is, a word not composed of existing particles), whose acquired meaning has become dense in our puffing modern world. It probably stemmed from verbal doodling. The rest of us have to make do with the materials to hand. As Jencks and Silver explain, 'all one has to do is stumble upon these ready-made subsystems and combine them in a new way'.[8] All this is part of our instinctive urge to rewrite the received script, to expand the linguistic map. Adhocism is closely related to *bricolage*: both encourage the do-it-yourself attitude. Words (archaism, slang, dialectisms, blends) can be reformulated, just as ideas can be recycled or clichés twisted productively. Just as quotations can profitably be used out of context, so we can resituate words, extrapolate. Language is a permanent jumble sale where we can pick and choose, re-use, give a second or further life. I mentioned earlier the concept of 'surgical linguistics'. Language can be extended and refurbished by artificial limbs, spare-part surgery: 'prothesis' and 'prosthesis' are close kin. Patchwork and mosaic are extensions of the same activity. Michel Leiris illustrates this beautifully. He defines *bricolage* as 'de bric et de brac, agile collage'.[9] He is alert to the perpetual suggestiveness of words; we speak words less than they speak to us. All poets must believe, with Freud, that language is compliant, meets us half-way. As the whole game is hit-or-miss, some of Leiris's rewrites or break-downs are more persuasive than others. Some are anagrams, puns, glosses, epigrams, alliterations, neologisms: all are approximate, as this is the science of the near-miss. Many are purely self-indulgent and passably meaningless ('Homere: Ô mers d'alors [Ô, merde alors]' (p. 32).) All in all, words for Leiris are the substratum of thoughts, the basis of thoughts and not merely their envelope (p. 103). Ogden Nash, in a more frankly playful vein, feigns to bewail, while practising it, neology in the present age:

> Coin brassy words at will, debase the coinage;
> We're in an if-you-cannot-lick-them-join age,
> A slovenliness provides its own excuse age,

Where usage overnight condones misusage.
Farewell, farewell to my beloved language,
Once English, now a vile orangutanguage.[10]

In both senses Céline was a master coiner. (1) '*Alibibi*: tricherie, alibibi
... théâtre ... rodomontades' (cheating, alibibi, theatricals,
braggadocio).[11] This coinage conjoins *alibi* and *bibi* (in slang: me,
number one), and hence denotes a process of selfishly acquiring a clear
conscience. (2) '*S'embrouillonner*'; *bouillonner* + *s'embrouiller* – to become
so boiling with rage that you get confused (a perfect description of
Céline's own style).[12] (3) 'Foudre d'escampette': *foudre de guerre* + *poudre
d'escampette* (hawk + rabbit-run).[13] (4) 'Goncourtiser': to practise *l'écriture artiste* like the Goncourt brothers, and to woo the Académie
Goncourt for a prize.[14] Céline's great predecessor, Rabelais, is celebrated by Spitzer in these terms, after Spitzer has reminded that the
'ever-waning expressivity of language needs the tonic of neologisms'; 'It
is always as though the rails of words running on the solid ground of the
established language and thus firmly linked to reality suddenly continued
into empty space, hanging in the air, as it were, above the abyss of
irreality.'[15] Thus suggests very aptly the more than utilitarian function of
new words. Even a word like 'windcheater' is more poetic than it strictly
needs to be. One largish area of neologism is the invention of previously
non-existent opposites ('couth', 'kempt', 'shevelled'); these occur particularly to those who opt to think against the grain, like Huysmans with
his *maléolente*.[16] In an even more nuancing fashion, Poe suggested that
'suspectful' be used to differentiate between the active and the passive
meanings of 'suspicious' (possibly honourable and probably
dishonourable).[17]

Many linguisticians are snooty about coinages, and use headings like
'unpredictable formations' or 'oddities'. 'However frequent these formations may be', one of them confesses, 'they are very awkward from the
point of view of generative grammar.'[18] Mountains labour over mouse-
like truisms: 'Irregularity is a manifestation of an important regularity of
language: change.'[19] Linguisticians talk cheerlessly of 'rule-governed
innovation'. I myself prefer to cheer or hiss what has been created,
however much of an awkward customer, rather than to hogtie the future.
All of us, in respect of language virtuosity, are more or less cack-handed
bricoleurs, DIYnicks. This *Sprachügefhl* (linguistic intuition) of most
speakers receives inadequate recognition from most professional commentators on language. Except with published writers or public figures, it
is of course generally impossible to track down the author of coinages,

hence the term 'phantom coinage' for a word or phrase created by an unknown chorus.[20] Pearsall Smith speaks of 'the ever-active mint of the popular vernacular', and, as the products are generally short words, 'these penny-pieces of popular coinage'.[21] Migliorini, at the other extreme, is unabashedly elitist. His premiss is that 'much of what was believed popular creation is a cultural patrimony which has descended by imitation to lower strata'.[22] It is, he believes, individuals or small groups who coin or adapt words, which are then taken over and circulated by the rest of us; he seems ungrateful for this essential propagating stage. Even the more democratic Pearsall Smith admits that acceptance of neologisms is always a problem, and is better assured if a famous person lends his name to a new thing or concept (for example, Ohm, Watt and Volt).[23] The vigorous but failed attempt to impose a common gender pronoun illustrates this difficulty.

No one can monopolize a word or an idea, as we saw when we examined plagiarism. The very fact of uttering, writing down or publishing distances the product from the begetter and places it into the common stock. Every coiner has to watch his or her child go out into the world and make its own way. A twelve-million-dollar lawsuit was brought against the Walt Disney organization over the word *supercalifragilisticexpialidocious* by two songwriters claiming to have used the word in a song sixteen years before *Mary Poppins* appeared on the screen. Algeo comments: 'It is so unlikely that two persons could have independently invented such an improbable vocalism that its use might be taken as evidence of plagiarism.'[24] In the event, Disney won. These are known as 'tall words', as in that famous Welsh railway-station name.

According to tabulators, the main methods of creating neologisms are: progressive derivation, regressive derivation, analogy with existing words (including deformation of the same), shortening, blending and compounding, making words from acronyms, and borrowing foreign words. As prefixes and suffixes are particles whose meanings are largely stable, I will mainly discount them in my examination of word-creation as of lesser interest. As for criteria, the commonly accepted ones are: necessity (but what of play? And isn't play a necessity?); harmony with the existing language; and clarity. In addition, new meanings can be attached to old words. As already noted, an infinitesimally small number of words have been created from scratch. Though it seldom troubles scientists, one catch in using a method of derivation, especially from Latin or Greek, is that you end up with long words. Even allowing for the observable fact that many French people seem less troubled than us by long Latinate terms (like *rhinopharyngite* for a sore throat), longer words obviously take up more room in the limited space of speech and are less memorizable. In addition, and for similar reasons, coined adjectives are less common than nouns.

Like puns, like Freud's 'dream-work' which so often operates by punning, neologisms often condense information, especially nowadays when we have grown used to miniaturized circuitry. Freud was fond of citing Hamlet's words: 'Thrift, thrift, Horatio!'[25] Literal-minded people find that condensation mists up their vision. Freud also spoke of 'the analysis and synthesis of syllables – a syllabic chemistry, in fact, which played a part in a great number of jokes'.[26] As well as composing words, we decompose them; and, indeed, to build up a neologism, you generally need to break off bits of existing words and recompose them. Like middens and humus, linguistic decomposition is a fruitful activity, if sometimes aurally, visually or nasally an offensive one to some.

Among the many erotic aspects of human relationship with language is the urge to interfere with it, for instance, to play at rearranging the letters assigned to words. The manipulation of orthography, especially in advertising copy, no doubt owes part of its appeal to simplified systems (phonetic spelling) – a trade-name needs to be easily recognized and remembered in overseas markets, hence a kind of Esperanto spelling – and to the insecurity of many people as to correct spelling. Seeing orthography maltreated in public displays reassures, avenges and delights all but stiff-necked pedagogues. For a keen student of 'commercial linguistics', Louise Pound, such audacities are also due to 'the general "jazzing" of language', since the 1914–18 War, 'the fading of awe for formalities and conventions'.[27] Making new, so as to be eye-catching, involves making strange, at first. But a neographism leads to refamiliarization, for repetition takes the initially blinding gloss off. Phiteezi shoes refer to a known value in a new form. In case advertisers seem merely perverse, it should be stressed that creative/barbaric misspellings in trade-names are forced on manufacturers by the law prohibiting descriptive names for products. You cannot simply call a spot-remover SPOT-REMOVER, as that would seem to eliminate all rivals; it would have to become SPOTTREEMOOVAH. This is a kind of code or circumlocution, a circumventing of a taboo imposed by law. By the same process and logic, joky advertising copy evades the charge of excessive claims and misrepresentation by blatant exaggeration, ironic litotes ('probably the best lager in the world'), self-mockery and so on. As always happens in advertising, bandwaggoning, 'Simon says', invariably ensues. An interesting but probably unanswerable question is whether commercial respelling has affected non-commercial practice, or whether, as in so many instances of dual register, the majority of people are bi-orthographical. Such creative spelling of course has its dubious sides, as does creative accountancy. But it offers many joys as in 'eyesoar', for the London Post Office Tower.[28] A common metaplasm, an oxymoron in that it manages to say opposite things at once, is 'sacreligious'. Pound remarks on, but does not amalgamate, the fondness for substituting the letter K in advertising and the fixation of the Ku Klux Klan on this letter.[29] Creative spelling can of course also conceal (as in DUNROVIN on a house name-plate) a cliché. Flaubert, the cliché-expert, used to pile on connotation (scorn, love of hyperbole) to the word *énorme* by writing it *hénaurme*. He first refreshed and then spoilt the point by overuse.

It might seem that the opposite of neologizing is disinterring archaisms, but such resurrecting can beget born-again words. By the pedantic criteria of chronology, both are improper, out of step. Like a borrowing, a grubbed-up archaism is a ready-made, as are a suit or a ship brought out of mothballs. A variant is to lift words out of regional lexis, 'emprunt interne' (in-house borrowing), but, especially in France, with its highly centralized culture, such initiatives have been rare. Another way in which creativity can go backwards, as some babies do when starting to crawl, is by back-formation. This is the verbal equivalent of the cinematic double-take. Why, indeed, not 'chalant', 'couth', 'kempt', 'shevelled'? 'It is strange', said one Hollywood magnate, 'what some authors auth.'[30] Such back-formation has links with popular or 'folk' etymology, so constantly eager to remotivate and reinterpret, to get back, with whatever wrench, to basics. Just as many people, confronted with non-figurative art or flames in a grate read familiar shapes into them, so man, for Palmer, 'abhors the vacuum of an unmeaning word'.[31] He allows, as he must, frequent doses of humour in such creative seeking of origins. Folk etymology is opposite to the mainly artistic tactic of defamiliarization, for it attempts to naturalize the alien. We make up origins, as did Stendhal's Julien Sorel when inventing himself an aristocratic father whose existence, if it were true, would explain both Julien's sense of superiority over his siblings and neighbours, and his requited dislike for his official family. The Marquis de Bièvre was a notorious pun-machine. In old French, *bièvre* meant beaver. The ancient legend of the beaver, when cornered, biting off its own testicles, comes from the pseudo-etymology 'Castor a castrando'. If you can't beat them, disjoin them. The French find all this hilarious: 'C'est à se les mordre' (It's enough to make you bit them off; crazy, man!) I have never felt that amused by anything in my life. What Barfield says of the nineteenth-century philologist, Max Müller, could be applied to many academic misusers of etymology:

> There is indeed something painful in the spectacle of so catholic and enthusiastic a scholar as Max Müller seated so firmly on the saddle of etymology, with his face set so earnestly towards the tail of the beast. He seems to have gone out of his way to seek for impossibly modern and abstract concepts to project into that luckless dustbin of pseudo-scientific fantasies – the mind of primitive man.[32]

Such erudite archaizing links up with popular etymology in that the findings (inventions) of both are probably better than totally made up words, in that some echoes still operate.

As Jespersen amongst many pointed out, 'borrowing' is a misleading term. 'The lender does not deprive himself of the use of the word,... and the borrower is under no obligation to return the word at any future time. Linguistic "borrowing" is really nothing but imitation, and the only way in which it differs from a child's imitation of its parents' speech is that here something is imitated which forms a part of a speech that is not imitated as a whole.'[33] We do not even have to pay any interest on loan-words. As well as such financial metaphors, images from immigration and demography recur. Many would want to place quotas on, erect tariff walls against, such alien invasion, so as to protect the purity of the native stock. Others favour an open-door or melting-pot policy. Probably too much credit is attached to borrowings. Two other metaphorical areas often involved are botany: imported plants supplanting home growths, grafts, or grafts not taking; grafts are also surgical, and the second metaphor is that of transfusion, new blood, and anaemic language seen as benefiting from the world word-bank.

We are to a very large degree constrained and disciplined, as well as quite literally constructed, by our native language. We can feel freer in speaking or writing foreign languages, because the weight of responsible behaviour reduces, as it does for many foreign holiday-makers; unless we have a professional commitment to the foreign tongue, we can vacation in it. Here we are 'borrowing' a whole language, or as much as we can muster or master of it. No one language can express everything that humanity has conceived. In this perspective, every national or tribal tongue is a dialect, cant or jargon, in relation to a non-existent world language. Just as by definition metaphors transfer, so all language constantly shifts across, interchanges. Like population movements, language has to be in flux. The most pressing reason for borrowing words or phrases is to fill a gap. Less urgent reasons include the urge to circumvent taboos and to display gentility (as in calling the buttocks 'derrière'); and luxury imports, especially from *haute couture, haute cuisine* and *haute culture*. Sometimes it is the very imprecision of the alien term (e.g. 'problematic') which gives it prestige. The paradox here is that certain words are selected for their richer sound, but they in fact can impoverish or blur the host language. Apart from truly needed technical terms, many borrowings are of foreign idioms – a neat expression of a notion which the home tongue cannot manage to express but which it recognizes. As we saw earlier, idiom veers towards cliché (which itself relies entirely on borrowing), though of course linguistic loans, like filched ideas, can be enriching. The borrowing of foreign words often underscores their conventional nature, for people tend to take over only what is proven, whether ideas or lawnmowers. Jespersen spoke of imitation; etymologically 'borrow', 'preserve' and 'bury' come from related roots. Borrowings, like archaisms, are ready-mades. They are new words only in the sense of looking new to fresh users. In reality, they have served their time; they are old lags.

Durable loan-words are gradually naturalized, that is, made familiar, even if an initial reason for bringing them in is one of shocking, of defamiliarizing. The rogue-word is tamed. Every language has its system, as instinctive and internalized as its grammar, for assimilating the foreign: changes of pronunciation, stress, spelling or usage. The trickiest problem is indeed how to pronounce the foreign word. If pronounced authentically, it will sound strange and snobbish in the midst of native sounds. If approximately, the variance might be so great that it impairs understanding. Yet the process never stops. A community has to be totally cut off from surrounding ones to avoid any linguistic interchange at all.

A major motive for borrowing is the desire for a change. People periodically get fed up with the same old words, or clothes, and kit themselves out with a new wardrobe, or at least a few fresh accessories. Calques are a special branch of borrowing: semantic take-over (as when French adopted *saison* in its football sense) or loan-translations. These are often inventive, as when the French render 'paper-chase' by 'rallye-paper'. Calque means basically a tracing, and a calque is a plagiarism, a theft lifted from the original language. Here are two lines overlapping English and Latin:

> In candent ire the solar splendor flames;
> The foles, languescent, pend from arid rames.[34]

This is very close to inkhorn creation, *mots savants*. Students of languages often float between two, as in this example: 'There is a lack of fundament in Hugo's characters.' Or the probably apocryphal 'nocturnal emissions of the BBC'. Some borrowings are ill advised, as in the French sports-footwear chain called 'Athlete's Foot'.[35] The French have concocted: *un smoking* (which suggests a jacket in flames), *un wattmann* (a character from Beckett's fiction), *le footing* (something apparently less energetic and more seductive than the supposed English original), *le talkie-walkie* (back-to-front and typically French in putting verbalization before locomotion), and *le lifting* (which sounds more akin to barbells than to plastic surgery). Yet such calques are creative borrowings, and a way of writing off part of the debt. No doubt, too, there is an element of Gallic cussèdness in thus reshuffling, truncating, (*un self*, *un night*), adapting English words.[36] It is also reminiscent of children's mistakes or mis-placed logic: if we have *le racing* why not *le footing*? There are false *faux amis*, like *pullupper* which, as the word does not suggest, means to gallop along. In all this, the dialectical process of language is active, as is shown by the term 'lexical interference'. Borrowings (indeed the name itself tells why) are rarely imposed, and so purists' complaints about foreign dumping or native passivity are generally groundless. As Hope says, 'It is sounder practice linguistically (and historically too, no doubt) to think of human beings welcoming or accepting new ideals, sources of inspiration or forms of behaviour from outside rather than external cultures bestowing them.'[37] The Welcome Waggon rather than Lady Bountiful.

By a reversal of *xenophobia*, the borrowing of foreign words has been called 'philoxénie verbale'.[38] The impulse to welcome the stranger can betray favouritism. Equally, and it is especially ironic in the case of the committed anti-racist, Etiemble, such overseas arrivals can provoke alarm and alarmism. He takes, in his influential study,[39] the whole phenomenon as a personal-cum-national insult. Throughout, he has a lot of often heavy-handed fun demonstrating how illiterate and cloth-eared are many take-overs from 'le sabir atlantique' (transatlantic lingua franca). He does put his finger on a common occurrence in borrowing – over-hastiness. Especially in trade and scientific affairs, the problems of coping with huge quantities of translations are so costly that often it is easier and saves money to take across the foreign term. But this imperative seems to function with excessive alacrity. He mocks in particular the invention of pseudo-English words like *tennisman*. Evading the native term, the French borrow a non-existent word. He would settle for Gallicized spelling (*lobe* for *lob*) of unavoidable imports, though he strives wherever possible to find a French equivalent, archaic or regional often, or to combine native words to cover the new meaning. The method of Etiemble, whose crustiness in his numerous other writings is generally of the most tonic variety, is reminiscent of those scientists who cram mice with tons of saccharine and prove thereby that this product is carcinogenic. A further irony is that there are many spurts of *franglais* in his own prose.[40] Etiemble's deepest regret is that France is in danger of becoming *cocalcoolique*, a Creolized colony of the United States.[41] (Americans seem more relaxed about Spanglish, especially in their South-West, or the longer-established Yinglish.) One benign example of *franglais* is the osmosis between *go-go* and *à gogo*, which nicely marries abundance and drive. The bilingual George Du Maurier, in his novel *Peter Ibbetson* (and this is no doubt why Queneau translated it), offers a ludic antidote to Etiemble's contagious and protectionist argument: 'Anglicizing French nouns and verbs and then conjugating and pronouncing them Englishly or *vice versa*.' This two-way game, Frankingle and Inglefrank, is played between an English boy and a French girl – a perfect *entente cordiale*. 'Dispeach yourself to ferm the feneeter, Gogo. It geals to pier-fond! we shall be inrhumed!' Or, 'Gogo, il frise à splitter les stonnes – maque aste et chute le vindeau; mais chute-le donc vite! Je snize déjà!'[42]

A key reason why French borrows so heavily from Anglo/American stocks is that its own genius is for abstraction, in both senses: making abstract, and making an abstract – quintessentializing, epigrammizing. It suffers from concrete-deficiency, and not just in the obvious areas of scientific novelties or commercial innovation, but in everyday life. As Duneton argues, the development of French was for so long in the exclusive hands of the upper classes that it lost contact with thinginess, which, for him, is better served and preserved in Occitan. German *sounds* more concrete, because of consonantal clanginess, even when it veers towards abstraction. In addition, there is in French a wider gap between the written and spoken forms than in English. The resulting paradox is that the French, reputed by many Englishmen to be the least welcoming of Europeans, have welcomed Anglicisms and Americanisms with open mouths. Some students of the process try to slow it down by classifying it into stages: *xénisme, pérégrinisme, emprunt* – the middle stage representing the point at which a foreign word is as yet unassimilated.[43] Turning the tables, the French should praise themselves for persuading some literary critics in Britain or America to foster French critical terminology, often plonking it uneasily into their own language. A fair exchange: the Americans export material goods, and the French immaterial ones.

English owes a huge debt to French, but it happened, mainly, so long ago that the most fervent restrictionists do not complain. It is recent borrowings that conservatives object to, even though the ruling Tories enabled a credit explosion. The English are notoriously easy-going about language, as they are about public cleanliness and food-standards, and suffer rarely, on home ground at least, from xenoglottophobia. Living on an island does not necessarily produce insularity, which is even more to be found in demoted, once-powerful nations such as France. Many French imports are used jocularly, or, if employed seriously, are received jocularly by hearers. The renowned, Eskimo-like, hospitality of the English tongue to all-comers, even if frequently not matched by that of the people towards immigrants, is a fact of linguistic life. Borrowing from a more ancient source, Latin or Latinate roots, is, according to Burchfield 'part of the process of filling real or fancied cavities', though I wonder how the guiding spirit of the OED thinks imaginary gaps can be plugged.[44] Many languages borrow from Latin or Greek in order to make up new words, but this is seldom so much resisted as is taking from living tongues. 'Nil de mortuis nisi bonum' could be translated as 'nothing but good comes from the dead (languages)'. Palmer likens the rapid Anglicization of foreign words, the re-garbing of the alien, to the 'protective mimicry', or camouflage, practised by the creatures of Nature.[45] The English seem particularly adept at false derivation, thus cooking the books of philology and faking family-trees, as if the demon of analogy were the patron saint. In the linguistic Cruft's Show, the hardiest mutt wins: mongrel English. As for the United States, Mencken laments the widespread tendency to think of language movement in terms of one-way traffic, instead, as common sense would instruct, of shuttling. Some Americanisms are, he points out, English archaisms, preserved longer over there, long enough sometimes to feed back into English usage, for instance 'notify' (used of a person 'to notify someone' instead of for a thing, 'to notify something to someone').[46] The English, quite cosy in their anti-Americanism, hardly begin to understand the logic of American Anglophobia.

As Farb stresses, 'even unlimited borrowing can never render a language bland and homogenized'.[47] It is clear that people of all walks are too cussèd, too prone to errors, too ready to play with and to revamp loan-words, ever to submit passively to their dominion. Indeed, the person in the street handles borrowings as Molière's Monsieur Jourdain engendered prose, without realizing.[48] Most linguisticians worth their salt protest what one of them, Bréal, called 'the determination to consider purity of language as something akin to purity of race'. More particularly, 'the Hellenic philologists who banish Turkish words from the vocabulary are continuing after their own fashion the War of Independence'.[49] This variety of punning can be lethal, and jumping to conclusions can lead, as in fascist regimes, to goosestepping to final solutions. 'Home is Best' is interchangeably an honourable sentiment and a dangerous slogan. A siege-mentality houses both heroic resistance and persecution complexes.

17

Subtle Blends

Linguistic racists are worried, as we have just seen, by cross-breeding, and yet *croisement de mots* is well installed among the array of French terms for blends. Like puns, blends hibernate in a language until someone awakens them, sees a connection, puts the bits together.[1] In 'la horde abjecte cinéphage', Céline spotted a providential link between *cinéma* and *-phage*, and wedded them, to his anti-democratic purposes.[2] An old (1573) blend 'witcraft' (only a breath away from witchcraft) would serve as an honorific title for blends.[3] When we think of the multitudinous spaces available for inscription today: sky-writing, graffiti, posters, labels, screens, stickers, badges, banners, as well as paper; when we recognize the present need to economize on space and time, visible in slogans, mottoes, condensed manifestos of all kinds, we can begin to understand the reasons for the wide spread of compression. The blender is the Renaissance Man of the kitchen. Blends, which are hybrids, name hybrids: liger, tigron, zebrule, tangemon, brunch. 'Meld' is a meld (of 'meet' and 'weld'). Having described blends as one of the most unpredictable categories of word-formation, Cannon admits 'the extreme difficulty in devising a taxonomy of absolutely discrete categories'.[4]

Gamely, Algeo has tried to break down blending.

In popular use the term *blend* is used for any word formed by shortening one word and combining what is left with all or part of another. There are, however, three distinct subspecies: portmanteaus [he cites 'chopter', chopper/copter], which combine words that might substitute for one another; telescopes ['administrivia'], which combine words that occur side by side in [a set phrase]; and jumbles, which combine words between which there is some association, although they are neither properly substitutes nor the sequential elements of a structure ['hashaholic', 'tripewriter', i.e. one used exclusively for political speeches].[5]

Perhaps appropriately, for it is an umbrella-term, it is the third-named, jumbles, which seems to embrace most examples of what have been

Earl of Crewett from *What a Life! An Autobiography* by E. V. L. & G. M. (Collins, 1987, p. 43) reproduced by kind permission of the publisher

called 'newly-wedded words'.[6] Jumbles, however, suggest chaos, whereas most blends want to communicate quickly. Hence the clipping ('edbiz'), often highly necessary, especially in the area of scientific terminology (e.g. 'phorate' condensed from '*ph*osph*o*radithic*ate*'). Pollarding can reinvigorate a tree; lopping part of a word may promote fresh growth.

When Lewis Carroll's Humpty Dumpty talks of packing two words up into the portmanteau (which in his day had the active meaning of a clothes trunk which opened up into two equal parts), he suggests a certain amount of force; cramming, as when we try to close a suitcase. The point of portmanteau words, or blends, is to enable an ellipsis of meaning, a shortcut – sometimes as a means of resisting that other form of cramming: brainwashing, indoctrination. The urge to stuff in more meaning possibly stems from a horror of a semantic void (and even

Illustration from *The Annotated Alice* by Lewis Carroll (Penguin Books Ltd., 1978, p. 271) reproduced by kind permission of the publisher

nonsense blends do not escape making some kind of sense). As well as packing meaning tight, blends (like protesting suitcases) can spill over. (In general, besides, rhetorical devices sprawl, practise incest, or canni-balism; they do not stay neatly regimented in the rows of the garden of rhetoric.) As the pun collocates two meanings, the blend puts together two meaningful segments. Many blends are puns, and vice versa (e.g. 'racqueteer', a tennis bum, or 'syphilization', which virtually repeats the sound of the target word 'civilization').[7] As Wentworth states, many blends present to the reader 'a readily-solved puzzle'.[8] As with puns, the receiver needs to decode with only a slight time-lag. Again, like a pun, a blend by no means has to be funny, though very many are.

There are several popular ways of talking about blending: metaphors we operate by. Stitching together, patchwork. Mosaic, collage, as in Max Ernst's *phallustrade*, which is 'an alchemical product made up of these elements: autostrada, balustrade and a certain amount of phallus. A phallustrade is a verbal collage.'[9] Welding, or melding ('The only thing a morpheme is good for is to be melted down and recast in a word');[10] dovetailing. Blends, like puns, are double-barrelled (even if they usually fire only one cartridge). Contamination (of which more later, when I look at lapsus; this is a metaphor favoured by the unconvinced, who dip only one portmanteau in the water. A whole host of metaphorical admixtures: cocktail, pot-pourri, gallimaufry, farrago, olla podrida, salmagundi – the nations unite beautifully to name hotchpotch. Hybrid, crucible, melting-pot, amalgam; a multicultural society should be prolific in blends. Hitched or bracketed words, happy couples, *conjoints*.[11] Telescope, copula. Pivot-words, where the central, shared letters are the fulcrum.

Agglutination, or concertina-words, which Queneau plays ambidextrously. Noting the phonetic coagulation of spoken French (or indeed of most languages),[12] Queneau in *Zazie dans le Métro* inserts a score of such forms into his text. This defamiliarizing, then refamiliarizing, tactic serves an organic function, for a key motif in this novel is disguise, and the action happens in sudden spurts, involving many collisions (of cars, viewpoints, wills). Suspicious of all systems, including his own, Queneau recognized that to have written the whole novel, or even sizeable chunks of it, in concertina-language would have produced something unreadable, for we have to read his contraptions aloud for the sou to drop. The whole device forcibly reminds readers what they tend to forget when devouring a novel: that people do not often talk like (spaced-out) books. Another Frenchman, Deleuze is less sportively spoilsport when he breaks down the portmanteau (*mot-valise*) into a 'disjunctive synthesis'.[13] This suggests pulling-and-pushing. An example is *philanthrophagie*: the generous offering by an altruistic literary crank, Paulin Gagne, of his own flesh to the starving.[14] Twisting the Gallic screws still further, Dupriez points out that the opposite of *le mot-valise* is *le mot dévalisé*.[15] *Dévaliser* means to burgle, to break into – a house or a whole existing word, and there to create havoc, as in Leiris' practice of unblending, decomposing an existing word: *sangloter* (to sob); *ôter les sangles* (to strip off the straps).[16]

I now offer a sampling of blends in French and English, so that readers can decide on their virtues or demerits. *Pudibondieuserie* (*pudibond + bondieuserie*); an emphatically bigoted prudery.[17] *Nostalgérie*: the homesickness of *pieds-noirs*.[18] *Gestapette* (*Gestapo + tapette*): a homosexual collaborator in Occupied France.[19] On the basis of *bikini*, the minimal version, *zérokini*, and *kakhikini* (army issue trunks). An automatic holy wafer dispenser: *eucharistomat*.[20] *La Gauchunie*, where the fusing of two words enacts the desired political alliance. As well as *la cocacolonisation* we encountered earlier, of which French professional anti-Americans are so fond, there is the more thoughtful and inward-turned *cocoricolonisation*, coined to typify de Gaulle's crowing patriotic discourse at the provincial capital, Strasbourg; imperialists can come from the metropole as well as from abroad.[21] Writing in French, I have coined *maladroiture* (*maladroit* + *droiture*), to describe that fiasco-prone truth-teller, Jules Vallès; *morigénitrix* (*morigéner* + *génitrix*) for a constantly chiding mother; *claironronner* (*claironner* + *ronronner* (to purr)), to blow one's own trumpet with a mute in; and *quelconqueté*, as French does not have a word for 'ordinariness', except the loaded *banalité* (*quelconque* – any old).

Some blends are strictly functional, such as Benelux, which saves quite a mouthful. Many have caught on, and inevitably veered towards cliché: 'guesstimate' (indispensable in this age of aleatory economic forecasting), 'slanguage', the venerable 'Oxbridge' and 'Yarvard', and 'Chunnel', which bridges two words more easily than two countries. Those who make a meal of alternative life-styles patronize a 'psychedelicatessen'.[22] Harman and Ising's musical cartoons ineluctably begat 'Harmanising'. The body politic is riddled with 'red tapeworms', and the Windy City periodically by 'Chicagorillas'.[23] 'Narrowcast' twists the familiar. 'Ventriloquacity' puts a lot of words into others' mouths. That word for a major American obsession, 'flunk', may be a blend (word historians fail to agree) of 'fail' and 'funk'. A 'shamateur' has long been around in vicious sporting circles.[24] 'Balloonatic' reminds us of the 'loon' in the first word. 'When identical twins named Fritz and Max had been confused very often, it became prudent to call each one of them Frax.'[25] Usefully, Swift cross-fertilized 'trite' and 'critical' to coin 'tritical'. 'Shampagne' is an honest blend. A brutal theatre critic has been termed a 'dramassassin'.[26] From my own (*petit*) *cru*, I offer 'martyrant' for a melodramatically possessive love. This is unpronounceable, and, in many circumstances, unspeakable. Incensed feminists might or might not be pleased by the title of 'energuwomen'.

Blends or portmanteaux are generally more telescoped compounds. Compounding is possibly the commonest way of creating new words, almost without noticing, like nose-picking. The virtual abolition of hyphens in American usage might be thought inimical to the spirit of compounding, for it tends to produce a blur instead of a marked encounter of two words that makes you stop and think. But like all mysteries, blurs may also give pause for thought. A hyphen can be a separator as well as a joiner, for example as an aid to pronunciation and stress: 'jack-knife', 'well-lit', 'set-to'.[27] In his novel *Les Météores*, Michel

Tournier uses hyphens extensively, for, given its obsessive theme of twinhood, and the desperate and unavailing emulation of his twin nephews by the homosexual uncle, Tournier yokes words, ideas, places, events; the whole book swivels between forced and longed-for approximation.[28] On a more everyday level, there are sandwich-words, or infixes (that is, two parts of one word enclosing an entire word). These are usually used in emphatic or emotional contexts: 'abso-one-hundred-per-cent-lutely', 'abso-bloody-lutely'.[29] A longer standing practice is to rhyme coupled words: 'brain-drain', 'culture-vulture', 'flower-power', 'gang-bang', 'nitty-gritty', 'stun-gun'. And the variant, the ablaut, or vowel-change: 'flip-flop, riff-raff, zig-zag, wishy-washy, shilly-shally'.[30]

While compound-words can be formed more readily in English than in French, because of the habit of omitting prepositions, we do not have quite the German facility. In addition, English/American concern to save breath means often that compounds are abbreviated ('motor-car' to 'car'). Bréal comments: 'English and German have the resource of compound-words: but an unsuccessful compound, such as is made every day in both those languages, possesses fewer drawbacks than other neologisms, since the two terms thus momentarily associated separate again at once, while these French abstract nouns, welded together by means of suffixes, seem to be forged for perpetuity.'[31] This exaggerates the discardability of the former and the durability of the latter, yet makes a valuable distinguo. The apparently infinite extendability of serious German compounds provokes outsiders' hilarity. Ferdière quotes an unattributed opinion that Germans regret deep down not being able to house all speech in a single word.[32] As barriers grow less rigid, French shows some tendency not only to take over English words but also word-order, which in French has traditionally been 'progressive' (*salle à manger* for 'dining-room'). This is in part also due to advertising practice, which needs to save space and to be zippy in expression. More commonly today, French promotes two words hyphenated instead of a more periphrastic construction (*lave-linge* instead of *machine à laver*). This change is also more concrete and less generalizing.

'*Time* abhors a hyphen.'[33] In the early period of its rise, the editor Briton Hadden's taste for Homer and compound Homeric epithets, and his relentless demand for terseness, produced a spate of blends, though later the house-style proliferated into much fancier and more verbose language. One example: 'The custard-piety of Chaplin's *The Pilgrim*.'[34] Though 'pilgrim' might induce 'piety', this blend is semantically fairly pointless (it would not be if it implied a critique of Chaplin's unthinking use of worn-out comic devices but it seems this was not intended.) For a critic, this kind of impractical yoking is 'infused with cock-sure smart-ness', and manages to combine 'disrespect for authority and reverence for success'.[35] Many of its blends are, to use one of them, 'barococo'.[36] Taking the longer view, Kenner says: '*Time*, the exhalation of the linotype machine, does not talk, it compresses. Its very neologisms (cinemactor, Americandidly) carry their wit to the eye alone.'[37] It was not only *Time* but numerous other American publications which drew this rejoinder: 'Nouns are telescoped to such an extent that a sentence looks like a railway accident.'[38] Another observer comments: 'With the rise of the mass media and syndicated columnists [in the nineteenth century], the blending became exceedingly popular. The rapid spread of education and publications created an indefinite supply of blenders who plied their skill with metronomic ease.'[39] The habit can be seen in many areas: the wedding of two names to baptise a locality on the boundary of states (Calexico) – given the huge size of most states in North America, anything that promotes cosy proximity is grasped at; the widespread taste in the United States for uniformity which, because it is a crucible-society, encourages the abolishing of differences; the smart-ass tradition, on both the East and West coasts; the habit of fusing two parental names for offspring (Charlene); the constant mergers and take-overs of corporations, tradenames, etc.; in connection with this, the practice of ever-'improving' mechandise and the consequent need for new names; and above all the telegraphic imperative: the necessity of compressing information. As befits a democracy, even the Ku-Klux-Klan has its own blended language, its rotgut moonshine: Kleagles, for its dignitaries, Klonklaves, for its meetings, and the Kloran, for its holy writ.

The law of least effort rules in advertising, which habitually collapses longer words or groups, either via hyphenation or blends; the economy of the big spenders. The obsession with newness in advertising claims, the cult of the 'born-again' in American religiosity, which relies heavily on well-publicized fund-raising campaigns, alike promote neologisms. It is notorious that words inaugurate, as well as reflect or endorse, a reality. Shock-effect and easy memorability are the targets, as in the spicy seafood soup promoted as 'not for blandlubbers'.[40] As advertising discourse relies generally on *bricolage* and collage, using any means to hand, recycling words and ideas, it is prepared to run segments together in makeshift fashion.

The urge to combine, often opposing things or concepts, is ancient. Hermaphrodite was the fruit of the union of Hermes and Aphrodite (the god of speech and the goddess of beauty): a youth with womanish breasts and long hair, whereas the androgyne was a bearded woman. For Graves such hybrid creatures mark the transition from matriarchy to patriarchy.[41] In zoology and botany, 'hermaphrodite' signifies an animal or plant possessing both male and female reproductive organs. True hermaphroditism rarely occurs in humans; pseudohermaphroditism is commoner, in which secondary characteristics of the opposite sex are developed. Oxymorons keep the ancient tradition of melding opposites alive: pianoforte; and blends can be oxymoronic: 'banksters', which usefully suggests hoodlums in pin-stripe suits. As Algeo notes, portmanteaux, as well as combining synonyms, can also combine words of contrastive meaning: 'The resulting word unites both the forms and the senses of the sources into a hermaphroditic tertium quid.' He cites 'beautility'.[42] In 'science- fiction', it may be wondered whether the two contributors to the compound are in fact always opposites.

As was shown earlier by the blend 'bromidiom', such coinages can veer into cliché. By the familiar mechanism of bandwaggoning, blends like 'dancethon', 'walkathon', 'telethon' have proliferated on the base 'marathon'. As such forms multiply, any sense of the original particle fades. The -*rama* words in French, last century, showed the same process of the largely empty suffix. In such ways, pattern-making takes over from invention.[43] Many combinations are more like bloomers, though as one linguist ruefully admits in a good pun, 'l'usage a toujours raison, même quand il a tort' (Usage is always right/always comes out on top, even when it's wrong).[44] Some blends unsimply say the same thing twice ('gigolothario', 'hintimation', 'aggranoying').[45] Others fail because of over-compression ('dawk' (dove/hawk) inferior to 'wargasm'; 'geep' (goat/sheep) inferior to 'shoat'). Some are ambiguous: one of *Time*'s, 'cinemadman', refers to Harpo Marx, but it could be a screen-advertising executive. Such ambiguity becomes acute when things are run together on a foreign model; for example 'vacances-couleurs', which could mean many things, was supposed to denote painting the house in one's holidays.[46] Some blends work only in the written form: 'dumbelle'[47] (a stupid and beautiful woman), as, when spoken, this sounds identical to 'dumb-bell'. A good many are merely flashy and unproductive, as in McLuhan's 'collideoscope' (filched from Joyce, anyway).[48] Purists tend to flinch from blends, which they relegate to fantasy, and complain when they are erected to the status of a regular lexical procedure.[49]

Blends can be put to serious work. The composite name encapsulating the grandparents in Sartre's *Les Mots*, 'Karlémami', is the first occurrence in that text of the phenomenon which dictates the book's title: the power of words to forge reality. Linked phonically by their telescoped names, these grandparents seem to be linked intrinsically, and so to form an indissoluble couple or essence. Wordplay takes sounds for substances. A true unity is absent from the actual marriage, but this is camouflaged by the blend-word. In Orwell's *Nineteen Eighty-Four*, the 'B vocabulary' (that is, words deliberately fabricated for brainwashing purposes) is composed of 'words which not only had in every case a political implication, but were intended to impose a desirable mental attitude upon the person using them.' All of these words are portmanteaux (Orwell calls them 'compound words'). 'They consisted of two or more words, or portion of words, welded together in an easily pronounceable form.' Examples: 'goodthink', 'Miniluv'.[50] The oligarchy in Orwell's dystopia wants a watertight system, and telescoped terms fit the bill.

Among the dangers in blending is that of changing one letter (to make a better fit), or that of using a cluster of consonants, and thus creating something that passes unnoticed. Our habit of skimming, of 'reading for meaning', ensures that we read generally for the most obvious, the handiest, meaning. Subconsciously and automatically, we often emend an assumed inaccuracy. This is the hasty inertia of corniness. We need, then, at times to rebecome beginners, to leave rapid scanning to computers, and to read in slow-motion (with action-replays). The best coinages, whether single words or blends, derut us. These hybrids offer the comfort of familiarity and the shock of the new; above all, the pleasure of the appropriate. Among the many French counterparts to portmanteau or blend, I cherish *signifiancés*.[51]

'On peut s'intoxiquer aux mots-valises.'[52] Some, inevitably, are teetotal in this area. Statistically, no doubt, Cannon is correct in talking of the 'low viability of blends'; few survive, though he stresses that they have existed in English since its earliest forms.[53] Many new forms pass quickly through the system; they lack roughage. The productivity is enormous:

> Slips and other oral nonce-forms are pouring out from perhaps millions of businesses and people who are enjoyably indulging their linguistic individuality, in a kind of dynamic, impermanent word-formation... This very old process is one of the most ramified, interrelated, and personally creative of all word-forming categories, with a significant role in language development and probably in language evolution. [54]

It is this fact of linguistic life, no doubt, that makes Algeo prophesy: 'Blending may look like a long shot, but the smart money will keep an eye on it.'[55] I am more drawn myself to pointed, intentional than accidental blends. We all do the latter; it takes skill to achieve the former.[56] Yet impromptu assemblies are more often pleasurable and profitable than highly structured ones, and the more natural-seeming the blend, the better. Like all forms of artful dodging, blending cannot be swallowed whole. Whether specious or genuine, blending is instinctive and permanent.

'We are more ready to try the untried when what we do is inconsequential. Hence the remarkable fact that many inventions had their birth as toys.'[57] Illusion, allusion, collusion and delusion all contain the notion of play. Serious play and ludic gravity can powerfully and osmotically coexist, as this whole book has tried to prove in action. The Divine Marquis whipped me on to coin the word 'iconocataclysm', for he urged that the breaking of idols should be a disaster playground.[58] As Barthes exulted, 'neologizing is an erotic act, which is why it never fails to attract the blue pencil of killjoys'.[59] This link of sex and coinage is at its most naked in limericks; Legman has termed it 'unexpurgaiety'.[60] With Barthes the pleasure of the text and pleasuring the text seem close bedmates. Blends are copulatory (cf. the Surrealist game, 'l'un dans l'autre'). 'D'une curiosité de voyeur, je pétille et m'électrotise' (*érotisme + électriser*).[61] To talk of Joyce, the supreme blender, that *calembourreau* (*calembour + bourreau* – torturer),[62] Clive Hart resorts to the notion of anastomosis (the joining of blood-vessels so as to intercommunicate): to provide with a mouth, to inter-osculate.[63] I have respelled 'Eurogenital', to describe the multinational skinflicks, and 'Eurotoxic' for the Rhine. To express the belief that fathers, if they cannot bear, can still mother children, we could coin the epithet 'androgynaecological'. New words can be seminal ('neolojism'), as well as simply gimmicky ('neologizmo').

Nobody needs scholars to tell them of the versatility of words. Any word, via innuendo, can serve a sexual function in a helpful context ('Show me your qualifications'). 'It' and 'thing' can be euphemisms. Though new words are sometimes coined so as to avoid roundabout speech, to smarten up the host language's clumsiness, they can like any other become euphemisms (especially, for instance, in military jargon). Céline coins *circonlocutasserie* in order to mime and thereby criticize lengthiness of speech.[64] A sub-branch of neology is the invention of fanciful meanings for existing words, as when *un bordel* is defined as a Bordeaux word for cradle, or *cyclamen* as tandem-lovers.[65] Neology recycles like puns, and both are acts of linguistic ecology. Humour is clearly a prime mover behind much linguistic creation. Linguisticians fall into the same trap as laymen: thinking that seriousness excludes play. Adams, for one, declares that in past centuries blends were made 'most often for the fun of it', whereas in our century such activities can 'on occasion produce serious and permanent additions to the vocabulary'.[66] Why not the grave and the jocal simultaneously (as in the coinage *mélan-comique*)?[67] Like slang, neology can be the wanton product of 'the exuberance of mental activity, and the natural delight of language-making'. Mencken counterposes to these generous words of Whitney the more hard-hearted opinion of Shorey that 'the unconscious genius of the people no more invents slang than it invents epics. It is coined in the sweat of their brow by smart writers who, as they would say, are *out for the coin*'. In his own name, Mencken adds: 'Or, if not out for the coin, then at least out for notice, *kudos*, admiration.'[68] Big-city wits obviously do not want to credit common people with creativity, but we all possess language, and anybody can be exuberant (as in 'parastreak', to sky-dive in the nude).[69] And it is probably the sophisticates or their plagiarists who practise neological bandwaggoning, as in the *-nik* vogue which followed the exploits of Sputnik (for example, 'muttnik', for the orbiting Soviet dog). Today we have the respectable 'refuseniks'. Jokes can breed seriousness, as well as vice versa.

All in all, blends make ends meet: a device of economy, but also a seductive goal for many kinds of minds.

18

Controlled Appellations

Neologists are would-be new Adams, re-naming the world and expanding Adam's no doubt skimpy lexis. Ever since Adam, naming has been, for pessimists, a losing battle (for words are one thing and things another), or, more positively, a production-line. All newborn beings need to be baptized, and some parents choose to underline the novelty of the event by making up a name (usually by combining particles from existing ones), or by conscripting common or proper nouns from the heavens, the months of the year, places, etc. As the child grows, it frequently attracts a nickname, a rechristening; if the person is unpopular, an Old Nick name. Invented names and titles, as any child knows in his bones, are choice weapons of insult and aggression, as is getting a name wilfully wrong in order to ridicule or intimidate the bearer. Heath remarks on the derision implicit in the constant mangling of names in Joyce, which seems to me to form part of the frequent regression to baby-talk in *Finnegans Wake*.[1] Less vicious sport can be had in this area, which Gracián called 'agudeza nominal' (nominal wit). I have elsewhere coined the blend 'onomastication' for this perpetual chewing over of names, whether of anxious parents awaiting a birth, or anybody eager to read meaning into the arbitrary sequence of sounds that is a proper name.[2] Many creative, or criminal, individuals resort to pseudonyms (*noms de plume, noms de guerre*), or cryptonyms, as an alias, for self-protection.

Onomatopoeia, which Puttenham called the 'Newnamer' and rhetoric *procreatio*, is, like interjection and ejaculation (premature or punctual), a form of coinage in which imitation rules. The mind sets up a relationship (called by linguisticians 'motivation', and also active in etymology and wordplay) between a form and its meaning. The process is heavily arbitrary, as the great dictator Humpty Dumpty makes clear when he browbeats Alice with '*My* name means the shape I am ... With a name like yours, you might be any shape, almost'.[3] Indeed Alice does assume various shapes in the course of the narrative, as befits her bewilderment.

Although we like feeling creative, and delight in reading meaning into sets of letters, our laziness and taste for shortcuts also leads to the manufacture of acronyms (etymologically, 'tip of name') and acrostics. VIBGYOR, the order of the prismatic colours, shows that, however addicted to grand titles and big words, we bite them off for convenience. Soviet Russia from its inauguration bred a plethora of acronyms: *Intourist*, *OGPU*. Not only administrators, but also aesthetes like the Russian Futurists, made new words to name their new world, a strongly centralized society. Algeo reminds how ancient the practice is.[4] Kabbalistic interpretation of the Torah is a form of acronymic exegesis. 'Cabal' itself is said to be formed from the initial letters of the group within Charles II's Privy Council (Clifford, Arlington, Buckingham, Ashley (Earl of Shaftesbury) and Lauderdale), associated with intrigue. In his letters to Stella, Swift uses initial abbreviations for the 'little language' of lovers, as many before and since. We have already encountered the acronymic term which links adhocism and neology, 'rejasing'.

In the modern world, shortage of time and space and the multiplicity of organizations all breed acronyms, which aim at being easily retained in the memory, sawn-off and significant (like the 'canting names' of heraldry). PLATO (a teaching machine) comes from 'programmed logic for automatic teaching operations'. WITCH: Women's International Terrorist Conspiracy from Hell. The second hints at the esoteric aspect of acronyms: a puzzle to be solved by select groups, although the present-day need among pressure-groups for publicity militates against total opacity of nomenclature. It is likely that many are formed backwards. An arresting acronym is chosen, and then meaningful constituent words arranged to fit the pattern. A high-powered computer at Euratom was nicknamed ZAZIE: Zahlen Analyser Zur Informazione Exploitation. This German/English/Dutch/Italian/French conglomerate must have pleased the polyglot Queneau. Initialese aids euphemism, as in SNAFU, though here the coyness rapidly became blatant. Much the same happens with TB, The Big C, DTs, WC, SOB, BO and VD. Sometimes second thoughts become necessary as the choice of letters proves unfortunate. CINCUS (from Commander in Chief, US Fleet) was hastily dropped and SOD (for Secretary of Defence) abandoned for SECDEF.[5] COCU, the acronym of the Consultation on Church Union, would delight an anticlerical Frenchman. There are some accidentally pointed coincidences. PTA serves both Parent–Teacher Association and Prevention of Terrorism Act. Mental shorthand in excess can cook up what has been called 'alphabet-soup', though acronyms add to the permutations available and so can engender new words based on themselves. Algeo sums up eloquently: 'Acronyms are playthings for the poet, icons for the mystic, tools for the bureaucrat, and data for the linguist. And anything that can serve all these ends has its future assured.'[6]

Business likes simultaneously to claim a philosophy and to stimulate impulse-buying; perhaps that is why in the United States haberdashery is often called 'notions'. Souriau stresses the double function of trade-names, 'at one and the same time siren-words and index-cards, stemming from the twin aims of seducing and classifying'.[7] In reply to the Comptroller of the British Patent Office, George Eastman justified his trade-name, Kodak, in these words: 'It is short. It is not capable of mispronunciation. It does not resemble anything in the art and cannot be associated with anything in the art except the Kodak.'[8] This could sound like a definition of Godhead. The care he took to fence off his coinage did not prevent many people using 'kodak' as a synonym for camera, while ceasing to exhibit any loyalty to the brand itself. Much the same happened with Frigidaire and Hoover. As soon as such trade-names pass into common parlance, much of the unique value is lost: the originator's product is no longer distinguished from its competitors. Nominal ownership is no more legally invulnerable and proof against plagiarism or vulgarization than intellectual property. Yet trade-names are one of the few domains where creation *ex nihilo* is practised. Computer programs have been used to provide etymology-free names, like the Du Pont de Nemours products Dacron, Lycra, Orlon and Teflon (though the machines have obviously been fed some leads). On the other hand, a possibly apocryphal story relates that NYLON was derived from the acronym 'Now you lousy old Nippon', uttered by a triumphant chemist at Du Pont on discovering a synthetic fabric to rival Japanese silk.[9] Trade-names are often, as in MacNuggets, agglutinated, a word which frequently describes accurately the texture of such products.

I said at the outset of this Neologism section that purely workaday scientific coinages would not come into the purview. This now needs some qualifying. I had in mind the myriad long words constantly spawned in the language of science to keep pace with inventions or discoveries. I share Pearsall Smith's opinion that much nomenclature of this type demoralizes more inventive coining. He believes in particular that the assumption that a scientific name should be self-defining (that is, contain its own meaning) is misleading and gives rise to many cumbrous syllables. Words are 'labels and not explanations'.[10] Scientists, of course, see a far more pressing need for a terminology, if not a whole language, easily understandable across national frontiers. (This fact of life also concerns the military, international transport and, above all, multinational manufacturers and distributors, and the publicity that supports them.) Condorcet dreamed of a 'linguistic algebra'.[11] In fact, mathematical language transcends boundaries better than most words. Most scientific neologisms derive from Latin and Greek roots; and for a long time there was an active taboo on mixing the two, though 'automobile' and 'television' put paid to that. Why turn to the 'dead' languages for new words? Among the possible motives: innate conservatism (tradition, old = authoritative); snobbery (*we* know what this word means, but most of *you* do not); a need to ritualize, which gives birth to 'medicine-man words' cut off from the 'words of the tribe'; ecumenism (Latin/Greek as lingua franca); the desire among some scientists to prove they are also humanists and possibly human; a recognition that human beings can work only with the given, the materials to hand: the new must take off from the old; a wish to couch the newfound in the (relatively) familiar. And yet in the supposedly sure sciences, the netherworld of particle physics fastbreeds an oxymoron like 'heavy lepton' (*lepton* = lightweight), or a pun like 'charmed quark': charmed, both because aesthetically satisfying and because the term aims at warding off the evil eye of incomplete theories. An earlier state of the art picked 'atom' (= indivisible), the most basic oxymoron of all.[12] Hydrogen should really be called oxygen, if etymology were respected. Scientific terminology is stereotypically precise, but think of the 'inflammable'/'flammable' ambiguity, which must have jeopardized, and curtailed, some lives. 'Flukicide', a chemical to destroy flatworms, sounds like accidental hara-kiri.

Scientists are capable of humour, as in choosing the word 'barn' as a unit of measure for the infinitely small, or in naming the Perhapstron. They are always mixing it, and so often blend (for instance 'bit' in computerese is taken from 'binary digit'). Computer jargon has frequently a homely, colloquial flavour (as perhaps befits the new upwardly mobile operators of such machines); bit, byte, bug, chip, software, hardware. As Bolton comments, computerese 'employs standard English phonology and grammar to build a small technical lexicon, borrowing some words with changed meanings, creating some new ones by compounding, and acronyms, employing a genial sense of humour in figures of speech. The resulting vocabulary is more compact and precise than the loose paraphrases it replaces'.[13]

The question of scientific vocabulary appears different from the standpoint of a rearguard resister like Etiemble. Indeed, the English take-over is now overwhelming in most international scientific conferences and publications. In his *Le Jargon des sciences*, Etiemble, who is in general anything but hostile to either science or novelty, voices his complaint against the more unthinking kind of mass-borrowing from English into French. We should feel some guilty sympathy for his lost cause, as it is our language which has acted imperialistically. To the common argument that foreign loan-words fill a gap and promote clarity, Etiemble responds by pointing out with great glee the polysemy of many Greek roots. It is a Babel. One root, *car*, can mean, in different compounds: head, deep sleep, hair, cummin, to lack, dear and vehicle.[14] On this basis, he jokes, 'autocar' means an egocentric. As Vallès's unemployed *baccalauréat*-holder finds out, you can starve on a diet of Greco-Roman roots. Etiemble makes the valid point that borrowing often reduces variety; the foreign import is made to work overtime and displaces several native words.[15] Reducing synonymy is generally a bad thing for language, if popular with dictators. Etiemble's positive counter-strike is to propose calling up dialect words and inserting them into new contexts. Exploit unutilized series of parallel sounds: on *lune*, make *bune*, *bunaire*, *bunatique*, and press them into service. It is, he argues, less arbitrary than making up polysyllabic, ugly-sounding new words mainly by derivation, or borrowing difficultly assimilable foreign terms (p. 121). He is surely right to remind us that language is not private property, for arrogant scientists to bend to their will, nor class-property (that is, jargon).

Much more esoteric than most scientific words are inkhorn terms, learned words (*mots savants*), also known as hothouse-words. Kennedy surmises that many of these, such as 'doctiloquent', probably exist only in dictionaries.[16] At least in social terms, a learned word is often a sign of ignorance, or at least tactlessness. Such coinages seep from neologor-rhea, can give rise to neologomachy which sets the contenders at neologgerheads.[17] In *Palimpsestes*, Genette argues that his forging *hyper-textualité* has the advantage that everyone (!) at least can agree on the meaning, unlike, for example, *parodie*, which has been around for centuries and means many if not all things to all (!) men. He cannot be serious. At the same time, French culture is so inbred that there is less chance of one-offs remaining such; they are generally taken up and bandied about, if only in derision, by other writers. It should be evident that technical, archaic or rare words are just as foreign to the uncompre-hending reader or listener (that is, each one of us at some time) as borrowings from alien tongues. Queneau sports with the serious idea that maybe all tongues are foreign by Gallicizing the Italian *lingue forestiere* into *langues forestières*.[18] Bertelé's term for poetic coinages is 'esperanto lyrique', but the inconvenience is that this lingo cannot be learnt like

Esperanto itself.[19] Most inkhorn terms, however, scarcely hope to survive a first glance. Brander Matthews's coinage 'osteocephalic' (bone-headed) was 'devised to bestow a flavour of the ancient world upon a word created by the modern world'.[20] The Duke of Edinburgh is credited with 'dontapedology': foot-in-mouth disease, by which he has been afflicted on occasion. I cherish Fritz Spiegl's 'pollexocracy' – rule of thumb.[21]

Inkhorn-terms are often nonce-formations, 'fly-by-night jargon'.[22] Many neologisms are, frankly, verbal stunts, and often meant to be one-off performances. 'If a nonce-word should happen to crop up a second time, should it be called a *deuce word*? Now *deuce word* is my own coinage and is itself a nonce word.'[23] A related category is 'opportunistic words', as when ludic journalists competed to coin terms in the hope that the *New English Dictionary* would pick them up in its trawl-net.[24] Perhaps, by analogy with inkhorn-terms, we might update these as 'dactylograph-emes'. Nonce-words that might usefully be taken over into the common stockpot, if only other people could be bullied or coaxed to accept them, include Makkai's 'transmote' to describe an employee who is neither promoted nor demoted, but moved out of the way – especially suitable in those institutions where nothing short of gross moral turpitude will ensure dismissal; and 'to prosist' – to insist on behalf of somebody else, which would make a nice change.[25]

A *hapax legomenon* (usually truncated to *hapax*) is a true nonce-word, one occurring only once in the language. Mallarmé's 'sonnet en-yx' ('Ses purs ongles très haut dédiant leur onyx') features the non-existent word *ptyx* (though its etymology could suggest a fold, *ptux* in Greek). It is a poem of absence, 'un sonnet nul', where negatives predominate. Mallarmé said in a letter that he had been assured the word did not exist in any language, which suited him perfectly, as it gave him the magical chance to create it by the sorcery of rhyme.[26] Or, as Riffaterre puts it, 'a pure ad hoc product of the sonnet's rhyming constraints'.[27] He goes on: 'With its outlandish spelling and its boldly non-French initial consonantal cluster, *ptyx*, like everything else in the sonnet, combines high visibility, an almost obtrusive physical presence as a form, and an equally obtrusive absence as meaning.'[28] A word created then to abolish signification, a red-herring, a non-existent mystery. In this poem Mallarmé pre-empts the strike of deconstructionists; the text talks only about itself; it is high-cultural megalomania. As Palmer says, and numerous critics and readers of this piece bear this out, 'man abhors the vacuum of an unmeaning word'.[29] On a less ethereal level, Ogden Nash illustrates the category of rhyme-engendered nonce-words with:

> Farewell, farewell, you old rhinoceros,
> I'll stare at something less prepocerous.[30]

A fanciful word, of obscure origin, to denote a fantasy-bird or a tall story, is *coquecigrue*.

Finally, there are nonce-phrases. I mentioned earlier the request, in an experiment, to 'do a Napoleon'. The experimenters also encountered a much more enigmatic invitation to 'do a Chomsky'. This shorthand meant opening a car-door for an encumbered fellow-passenger, as the great man had courteously done for the speaker the week before. This instance proves we can create meaning (whoever outside of a laboratory thought we could not?), as well as selecting it prepacked from our mental lexicons. While the listener has still to 'parse' the nonce-phrase correctly, we can collectively make sense of nonce-sense.[31]

19

High Neologism

A word is dead
When it is said,
Some say.
I say it just
Begins to live
That day.

Emily Dickinson[1]

Mallarmé's *ptyx* already offered us a fine example of high coinage. In this study of the supply and maintenance of new words, or neologistics,[2] I now turn to the claimed experts, the writers of high literature. Do authors re-use, plug, their coinages? If not, perhaps, like Mallarmé, they see them as nonce-formations, although the occasion, however brief, is a special one. Do they want them to be taken up by others, or do they act proprietorially? How can they, since what is printed passes, whatever the law says, into the true public domain, readers' minds and memories? Poets especially have traditionally been granted the (poetic) licence to coin new words, like fresh metaphors. And many neologisms are indeed akin to metaphors, in that (particularly in the form of blends) they compress previously disparate material. For Riffaterre, literary neologism differs from the everyday variety; the latter is fabricated to express a new meaning, generally by linking a word and a thing; and it does not necessarily strike the hearer as unusual. The literary neologism, on the other hand, 'is always perceived as an anomaly, and used for that very reason ... It cannot fail to seize our attention ... It obliges the reader to become conscious of the form of the message he is decoding, and this act of consciousness is the very essence of literary communication'.[3] This is to see neologisms as the sleeping policemen on the highway of literature, jolting us out of the automatism of cruising through the texts. Literary neologisms are unlikely, on the whole, to pass into the common language. Advertising coinages are midway between literary and everyday neologisms in that they aim to be striking, like the former, but also to be memorized and to become part of current usage, like the latter, quite literally household words.

Writers fill up the shelves, as they were born or made to do, but also, like supermarket assistants, because they notice the gaps. Neology can take the form of extending grammar as well as lexis. Ponge, for example, invents a string of reflexive verbs in order to concretize his point that nature acts on itself, even though our anthropomorphic gaze lends it humanoid traits: 'Dès le matin, le ciel se dalle, se marquette, se pave, se banquise, se glaçonne, se marbre, se cotonne, se coussine, se cimente, se géographise, se cartographise.'[4] Ironically and knowingly he has to use largely man-made substances to make this point: the sky, flagstones, inlays, paves, icefloes, icecubes, marbles, cottons, cushions, cements, geographizes, cartographizes itself. Of his own fabrication *implexe*, Valéry wrote: 'Très suggestif. Je ne sais pas trop ce qu'il suggère; mais il suggère énormément.'[5] He is not too sure what it suggests, but certainly a great deal. Here we are very close to kabbalistic word-charms, or magic nonsense like 'Abracadabra' – mystery words where the connotation is left up to the receiver. Balzac is even more barefaced in his effrontery: 'The French language has accepted the new words of my predecessors; it will accept mine. Upstarts will become aristocrats in time.'[6]

In discussing classicism in the first part of this book, I spoke of those writers who aspire to a style like varnish. Such are generally hostile to neology, which they imagine as producing clotted language which draws too much localized attention to itself, to the detriment of the overall meaning. They are, besides, presumably satisfied with the existing lexical stock (though this itself of course expands daily). In between the conservationists and the inventors come those prepared on occasion to ransack the past or the regions, to raid foreign stocks, for words that they need. In terms of statistics, 785 neologisms have been counted in Céline's *Bagatelles pour un massacre*, whereas the entire and voluminous works of Jules Romains and André Maurois yielded only one.[7] For Rogers, even a writer like Fielding, in a neo-classical age, does not set out to transcribe usage (for instance in his rendering of Mrs Slipslop's fractured English) but often to create it. 'Fielding could never have used such forms if he'd heard them as common (street) usage, as the joke would have been lost.' I can only agree with Rogers's argument that 'lexicography is too prone to believe there should be demotic fire behind all neologistic smoke.'[8]

Although writers were coining centuries before the press was invented, as much of literature (especially of the Naturalist, sociological or politically committed variety) drew closer to journalism in the nineteenth century, the readiness of newsmen to invent words transmitted itself even to poets, who until then had used their licence sparingly. Regarded as a key innovator by Modernists such as Eliot and Pound, Laforgue was credited by the last named with 'the dance of the intellect among words', or 'logopoeia'.[9] Laforgue himself defined his fusions as 'cet accouplement de mots qui n'ont qu'une harmonie de rêve mais font dans la réalité des couples impossibles, et qui ont pour moi le charme insoluble, obsédant, entêtant des antinomies en métaphysique' (this mating of words which click only in dreamland, but beget in reality impossible pairings which have for me the unsolvable, captivating and insistent charm of paradoxes in metaphysics). He adds: 'wordplays, but so aesthetic'.[10] There is here a whole complex of attitudes: Laforgue's no-hope but stubborn eroticism; his longing for a true and durable love-partner; his fascination with *chimères*, hybrids, *mots-centaures* (he married an Englishwoman, the breed which for him constituted a third sex, neither male nor female); his constant linking of the quotidian and the transcendent. Some examples of his practice: *spleenuosités* (a splendid furthering of the vogue loan-word 'spleen', suggesting the ramifications, as in 'sinuosities', of this richly melancholic state); *voluptés à vif* (*viol* + *voluptés*: rapeture on edge); 'ces vendanges sexcriproques' (these sex-ciprocal wine-harvests); 'hontes sangsuelles' (leecherous shame); 'grosses plaisanteries éléphantaisistes'; 'O rancoeurs ennuiverselles!'; 'massacrilège-moi!'; 'la céleste Eternullité'.[11]

The 'ego-futurists' in Russia produced some whole poems consisting solely of neologisms, sometimes so as to block foreign borrowings, sometimes in order to 'explore the inner life of the word':[12] a kind of verbal microscopy. A new society needed, they believed, a new language. I take it on trust from students of science-fiction that the same notion, in that realm, has produced mainly banality. Angenot claims that, such as they are, neologisms in science-fiction fall into two main categories: words supposed to anticipate a future state of the language of the narrative, or words supposed to belong to a parallel linguistic universe; or words 'borrowed' from an extraterrestrial tongue.[13] As for those other would-be openers-up of a new world, the Surrealists, Breton himself admitted that very few neologisms occurred in automatic-writing sessions.[14] It remains ambiguous whether this shows how uninventive was the subconscious of the Surrealist Pope and his acolytes (and his sniffiness about humour and puns suggests that it was), or whether the dearth proves how deliberate an exercise is most coining.

Queneau was one such conscious coiner. Whereas the frantic neologizer

Céline, one of Queneau's gracefully admitted precursors in the field of language renewal, talked of the urgent need to reanimate a dead idiom, less drastically Queneau spoke of acting as a midhusband at the birth of *néo-français*. He was eager to add to the stock of the French language, to fill in some of its gaps, to articulate some of the things it was previously unable to convey in quite so economical a way. For many, besides, the French tongue is looking peaky, and needs all the tonics it can get. If this midhusband operates on a dying language, it is in order to save the child alive and kicking in its womb and, in so doing, to rescue the mother as well: a Caesarian.[15] The same sounds can mean different things: in *Zazie*, as in all guide-books, the Sainte-Chapelle is platitudinously 'un joyau (jewel) de l'art gothique'; *Zazie* itself is 'un joyau de l'argotique'.

Some examples: *conneversation* (a stupid chat, with a nod towards *malversation*: embezzling); *phallucination* (a naïve heroine warns herself to stop looking at men's flies in 'une espèce de mysticisme avec des phallucinations'. This clever-dick blend hints that such conduct is saintly). *Ontalgie*: 'maladie existentielle, ça ressemble à l'asthme mais c'est plus distingué.' The Duc d'Auge, centuries ahead of his time, invents *sieste, mouchoir, péniche* (barge). When queried as to whether he practises neologism, he responds: 'Ne néologise pas toi-même: c'est là privilège de duc' (Vaugelas would agree). Auge justifies himself: 'Je dérive [mouchoir] du bas-latin *mucare*, un vocable bien françoüe selon les règles les plus acceptées et les plus diachroniques.'[16] Queneau constantly plays elegance and the vernacular off against each other, so that each scores points against the opponent, but neither wins outright; he loves pedantry as much as slang, as all true philologers must. *Procréfoutre*[17] cross-breeds *procréer* and *foutre*, and the medical/theological and the demotic. He likes making silk purses out of sows' ears. In so doing, Queneau illustrates the two-way, up/down action of parody. He aims to ennoble slang as much as to debag poshness. As a result, his readers need to be bilingual.[18] As well as increasing the stock, Queneau sometimes clips words, so as to make new: *l'orama* is a more limited panorama, and suitable for a fictional world where the emphasis falls often on lesser, streamlined living. Gallicizations offer another way of making strange: *le baïlle-naïte* (Paris By Nights tours, yawn-making). *Apibeursdé touillou*: such take-overs do not make the import look any more French or natural; they create in fact a new and intriguing monstrosity.[19] In *Les Fleurs bleues*, where there is much talk of talking horses and of alchemy, the blend *chevalchimie* falls pat.

Any attempts at rethinking and reformulation are, in effect, an attempted *Verfremdungseffekt* – an effort to see the old with fresh eyes, as with recycled clichés. The very fact of being attentive and critical about language is a kind of defamiliarization. Disassociation and reassembly break old associations of ideas, derail trains of thought or reroute them.

> Oft from new truths, and new phrases, new doubts grow,
> As strange attire aliens the men we know.[20]

Few writers have made stranger, more outlandish, than James Joyce.

Joyce minces words and makes long sausages out of them. Is it all baloney? *Finnegans Wake* is virtually one continuous act of neology. (Neologeewhiz, as American Joyceans tend to exclaim.) Or one vast nonce-word, an unrepeatable offer? Self-admittedly and boastingly, this text is 'sentenced to be nuzzled over a full trillion times for ever and a night till his noddle sink or swim by that ideal reader suffering from an ideal insomnia.'[21] Let us listen first to those self-appointed but encouraged cheer-leaders of *Our Exagmination* . . . , the pom-pom crew, and their numerous successors, especially in France. (Was ever a writer better surrounded by minders? It is the merely solo gainsayers who appear the underdogs; the claque sets up a pale.) Beckett claims strangely that 'Mr Joyce has desophisticated language.'[22] Robert McAlmon speaks of 'philological "rag-picking" . . . Joyce wishes to originate a flexible language that might be an esperanto of the subconscious'.[23] For Stuart Gilbert, 'the word-building of *Work in Progress* is founded on the rock of petrified language, of sounds with solid associations.'[24] Joyce's fear of the commonplace (and yet total reliance on it) is visible in these words from *Stephen Hero*: 'He was determined to fight with every energy of soul and body against any possible consignment to what he now regarded as the hell of hells – the region, otherwise expressed, wherein everything is found to be obvious.'[25] As Margot Norris has said: 'Although *Finnegans Wake* is thoroughly original . . . it may also be the most self-consciously unoriginal work in the language.'[26] Joyce himself called it 'an epical forged cheque' and 'the last word in stolentelling'.[27] Defenders of Joyce, like Stephen Heath, stress the discontinuity, the endless openness of this text, its refusal of stable meaning, and to that end Heath uses the Joycean blend 'ambiviolence' – which suggests both aggression and hesitancy.[28] Yet even champions of Joyce like Anthony Burgess acknowledge that 'he crams the portmanteau sometimes to bursting.'[29]

In Butor's view, Joyce did not write only for English readers, but for all who knew English: 'There is in Joyce, and it's crucial from the outset, a wild determination to *detach the English language from its nationality*.'[30] This sees Joyce's language as aiming to be a lingua franca, or an

Esperanto – a synthetic language based on many existing ones: 'this piggybacking of languages and cultures', in McLuhan's words.[31] Undoubtedly, Joyce gave himself more to play with by his multilingual borrowings: 'Polyvalent because polyglot'.[32] As Hartman says, 'Joyce dramatises the language jam in which we are stuck, the intrinsic duplicity, racial mix, and historically accreted character of living speech.' He goes on to say that 'English is equally prone to this happy impurity, not having suffered, like French or Italian, a decisive neoclassical sublimation of the vernacular.'[33] And yet, while applauding much of Joyce's motivation, I take only spasmodic pleasure in the result. I admire Molly Bloom's 'soliloquacity',[34] but remain sceptical of so much that is unrepeatable in Joyce's work; it so often seems a sterile planet. 'Joycean blends are bound to their contexts – one could hardly use his inventions elsewhere – and there is frequently no obvious semantic link between the source words of the splinters which are combined. "Everscepistic" has no "meaning" as a unit: it is simply a compression of four disparate notions. This "atomised" quality sets Joycean blends apart.'[35] Everest, sceptic, septic, pistic (= pure):[36] the nonce-word here is very close to nonsense. George Steiner sums up the doubts: 'There have been no genuine successors to Joyce in English; perhaps there can be none to a talent so exhaustive of its own potential. What counts more: the treasures which Joyce brought back to language from his wide-ranging forays remain piled glitteringly around his own labours. They have not passed into currency.'[37] That flight from the obvious, as from the plague, made Joyce by choice into a kind of linguistic leper.

Just as I prefer printed puns, so I relish most neologisms with a real bite. Such as Hervé Bazin's *maternite*, which like other words with the same ending (*-itis*) suggests an inflamed condition.[38] Or Rimbaud's *patrouillotisme*, his jibing coinage to denote citizens putting on a show of militaristic patriotism (*patriotisme, patrouille* – and *trouille* (funk) is buried in it).[39] Or Ponge's *amphibiguïté*: the state of being neither fish nor flesh.[40]

'New-fangled', etymologically, bears traces of seizing, and of gewgaws. Neology embraces appropriation and whimsy. The urge towards defamiliarization can lead to mere ornateness, periphrasis; rephrasing can entail going around (as in 'Martian' poetry), and other forms of preciosity. The whole process can give rise to much 'picayunity'.[41] In addition to its meaning of 'fashion', neophilia has also been used to describe the provision of challenging mazes to rats in experiments. Whether applied to demagogues, way-out critics, or families having a row, diarrhetoric can strike anywhere. I called this section 'High Neologism', and 'high' can also signify overripe, drunk or drugged. Or, of course, arrogant, as in 'high-and-mighty'. Symbolist writers deliberately practised a kind of reserved language, intended to sever them from naturalist or populist authors and their popular audiences; and also to throw the reader. Edmond de Goncourt expressed horror at the very idea of having to descend to speaking 'the omnibus language of news items'.[42] Mallarmé's aversion for 'the language of the tribe', and the need he felt to fumigate it are well known. Neologisms can thus be hermetic, a club-language. At the apparent other extreme, Céline's violently demotic coinages have been described as back-to-front elitism, inverted preciosity.[43]

Salmon describes thus the licence given to writers of high culture: 'Verbal creation, author's neologism, joky coinages, word-magic, verbal fantasy, all of these in other hands would be condemned out of hand as barbarisms or trickery.'[44] He sees neology as an assertion of the will-to-power, a way of violating language, giving it children against its will, dominating it, and generally making sport of its rules, or at least choosing to believe this. This is a counterblow to alleviate the sense of having to deal with a medium not our own, which we have had to inherit as a totality. Salmon goes on to assert that such individual acts of expression enact some of the aspirations of the collective unconscious. I would like to believe that, but feel it safer to echo Isaac Disraeli's claim: 'Certain it is that in highly cultivated ages we discover the most refined intellects attempting neologisms.'[45] I am grateful for the recognition by the linguist John Algeo that 'while linguists study language, poets renew it.'[46]

20

Looking Round the Bend

After the elite, the marginalized: children, women and lunatics. Women, children, the mentally deranged and emergent nations are all trying out their voices and attempting to find a language to call their own, with which they can catch up and possibly surpass the mainly male discourse of adulthood and advanced-nation status. 'Lexical creativity is common in children's speech,' notes one student, Eve Clark.[1] Another, Bréal, talking of extensions to vocabulary, notes that 'children have a part in it which is by no means small: as they take up the language at the point to which the preceding generations have brought it, they generally are ten or twenty years in advance of their parents':[2] this puts an interesting slant on the generation-gap. In language as in all else, children should never be dismissed as passive consumers or mere regurgitators. They adapt or invent words for their own (often impenetrably enigmatic) purposes. This is a tricky area, for parents and other grown-ups of course interfere, interpret sounds, read into sayings, all along adult patterns of thought, whereas creating words is part of the semi-magical early stages of language acquisition and control; mystery before mastery. One chastened observer heard his six-year-old son, by then used to the grown-up noting all his idiosyncratic utterances, say after one such: 'You can write that one down!'[3]

It must be true that many coinings by children are under semi-control, and often the result of mis-analogy, mis-generalization, mishearing or mispronunciation. Such innovations are technically wrong often, as are similar adult slip-ups in a careless, distracted or anxious moment. But such solecisms are on the right track. 'The child spontaneously coins neologisms, thus showing that he has mastered the mechanics of analogy. It is in this sense that some have argued that children's "mistakes" are in fact the proof in action of their linguistic competence as it develops.'[4]

Women, from whom most children learn the bulk of their early language, face different prejudices, profoundly rooted. In response, militant feminists seek both to block, to censor and to innovate (new pronouns and possessive adjectives, redesignated terms for jobs and activities): they seek both to abort and to give birth. We have already seen in other areas the impossibility of imposing neologisms by diktat or of banning unwelcome language. Feminists here share the dilemma of linguistic protectionists in France and elsewhere. As for truly radical feminists who dream of creating a totally female language, if neology as a general phenomenon can teach us anything, it is that no new order can be constructed except on the basis of the existing one. In addition, the question of how to create an audience and how to make the new language comprehensible to it presents insuperable difficulties. Indeed, here as so often elsewhere, women are in a Catch-22 situation. This new language would have to be born, thus creating the new woman, before it can be conceived. I am, of course, ineluctably using male logic and referring to an undeniably male-dominated sequence of thinking here. Women may well think differently.

Women are commonly amalgamated with lunatics in throwaway generalizations. Another stereotype that needs its head examined is that sane word-coiners create calm, deliberate neologisms, whereas the mentally adrift spawn frantic, compulsive monstrosities. This neo-logomania is termed 'neologistic jargon aphasia' by professionals who encounter it in their work. Buckingham and Kertesz define such activity as

> a phonological form produced by the patient for which it is impossible to recover with any reasonable degree of certainty some single item or items in the vocabulary of the subject's language as it presumably existed prior to the onset of the disease. It is often possible to relate one neologism to some other neologism, but this is possibly only because of structural phonological similarity and not necessarily due to any meaningful semantic variable.[5]

Here, the gap between nonce-sense and nonsense, to put it very roughly, is very short. For another professional, far more oriented towards poetry, Ferdière, 'there is not the slightest difference between sanity and mental illness on the score of verbal invention. An inkhorn term, lengthily and meticulously elaborated in the study is indistinguishable from a neo-logism "springing fully armoured" from the depths of the unconscious on the lips of a child or somebody raving.'[6] Some Surrealists tried unavailingly to ape madness, and I quoted earlier Breton's admission on the dearth of neologisms in automatic writing. In the discussion of stupidity in the first part of this book I also declared that there were more colloquial words for madness than for any other area of existence but sex.

In France in the eighteenth century, there was a spurt of-*manie* formations: *bibliomanie, étrangéromanie, jardinomanie.*[7] Guiraud points to joky creations for fools and loonies: *un navet* (turnip), from *naïf; une tarte* (dolt/pie), from *tart* (slow, tardy).[8] Thus the *minus habentes* acquire invented words to stigmatize them, as well as contributing their own, in an attempt at self-explanation.

Henri Michaux argues that

> certain inmates are forced by inner necessity to coin a word for their double or multiform misery. For instance, one patient said repeatedly she was 'penetroversed', that is, penetrated and traversed at the same time. This word forced itself on her, a word for new needs. She didn't have to read books in order to construct it.[9]

For his own part, Michaux said his invented words and imaginary creatures were invented 'nervously'.[10] By this he seems to mean that he invented them in sympathy or by analogy with mentally disturbed creations. Thus, anti-snobbishly, he holds that his coinages are not peculiar to him (the root meaning of 'idiotic' is private), but that they have a social dimension.[11] What I have seen of Artaud's neologisms appear to lack this bridge and extension. For Grésillon, portmanteaux in particular enable the patient to articulate his suffering, and he cites: 'Cher merdessein: est-ce que j'ai une tu-meurs?' (Dear Doctor, have I got a tumour?)[12] The doctor is folded up with shit (*merde*) and has sinister designs (*desseins*); the dreaded verdict is: you are dying ('tu meurs'). There is here a method in the madness, a sense-making amid the apparent jabbering. It is impossible to know how desperate or triumphant was Jung's patient who called her coinages 'power-words'.[13]

The very disturbing *fou littéraire*, Jean-Pierre Brisset, points up the ambiguity of the phrase 'making sense': conforming to orthodox meaning, and fabricating new significance. (Similarly, 'Seeing things' registers reality and injects unreality.) He strove in several works to rewrite present language backwards, to invent its origins, in a kind of reverse God-pride: a sustained act of back-formation. In the process he claimed the impossibility of neologizing.

> The most modern new names were created before Man. 'Telephone' is formed from 'Teu ait l'ai faune', and we see fauns using the air or water as a telephone. Man is incapable of creating an intelligible new sound, and furthermore is banned from creating a new word. Even the most barbaric forms of slang are cries coming from our ancestors; for millions of years they uttered so many cries that assuredly all possible permutations were known to them.[14]

This curiously static or back-pedalling view is essential to Brisset's strange medley of emancipation and prohibition. It did not stop him from coining himself, as when he proposed to replace Graeco-Latin derivations with French ones: *loinisser* (from *loin*, distant) instead of *télégraphier*.[15]

Glossolalia, the coining of a whole new language (or at least specimens, and usually very cloudy ones), seems to stem from the urge to distort or otherwise adapt one's own native tongue, and to incorporate into this whatever fragments of foreign language have been more or less consciously picked up. The need for a consenting and supportive audience is very high. The quite widespread recurrence of glossolalia suggests a permanent human need for strangeness and indeed for intriguing opacity, as if many ordered: 'amaze us'. Joyce's carillons of sound, echolalia in certain deranged conditions, the frequent desire to regress to childhood, the undoubted attempt by some to mystify others, claims to have escaped mortal bonds and terrestrial boundaries – all these phenomena seem to criss-cross or clang together. Those who boast of speaking in tongues make out that what is a pseudo-language and often an accident (a popping up or out) of sound is a sign of supernatural inspiration. Leiris prefers to play with the word: 'Glossolalie (la glotte y sonne un hallali)' (Glossolalia: the glottis sounds the mort).[16]

In the vernacular of French psychiatry, internees are sometimes referred to as *colloqués*: that is, the relegated, the palmed off. (Participants at colloquia melodramatically imagine on occasion that they have comparably been banged up.) In their enforced exile, their generally unhappy autarky, their imaginably unwilling hermeticism, some patients resort to graphic figurations of their preoccupations. In one such, we can see the progressive complication of both shapes and words. The artist's obsession was cybernetics, which begins to explain the mechanization of the monster-figure created. The professional witnesses call these 'dessins-valises', or portmanteau-drawings. They are convinced that a pronounced playful spirit also inhabits the sketches, but that the total effort represented an attempt at self-affirmation and self-defence against anguish.[17] As Diderot, one of the sanest as well as one of the most split minds of the Enlightenment, said: 'The World sometimes seems to me peopled entirely by monstrous beings.' We are all monsters, exceptions. As Cardinal says of a drawing by August Klotz: 'Like a dream that can manage a marvellous concentration of disparate mental events, the drawing depicts four superimposed locations ... [This] demonstrates the same principles of condensation, superimposition and contamination familiar to students of dream-work and Freudian analyses of speech-errors and jokes.' Another Klotz picture 'combines two contradictions ... This

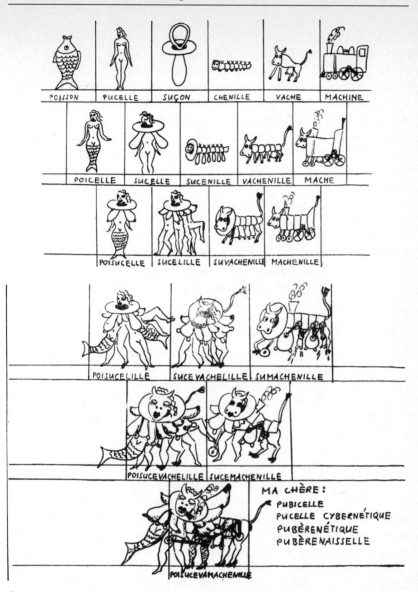

Poisucevamachenille, from Les 'druses' écrites et dessinées (Kontaminationen, blendings); pathogénie de certains néomorphismes by Jaroslav Stuchlik and Jean Bobon, published in *Acta Neurologica et Psychiatrica Belgica Fasc. 6, 1960, pp. 529–550*. Reproduced by kind permission of Jean Bobon.

suspension of oppositions is like an arrested dialectical process, a having-both-ways rather than a compromise or synthesis, and seems to typify the thought-processes of schizophrenia'.[18]

I cross-fertilize 'neologanberry' (and the loganberry is already a hybrid). 'Monster' seems to contain the idea of show (as when spectacles are made of freaks), though the derivation is really from *monere*, to warn. Sirens (women/birds), tritons (men/dolphins), mermaids (women/fish), harpies (women/birds of prey), monotaur (man/bull), Sphinx (woman/lion/bird of prey), satyr (man/goat): mythology is a madhouse of imaginary cross-breeds. Balzac fashioned the idea of 'l'homme à deux têtes', the supercharged creature formed of two powerful wills and ambitions. And modern technology spawned the frogman. Mongrels are notoriously tougher than thoroughbreds (and 'hybrid vigour', or heterosis, is a scientific fact in some cases). The urge to miscegenate counteracts racism. A French term for portmanteau, *mot-centaure*, is especially apt, as Chiron the centaur was already a composite mythological figure, a great pedagogue whose pupils included Hercules, Achilles, Theseus and Jason. The imagining of fabulous beasts reveals, apart from the urge to blend, to be eclectic, that of quintessentialization. The unicorn is a right hotchpotch and, as such, eminently befitted to symbolize Britain, and the English language. The legs of a buck, the tail of a lion, the head and body of a horse, and a single white, red and black curly horn in the middle of the forehead. This might suggest a semi-cuckold, though the unicorn is usually associated with virginity (which might of course be the cause of cuckoldry).

Just as some *salon*-revolutionaries waved corpses or skeletons (clichés) at us in the first part of this book, so their partners revel in talking of neologisms (especially blends) as deviants, criminals or monsters – a whole teratological diagnosis which sees word-creation as paraplasm, or malformed tissue. But verbal *monstricules* (monsterettes)[19] can be pointed, ludic, or both simultaneously. As well as the fabulous beasts of mythology there is the pantomime horse, or the Chinese dragon (people inside animal shapes). If the camel is a horse designed by a committee, things inaugurated by such bodies often have, like the camel, remarkable endurance and unkillability. The 'donkophant',[20] a cross between a Democrat and a Republican, made from their respective mascots, the donkey and the elephant, is still alive and with us. The jazzy 'Anglo-saxophone' seems very suitable for our syncopated, gaudy language.[21] A creative bit of *franglais*: the 'exégète-set',[22] which nicely pinpoints the profits to be made from critical modishness, at the non-stop conferences of David Lodge's *Small World*. Monster-words, verbal ogres, remind us, like the whole mode of the grotesque, of how far from being properly human we often are. The grotesque makes strange to bring home.

Deformity is often thought of as an accident of nature (or act of God – not only a sadist but also a let-out clause on insurance policies). I want to end with the domain of lapsus, the area where we can all seem momentarily unhinged. The sign that the dubious hero of Sartre's 'La Chambre' has finally started to collapse into unarguable madness, after play-acting it to some extent, occurs when a word just plops out of his mouth, like a baby dribbling, or a spluttering adult. I am, however, more taken with the production of sense, the creativity of accident, than with fiasco *per se*, about which not much, so inherent is it in living, can be said. The area of lapsus is that of humankind with its flies open or its knickers dropping.

'Name the greatest of all the inventors. Accident.'[23] Scientists would partly agree, but culinary experts have their doubts, despite various legends about recipes *after* the event. As Jane Grigson remarks, absent-minded creation might not, by definition, be repeatable.[24] Chefs are not enamoured of nonce-dishes. Perhaps it is safer to claim, with the adhocists Jencks and Silver, that 'all recipes are recombinations of similar parts in similar ways'.[25] Yet if, as some scientists drawn to the idea of chaos maintain, creation itself is something of a cock-up; if, more generally, from a myriad of mistakes, some form of natural selection picked the fittest for survival, then the poets' intuition was on the right lines. Ponge acclaimed the goat as 'an error and the perfection of this error'.[26] Randomness bothers mainly pedants. While some linguisticians have paid attention to parapraxes, a more common response is that of Makkai: 'Insofar as they still occur for reasons a linguistic study cannot consider its proper task to analyse, they can be called occurring non-occurences.'[27] (I suppose, after all, it was human beings who invented the concept of non-persons.) I would have thought that it was blatant to every user that much in language is precisely accidental. Words overlap, contaminate and magnetize each other. Impingement and infringement are central facts of linguistic life (and a dictionary tells me these two words are now synonyms; that spill-over or coincidence had crept up on me unawares). 'Contamination' suggests pollution, but in practice, like analogy and like compromise, it seems entirely natural and unworthy of censure.

Half or fully accidental blends like 'smothercate' can be caused by excess material: we try to choose between competing words and often conflate them; half-knowledge (we think two terms are related); or ignorance (we flounder). According to Bolinger, such blending may be the source of many – if not most – of the words now listed in dictionaries with 'source unknown'.[28] If many such chance coinages survive, they must have a certain inevitability. For Aitchison, synonymy confuses us. (This must be especially likely with a rich vocabulary like that of English.) She keeps stressing the role of informed guesswork in the operations of the 'mental lexicon'. She might profitably have added: in linguistic enquiry. 'Freudian slips,' she says: 'More words are prepared than normally surface. Usually the unwanted ones are suppressed but occasionally they pop up inconveniently.'[29] This is what Joyce in *Finnegans Wake* (p. 411) calls a 'freudful mistake', a useful deviation which enacts the lapsus and possibly mocks the analyst. Freud himself talked of

> a similarity of any sort between two elements of the unconscious material – a similarity between the things themselves or between their verbal presentations – is taken as an opportunity for creating a third, which is a composite or compromise idea ... The formation of substitutions and contaminations which occurs in slips of the tongue is accordingly a beginning of the work of condensation which we find taking a most vigorous share in the construction of dreams.[30]

Phonological similarity frequently causes confusion between words. No doubt some spoonerisms are simply non-, as well as nonce-, words ('flee runch' for 'free lunch'). For Fromkin such errors are difficult to reconcile with Freud's insistence on motivated slips. This seems to me too literal-minded. If we are trying simultaneously to cloak and to flash our secret desires, it is entirely likely that the strain will produce non-words, but these ought to give a clue that we indeed have something to hide. Psycholinguists are suspicious of Freud, and strike back with talk of his 'unconscious filter', *his* Freudian slip in effect, which made him want to find all parapraxes secretly meaningful. They neglect the writerly imperative. Like the good writer he was, Freud wanted his sample slips of the tongue to be interesting, which is more than can be said of the material furnished by psycholinguists, neurologists or speech-pathologists who write on this area.[31] The poet knows better. Sir John Squire, in his 'Ballade of Soporific Absorption':

> My feech will not spalter the least little jot ...
> But I'm not so think as you drunk I am.

John Skinner claimed that Lewis Carroll's well-attested stutter, together with his shyness and consequently precipitate delivery when he did speak, was instrumental in his production of portmanteau-words. Despite the squashing of this opinion by two French speech pathologists, Ferdière obviously likes the idea for its poetic suggestiveness, in which a deficiency becomes a bonus.[32] I spoke earlier of the muddling of idioms and clichés. B. F. Skinner believes that the blending of phrases is possibly commoner than that of single words (for example: 'There is no crime against it; it's no crime / there's no law against it').[33] The cause, no doubt, is the pressure of deadlines (originally, the line in a military prison on going beyond which a prisoner was liable to be shot), not just on journalists but on all of us in everyday talk. How often in conversation it is a matter of who will get in first or, once in, will hog the stage. In these circumstances, language is rushed, sound often takes precedence over sense, we anticipate a word before the sentence is ready for it, and gabbling sets in. Gaffes, 'foot-in-mouth disease', easily arise. But they can be 'blunderful'. As Hackett says, 'all speech, smooth as well as blunderful, can be and must be accounted for essentially in terms of three mechanisms ... analogy, blending, and editing'.[34] I would prefer not to think of three such dynamic processes (and note how primordial is blending) as mere 'mechanisms'. If many fine neologisms are the result of reflection and maturation, we must allow that panic can produce interesting parapraxes, as well as regression to cliché. Coleridge noted that 'it is a tendency of all languages to avail them of the opportunity given by accidental differences of pronunciation and spelling to make a word multiply on itself'.[35]

Even or especially when we mishear, we labour to make a kind of sense (as when trying to make out an imperfectly understood foreign language). Slips of the ear as well as of the tongue, mind or pen. Of course, we can mishear deliberately, as Cotgrave's gloss on a French idiom shows: '"Il fait de l'entend-trois": He answers (of purpose for the purpose) as though he understood not the question; or, he seems to listen to somewhat else; or, makes as if he had three to answer at once and therefore cannot satisfie every one.' Cotgrave calls this 'an equivocation of doubtful, of double meaning'.[36] There is a strong link here with tendentious wit, pointed punning. Spoonerism, that mixture of chiasmus, rhyme, transposition of thought and distraught mentality, can create disturbing collocations of sounds and sense, and nonce-words ('kinquering congs'), or blends (the trade-name of a sun-lotion, Tanfastic – very much a controlled skid.) A related phenomenon is the malapropism, in which someone has previously misheard, and then misquotes or mis-applies. Children coin these prolifically, as students under pressure beget howlers. 'When Molière's hero is flattered by his servant, we see him pruning himself.' This no doubt is Don Juan's castration-complex. 'The eighteenth-century episcopal novel' is presumably the genre where bishops say and do things to actresses. A perfect in-several-minds compound: 'The emphasis is by no means under-exaggerated.' An Irish bull from an English examinee: 'Mauriac's hero suffers from an over-bearing inferiority-complex.'[37] Major Richard Daley of Chicago was celebrated for malapropisms: 'harassing the atom', 'rising to the higher platitudes of achievement' (plateaux + planes + altitudes?).[38] The joy of such errors is itself a compound of superiority and fellow-feeling: we know we are equally prone to such stumbles. In French, the malapropism is often called *le pataquès*, which also means *un cuir*, or faulty liaison. We are all capable of *liaisons dangereuses*. An anxiously vigilant lady said 'on était sur le cul-vif' (for *qui-vive*: look-out): my pants were hot.[39] As Bolinger and Sears suggest, 'a folk etymology is a kind of auditory malapropism'.[40] Bolinger explicates a blend like 'glob' – 'probably a blend of "gob" and "blob". Like a swarm of bees, the swarm of words becomes self-governing, with internal forces as strong as external ones' – by claiming that it is, too, a kind of malapropism: 'When something is *protuberant* it *protrudes*, and one is tempted to say *protruberant*.'[41] We are often not at home in our native language. We domesticate, by corrupting them, loan-words, but often we fail to recognize or apply appositely obsolete or abtruse native words, and treat them too as aliens.

Finally, and appropriately (a prayer addressed to the typists and printers of this book): literals, gremlins, devils, typos (those bugs of the pre-computer age). Printers' errors are often caused by trying to make sense of the surprising. They are thus a force for cliché; printers are conditioned by stereotypes. George Orwell said in a letter to a friend: 'As there are a lot of neologisms there are bound to be many printers' errors of a stupid kind.'[42] If it is any mitigation, lexicographers too can bring chaos where none existed. 'Bycoket', the cap of state formerly worn by English kings, has been progressively garbled across many dictionaires into 'abacot'.[43]

> Be subtle, various, ornamental, clever,
> And do not listen to those critics ever
> Whose crude provincial gullets crave in books
> Plain cooking made still plainer by plain cooks,
> As though the Muse preferred her half-wit sons;
> Good poets have a weakness for bad puns.
> 　　　　　　　　　　　W. H. Auden[44]

It must be obvious by now that, though I aim to be frank, I hold no brief for plain speech, partly because I am not convinced it can ever exist.

Conclusions are full of Ogden Nash's useful coinage, aft-bodings (at last an equivalent for *l'esprit de l'escalier*): being wise, or witty, after the event.[45] I have talked of different forms of word-emergence, but said little about obsolescence, except indirectly in speaking of resurrected archaisms. No doubt millions of words have died throughout human history, each of them a neologism on its first use. Thousands have changed or added to the original meaning. Neologizing is a permanent growth-industry, and, for each of us, an endless and hopeless catching-up exercise. Dictionaries, too, cannot keep up with neologisms any more than with expanding and altering reality. If everybody went in for making up words, no doubt chaos would ensue. Some sort of tacit quota-system, or natural selection or wastage, imaginably prevails.

Why do so many feel the need, as with puns, to apologize nervously for creating new words, as if the activity were thought obscurely blasphemous, or, less ethereally, surplus to requirements? Eco, describing the Museum of the City of New York and its reconstruction of the historical Manhattan purchase-contract, writes: 'It isn't a facsimile, but – excuse the neologism – a fac-different.'[46] Using one of the oldest rhetorical metaphors, Louise Pound pleads only moderately: 'Weeds too have their place in linguistic gardens.'[47] A further qualifying approach is, again as with puns, to argue that the best neologisms are anonymous and spontaneous.[48] I admit that, like puns, good neologisms are rare birds, though I think they will never be an endangered species. In neology, the (former) Empire (the United States, the ex-subject races of the Commonwealth about whose large contribution to the constant evolution of English I have said nothing) strikes back. In my love of coinages, I may well give the impression that I mistake happy turns for full bliss; but, just as the tears of things are made up of multiple little miseries, so linguistic happiness is composed of many small felicities.

As conscious blends and accidental creations have taken us into the area of coalescence or collision, I have tried to persuade that this area is a central fact of linguistic, and indeed of social, life. Folk-etymology (and here scholars are often common folk) illustrates the human urge towards analogy, drawing together and, in a non-pejorative sense, contamination. The love of uniformity visibly at work in this vast area breeds both neologisms and clichés. It is appropriate to end with some colliding, and potentially merging, views.

Whereas, instinctively and after bitty reflection, I see neology as healthy, is it tenable to see it as a sickness in language, a cancerous growth? In this perspective, neology could be considered one of the clichés of the modern age, with its cult of the new (in advertising or in high art), its neophilia: 'Is not neological delirium becoming an attested perversion, valued as the highest intellectual refinement?'[49] Against this, Grandjouan's belief that 'the neologism is the oxygen of vocabulary', and, by implication, indispensable for life itself.[50] Foucault resorts to an oxymoron, to catch the paradoxical 'rich indigence of language'.[51] Bréal declares, and I cannot but agree: 'We all work more or less at the vocabulary of the future, whether we are scholars or unlettered.'[52] We all muck in, as we do with clichés. Finally, and soberingly, Eve Clark: 'Innovations are governed by conventions.'[53] But she has forgotten chance, slips and all the other ways language bursts out of the corsets forced on it by the very ones who should be grateful for its diversity.

21

Coda: When All is Said and Done

> Master of the word you are about to utter, slave of the word you have just spoken.
>
> Jean Paulhan[1]

The epigraph snares exquisitely our love–hate, master–slave oscillation with respect to language; and it links the two poles of this book, neologism and cliché, innovation and dependence. I have shuttled between old and new, parasitic and creative, because I am fascinated, like Sartre among many others, by the question: what do we do with what is done for and to us? Just as 'l'amour, c'est beaucoup plus que l'amour', so this study has tried to be something else. Readers may well think that there was no problem to begin with; and may have hummed

> I'll be seeing you,
> In all the old familiar places,
> That this heart of mine embraces.

Perhaps inevitably much of what I have said will have seemed like trying to teach the grandmother-reader to suck eggs. I do not apologize, although I am sorry, if this is so. I do not and cannot know what or how much you readers already know, nor to what extent you know better than I. Most orthodox conclusions of books are full of truisms (even if recently coined ones). They repeat what has already been amply demonstrated. I prefer to start a few more hares. It is one way of suggesting that nothing is fixed and final, that conclusions can be con-clusions.

The practice and the structure of this book resemble a cento. Or (that hybrid) a centaur. Or a pantomime-horse.

> And oftentimes excusing of a fault
> Doth make the fault the worser by th' excuse.[2]

Have I achieved (and would I want to?) Eliot's 'easy commerce of the old and new'? I tend to find, given my proneness to lateral lurches, all sustained thinking rather like running round a squirrel-cage. In trying to think the unthinking, I may well have not focused my thoughts steadily. I do not share the simian taste for nit-picking, though undoubtedly I fiddle and harp in other ways. I have little sympathy for those who fear bittiness. Reality is broken up. In his study of antisemitism, Sartre said that what labellers were afraid of was the very shape of reality, an object of unending approximation.[3] Fragments often have a glittering or multi-coloured beauty; a diamond is a faceted shard. I like being a magpie, but others may feel I flash my poetic licence overmuch. A book is a small self writ large. Defending puns last time out, pleading specially for clichés and neologisms this one – I could end up like Camus's Clamence, vaingloriously championing widows and orphans, after being beached by verbal and moral alcoholism in an infernal bar in Amsterdam. The danger is more apparent than real, like much in life; and the prime lesson I extract from that truth-telling and ambiguous novel is that 'nous ne sommes qu' à peu près en toutes choses' (we are but near-misses at everything).[4]

All of us recycle words, experiment with their etymological shiftiness, their unstable connotations, just as all writers feed off and adapt previous literature. We, like them, dip into public treasures; we are alike remembrancers. This naturally man-made resource, unlike fossil fuels, is inexhaustible. Clichés can have surprising vitality and long life; many neologisms die in their infancy. Does this suggest that criss-cross is the basic pattern of existence? Is it Sod's Law? Is it the price of progress? Is it yet more proof that overlap rules? 'Is it even always an advantage to replace an indistinct picture by a sharp one? Isn't the indistinct one often exactly what we need?[5] Of course, the fact that the great Ludwig said this gives it no automatic truth-value. When Sir Thomas Browne spoke of 'arthriticall analogies',[6] he was actually referring to elephants' joints, but he may also have had in various parts of his capacious mind a deep-rooted human antic. Language plays with itself, but has not yet gone blind. The funny-bone, for instance, is so called perhaps because of its *proximity* to the humerus; and more perversely because it rarely tickles when you bang your elbow. 'Tolerance', in science, industry or commerce, is a permissible deviation from the norm. The world should be one vast 'maison de tolérance'. As the French proverb has it: '*Presque* et *quasiment* empêchent de mentir' ('almost' and 'near enough' keep us from lying). The more brutal Anglo-Saxon equivalent is 'Almost was never hanged'. The medieval Latin term for this area of acceptable play or leeway was *remedium*. It could be our panacea, our placebo, our nostrum for, at root, all nostrums are ours, for the taking. Rounding up or rounding down are everyday practices in statistics, those numerical metaphors. 'Although this may seem a paradox, all exact science is dominated by the idea of approximation,' said Bertrand Russell.[7] A distinguished French mathematician, Guillebaud, wrote a book of which I understood the title better than the text: *Leçons d'à peu près* (Lessons in Rough Measures).[8] As a man of letters, Michel Tournier has a splendidly cavalier way with arithmetic. Wanting to yoke, as is his wont, far-fetched units, in the course of finding an analogy between Canada and the Sahara, he gives-or-takes two million square kilometres.[9] Analogies and metaphors make liaisons, and these can be dangerous. Tournier's *Le Roi des Aulnes* is built on funambulism.

'As near as dammit,' we say; French has 'il était moins une' (it was one short). Rigour is best left to corpses. Many scientists, and literary enviers of science, are unhappy with fuzzy edges. They dispute demarcation, like so many boiler-makers. Yet the brain itself is a grey area. I have the Scouse, and scouse, view of history and reality: chuck in the left-overs, make do. The French term for a near-pun (the commonest and usually the best kind) is *un à peu près*. We need a counterpart. Perhaps a 'wanton'. Loose, libidinous, and sometimes not up to the mark, as in 'she found me wanton'. As Viola says to Feste: 'They that dally nicely with words quickly make them wanton.'[10] For choice, I wear baggy trousers; I prefer loose fits. To conclude this credo of elbow-room at a loose end (the opposite of tight-end, those backward young male fannies that appeal so to forward women fans), are my themes bull or bullion?[11] I cannot answer that, and return to Browne: 'There are many things to be taken in soft and flexible sense, and not to be called unto the rigid test of reason.'[12] Perhaps the bull is at best or at least Irish (as I might be if my family-tree were not of the bonsai variety). I would say that approximating wordplay keeps the mind and the ears on their toes. For Plato in his *Cratylus*, language had origins both criminal (Hermes the thief as well as the communicator) and sensual (Pan the son of Hermes). Language is originally slang or cant, a secret tongue shared by all. Of course, Hermes (or Mercury) is ambiguous, mercurial. He sometimes told the truth, so that no one was ever quite sure where they were with him or it. Mercury is both slippery and poisonous. Yet the underhand can still be above board. Despite my imaged style and double meanings, I hope I have written an open book. It takes a leap – of imagination, fellow-feeling, audacity, recognition – to make or to register the play of words, to bridge these loose connections.

Rhetoric is encroachment, incest, continuum; it has no watertight compartments. All interpretation, sign-reading and evaluation are inescapably rough-and-ready. 'Proxime accessit' is humanity's best grade; we never do full justice to anything or anyone. 'Near-miss' can be pejorative (a failure) or meliorative (an honourable shot). Some people are so obsessed with the fireproof, the impeccable that you feel that, when they die, they wish to be buried in the symmetry. Taxonomists want to put all their Basques in separate exits. I would rewrite the declaration of independence as the pursuit of slap-happiness. In putting so much stress on overlap and what the French call *bavure* (slobber), however, I do not want to smudge distinctions. Cliché, however permanently with us, can damage the brain; and new words do not solve old problems. We end where we began, in messiness and the altogether.

> The climate of thought has seldom been described ...
> In thought the seasons run concurrently.[13]

My vision has multiple blind spots. Call me Lily of Lacuna.

Language is a tool. It is also a musical instrument, an old tin-can, a dustbin, a box of tricks. 'Language is a Trojan horse by which the universe gets into the mind.'[14] I oscillate between finding this sentence vacuous and enriching. Clichés will not go away, nor should we even desire them to. Use them. Know them. Use them knowingly. Neologisms are a test of our relationship with and concern for others (one test among hundreds). We have, in making new, to make ourselves understood.

I have said my piece. Everything in this garden of rhetoric, adorned by its neologgia, is lovely.[15] I await those agents of chastisement, the snakes in the grass.

Notes

CHAPTER 1 DECLARING AN INTEREST

On the title-page, the Myles na Gopaleen (Flann O'Brien) quotation is from *The Best of Myles* (Picador, London, 1979), p. 223; the Goldwyn from *The Observer*, 24 October 1948; the Pascal from *Pensées et opuscules*, ed. Leon Brunschvicg (Hachette, Paris, 1957), p. 329; the Bloy from *Exégèse des lieux communs*, ed. Jacques Petit (Gallimard, Paris, 1968) (1902–13), p. 419.

1   The conspiratorial we has also been called the 'co-optive we'.
2   Selwyn G. Champion (ed.), *Racial Proverbs* (Routledge, London, 1938), p. 8.
3   John Gross, *New York Times*, 4 April 1985, C 12.
4   Paul de Man, 'The Epistemology of Metaphor', in *On Metaphor*, ed. Sheldon Sacks (Chicago University Press, 1979), p. 16.
5   Sir Thomas Browne, *The Major Works*, ed. C. A. Patrides (Penguin, Harmondsworth, 1984), p. 60.
6   The philologist Gildersleeve, quoted in Brander Matthews, 'The Art of Making New Words', *The Unpopular Review*, IX (1918), p. 60.
7   T. E. Hope, *Lexical Borrowing in the Romance Languages* (2 vols, Blackwell, Oxford, 1971), vol. 2, p. 561.
8   Dwight Bolinger, 'Fire in a Wooden Stove: On Being Aware in Language', in *The State of the Language*, eds Leonard Michaels and Christopher Ricks (University of California Press, Berkeley, 1980), p. 387.
9   Ibid., p. 380.
10 Roland Barthes, *S/Z* (Seuil, Paris, 1970), p. 17. How really modest is this claim? Or is Barthes, like Sartre at the end of *Les Mots*, boasting of his commonalty?
11 Edwin Newman, *Strictly Speaking* (Bobbs-Merrill, Indianapolis, 1974), p. 17.

CHAPTER 2 LANGUAGE SCHOOLS, OR GROUNDING IN CLICHÉ

1   Lawrence Lerner, 'Cliché and Commonplace', *Essays in Criticism*, VI, 3 (1958), p. 251.
2   Michel de Montaigne, *Essais*, ed. Maurice Rat (3 vols, Garnier, Paris, 1962), vol. 2, p. 486.
3   Paul Pickrel, 'Identifying Clichés', *College English*, 47, 3 (1985), p. 261.

4   Charles Sorel, *Histoire comique de Francion*, ed. E. Roy (Hachette, Paris, 1926 (1622)), vol. 2, pp. 2–3. The schoolboys' notebooks were called *raptaria*.

5   See Antoine Albalat, *La Formation du style par l'assimilation des Auteurs* (Colin, Paris, 1901), p. 6. Among Richesource's publications was *Le Masque des orateurs* (Paris, 1667).

6   Michel Bréal, *Quelques Mots sur l'Instruction publique* (1872), quoted in Antoine Prost, *Histoire de l'enseignement en France (1800–1967)*, 2nd edn (Colin, Paris, 1968), p. 53. Prost himself talks of 'cette pédagogie du lieu commun [commonplace]: c'est dans les banalités que s'illustrent les parfaits rhétoriciens'. Ibid., p. 53.

7   Albalat, *La Formation du style*, pp. 67–8.

8   Ibid., p. 7.

9   Ibid., p. 5.

10 Claude Duneton, *Parler croquant* (Stock, Paris, 1982), p. 225. My colleague Geoffrey Strickland informs me that, in the seventeenth century, pupils of the Jesuits were taught both simple and ornate styles, how to tell the difference and when best to use each.

11 Louis-Ferdinand Céline, *Bagatelles pour un massacre* (Denoël, Paris, 1937), pp. 166–7.

12 Sister Joan Marie Lechner, OSU, *Renaissance Concepts of the Commonplace* (Greenwood, Westport, Conn., 1974), pp. 157–9.

13 See Richard Lederer, 'Trite as a Cliché', *Wordways*, 15, 1 (1982), pp. 11–12, 62.

14 Charles Lamb, *Works* (Simpkin, London, n.d.), p. 222.

15 Footnotes, of course, are frequently pedantic, and possibly a variant form of shoe-fetishism.

16 Dwight Macdonald, *Against the American Grain* (Gollancz, London, 1963), pp. 362–3.

17 Ibid., p. 365.

18 Parts of this paragraph are based on Macdonald, pp. 391–2; Freud, *Standard Edition*, tr. James Strachey et al. (Hogarth, London, 1955), vol. 18, pp. 264–5; and Ernest Jones, *Sigmund Freud: Life and Work* (Hogarth, London, 1956), pp. 270–1. Börne's *Sämtliche Werke* were published in New York in 1858.

19 Raymond Queneau, *Les Fleurs bleues* (Gallimard, Paris, 1978), p. 19.

20 Quoted in William Safire, *The New Language of Politics* (Random House, New York, 1968), p. 30.

21 Philip Howard, *Weasel Words* (Hamish Hamilton, London, 1978), p. 3.

22 H. L. Mencken, *The American Language* (Kegan Paul, London, 1952), Supplement 1, p. 412.

23 Dwight Bolinger, *Language: The Loaded Weapon* (Longman, London, 1980), p. 127.

24 Nathan Silver, 'Architect Talk', in *The State of the Language*, p. 325.

25 Neal R. Norrick, 'Stock Similes', *Journal of Literary Semantics*, 15, 1 (1986), p. 44.

26 Bolinger, *Language*, pp. 125–6.

27 Eric Partridge, *Usage and Abusage* (Penguin, Harmondsworth, 1963), p. 213.

28 Richard Dean Rosen, *Psychobabble* (Wildwood, London, 1978), p. 11.

29 Søren Kierkegaard, quoted in Rosen, p. 11.

30 Rosen, p. 36.
31 Ibid., p. 45.
32 Ibid., p. 68.
33 'Bafflegab' is recorded in Safire, *New Language of Politics*, p. 26.
34 Quoted in Mencken, *American Language*, Supplement 1, p. 414.
35 Bolinger, *Language*, pp. 135–6.
36 Ibid., p. 136.
37 Ibid.

CHAPTER 3   HOWLING WITH THE WOLVES

The Hulme quotation is from 'Romanticism and Classicism', *Speculations* (Routledge and Kegan Paul, London, 1977), p. 132.

1 Albert Camus, *La Chute* (Gallimard, Paris, 1956), p. 77.
2 Montaigne, *Essais*, eds Albert Thibaudet and Maurice Rat (Gallimard, Paris, 1962), p. 1045.
3 Oscar Wilde, *An Ideal Husband*, in *Plays* (Penguin, Harmondsworth, 1981), p. 168.
4 Jean-Paul Sartre, *La Nausée* (Livre de poche, Paris, 1956), p. 17. *Exister* is a swear-word in this novel. Whether it means at one moment to solidify oneself into a group-sculpture, or at another to proliferate amorphously like tree-roots, it is the very opposite of what the hero pursues: an immaterial essence, symbolized by music, the highest and wordless art. I am not equipped to discuss cliché in music, though it is full of the same old tunes.
5 Michel Schneider, *Voleurs de mots* (Gallimard, Paris, 1985), p. 229.
6 Jonathan Raban, 'Continental Divide', *The Observer*, 8 February 1987, p. 28.
7 Evan Esar, *Comic Dictionary* (Horizon, New York, 1960), p. 314.
8 Quoted by Joseph Priestley, *Memoirs* (Johnson, London, 1806–7), p. 572.
9 Anton Zijderveld, *On Clichés* (Routledge & Kegan Paul, London, 1979), p. 17.
10 Ibid., p. 26.
11 Ibid., p. 43.
12 Christopher Ricks, 'Clichés', in *The State of the Language*, p. 58.
13 Zijderveld, *On Clichés*, p. 46.
14 Ibid., p. 69.
15 Eric Partridge, *Eric Partridge in his Own Words*, ed. David Crystal (Deutsch, London, 1980), p. 134.
16 Schneider, *Voleurs de mots*, p. 136.
17 Nicholas Bagnall, *A Defence of Clichés* (Constable, London, 1985), p. 85.
18 Alfred Lord Tennyson, 'In Memoriam', VI.
19 Noah Jonathan Jacobs, *Naming-Day in Eden* (Gollancz, London, 1958), pp. 129–30.
20 D. J. Enright, *The Alluring Problem: An Essay on Irony* (Oxford University Press, 1986), p. 152.
21 Stirling Haig, *Flaubert and the Gift of Speech* (Cambridge University Press, 1986), p. 68.
22 Samuel Butler, *Note-Books*, ed. H. F. Jones (Fifield, London, 1919), p. 268.

23 Pierre Guiraud, *Les Gros Mots* (Presses Universitaires de France, Paris, 1976), pp. 114, 122.

24 Remy de Gourmont, *Le Problème du style* (Mercure de France, Paris, 1907), p. 112.

25 Jean Paulhan, *Les Fleurs de Tarbes* (Gallimard, Paris, 1973), p. 88. Such words are 'transparentes ou invisibles' (p. 92).

26 Jean-Noël Kapferer, *Rumeurs* (Seuil, Paris, 1987), p. 12. I am very much indebted to this excellent study.

27 Napoleon, *Maximes et pensées*, no. 13.

28 Kapferer, *Rumeurs*, p. 68.

29 Ibid., p. 74.

30 This whole book's foundation rests on such a pious hope.

31 Kapferer, *Rumeurs*, p. 192.

32 Gustave Flaubert, *Lettres inédites à Tourguéneff* (Editions du Rocher, Monaco, 1946), p. 105.

33 Havelock Ellis, *The Dance of Life* (Constable, London, 1923), p. 269.

34 Chamfort, *Maximes et pensées*, ed. G. Renaux (Livre de poche, Paris, 1970), p. 52.

CHAPTER 4   SWINGING BETWEEN THE POLES

The Lerner quotation is from his 'Cliché and Commonplace'. The Enright from 'Quotations', *Collected Poems 1987* (Oxford University Press, 1987), p. 344.

1 Paul Valéry, *Oeuvres*, ed. Jean Hytier (Gallimard, Paris, 1960), vol. 2, p. 801.

2 Norman Bryson, *Tradition and Desire* (Cambridge University Press, 1984), pp. 15, 30.

3 Walter Gropius, *The New Architecture and the Bauhaus* (Faber, London, 1935), p. 37.

4 Roger Ascham, *The Schoolmaster*, ed. L. V. Ryan (Cornell University Press, Ithaca, 1967), p. 50.

5 Aristotle, *Poetics*, 1448b.

6 Thomas H. Greene, *The Light in Troy* (Yale University Press, New Haven, 1982), p. 57.

7 Richard Rainolde, *The Foundacion of Rhetorike*, quoted in Lechner, *Renaissance Concepts*, p. 17.

8 Cassiodorus, Roman grammarian, quoted in Lechner, p. 38.

9 Lechner, pp. 232–3.

10 Walter Ong, *The Presence of the Word* (Yale University Press, New Haven, 1967), p. 57.

11 Ibid., p. 83.

12 Jean de La Bruyère, *Les Caractères*, eds G. Servois and A. Rébelliau (Hachette, Paris, 1906), p. 25.

13 Lautréamont, *Oeuvres complètes*, ed. M. Saillet (Livre de poche, Paris, 1963), p. 426.

14 Edmond and Jules de Goncourt, *Journal*, ed. Robert Ricatte, (Fasquelle/ Flammarion, Paris, 1956), vol. 2, p. 331.

15 Guy de Maupassant, 'Le Roman', in *Pierre et Jean*, ed. Bernard Pingaud (Gallimard, Paris, 1982), p. 56.

16 Harold Bloom, *The Anxiety of Influence* (Oxford University Press, New York, 1973), p. 148.

17 Ibid., p. 56.

18 Schneider, *Voleurs de mots*, p. 45. He is referring to La Fontaine's debonair exploitation of Aesop's fables.

19 As we will see in the Neologisms section, the modernizing of the language also became at this time a key issue.

20 Gourmont, *Le Problème du style*, p. 27.

21 As in all ages, however, the dominant genres did not kill off mixed ones like burlesque, the serio-comic, etc.

22 Michel Tournier, *Les Météores* (Gallimard, Paris, 1981), p. 101.

23 Michel Riffaterre, *Essais de stylistique structurale* (Flammarion, Paris, 1971), pp. 172–3.

24 Boris Pasternak, *Dr. Zhivago*, trs M. Hayward and M. Harari (Collins/Harvill, London, 1958), p. 394.

25 Gérard Genette, *Figures II* (Seuil, Paris, 1969), p. 136.

26 Schneider, *Voleurs de mots*, p. 333.

27 Charles Lamb, letter to B. W. Procter, 22 January 1829.

28 Rev. Charles Caleb Colton, *The Lacon* (Longman, London, 1822), vol. 2, p. 112.

29 Ibid., p. 229.

30 This point was made by Godfrey Goodman, *The Fall of Man* (1616), quoted in Robert K. Merton, *On the Shoulders of Giants: A Shandean Postscript* (Free Press, New York, 1965), p. 46.

31 Ibid., p. 74.

32 T. S. Eliot, Introductory Essay to *London* and *The Vanity of Human Wishes* (Etchells and Macdonald, London, 1930), p. 11.

33 Henry Miller, 'With Edgar Varèse in the Gobi Desert', *The Air-Conditioned Nightmare* (Grafton, London, 1986), p. 115.

34 Edward Young, *Conjectures on Original Composition*, ed. E. J. Morley (Manchester University Press, 1918), pp. 9, 13. Further references are bracketed in the text.

35 Ruth Amossy and Elisheva Rosen, *Le Discours du cliché* (CDU/SEDES, Paris, 1982), p. 27.

36 Alfred de Musset, *Oeuvres complètes en prose*, eds M. Allem and P. Courant (Gallimard, Paris, 1960), p. 301.

37 Musset, 'La Coupe et les lèvres', *Premières Poésies*, ed. M. Allem (Garnier, Paris, n.d.), p. 164.

38 Musset, 'Namouna', ibid., p. 281.

39 Lerner, 'Cliché and Commonplace', p. 265.

40 Milton, *Paradise Lost*, 1, 16.

41 Ernst Robert Curtius, *European Literature and the Latin Middle Ages*, tr. W. R. Trask (Routledge & Kegan Paul, London, 1953), p. 95.

42 Ibid., p. 96.

43 Ibid., p. 251.

44 Samuel Johnson, *The Rambler*, 2, 24 March 1750.

45 Samuel Butler, *Selections from the Note-Books*, ed. A. T. Bartholomew (Cape, London, 1930), p. 74.

46 George Steiner, *After Babel* (Oxford University Press, 1975), pp. 465–6. My italics.

47 Geoffrey Strickland, letter 7 July 1986.

48 Richard Hoftstadter, *Anti-intellectualism in American Life* (Cape, London, 1964), p. 418.

49 Wilbur S. Howell, *Logic and Rhetoric in England, 1500–1700* (Princeton University Press, 1956), pp. 23–4.

50 T. S. Eliot, *Four Quartets*, in *Collected Poems, 1909–1962* (Faber, London, 1977), p. 221.

51 Stuart Chase, *The Tyranny of Words* (Methuen, London, 1950), pp. 34, 38.

52 Ashley Montagu, 'The Language of Self-Deception', in *Language in America*, eds Neil Postman et al. (Pegasus, New York, 1969), p. 82.

53 Jean Paulhan, *Les Fleurs de Tarbes*, p. 105.

54 Ibid., p. 103.

55 Ibid., p. 108.

56 Ibid., p. 121.

57 Schneider, *Voleurs de mots*, p. 83.

58 Lerner, 'Cliché and Commonplace', p. 252.

59 I am paraphrasing freely from a source I cannot trace, possibly the Spanish poet Juan Ramón Jiménez.

CHAPTER 5 SCALING THE HEIGHTS

The Don Marquis quotation is from *Archy's Life of Mehitabel* (Doubleday, New York, 1933). It takes a lower form of life, a cockroach, to be frank in this way. The Goethe quotation is from 'Epilog zu Schillers Glocke', *Sämtliche Gedichte* (dtv, Munich, 1961), vol. 3, p. 79.

1 Viktor Shlovsky, 'Art as Technique', in *Russian Formalist Criticism*, eds L. T. Lemon and M. J. Reis (University of Nebraska Press, Lincoln, 1965), p. 7.

2 Schneider, *Voleurs de mots*, p. 60.

3 Paulhan, *Fleurs de Tarbes*, p. 36.

4 Shakespeare, *Timon of Athens*, IV, 3, 438–46.

5 Edward Ravenscroft (a prolific plagiarist and adapter), prologue to *Titus Andronicus* (1687), quoted in Alexander Lindey, *Plagiarism and Originality* (Harper, New York, 1952), p. 239.

6 Quoted ibid., p. 63.

7 Walter Ong, 'Commonplace Rhapsody: Ravisius Textor, Zwinger and Shakespeare', in *Classical Influences on European Culture, 1500–1700*, ed. R. R. Bolgar (Cambridge University Press, 1976), p. 124.

8 But see Harold O. White, *Plagiarism and Imitation during the English Renaissance* (Harvard University Press, Cambridge, Mass., 1935), p. 103, who argues that Greene was referring to Shakespeare's versatility as an actor, and not to his plagiarism, which was common in a melting-pot culture.

9 Alfred Lord Tennyson, 'Locksley Hall Sixty Years After' (1886).

10 William Wordsworth, 'To the Same Flower', *The Poems*, ed. J. O. Hayden (Penguin, Harmondsworth, 1982), p. 538.

11 George Wither, *The Shepherd's Hunting* (1615), Eclogue IV, 366ff.

12 Margery Sabin, *English Romanticism and the French Tradition* (Harvard University Press, Cambridge, Mass., 1976), pp. 153–8. 'L'Unité' is from *Contemplations*.

13 As Henry James said of Zola, *Selected Literary Criticism*, ed. Morris Shapira (Heinemann, London, 1963), p. 245.

14 Honoré de Balzac, *Les Illusions perdues*, ed. Antoine Adam (Garnier, Paris, 1954), p. 422.

15 Gustave Flaubert, 'Dictionnaire des idées reçues', in *Bouvard et Pécuchet*, ed. C. Gothot-Mersch (Gallimard, Paris, 1979), p. 537.

16 See my *Puns* (Blackwell, Oxford, 1984), pp. 55–6, for a similar process in the life of the pun-machine, the Marquis de Bièvre. Much the same happened later, after *Ubu Roi*, to Alfred Jarry.

17 For this and much other useful information on Monnier, see his *Scènes populaires*, ed. A.-M. Meininger (Gallimard, Paris, 1984).

18 Jonathan Culler, *Flaubert, The Uses of Uncertainty* (Elek, London, 1974), p. 163.

19 Flaubert, *Correspondance* (Conard, Paris, 1927), vol. 3, p. 338. Flaubert's italics.

20 Ibid., p. 359.

21 Flaubert, *Madame Bovary*, ed. P. Vernière (Cluny, Paris, 1938), p. 201.

22 Harry Levin, *The Gates of Horn* (Oxford University Press, New York, 1963), p. 258.

23 Flaubert, *Correspondance*, vol. 4, pp. 61–2.

24 *Correspondance*, vol. 8, p. 400, and vol. 1, p. 192.

25 Spinoza, *Ethics*, Part 3, Proposition VII.

26 Flaubert, *Correspondance*, vol. 2, p. 451.

27 *Correspondance*, vol. 4, p. 46.

28 *Correspondance*, vol. 3, pp. 153–4.

29 See Jean-Paul Sartre, 'Une Idée fondamentale de la Phénoménologie de Husserl: L'Intentionnalité', *Situations I* (Gallimard, Paris, 1947), pp. 31–2, for his attack on 'philosophie alimentaire'. *La Nausée*, it should be said, also houses the sublime cliché that art is salvation. The proto-Existentialist yields here to essentialism, though admittedly the credo is full of *dubito*.

30 Sartre, *L'Idiot de la famille* (3 vols, Gallimard, Paris, 1971), vol. 1, p. 617. Flaubert's conversion of people into objects and his humanization of things Sartre likens to his own concept of 'le pratico-inerte', in *Critique de la raison dialectique*.

31 Sartre, *L'Idiot de la famille*, p. 632.

32 Flaubert, *Correspondance*, vol. 2, pp. 243–4.

33 James, *Selected Literary Criticism*, p. 152.

34 Flaubert, *Par les champs et par les grèves*, in *Oeuvres complètes*, ed. B. Masson (2 vols, Seuil, Paris, 1964), vol. 2, p. 484.

35 Sartre, *Situations I*, p. 115, on Albert Camus, *Le Mythe de Sisyphe* (Gallimard, Paris, 1942), p. 29.

36 Flaubert, *Correspondance*, vol. 4, p. 96.

37 A fragment in Charles Baudelaire, *Les Fleurs du mal*, ed. Enid Starkie (Blackwell, Oxford, 1953), p. xiv.

38 Flaubert, *Correspondance*, vol. 1, p. 1.

39 Sartre, *L'Idiot de la famille*, vol. 1, pp. 633–5. An example: 'Brunettes are sexier than blondes (see Blondes): 'Blondes are sexier than brunettes (see Brunettes).' Like barbers' mirrors before and behind, this referential pingpong gets us nowhere, except into infinite regress.

40 Sartre, *L'Idiot de la famille*, p. 646.

41 Marcel Proust, 'A propos du style de Flaubert', *Contre Sainte-Beuve* (Gallimard, Paris, 1971), p. 587.

42 Shoshana Felman, *La Folie et la chose littéraire* (Seuil, Paris, 1978), pp. 164–5. Felman mentions the probable derivation of *perroquet* from the Italian diminutive for a parish-priest, *parrochetto*. Julian Barnes, *Flaubert's Parrot* (Picador, London, 1985), p. 58, cites the case of a man who believed he had become a parrot, after losing his pet; he started perching, flapping and squawking.

43 Mary McCarthy, 'On *Madame Bovary*', *Partisan Review*, 2 (1964), p. 178.

44 Flaubert, *Correspondance*, vol. 4, p. 74.

45 Felman, *La Folie*, p. 212.

46 Hugh Kenner, *Flaubert, Joyce and Beckett: The Stoic Comedians* (W. H. Allen, London, 1964), p. 19.

47 I have not checked this, but I know it for a fact.

48 Champion, *Racial Proverbs*, p. 238.

49 Guy Bechtel and Jean-Claude Carrière, *Dictionnaire de la bêtise* (Laffont, Paris, 1983), p. 11. Further references to this marvellous rag-bag are bracketed in the text.

50 Ogden Nash, 'Oh, Stop Being Thankful All Over the Place', in *New Pocket Anthology of American Verse*, ed. O. Williams (Pocket Books, New York, 1955), pp. 340–1.

51 George Eliot, *Middlemarch* (Signet, New York, 1964), p. 191.

52 From George Novack and Arthur Zipser (eds), *Who's Hooey: Nitwitticisms of the Notable* (Dutton, New York, 1932).

53 Flaubert, *Correspondance*, Supplement 3, pp. 56–7.

54 Léon Bloy, *Exégèse des lieux communs*, p. 335. Subsequent references are bracketed in the text.

55 Bloy's, *Journal*, ed. J. Bollery (Mercure de France, Paris, 1956), vol. 1, p. 27. Bloys' italics.

56 *Journal*, vol. 3, p. 314.

57 Bloy, *Lettres à Philippe Raoux* (Desclée de Brouwer, Paris, 1937), p. 156.

58 Donat O'Donnell (Conor Cruise O'Brien), *Maria Cross* (Chatto & Windus, London, 1954), p. 214.

59 Raymond Queneau, *Bâtons, chiffres et lettres* (Gallimard, Paris, 1965), p. 114. cf. other ironically praising terms for boners: gems, peach, as well as pearl.

60 Queneau, *Pierrot mon ami* (Gallimard, Paris, 1959), p. 123.

61 Ibid., p. 69.

62 Queneau, *Le Chiendent* (Gallimard, Paris, 1974), p. 22.

63 Queneau, interview with Marguerite Duras, 'Uneuravek', *L'Express*, 22 January 1959, p. 27.

64 Queneau, *Saint Glinglin* (Gallimard, Paris, 1975), p. 32.

65 Ibid., p. 33.

66 Queneau, *Les Fleurs bleues*, p. 102.

67 Ibid., p. 69.

68 Queneau, *Exercices de style* (Gallimard, Paris, 1982), p. 79.

69 Queneau, *Bâtons, chiffres et lettres*, p. 182.
70 For some bright, and darker, thoughts about quotation, see the section on it in ch. 6.
71 D. H. Lawrence, quoted in Jennifer S. Levine, 'Originality and Repetition in *Finnegans Wake* and *Ulysses*', *PMLA*, 94, 1 (1979), p. 108.
72 Levine, 'Originality and Repetition', pp. 109–10.
73 Margery Sabin, *The Dialect of the Tribe* (Oxford University Press, New York, 1987), p. 286.
74 Levine, 'Originality and Repetition', p. 114.
75 Marshall McLuhan, *From Cliché to Archetype* (Viking, New York, 1970), p. 126.
76 See *Puns*, pp. 166–9.
77 Gérard Genette, *Palimpsestes* (Seuil, Paris, 1982), p. 156. Michel Tournier likens the Surrealists to junior teachers behaving as autocrats, *Le Vent Paraclet* (Gallimard, Paris, 1977), pp. 112–13.
78 Julien Gracq, *André Breton: quelques aspects de l'écrivain* (Corti, Paris, 1948), p. 94.
79 Quoted in Amossy and Rosen, *Le Discours du cliché*, pp. 130–1.
80 Anthony Haden-Guest, *Down the Programmed Rabbit-Hole* (Hart-Davis, MacGibbon, London, 1972), p. ix.
81 Sartre, *'Portrait d'un inconnu'*, *Situations IV* (Gallimard, Paris, 1964), pp. 10–11.
82 Nathalie Sarraute, 'La Littérature aujourd'hui (II)', *Tel Quel*, 9 (1962), p. 49.
83 See Simone de Beauvoir, *La Force des choses* (Gallimard, Paris, 1963), pp. 291, 650.
84 Lewis Carroll, *The Annotated Alice*, ed. Martin Gardner (Penguin, Harmondsworth, 1978), p. 121.
85 Susan Sontag, *Against Interpretation* (Eyre & Spottiswoode, London, 1967), pp. 119, 121.
86 I come back to kitsch in ch. 11.
87 Alexander Pope, 'The Dunciad', *Poetical Works*, ed. H. Davis (Oxford University Press, 1978), p. 562.
88 Owen Barfield, *Poetic Diction: A Study of Meaning* (Faber, London, 1952), p. 134.
89 Jacques Audiberti, *Dimanche m'attend* (Gallimard, Paris, 1955), p. 75.
90 Paulhan, *Fleurs de Tarbes*, p. 107.
91 Myles na Gopaleen, *The Best of Myles*, p. 206.
92 Inverted commas often betoken a mistake or howler (cf. *sic*); and of course often *are* a mistake, as in innumerable notices such as 'Cauliflower's: 75p each'.
93 Haig, *Flaubert*, p. 117.
94 Culler, *Flaubert*, p. 165.
95 Amossy and Rosen, *Le Discours du cliché*, p. 145.

CHAPTER 6   PLUMBING THE DEPTHS: PLAGIARISM

Robert Graves's poem 'The Thieves' is from *Selected Poems*, ed. Paul O'Prey (Penguin, Harmondsworth, 1986), pp. 142–3.

1 Robert Burton's superb *Anatomy of Melancholy*, which he himself called a cento, relies on continuous interlarding.

2 Stuart Gilbert, 'Prolegomena to *Work in Progress*', in *Our Exagmination ...*, by Samuel Beckett et al. (Faber, London, 1972), p. 50.
3 Lucretius, *De Rerum Natura*, 1, 155–6.
4 Luis Buñuel, *My Last Breath*, tr. A. Israel (Fontana, London, 1985), pp. 69–70.
5 White, *Plagiarism and Imitation*, p. 10.
6 Ibid., pp. 13–14.
7 Colton, *The Lacon*, p. 229.
8 Quoted in Lindey, *Plagiarism and Originality*, p. 222.
9 Schneider, *Voleurs de mots*, pp. 86–90.
10 Ibid., p. 71.
11 André Gide, *Journal des 'Faux-Monnayeurs'*, (Gallimard, Paris, 1927), p. 85.
12 Roland Barthes, *Le Degré zéro de l'écriture* (Seuil, Paris, 1972), p. 16. On the same page he goes on to say, naïvely, that no writing is ever innocent.
13 Sir Philip Sidney, *Astrophel and Stella*, lxxiv.
14 Martial, *Epigrams*, tr. W. P. Ker (Heinemann, London, 1961), 1, 53.
15 Schneider, *Voleurs de mots*, p. 305.
16 Gourmont, *Le Problème du style*, pp. 142–3.
17 Colton, *The Lacon*, p. 142.
18 Frances Yates, *The Art of Memory* (Routledge & Kegan Paul, London, 1966).
19 Mark, II, 2.
20 Yates, *Art of Memory*, p. 274.
21 Flaubert, *Bouvard et Pécuchet*, p. 190.
22 Ernest Jones, *Sigmund Freud*, vol. 1, p. 7, mentions the anonymous paper. When Freud visited the Père Lachaise cemetery, the only graves he sought out were those of Börne and Heine (who is buried, as it happens, in the Montmartre cemetery) (Jones, p. 271). A Freudian slip with no undertones that I can detect.
23 Thomas de Quincey, *Confessions of an English Opium-Eater*, ed. A. Hayter (Penguin, Harmondsworth, 1976), p. 249.
24 See my test-score mentioned earlier.
25 Schneider, *Voleurs de mots*, p. 35. Subsequent quotations are bracketed in the text.
26 The play on the root-verb *tenir* (to hold) here is far more winning and to the point than Lacan's tortured wordplay.
27 See Jean Cau (at that time Sartre's secretary), *Croquis de mémoire*, (Julliard, Paris, 1985), pp. 91–2. The anecdote is preceded by a lethal description of Lacan's uncoordinated, frenetic keep-fit sessions in a gym, a barking creature threshing around in an invisible net (p. 89).
28 Quoted by Robert Georgin, 'Le Linguiste du monde occidental', in *Jakobson, Cahiers Cistre*, 5 (L'Age d'homme, Lausanne, 1978), p. 12.
29 Roland Barthes, *Le Plaisir du texte* (Seuil, Paris, 1973), pp. 37–8.
30 George Steiner, *Language and Silence* (Faber, London, 1967), p. 82.
31 Mark Twain, *Notebook*, ed. A. B. Paine (Harper, New York, 1935), p. 312.
32 Vladimir Jankélévitch, *L'Ironie* (Flammarion, Paris, 1964), p. 30.
33 Blaise Pascal, *Pensées et opuscules*, p. 541.
34 See Pascal, ibid., p. 327 re 'Salomon de Tultie', an anagram of Pascal's pseudonym, Louis de Montalte. My remarks here owe much to Antoine Compagnon, *La Seconde Main* (Seuil, Paris, 1979), pp. 307–9.

35 Compagnon, p. 218. Further references are bracketed in the text.
36 Ibid., p. 304. Compagnon here himself encroaches on his subject and impersonates Montaigne by using the first person to speak of him.
37 See Montaigne, *Essais*, vol. 2, pp. 387–8.
38 Compagnon, *La Seconde Main*, pp. 321–2, citing the anonymous *Parterre de la rhétorique* (C. La Rivière, Lyon, 1659), p. 38.
39 E. E. Kellett, *Literary Quotation and Allusion* (Heffer, Cambridge, 1933), p. 3.
40 Gérard Genette, *Figures II*, p. 273, referring to Proust, *A la Recherche du temps perdu* (3 vols. Gallimard, Paris, 1954), vol. 2, p. 941 and vol. 3, p. 278.
41 See Compagnon, *La Seconde Main*, p. 369, citing Baltasar Gracián, *Agudeza y Arte de ingenio*, (Aguilar, Madrid, 1907), pp. 402–4.
42 Montaigne, *Essais*, vol. 3, p. 1034.
43 The role of clichés in oral cultures is discussed in ch. 9.
44 Merton, *On the Shoulders of Giants*, p. 106.
45 Sabin, *The Dialect of the Tribe*, p. 192.
46 Kellett, *Literary Quotation*, p. 14, antedating Kristeva and company by forty years.
47 Ralph Waldo Emerson, 'Quotation and Originality', *Works* (Bell, London, 1884), vol. 3, pp. 213, 217, 224.
48 Lindey, *Plagiarism and Originality*, pp. 2, 204, 24.
49 Several of the reviewers of my *Puns*, by unacknowledged quotation, managed to appear as if they were expressing their own ideas. But, as many of mine were not mine to begin with ...
50 Melvyn Bragg, letter to *TLS*, 20 March 1987, p. 297.
51 Montaigne, *Essais*, vol. 3, pp. 1045–6.
52 Michael Edwards, 'Reports from the New Frontier', *TLS*, 21 August 1987, p. 892.
53 Schneider's *distinguo*, *Voleurs de mots*, p. 93.
54 See Ong, *Presence of the Word*, p. 85.
55 Jonathan Swift, 'Digression in Praise of Digression', *'A Tale of a Tub' and Other Satires*, ed. K. Williams (Dent, London, 1982), p. 93.
56 Ong, 'Commonplace Rhapsody', p. 93.
57 Ibid., p. 126.
58 Ibid., p. 118.
59 Ibid., p. 100.
60 Ibid., p. 101.
61 I will discuss in more detail such re-use of material in ch. 12.
62 Barthes, *Le Plaisir du texte*, pp. 45–6.
63 Barthes, 'La Mort de l'Auteur', *Mantéia*, V (1968), p. 13. D. J. Enright punctures this suave modernist naivety with his line: 'The Death of the Author: alas, an eternal verity.' 'Cross Words', *Collected Poems 1987* (Oxford University Press, 1987), p. 325.
64 Schneider, *Voleurs de mots*, p. 35.
65 Paulhan, *Fleurs de Tarbes*, pp. 34–5. Free indirect speech is a comparable alibi: 'It's up to you to guess who is thinking this.'
66 Heraclitus, fragment 2.
67 Steiner, *Language and Silence*, p. 286.
68 Schneider, *Voleurs de mots*, pp. 142–3.
69 Ibid., p. 130. Freud quoted a strange French saying which I have failed to

track down: 'Coquin qui donne plus qu'il n'a' (Anyone who gives more then he has is a rogue). See the *Freud-Jung Letters*, tr. R. Manheim, ed. W. McGuire (Hogarth/Routledge & Kegan Paul, London, 1974), pp. 28, 40. The project anticipated by a couple of decades the Surrealists' attempt at collective operations.

70 Eudora Ramsay Richardson, 'The Ubiquitous Plagiarist', *Readings in Present-Day Writers*, ed. Raymond W. Pence (Macmillan, New York, 1933), p. 324.

71 Lindey, *Plagiarism and Originality*, p. 26. The judge ruled that Curwood enjoyed no monopoly over this area.

72 Schneider, *Voleurs de mots*, p. 39.

CHAPTER 7   THE MODES OF PLAGIARISM

The epigraph is from Lord Chesterfield, *Letters to his Son* (Dent, London, 1929), p. 151.

1 Schneider, *Voleurs de mots*, p. 75. (The texts are Gérard de Nerval, 'Angélique', *Oeuvres*, eds Albert Béguin and Jean Richer (Gallimard, Paris, 1952), vol. 1, p. 239, and Charles Nodier, *Histoire du roi de Bohème et de ses sept châteaux* (Plasma, Paris, 1980), p. 27).

2 Bagnall, *A Defence of Clichés*, p. 8.

3 Genette, *Palimpsestes*, p. 438.

5 Peter Ouspensky, *The Psychology of Man's Possible Evolution* (Hodder & Stoughton, London, 1951).

5 Lindey, *Plagiarism and Originality* p. 280. Many others than myself must have felt that this was one of the Creator's less creative and more narcissistic acts.

6 Denis Diderot, *Eléments de physiologie*, in *Oeuvres complètes*, eds J. Assézat and M. Tourneux, (Garnier, Paris, 1875), vol. IX, p. 354.

7 T. S. Eliot, 'Philip Massinger', *Selected Essays* (Faber, London, 1951), p. 206.

8 Schneider, *Voleurs de mots*, p. 308.

9 Umberto Eco, *Faith in Fakes*, tr. William Weaver (Secker & Warburg, London, 1986), p. 46.

10 Eric Hoffer, *The Passionate State of Mind* (Harper, New York, 1955), p. 21.

11 Colton, *The Lacon*, p. 113.

12 Gabriel Tarde, *The Laws of Imitation* tr. E. P. Parsons (Peter Smith, Gloucester, Mass., 1962), p. xvii.

13 See Paul Nizan, *La Conspiration* (Gallimard, Paris, 1938), p. 166.

14 Though we heard earlier Queneau's dissident parrot, Laverdure. Flaubert called parrots 'winged apes' (quoted in Luc Dariosecq, 'A propos de Loulou', *French Review*, XXXI, 4 (1958), p. 322).

15 Stuart Chase, *The Tyranny of Words*, p. 34.

16 This parrot folklore is paraphrased and embroidered upon from the incomparable Gershon Legman's *Rationale of the Dirty Joke* (Panther, London, 1972), vol. 1, pp. 205–9.

17 Robert Louis Stevenson, *Memories and Portraits* (Heinemann, London, 1924), pp. 29–30.

18 On a lower but still useful level, learning to write through paraphrase has its point.

19 Proust, *Contre Saint-Beuve*, p. 594.

20 Proust, *Correspondance générale* (Plon, Paris, 1933), vol. 4, p. 230.

21 See Proust, *Pastiches et mélanges*. Lemoine swindled De Beers with his claim of having discovered how to fabricate diamonds.

22 See André Malraux, *Les Voix du silence* (Gallimard, Paris, 1951), p. 210.

23 W. H. Auden, *Collected Poems*, ed. E. Mendelson (Faber, London, 1976), p. 471.

24 Genette, *Palimpsestes*, pp. 177–81. When I translated into French a genuine novel written in English by a French writer, Georges Darien (*Gottlieb Krumm, Made in England*), this story of a con-man was suspected by some French reviewers of being a forgery.

25 Dwight Macdonald, *Parodies* (Faber, London, 1960), pp. 567, XV.

26 Claude Bouché, *Lautréamont, du lieu commun à la parodie* (Larousse, Paris, 1974), p. 188.

27 See John Fowles, for instance, *The Ebony Tower* (Little, Brown, Boston, Mass., 1974), p. 18, about an artist using parody to enrich his own canvases: 'Beneath the modernity of so many of the surface elements there stood both a homage and a kind of thumbed nose to a very old tradition.'

28 See Michel-Antoine Burnier and Patrick Rambaud, *Le Roland Barthes sans peine* (Balland, Paris, 1978).

29 René Bertelé, preface to Robert Desnos, *Corps et biens* (Gallimard, Paris, 1968), p. 7.

30 Aragon talks in these terms of his use of collages of quotations in his *Les Aventures de Télémaque*. See *Les Collages* (Hermann, Paris, 1980), pp. 120–1.

31 Kellett, *Literary Quotation*, p. 25.

32 Genette, *Palimpsestes*, p. 453, talking of 'squared literature' ('littérature au second degré').

33 Quoted in Linda Hutcheon, *A Theory of Parody* (Methuen, London, 1985), p. 5.

34 Ibid., p. 14.

35 Ibid., p. 27.

36 G. D. Kiremidjian, 'The Aesthetics of Parody', *Journal of Aesthetics and Art Criticism*, 28, 2 (1969), p. 242.

37 Hutcheon, *Theory of Parody*, p. 75.

38 See Macdonald, *Parodies*, p. 75.

39 Genette, *Palimpsestes*, p. 453.

40 Anthony Burgess, *Joysprick* (Deutsch, London, 1973), p. 146.

41 James Joyce, *Finnegans Wake* (Faber, London, 1975), pp. 181–2. On p. 170, Joyce alludes, via his 'sham' writer-figure, Shem the Penman, to the Victorian counterfeiter, Jim the Penman.

42 Schneider, *Voleurs de mots*, p. 310, referring to Freud's 'Analysis Terminable and Interminable', Standard edn, vol. 23, p. 236. With customary honesty Freud admits that analogy, here as so often, is a seductive and unreliable mode.

43 Julia Kristeva, 'Bakhtine, le mot, le dialogue et le roman', *Critique*, 239 (1967), pp. 440–1.

44 Laurent Jenny, 'La Stratégie de la forme', *Poétique*, 27 (1976), pp. 257–61.

45 In *Ficciones* (Alianza, Madrid, 1974). Page references are bracketed in the text.

46 Borges, 'About William Beckford's *Vathek*', *Other Inquisitions*, tr. R. Simms (Souvenir, London, 1973), p. 140.

47 Cf. the section on Börne, earlier.

48 Proust, *A la Recherche du temps perdu*, vol. 3, p. 436.

49 Ortega y Gasset, quoted by J. Marías, 'Metaphysics: Existence and Human Life', *Yale French Studies*, 16 (1955–6) p. 123. On one page Alain opines: 'He who does not imitate does not invent.' On another: 'It is by copying that we invent.' See Alain, *Propos*, ed. M. Savin (Gallimard, Paris, 1956), pp. 433, 221. Even Homer hiccups.

50 Sir Joshua Reynolds, *Discourses*, ed. J. J. Findlay (Blackie, London, 1906), pp. 72–3.

51 Joseph Roux, *Meditations of a Parish Priest*, tr. I. F. Hapgood (Crowell, New York, 1886), 4.40.

52 In St Jerome, *Commentary on Ecclesiastes*, 1.

53 Eco, *Faith in Fakes*, p. 146.

54 Schneider, *Voleurs de mots*, p. 16.

55 See Macdonald, *Parodies*, p. 74.

56 Rudyard Kipling, *Sixty Poems* (Hodder & Stoughton, London, 1939), p. 63.

57 Montaigne, *Essais*, ed. M. Rat (Garnier, Paris, 1958), vol. 1, p. 157.

58 Jean Giraudoux, *Siegfried*, 1, 6, in *Théâtre I* (Grasset, Paris, 1958), pp. 22–3.

59 Lautréamont, *Oeuvres complètes*, p. 402.

60 Young, *Conjectures on Original Competition*, p. 12. More arrogantly, he says later: 'Imitation is inferiority confessed; emulation is superiority contested, or denied' (p. 29).

61 Ogden Nash, 'The Japanese', in *The Penguin Book of Comic and Curious Verse*, ed. J. M. Cohen (Penguin, Harmondsworth, 1954), p. 87.

62 Walter de la Mare, 'The Ghost'.

63 D. J. Enright, 'Empire Games', *Foreign Devils* (Convent Garden Press, London, 1972), p. 17.

64 See Georges Maurevert, *Le Livre des plagiats* (Fayard, Paris, n.d.), p. 190.

65 Quoted in Nelson Adkins, '"Chapter on American Cribbage": Poe and Plagiarism', *Papers of the Bibliographical Society of America*, 42 (1948), pp. 171–2.

66 See La Fontaine, 'Le Geai paré des plumes du paon', and 'Epilogue' (Book 6), *Fables* (Crès, Paris, n.d.), pp. 122, 183.

67 Voltaire, 'Plagiat', *Oeuvres complètes de Voltaire*, (Baudoin, Paris, 1826), vol. 7, p. 357.

68 The Cavalier Marin, quoted in Lindey, *Plagiarism and Originality*, p. 238.

69 Eco, *Faith in Fakes*, pp. 174–5.

70 Schneider, *Voleurs de mots*, p. 101.

71 Paul Hazard, 'Les Plagiats de Stendhal', *Revue des Deux Mondes*, 65 (1921), p. 345.

72 Quoted in Ruth Finnegan, *Oral Literature in Africa* (Clarendon, Oxford, 1970), p. 396.

CHAPTER 8 LETDOWNS

1 The far from silent majoritarian, Anon, it would seem.
2 Hugh Kenner, *The Counterfeiters* (Johns Hopkins University Press, Baltimore, 1985), pp. 55–6.
3 Ibid., p. 48.
4 D. B. Wyndham Lewis and Charles Lee (eds), *The Stuffed Owl* (Dent, London, 1930), pp. x, xiii.
5 e. e. cummings, *collected poems* (Harcourt Brace, New York, 1938), p. 203.
6 Francis Ponge, *La Fabrique du pré* (Skira, Geneva, 1971), p. 278.
7 Don Marquis, quoted in Evan Esar, *The Comic Encyclopaedia* (Doubleday, New York, 1978), p. 553.
8 Flaubert, *Madame Bovary*, p. 304.
9 Ibid., p. 43.
10 Ibid., p. 107.
11 In Andrée Bergens (ed.), *Queneau* (Cahiers de l'Herne, Paris, 1975), p. 336.
12 See Peter Mullen, 'The Religious Speak-Easy', in *Fair of Speech: The Uses of Euphemism*, ed. D. J. Enright (Oxford University Press, 1985), p. 159.
13 Quoted in Safire, *New Language of Politics*, p. 112.
14 Quoted ibid., p. 484.
15 Whitney Bolton, *The Language of '1984'* (Blackwell, Oxford, 1984), p. 153.
16 Hugh Rawson, *A Dictionary of Euphemisms and Other Doubletalk* (Crown, New York, 1981), p. 1.
17 Jeremy Lawrence, *Unmentionables and Other Euphemisms* (Gentry, London, 1973), p. 11.
18 Ibid., p. 42.
19 Arther Herzog, *The BS Factor: The Theory and Technique of Faking It in America* (Simon & Schuster, New York, 1973), p. 178.
20 James Lincoln Collier, 'The Language of Censorship', in *Language in America*, p. 57.
21 See Queneau, *Oeuvres complètes de Sally Mara* (Gallimard, Paris, 1979), p. 22.
22 Robert Browning, 'Andrea del Sarto', *Men and Women*, p. 78. Adopted as a motto by the architect Mies van der Rohe.
23 Jean-Antoine Roucher, 'Les Mois' (1779), where, as in Thomson's *Seasons*, love of nature breeds commonplaces. Roucher was guillotined on the same day and scaffold as André Chénier, a black lesson in the superior powers of truncation.
24 Charles Dickens, *Little Dorrit*, ed. John Holloway (Penguin, Harmondsworth, 1971), p. 145.
25 Ibid., p. 152.
26 Joseph Wood Krutch, *If You Don't Mind My Saying So* (Sloane, New York, 1964).
27 Douglas Berggren, 'The Use and Abuse of Metaphor (II)', *Review of Metaphysics*, XVI, 3 (1963), p. 472.
28 Arthur Clutton-Brock, 'Dead Metaphor', Society for Pure English, Tract XI, 1924, p. 15.
29 Lerner, 'Cliché and Commonplace', p. 250.

30 William Empson, *Seven Types of Ambiguity* (Penguin, Harmondsworth, 1961), p. 25.

31 Karl Marx, preface to *Capital*, tr. B. Fowkes (Penguin, Harmondsworth, 1976), vol. 1, p. 91. The formula occurs in Pierre de l'Hommeau, *Maximes du droit français* (1614).

32 Mark Milner and Christopher Hulme, *The Guardian*, 27 October 1987, p. 1.

33 Quoted in Jeremy Lawrence, *Mix Me a Metaphor* (Gentry, London, 1972), p. 30.

34 George Orwell, 'Politics and the English Language', *Collected Essays* (Penguin, Harmondsworth, 1970), vol. 4, p. 164.

35 Evan Esar, *Humorous English* (Horizon, New York, 1961). See *Puns*, pp. 121–2 for further material on Irish Bulls.

36 See Lawrence, *Mix Me a Metaphor*, p. 37. This was apparent from Roche's papers.

37 Lerner, 'Cliché and Commonplace', p. 262.

38 Ong, 'Commonplace Rhapsody', p. 120.

39 Albert Camus, *La Peste* (Gallimard, Paris, 1947), p. 245.

40 Quoted in Bechtel and Carrière, *Dictionnaire de la bêtise*, p. 24.

41 Ogden Nash, 'A Visitor from Porlock, but, Alas, No Xanadu', *There's Always Another Windmill* (Penguin, Harmondsworth, 1972), p. 24.

42 James Rogers, *The Dictionary of Clichés* (Ward Lock, London, 1986), p. 64.

43 Horace, *Ars Poetica*, 365.

44 Jean-François Revel, *Le Style du Général* (Julliard, Paris, 1959), p. 31.

45 Susan Sontag, 'Notes on Camp', *Against Interpretation*, p. 284.

46 Quoted in Eric Buyssens, 'Tautologies', *La Linguistique*, 6, 2 (1970), p. 37.

47 Ibid., p. 42.

48 Pascal, *Pensées et opuscules*, p. 328.

49 Albert Camus, *La Chute*, p. 99.

50 See Bagnall, *Defence of Clichés*, p. 37.

51 Alfred North Whitehead, *Science and the Modern World* (Cambridge University Press, 1953), p. 5.

52 Rosemary Colie, *Paradoxia Epidemica* (Princeton University Press, 1966), p. 206.

53 Roland Barthes, *L'Obvie et l'obtus* (Seuil, Paris, 1982), pp. 45–55.

54 Ned Rorem, *Music from Inside Out* (Braziller, New York, 1967).

55 Jules Vallès, *Littérature et Révolution*, ed. Roger Bellet (Editeurs français réunis, Paris, 1969), p. 131.

56 François Mauriac, *Un Adolescent d'autrefois* (Flammarion, Paris, 1969), p. 30.

57 H. G. Wells, *The Happy Turning*, in *The Last Books of H. G. Wells*, ed. G. P. Wells (H. G. Wells Society, London, 1968), p. 22.

58 Haig, *Flaubert*, p. 17.

CHAPTER 9   A FEW WELL-CHOSEN WORDS

1 Oliver Wendell Holmes, 'A Visit to the Asylum for Aged and Decayed Punsters', *Soundings from the Atlantic* (Ticknor & Fields, Boston, 1864), p. 361.

2 Robert Louis Stevenson, *Virginibus Puerisque* (Heinemann, London, 1924), p. 18.

3   Max Jacob, *Conseils à un jeune poéte* (Gallimard, Paris, 1945), p. 19.
4   Carroll, *The Annotated Alice*, p. 269.
5   Olivier Reboul, *Le Slogan* (Complexe, Brussels, 1975), p. 18.
6   Ibid., p. 107.
7   Ibid., p. 24.
8   Quoted in Safire, *New Language of Politics*, p. 11.
9   Quoted ibid.
10 Compagnon, *La Seconde Main*, p. 284.
11 Cf. the earlier remark about the categorical infinitive in French.
12 Barthes, *Le Plaisir du texte*, p. 66.
13 Ibid., pp. 68, 70.
14 Adolf Hitler, *Mein Kampf*, tr. R. Manheim (Houghton Mifflin, Boston, 1943), p. 185 and passim.
15 Reboul, *Le Slogan*, p. 54.
16 Margaret Thatcher, interview with Anthony King, *The Listener*, 5 September 1974.
17 Thomas Carlyle, 'Chartism', *Selected Writings*, ed. A. Shelston (Penguin, Harmondsworth, 1971), p. 154. As Shelston remarks, the same references are 'used time and again to the point of cliché' (pp. 22–3).
18 Kenneth Hudson, *The Language of Modern Politics* (Macmillan, London, 1978), p. 105.
19 Ibid., p. 122.
20 Ivan Fónagy, 'Des Clichés politiques en tant que modèle d'érosion sémantique', in *From Sounds to Words*, eds K.-H. Dahlestadt et al. (Umeå, 1983), p. 112.
21 Bolinger, *Language*, p. 115.
22 Orwell, 'Politics and the English Language', p. 159. Subsequent page references are bracketed in the text.
23 Ricks, 'Clichés', pp. 55–6.
24 Orwell, *Nineteen Eighty-Four* (Penguin, Harmondsworth, 1956), p. 68.
25 Anthony Burgess, *1985* (Arrow, London, 1984), p. 43.
26 Ibid., p. 44.
27 Bolton, *Language of '1984'*, p. 152. A kind of backfiring homeopathy.
28 Lionel Duisit, *Satire, parodie, calembour* (Anma Libri, Saratoga, Calif., 1978), pp. 106–7. See also my section on advertising language in *Puns*, pp. 130–41.
29 Bolinger, *Language*, pp. 17–18.
30 Marie-José Jaubert, *Slogan mon amour* (Barrault, Paris, 1985), p. 11.
31 Reboul, 'Le Slogan et les fonctions du langage', *Le Français dans le monde*, 143 (1979), p. 26.
32 Pope, *An Essay on Man*, 348ff.
33 Barbara and Wolfgang Mieder, 'Tradition and Innovation: Proverbs in Advertising', *Journal of Popular Culture*, 1 (1977), p. 308. Subsequent references are bracketed in the text.
34 Ibid., p. 317, quoting Priscilla Denby, 'Folklore in Mass Media', *Folklore Forum*, 4 (1971), pp. 113–25.
35 Leo Spitzer, 'American Advertising Explained as Popular Art', *A Method of Interpreting Literature* (Smith College, Northampton, Mass., 1949), p. 127.
36 Champion, *Racial Proverbs*, p. 321.

37 Francis Ponge, 'My Creative Method', *Méthodes* (Gallimard, Paris, 1961), p. 38.
38 Champion, *Racial Proverbs*, pp. xv–xvii. Subsequent references are bracketed in the text.
39 Isaac Disraeli, *Curiosities of Literature* (Routledge, London, 1858), vol. 3, pp. 38, 34.
40 This excellent blend, by Carolyn Wells, is quoted in Harold Wentworth, 'Blend words in English' (Ph.D. thesis, Cornell University, 1934), p. 5.
41 Reboul, 'Le Slogan', p. 23.
42 Kenneth Burke, *The Philosophy of Literary Form*, 3rd edn (University of California Press, Berkeley, 1973), pp. 295–300.
43 Shakespeare, *Much Ado About Nothing*, V, i, 17. The speaker, Leonato, expresses scorn for such an idea.
44 Champion, *Racial Proverbs*, p. 321. A Swiss-German item.
45 Sabin, *Dialect of the Tribe*, p. 22. Haig (*Flaubert*, p. 25) coins the term 'theolocutives' for Flaubert's own more Olympian maxims.
46 Barthes, *Mythologies*, pp. 263–4.
47 Champion, *Racial Proverbs*, p. 360. A Spanish proverb.
48 Denis Saurat, 'Introduction to the Proverbs of France', in Champion, *Racial Proverbs*, p. xlvii.
49 Claude Roy, 'La Sagesse des nations', *L'Homme en question* (Gallimard, Paris, 1960), pp. 41–8.
50 Sartre, *L'Existentialisme est un humanisme* (Nagel, Paris, 1968), pp. 13–14.
51 Simone de Beauvoir, *L'Existentialisme et la sagesse des nations* (Nagel, Paris, 1963), p. 28.
52 I first heard this on Rowan and Martin's *Laugh-In*, but that joke factory recycled many used parts.
53 Jacobs, *Naming-Day in Eden*, p. 135.
54 Almuth Grésillon and Dominique Maingueneau, 'Polyphonie, proverbe et détournement, ou, un Proverbe peut en cacher un autre', *Langages*, 73 (1984), p. 116.
55 Quoted ibid., p. 122.
56 See Pierre Guiraud, 'Etymologie et *ethymologia*', *Poétique*, 11 (1972), pp. 408–9.
57 See Finnegan, *Oral Literature*, pp. 188–90.
58 Jean Paulhan, *Les Hains-Tenys* (Gallimard, Paris, 1939), p. 30.
59 Elinor Keenan, 'A Sliding Sense of Obligatoriness: The Polystructure of Malagasy Oratory', in *Political Language and Oratory in Traditional Society*, ed. M. Bloch (Academic, London, 1975), pp. 93–112.
60 Finnegan, *Oral Literature*, pp. 409–17.
61 Ong, *Presence of the Word*, p. 85.
62 Ibid., pp. 134–5.
63 Ong, 'Commonplace Rhapsody', p. 115.
64 Ibid., p. 108.
65 G. K. Chesterton, 'In Defence of Slang', *The Defendant* (Dent, London, 1907), p. 146.
66 Sabin, *Dialect of the Tribe*, p. 40.
67 Logan Pearsall Smith, *Words and Idioms* (Constable, London, 1925), p. 187. Further quotations are bracketed in the text.

68 Adam Makkai, *Idiom Structure in English* (Mouton, The Hague, 1972), p. 171.

69 Pierre Guiraud, *Les Locutions françaises* (Presses Universitaires de France, Paris, 1961), p. 7. Further references are bracketed in the text.

70 H. W. Fowler, *A Dictionary of Modern English Usage*, rev. Sir E. Gowers (Oxford University Press, 1983), p. 554.

71 O. Henry, *Whirligigs*, in *Complete Works* (Doubleday, New York, 1953), vol. 2, p. 126.

72 Eugène Ionesco, interview with Denise Bourdet, *Revue de Paris*, December 1961, p. 141.

73 Oliver Wendell Holmes, *Over the Teacups* (Sampson Low, London, 1891), p. 42.

74 Paul Valéry, *Cahiers*, ed. J. Robinson (Gallimard, Paris, 1974), p. 1079.

75 Théodore de Banville, *Petit Traité de poésie française* (Fasquelle, Paris, 1899), p. 76.

76 Philippe Martinon, *Dictionnaire des rimes françaises* (Larousse, Paris, 1962).

77 Raymond Queneau, 'Affreux mur', *L'Instant fatal* (Gallimard, Paris, 1966), p. 139.

CHAPTER 10   HABITS OF MIND/ODIOUS COMPARISONS

1 José Ortega y Gasset, *The Revolt of the Masses* (Allen & Unwin, London, 1961), p. 102.

2 Quoted in Etienne Souriau, 'Sur l'esthétique des mots et des langages forgés', *Revue d'Esthétique*, 18 (1965), p. 25.

3 G. W. Turner, *Stylistics* (Penguin, Harmondsworth, 1973), p. 112.

4 Bolinger, *Language*, p. 143.

5 Bolinger, 'Metaphorical Aggression: Bluenoses and Coffin-Nails', in *Language in Public Life*, eds J. E. Alatis and G. R. Tucker (Georgetown University Press, Washington, 1979), p. 261.

6 George Ade, *Hand-made Fables* (Doubleday, Page, New York, 1920).

7 George Crabbe, *The Borough*, 1, 138.

8 William James, *Psychology* (Macmillan, London, 1905), p. 143.

9 Bolinger, *Language*, p. 103.

10 Henri Bergson, *Le Rire* (Presses Universitaires de France, Paris, 1975), p. vi. Further references are bracketed in the text.

11 Diderot, 'De la Poésie dramatique', *Oeuvres esthétiques*, ed. Paul Vernière (Garnier, Paris, 1959), p. 218.

12 Diderot, *Correspondance*, ed. G. Roth (Minuit, Paris, 1956), vol. 2, p. 97.

13 The English counterpart is crambo, from Juvenal's *crambe repetita* (cabbage dished up again): stale repetition. (Juvenal, *Satires*, vii, 154.)

14 See Molière, *Théâtre complet*, ed. Robert Jouanny (Garnier, Paris, 1960), vol. 1, pp. 411, 486 and 501.

15 Flaubert, *Correspondance*, vol. 5, p. 95.

16 Paul Valéry, *Monsieur Teste* (Gallimard, Paris, 1946), p. 14.

17 Valéry, 'L'Idée fixe', *Oeuvres*, vol. 2, p. 206. Further references are bracketed in the text.

18 Quoted in Maurice Rheims, *Le Dictionnaire des mots sauvages* (Larousse, Paris, 1969), p. 542.

19 Walter Lippmann, *Public Opinion* (Macmillan, New York, 1947), p. 104.
20 Ibid., p. 156.
21 See Freud, *The Interpretation of Dreams*, ed. J. Strachey (Penguin, Harmondsworth, 1976), pp. 429, 438, 451, 564.
22 Lippmann, *Public Opinion*, p. 352.
23 Barthes, *Le Plaisir du texte*, p. 69.
24 Etiemble, *Racismes* (Arléa, Paris, 1986), p. 213.
25 Ibid., p. 216.
26 Edward W. Said, *Orientalism* (Penguin, Harmondsworth, 1985), p. 328.
27 Ibid., p. 326.
28 A. A. Roback, *A Dictionary of International Slurs* (Sci-Art, Cambridge, Mass., 1944), pp. 313–15.
29 Ibid., p. 338.
30 See Eric Partridge, *Dictionary of Historical Slang* (Penguin, Harmondsworth, 1978), p. 584.
31 See Christie Davies, 'Language, Identity and Ethnic Jokes about Stupidity', *International Journal of the Sociology of Language*, 65 (1987), pp. 39–52.
32 Gelett Burgess, *Burgess Unabridged* (Simpkin, London, 1914), p. 108.
33 See Jacques Le Goff, 'Les Mentalités, une histoire ambiguë', in *Faire de l'histoire*, eds J. Le Goff and P. Nora (Gallimard, Paris, 1974), vol. 3, pp. 83–4.
34 Roback's coinage for racial slurs. It presumably means 'seeing other races as inferior' (one of the several meanings of *phaulos*).
35 Peter Farb, *Word Play* (Cape, London, 1974), p. 185.
36 Valery Larbaud, *Sous l'invocation de Saint Jérôme* (Gallimard, Paris, 1946), p. 44.
37 Ibid., p. 74.
38 Freud, *The Interpretation of Dreams*, p. 663.
39 Pierre Guiraud, *Les Gros Mots*, p. 114.
40 I will discuss this topic further in the Neologisms section.
41 Sabin, *Dialect of the Tribe*, p. 12.
42 Amossy and Rosen, *Le Discours du cliché*, p. 14.
43 Rivarol, *Discours sur l'universalité de la langue française*, 1784.
44 Charles Bally, *Linguistique générale et linguistique française*, 3rd edn (Francke, Berne, 1950), p. 344.
45 Robert Graves and Alan Hodges, *The Reader Over Your Shoulder*, (Cape, London, 1955), pp. 29–30.
46 Richard Cobb, *A Second Identity* (Oxford University Press, 1969), p. 245.
47 Finnegan, *Oral Literature*, p. 447, quoting C. Hayford, *Gold Coast Native Institutions* (London, 1903), p. 70.
48 Gerald Brenan, *Thoughts in a Dry Season* (Cambridge University Press, 1978), p. 96. He goes on: 'French, on the other hand, being a language more given to abstraction, contains fewer of these poisons, which makes it a better language for purposes of exposition.'
49 George Santayana, 'Aversion from Platonism', *Soliloquies in England* (Constable, London, 1923), pp. 18–19.
50 James Thurber, in *Writers at Work*, ed. M. Cowley, 1st series (Mercury, London, 1962), p. 88.
51 Harold Rosenberg, *The Tradition of the New* (Thames and Hudson, London, 1962), p. 87. Further references are bracketed in the text.

CHAPTER 11   POP EYES

1 W. H. Auden, *The Dyer's Hand* (Faber, London, 1963), p. 100.
2 Herbert H. Clark and Richard Gerrig, 'Understanding Old Words with New Meanings', *Journal of Verbal Learning and Verbal Behaviour*, 22, 5 (1983), pp. 591–608.
3 Baudelaire, 'Salon de 1846', *Curiosités esthétiques*, ed. Henri Lemaître (Garnier, Paris, 1962), pp. 163–4.
4 Ibid., p. 173.
5 According to Edouard Fournier, *L'Esprit des autres* (Dentu, Paris, 1857), p. 1.
6 Philip Thompson, foreword to Philip Thompson and Peter Davenport, *The Dictionary of Visual Language* (Penguin, Harmondsworth, 1982), p. vii.
7 Ibid., p. 196. As I suggested earlier, repetition in adverts, also, is a battering-ram of banality.
8 Lawrence, *Unmentionables*, p. 70.
9 Thompson and Davenport, *Dictionary of Visual Language*, p. 163.
10 Louis Aragon, *Les Collages*, p. 119.
11 Ibid., p. 132.
12 Stefan Kanfer, *Time*, 7 September 1970, p. 63.
13 Marcel Duchamp, *Duchamp du signe*, eds M. Sanouillet and E. Patterson (Flammarion, Paris, 1975), pp. 181–2. Further references are bracketed in the text.
14 Eliane Formentelli, 'Notes sur la pensée rhapsodique', *Revue d'Esthétique*, 3/4 (1978), p. 75 – a special number on collage.
15 Bagnall, *Defence of Clichés*, p. 80.
16 Chris Baldick, 'From folk to fairy-tale', *TLS*, 29 January–4 February 1988, p. 108.
17 Zijderveld, *On Clichés*, pp. 88–9.
18 Curtis Brown, *Star-Spangled Kitsch* (Universe, New York, 1975), p. 38. Further quotations are bracketed in the text.
19 Gillo Dorfles, *Kitsch: An Anthology of Bad Taste* (Studio Vista, London, 1969), p. 53.
20 Eco, *Faith in Fakes*, p. 7.
21 Walter Karp, 'A Fascination with the Commonplace', *American Heritage* 37 (1986), p. 42.
22 Cabrera Infante, *Infante's Inferno* (Faber, London, 1985), p. 359.
23 James Bone, 20 December 1945.
24 Lerner, 'Cliché and Commonplace', pp. 254, 252.
25 Bob Hodge and Roger Fowler, 'Orwellian Linguistics', in *Language as Control*, eds R. Fowler et al. (Routledge & Kegan Paul, London, 1979), p. 17.
26 Bagnall, *Defence of Clichés*, p. 71.
27 Gelett Burgess, *Are You a Bromide?* (Huebsch, New York, 1908). Further references are bracketed in the text. In a footnote Burgess acknowledges a debt to Frank O'Malley for the blend 'bromidiom' (p. 22).

CHAPTER 12   A DEAD-AND-ALIVE HOLE

1 Baudelaire, 'Madame Bovary', *Curiosités esthétiques*, p. 644.
2 Louis Aragon, *Traité du style* (Gallimard, Paris, 1928), p. 66–7. I am tempted to change 'l'humanité' in the original to *L'Humanité*, to which Aragon soon after this text contributed much mindless copy.

3 Remy de Gourmont, 'Le Cliché', *Esthétique de la langue française* (Mercure de France, Paris, n.d.), p. 302. Further references are bracketed in the text.

4 Paulhan, *Fleurs de Tarbes*, p. 31. Other references are bracketed in the text.

5 Gustave Lanson, *L'Art de la prose* (Fayard, Paris, n.d.), p. 124. Jean de la Bruyère, 'Discours à l'Académie', *Les Caractères*, eds G. Servois and A. Rébelliau (Hachette, Paris, 1906), p. 512.

6 *Fowler's Modern Usage*, p. 44.

7 Bagnall, *Defence of Clichés*, p. 101.

8 Gérard de Nerval, *Aurélia* (Editions du Rocher, Monaco, 1946), p. 78.

9 Geoffrey Strickland, *Structuralism or Criticism?* (Cambridge University Press, 1981), p. 49.

10 Régine Pietra, 'Lieux communs', *Littérature*, 65 (1987), p. 105.

11 Ibid., p. 102.

12 Michel Riffaterre, *Essais de stylistique structurale*, p. 178, quoting Aragon, *Traité du style*, p. 87.

13 Ibid., p. 163.

14 Anne Herschberg-Pierrot, 'Problématiques du cliché: sur Flaubert', *Poétique*, 43 (1980), p. 335.

15 Samuel Beckett, *Watt* (Calder, London, 1963), p. 61.

16 A graffito, quoted in R. Reisner and L. Wechsler (eds), *Encyclopaedia of Graffiti* (Macmillan, New York, 1974), p. 162.

17 Dean Inge, *Wit and Wisdom* (Longmans, London, 1927), preface.

18 Thomas Bailey Aldrich, 'Originality', in *An Anthology of New England Poets*, ed. L. Untermeyer (Random House, New York, 1948), p. 509.

19 Schneider, *Voleurs de mots*, p. 358.

20 Ralph Waldo Emerson, 'Self-Reliance', *Works* (Bell, London, 1884), vol. 1, p. 19. Further references are bracketed in the text.

21 Sabin, *English Romanticism*, p. 20. To re-employ Orwell's heavily-used but still potent slogan: some are more equal than others.

22 Henry David Thoreau, *Walden* (New American Library, New York, 1960), p. 216.

23 See Anne-Marie Perrin-Naffakh, *Le Cliché de style en français moderne* (Presses de l'Université de Lille III, 1985), p. 525.

24 Baudelaire, 'Salon de 1859', *Oeuvres critiques* (Gallimard, Paris, 1976), p. 1043.

25 Baudelaire, *Curiosités esthétiques*, p. 482. Further references are bracketed in the text.

26 Bagnall, *Defence of Clichés*, p. 57.

27 Eugène Ionesco, *Le Rhinocéros* (Gallimard, Paris, 1959), p. 199.

28 Farb, *Word Play* (Cape, London, 1974), p. 222.

29 Lippman, *Public Opinion*, pp. 80–1.

30 André Gide, *Journal, 1889–1939* (Gallimard, Paris, 1951), pp. 897–8.

31 Ibid., p. 42.

32 Valéry, *Cahiers*, vol. 2, p. 1002.

33 Barthes, *Le Plaisir du texte*, p. 35.

34 Perrin-Naffakh, *Le Cliché de style*, p. 259.

35 Schneider, *Voleurs de mots*, p. 286.

36 Ibid., p. 333.

37 André Malraux, *La Condition humaine* (Livre de poche, Paris, 1946), pp. 46–7.

38 James Joyce, *Ulysses* (Penguin, Harmondsworth, 1971), pp. 197–8.
39 Roger Cardinal, 'Singular Visions', in *Outsiders* (Arts Council, London, 1979), pp. 21, 23.
40 Quoted in W. Jackson Bate, *The Burden of the Past and the English Poet* (Chatto & Windus, London, 1971), pp. 3–4. Further references are bracketed in the text.
41 Charles Jencks and Nathan Silver, *Adhocism* (Anchor, New York, 1973), p. 65. Like Koestler, to whom they confess a large debt, they speak of 'dissociation and recombination'.
42 Ibid., p. 27.
43 François Jacob, 'Evolution and Tinkering', *Science*, 196, 4295 (1977), p. 1164. A nice pun on 'stock'.
44 Ibid.
45 Ibid., p. 1166.
46 Examples from Advanced Level French Literature examination scripts.
47 See Claude Lévi-Strauss, *La Pensée sauvage*, (Plon, Paris, 1962), p. 26.
48 Arthur Yap, 'commonplace', *commonplace* (Heinemann, Singapore, 1977), p. 29.
49 Twain, *Notebook*, p. 237.
50 Victor Shlovsky, 'Art as Technique', pp. 12–13.
51 Ibid., p. 17.
52 William Empson, 'The Beautiful Train', *Collected Poems* (Hogarth, London, 1984), p. 64.
53 Cabrera Infante, *Infante's Inferno*, p. 252.
54 Jules Vallès, *Le Bachelier*, ed. Walter Redfern (University of London Press, 1972), p. 171.
55 There are variants of this attributed statement, but this one suits my purposes.
56 Attributed variously to John Buchan or H. E. Fosdick.
57 Jencks and Silver, *Adhocism*, p. 107.
58 Reisner and Wechsler, *Encyclopaedia of Graffiti*, p. 238.
59 C. Bürli-Storz, *Deliberate Ambiguity in Advertising* (Francke, Berne, 1980), p. 9.
60 George Bertram Milner, 'Homo Ridens: Towards a Semiotic Theory of Humor and Laughter', *Semiotica*, 1, V (1972), pp. 17–18.
61 Marcel Benabou, 'Un Aphorisme peut en cacher un autre', in *Bibliothèque Oulipienne*, ed. Jacques Roubaud (Slatkine, Geneva, 1981), pp. 281–97.
62 Pat Rogers, 'Swift and the Revival of Cliché', in *The Character of Swift's Satire*, ed. Claude Rawson (Associated Universities Press, London, 1983), p. 209. Further references are bracketed in the text.
63 Cabrera Infante, *Holy Smoke* (Faber, London, 1986), p. 50.
64 Gershon Legman, *No Laughing Matter: Rationale of the Dirty Joke* (Second Series) (Granada, London, 1978), p. 1121.
65 Zijderveld, *On Clichés*, p. 102.
66 Marcus Cunliffe, 'Newness as Repudiation', *TLS*, 30 May 1980, pp. 615–16.
67 Jesse Bier, *The Rise and Fall of American Humor* (Holt, Rinehart & Winston, New York, 1968), pp. 3, 339.
68 I can barely forgive the *Times Higher Education Supplement* for titling an article of mine championing puns 'Excuse the pun, but…'.

69 Pierre Reverdy, 'Aube sinistre', *Main d'oeuvre* (Mercure de France, Paris, 1949), p. 426.

70 Thomas Hood, 'Miss Kilmansegg and her Precious Leg', *Poetical Works* (Warne, London, n.d.), p. 588.

71 An excellent coinage, down to Keith Foley of Strathclyde University, in a letter, 18 June 1987.

72 Pope, footnote to *Dunciad*, p. 563.

73 Harriet Weaver, quoted in Macdonald, *Against the American Grain*, p. 140.

74 Ibid., p. 138.

75 Galen Strawson, 'Neither the Nice nor the Good', *TLS*, 8 February 1985, p. 140.

76 Christopher Ricks, *The Force of Poetry* (Clarendon, Oxford, 1984), p. 2.

77 *Freud/Jung Letters*, p. 220. Ernst Gombrich comments on this passage in *Tributes* (Phaidon, Oxford, 1984), p. 106.

78 S. A. Leavy, in *Interpreting Lacan*, eds J. H. Smith and W. Kerrigan (Yale University Press, New Haven, 1983), p. 13.

79 Evan Esar's definition of the pun in his *Comic Dictionary*, p. 237.

80 Arthur Schopenhauer, *Essays and Aphorisms*, tr. R. J. Hollingdale (Penguin, Harmondsworth, 1970), p. 201.

81 See Emerson, 'The Poet', *Complete Works* (Bell & Daldy, London, 1866), vol. 1, p. 162, and Max Müller, *Biographies of Words* (Longman, London, 1888), p. x.

82 George Lakoff and Mark Johnson, *Metaphors We Live By* (Chicago University Press, 1980), p. 8.

83 Ibid., p. 55.

84 Bagnall, *Defence of Clichés*, p. 62.

85 McLuhan, *From Cliché to Archetype*, pp. 58–9.

86 Riffaterre, *Essais de stylistique structurale*, p. 186.

87 Ricks, 'Clichés', p. 58.

88 Ricks, *Force of Poetry*, pp. 3–5.

89 McLuhan, *From Cliché to Archetype*, pp. 204–5.

90 Eco, *Faith in Fakes*, p. 209.

91 John Middleton Murry, *Countries of the Mind* (Second Series) (Oxford University Press, 1931), pp. 1–2.

92 Michael Frayn, *Constructions*, (Wildwood House, London, 1974), no. 219.

93 Henry de Montherlant, quoted in René Georgin, *Jeux de mots*, (A. Bonne, Paris, 1957), p. 147.

94 Max Jacob, *Conseils à un jeune poète*, p. 19.

95 André Gide, *Attendu que...* (Charlot, Algiers, 1943), p. 174.

96 Paulhan, *Fleurs de Tarbes*, p. 93.

97 Kenneth Hudson, *Language of Modern Politics*, p. 140.

98 Frank Sullivan, *Sullivan at Bay* (Dent, London, 1939), p. 24.

99 Camus, *La Chute*, p. 141.

100 Steiner, *After Babel*, p. 123.

101 George Moore, *Avowals* (Heinemann, London, 1924), pp. 285–6.

102 I purloin the title of J. P. Stern's book on Lichtenberg.

103 Bolinger, *Language*, p. 119.

104 Elbert Hubbard, *Roycroft Dictionary and Book of Epigrams* (Roycrofters, East Aurora, NY, 1923).

105 Schneider, *Voleurs de Mots*, p. 280.
106 Eric Partridge, *Eric Partridge in His Own Words*, p. 140.
107 John Bunyan, preface to *Holy War*, 1682.
108 Herschberg-Pierrot, 'Problématiques du cliché', p. 334.
109 Amossy and Rosen, *Le Discours du cliché*, p. 140.
110 Virgil, *Aeneid*, VI, 743.

CHAPTER 13   CHANGE OF GEAR IN THE MELTING-POT

1 Antoine de Saint-Exupéry, *Terre des hommes*, in *Oeuvres* (Gallimard, Paris, 1953), p. 169.
2 Friedrich Nietzsche, *The Will to Power*, tr. A. Ludovici (Foulis, Edinburgh, 1888), p. 55.
3 Cabrera Infante, *Infante's Inferno*, p. 284.
4 Walter Kaufman (ed.), *The Portable Nietzsche* (Viking, New York, 1975), p. 109.
5 Noam Chomsky, *Syntactic Structures* (Mouton, The Hague, 1975), p. 15.
6 Leon Mead, *Word-Coinage* (Crowell, New York, 1902), p. 49.
7 Flaubert, *Dictionnaire des idées reçues*, p. 543.

CHAPTER 14   FIRST WORDS

1 *Webster's Third New International Dictionary*, 1961.
2 Mencken, *American Language*, Supplement 1, p. 363.
3 Edgar Z. Friedenberg, *The Vanishing Adolescent* (Beacon, Boston, 1967), p. 3.
4 Spinoza, *Ethics*, III, xxii.
5 See George Orwell, 'New Words', *Collected Essays*, vol. 2, pp. 17–27.
6 Ferdinand Brunot and Charles Bruneau, *Précis de grammaire historique de la langue française* (Masson, Paris, 1933), pp. 170–5.
7 Quoted in Leo Spitzer, 'The Individual Factor in Linguistic Innovations', *Cultura Neolatina*, 16, 1 (1956), p. 72. Strict grammar would require here a hiccuping *est morte* in both parts of the phrase.
8 Hervé Bazin, *Le Matrimoine* (Seuil, Paris, 1967), p. 141.
9 Kristoffer Nyrop, *Grammaire historique de la langue française* (Picard, Paris, 1899–1930), vol. 1, p. 3.
10 Louis Guilbert, *La Créativité lexicale* (Larousse, Paris, 1975), pp. 49–50.
11 John Algeo, 'The Taxonomy of Word Making', *Word*, 29 (1978), p. 128.
12 Brander Matthews, 'The Art of Making New Words', p. 67.
13 Spitzer, 'The Individual Factor', p. 76. Further references are bracketed in the text.
14 Pierre Widal, 'Pour une physiologie du néologisme', *Meta*, 18 (1973), p. 357.

CHAPTER 15   ILLUSTRATION OF DEFENCE

1 Pope, 'An Essay on Criticism', *Poetical Works*, p. 73.
2 Keith Foley, letter of 1 May 1987. I would prefer the spelling 'neo-logarhythm', to avoid contamination with mathematics.
3 See Raymond Lebègue, 'Dépérissement et mort du néologisme (d'Henri II

à Louis XIII)', *Cahiers de l'Association Internationale des Etudes françaises*, 25 (1973), pp. 35–6.

4   Ibid., p. 39.

5   Ibid., p. 34.

6   Pierre Guiraud, 'Néologismes littéraires', *La Banque des mots*, 1 (1971), pp. 25, 27.

7   See Wendy Ayres-Bennett, *Vaugelas and the Development of the French Language* (Modern Humanities Research Association, London, 1987), pp. 127–8, 123.

8   Alexis François, *Histoire de la langue française cultivée* (Jullien, Geneva, 1959), vol. 1, p. 301.

9   Matthews, 'The Art of Making New Words', p. 61.

10 Bouhours, quoted in Ferdinand Brunot, *Histoire de la langue française* (Colin, Paris, 1911), vol. IV.1: *La Langue classique*, p. 444.

11 Ibid., p. 445.

12 See Jean-Pol Caput, *La Langue française: histoire d'une institution* (Larousse, Paris, 1972–5), vol. 2, p. 30.

13 See Jean-Jacques Rousseau, *Emile*, eds F. and P. Richard (Garnier, Paris, 1957), p. 402.

14 Pierre Choderlos de Laclos, *Les Liaisons dangereuses*, ed. René Pomeau (Garnier-Flammarion, Paris, 1966), p. 37.

15 Quoted in Brunot, *La Langue classique*, p. 448.

16 Ibid.

17 Ibid., p. 449.

18 Ibid., p. 514.

19 Jacques-Olivier Grandjouan, *Les Linguicides* (Didier, Paris, 1971), p. 270.

20 Brunot, *La Langue classique*, p. 515.

21 See John Wilkins, *Essay Towards a Real Character, and a Philosophical Language*, 1668.

22 Daniel Defoe, 'Of Academies', *An Essay upon Several Subjects*, 1702.

23 Joseph Addison, *Spectator*, 4 August 1711.

24 Lord Chesterfield, *The World*, 28 November 1754.

25 Eric Partridge, preface to his edition of Swift's *Polite Conversation* (Deutsch, London, 1963), p. 12.

26 Sverker Bengtsson, *La Défense organisée de la langue française* (Almqvist & Wiksells, Uppsala, 1968), p. 157.

27 Graves and Hodge, *The Reader Over Your Shoulder*, p. 18. cf. Napoleon's dictum, variously reported: 'Impossible n'est pas français', to General Lemarois, 9 July 1813.

28 J. Y. T. Greig, *Breaking Priscian's Head* (Kegan Paul, London, 1928), pp. 21, 96. Priscian (*c*. AD 500) was a Roman grammarian whose works were used as a model for teaching for centuries. For Greig, he epitomizes the baleful influence of Latin grammar and its dusty champions over usage.

29 Alexis François, *Histoire de la langue française* (Colin, Paris, 1932), vol. VI, 2:1: *La Langue postclassique*, pp. 1055, 1067, 1127.

30 Voltaire, letter of 31 August 1749.

31 François, *La Langue postclassique*, pp. 1153–4.

32 François, *Histoire de la langue française cultivée*, p. 45.

33 Charles Bordes, *Observations sur la langue française*, 1760.

34 Caput, *La Langue française*, vol. 2, p. 34.
35 Louis-Sébastien Mercier, *Dictionnaire d'un polygraphe*, ed. G. Bollème (Union Générale d'Editions, Paris, 1978), pp. 229–30, 238, 243, 289–90, 291.
36 Mercier, quoted in François, *La Langue postclassique*, p. 1155.
37 Michel Riffaterre, 'La Durée de la valeur stylistique du néologisme', *Romanic Review*, XLIV (1953), p. 286.
38 François, *La Langue postclassique*, p. 1150.
39 Mercier, introduction to his *Néologie*. Much of the material in this section is indebted to the excellent study by Mario Mormile, *La 'Néologie' révolution-naire de Louis-Sébastien Mercier* (Bulzoni, Rome, 1973).
40 Quoted in Robert Le Bidois, *Les Mots trompeurs, ou le délire verbal* (Hachette, Paris, 1970), p. 15.
41 Stendhal, *Mémoires d'un touriste* (Le Divan, Paris, 1929), vol. 1, p. 142.
42 Keith Foley has amassed a record collection of such verbs.
43 Pearsall Smith, *Words and Idioms*, p. 23.
44 Ibid., p. 24.
45 Mencken, *The American Language*, p. 10. Further references are bracketed in the text.
46 A. E. Sullivan, *Daily Telegraph*, 2 March 1935, quoted ibid., p. 174.
47 Burke, *Philosophy of Literary Form*, pp. 300–1.
48 Samuel Beckett, *Proust* (Grove, New York, 1970), p. 10.
49 Denis Donoghue, 'Radio Talk', in *The State of the Language*, p. 549.
50 Quoted in Rheims, *Le Dictionnaire des mots sauvages*, pp. 384, 398.
51 Jacobs, *Naming-Day in Eden*, p. 59.
52 Grandjouan, *Les Linguicides*, p. 284. The reworked old tag is from Publius Syrus, *Moral Sayings* (first century BC).
53 Charles de Gaulle, quoted in *Paris-Match*, 1 May 1965.
54 Andrew Joscelyne, 'French Language Planning, 1966–1986', *Language Monthly*, 36 (1986), p. 28. This article is an excellent survey of the question.
55 *Le Monde*, 19 January 1973, reacting to the ministerial decrees of that month.
56 Jacques Derogy, 'Les Inquisiteurs du bon français', *L'Express*, 23 November 1984, pp. 73–4.
57 Joscelyne, 'French Language Planning', p. 29, quoting Alain Fantapie.
58 Ibid.
59 Maurice Genevoix, 'L'Académie française et les commissions ministérielles de terminologie', *La Banque des mots*, 5 (1976), p. 8.
60 Aurélien Sauvageot, 'Valeur des néologismes', *La Banque des mots*, 1 (1971), p. 31.
61 Disraeli, *Curiosities of Literature*, vol. 3, p. 23.
62 Alain Touraine, quoted in *L'Express*, 17–23 August 1984, p. 16. The reference is to Balzac's novel about an inexorably shrinking shagreen hide.
63 Marcel Proust, *Sodome et Gomorrhe* (Gallimard, Paris, 1924), p. 176. The Narrator is here chastising himself for his snobbish corrections of the peasant servant Françoise's slips which, at heart, he knows to be signs of a living language.
64 Queneau, *Bâtons, chiffres et lettres*, p. 69.
65 Michel Tournier, *Le Vent Paraclet*, pp. 85–6.

66 Tournier, *le Roi des Aulnes* (Gallimard, Paris, 1978), p. 125.
67 Le Bidois, *Les Mots trompeurs*, p. 10. I relish the oxymoron.
68 Duneton, *Parler croquant*, p. 140.
69 Jean-Louis Bory, *Tout feu toute flamme*, (Julliard, Paris, 1966), p. 127.
70 Duneton, *Parler croquant*, p. 245. Literally, to drown a fish by playing it once hooked.
71 Ibid., p. 272.
72 André Martinet, 'Les Puristes contre la langue', *Le Français sans fard* (Presses Universitaires de France, Paris, 1969), pp. 28, 29, 31, 27.
73 R. E. Keller, *The German Language* (Faber, London, 1978), p. 611.
74 Ibid., p. 612.
75 Ibid.
76 Anna Laura Lepschy and Giulio Lepschy, *The Italian Language Today* (Hutchinson, London, 1977), p. 29.
77 Quoted in Silvia Scotti Morgana, *Le Parole nuove* (Zanichelli, Bologna, 1981), p. 91.
78 Jean-Claude Corbeil, 'Aspects du problème néologique', *La Banque des mots*, 2 (1971), pp. 132–6.
79 Valter Tauli, *Introduction to a Theory of Language Planning* (Almqvist & Wiksells, Uppsala, 1968), p. 26. Tauli is Estonian.
80 Charles Kay Ogden, *Debabelization* (Kegan Paul, London, 1931), p. 15.
81 *Times Higher Education Supplement*, 13 June 1986, p. 12, in a report on the supplement to the *QED*.
82 Pat Rogers, 'The *OED* at the turning-point', *TLS*, 9 May 1986, p. 488.
83 Ibid., p. 487.
84 Tauli, *Introduction to a Theory of Language Planning*, p. 16.

CHAPTER 16   NEW WORDS HOME AND ABROAD

1 Keith Foley, letter of 1 May 1987. A neologotype could also be a newly devised trade insignia.
2 But mints melt down old coins as well as new ore.
3 Anthony Burgess, *1985*, pp. 43–4.
4 Robert Graves, 'The Devil's Advice to Story-tellers', *Selected Poems*, p. 93.
5 Souriau, 'Sur l'esthétique des mots et des langages forgés', p. 48.
6 Mead, *Word-Coinage*, p. 153, quoting Robert Barr.
7 Ogden Nash, 'Taste Buds, En Garde', *There's Always Another Windmill*, p. 50.
8 Jencks and Silver, *Adhocism*, p. 70.
9 Michel Leiris, *Langage tangage* (Gallimard, Paris, 1985), p. 14. The title suggests pitching and tango.
10 Ogden Nash, 'Laments for a Dying Language', *Everyone but Thee and Me* (Little, Brown, Boston, 1962).
11 Céline, *Bagatelles pour un massacre*, p. 138.
12 Céline, *Guignol's Band* (Gallimard, Paris, 1952), p. 48.
13 Céline, *Les Beaux Draps* (Nouvelles Editions Françaises, Paris, 1941), p. 22.
14 Céline, *Bagatelles pour un massacre*, p. 11.
15 Spitzer, 'The Individual Factor', p. 78.
16 Joris-Karl Huysmans, *La Cathédrale* (Plon-Nourrit, Paris, 1898), p. 435.

17 Quoted in Mencken, *The American Language*, p. 175.
18 Laurie Bauer, *English Word-Formation* (Cambridge University Press, 1983), p. 232.
19 G. Hudson, 'The Representation of Non-productive Alternation', in *Historical Linguistics II*, eds J. Anderson and C. Jones (North Holland, Amsterdam, 1974), p. 224.
20 Safire, *New Language of Politics*, p. ix.
21 Logan Pearsall Smith, 'Needed Words', Society for Pure English, Tract XXXI, 1928, p. 322.
22 Bruno Migliorini, *The Contribution of the Individual to Language* (Clarendon, Oxford, 1952), p. 17.
23 Pearsall Smith, 'Needed Words', p. 323.
24 John Algeo, 'Where Do All the New Words Come From?' *American Speech*, 55 (1981), p. 265.
25 Freud, *Jokes and their Relation to the Unconscious*, trs J. Strachey et al. (Penguin, Harmondsworth, 1976), p. 77.
26 Freud, *The Interpretation of Dreams*, p. 405.
27 Louise Pound, 'Spelling Manipulation and Present-Day Advertising', *Dialect Notes*, V, 6 (1923), p. 226.
28 Jencks and Silver, *Adhocism*, p. 166.
29 Pound, 'Spelling Manipulation', p. 228.
30 Quoted in Louise Pound, 'Then and Now', *PMLA* LXXI, 1 (1956), p. 11.
31 A. Smythe Palmer, *Folk-Etymology* (Bell, London, 1882), p. xiv.
32 Barfield, *Poetic Diction*, p. 74.
33 Otto Jespersen, *Language* (Allen & Unwin, London, 1922), p. 208.
34 O. W. Holmes, *The Autocrat of the Breakfast Table* (Sampson Low, London, 1891), p. 263.
35 Quoted in William Ward, 'Tower of Babble', *The Observer*, 9 August 1987, p. 43.
36 On this topic see N. W. Spence, in *French Studies Bulletin*, 19 (1986), pp. 1–2.
37 Hope, *Lexical Borrowing*, vol. 2, p. 723.
38 Grandjouan, *Les Linguicides*, p. 150.
39 Etiemble, *Parlez-vous franglais?* (Gallimard, Paris, 1964). André Rigaud ('Les Mots-centaures', *Vie et langage*, 202 (1969), p. 55) claims to have coined this blend in *Le Quotidien* of Buenos Aires of 21 November 1955, but admits it would have died without Etiemble's boost. Etiemble himself credits a lexicographer, Maurice Rat, who introduced it in *France-Soir*, 26 September 1959.
40 Listed in Grandjouan, *Les Linguicides*, p. 279.
41 Etiemble, *Parlez-vous franglais?*, p. 327. A variant portmanteau is *coca-colonisation*.
42 George Du Maurier, *Peter Ibbotson* (Osgood & McIlvaine, London, 1892), p. 37. The doubt is placed in the preface as to whether the narrator is insane or not. What further attracted Queneau was the theme (re-used in his own *Fleurs bleues*) of two people sharing a dream-life. Miles Kington has resurrected this kind of *franglais*.
43 See Guilbert, *La Créativité lexicale*, p. 93.
44 Robert Burchfield, *The English Language* (Oxford University Press, 1985), p. 26.

45 Palmer, *Folk-Etymology*, p. x.
46 Mencken, *American Language*, p. 6.
47 Farb, *Word Play*, p. 308.
48 Louis Deroy, *L'Emprunt linguistique* (Belles Lettres, Paris, 1956). p. 17.
49 Bréal, *Semantics*, pp. 256, 263.

CHAPTER 17   SUBTLE BLENDS

1 In fact, Attridge sees the portmanteau as the basic element of all language: 'Every word in every text is, after all, a portmanteau of sorts, a combination of sounds that echo through the entire language and through every other language and back through the history of speech.' Derek Attridge, *Peculiar Language* (Cornell University Press, Ithaca, NY, 1988), p. 208.
2 Céline, *Bagatelles pour un massacre*, p. 186.
3 Ralph Lever, *The Arte of Reason, rightly termed witcraft*, 1573.
4 Garlon Cannon, 'Blends in English Word Formation', *Linguistics*, 24, 4 (1986), pp. 744, 749.
5 John Algeo, 'Portmanteaus, Telescopes, Jumbles', *Verbatim* II, 2 (1975), pp. 1–2.
6 Lester V. Berrey, 'Newly-wedded Words', *American Speech*, February 1939, pp. 3–10.
7 John Algeo, 'Blends, a Structural and Systemic View', *American Speech*, 52, 1–2 (1977), pp. 50, 60.
8 Wentworth, *Blend-Words*, p. 9.
9 Max Ernst, in *Dictionnaire abrégé du surréalisme* (Galerie des Beaux-Arts, Paris, 1938), p. 21.
10 Dwight Bolinger and Donald Sears, *Aspects of Language*, 3rd edn (Harcourt, Brace, Jovanovich, New York, 1981), p. 60.
11 See my *Puns*, p. 171, for a delectable French pun on *conjoint*.
12 Queneau, *Bâtons, chiffres, et lettres*, p. 81.
13 Gilles Deleuze, *Logique du sens* (Minuit, Paris, 1969), pp. 64–5.
14 See André Blavier, *Les Fous littéraires* (Veyrier, Paris, 1982), pp. 687–713.
15 Bernard Dupriez, *Gradus* (Union Générale d'Editions, Paris, 1980), p. 394.
16 Michel Leiris, 'Glossaire, j'y serre mes gloses', *Mots sans mémoire* (Gallimard, Paris, 1969), p. 108.
17 Jean-Paul Clébert, *Paris insolite* (Denoël, Paris, 1961), p. 83.
18 Henry de Montherlant, *La Rose de sable* (Gallimard, Paris, 1968) p. 7.
19 Patrick Modiano, *La Place de l'Etoile* (Gallimard, Paris, 1968), p. 80.
20 Quoted in J. Dierickx, 'Les "mots-valises" de l'anglais et du franglais', *Revue des langues vivantes*, xxxii, 5 (1966), pp. 457, 459.
21 See *Le Canard enchaîné*, 18 November 1964.
22 Quoted in Cannon, 'Blends in English', p. 741.
23 Examples quoted in Berrey, 'Newly-wedded Words', pp. 6–7.
24 Examples from Wentworth, *Blend-Words*, pp. 42, 48, 102, 158.
25 Ralph Levy, 'Haplologic Blends in French and English', *Symposium*, 4 (1950), p. 60.
26 Quoted in Margaret M. Bryant, 'Blends are Increasing', *American Speech*, 48–9 (1973–4), pp. 176, 169.
27 Jean Praninskas, *Trade Name Creation* (Mouton, The Hague, 1968), p. 29.

28 For further details, see my 'Approximating Man: Michel Tournier and Play in Language', *Modern Language Review*, 80, 2 (1985), pp. 304–19.

29 Harold Wentworth, '"Sandwich" words and Rime-Caused Nonce Words', *West Virginia University Bulletin*, Philological Studies, 3 (1939), p. 65. He contrasts these with other tinkerings, such as 'absotively' and 'posilutely'.

30 Both sets of examples from Bauer, *English Word-Formation*, p. 213. cf. the American vogue for a string of such rhyming pairs: 'Zoot suit with a reet pleat', etc.

31 Bréal, *Semantics*, p. 266.

32 Gaston Ferdière, 'Notes préliminaires sur les "Portmanteau words" de Lewis Carroll', *Acta Neurologica et Psychiatrica Belgica*, 57 (1957), p. 998.

33 Joseph J. Firebaugh, 'The Vocabulary of *Time* Magazine', *American Speech*, 1940, p. 237.

34 Quoted in Robert T. Elson, *Time Inc. (1923–1941)* (Atheneum, New York, 1968), p. 83.

35 Firebaugh, 'Vocabulary of *Time*', p. 242.

36 *Time*, 3 May 1971, p. 33.

37 Hugh Kenner, *Flaubert, Joyce and Beckett*, p. xv. Kenner, a shareholder in the Ong/McLuhan line, similarly battens on to the modern divorce between the spoken and the written word.

38 St John Ervine, in *The Observer*, 13 February 1938, quoted in Mencken, *American Language*, Supplement 1, p. 340.

39 Cannon, 'Blends in English', p. 737.

40 Quoted in Bryant, 'Blends are Increasing', p. 175.

41 Robert Graves, *Greek Myths* (Penguin, Harmondsworth, 1957), vol. 2, p. 73.

42 Algeo, 'Portmanteaus', p. 1.

43 See Dierickx, 'Les "mots-valises",' p. 457.

44 André Goosse, *La Néologie française aujourd'hui* (Conseil international de la langue française, Paris, 1975), p. 72.

45 The first example is from Berrey, 'Newly-wedded Words', p. 7, and the second two from Wentworth, *Blend-Words*, pp. 15, 57.

46 See Goosse, *Néologie française*, p. 30.

47 From Wentworth, *Blend-Words*, p. 95.

48 Marshall McLuhan and Quentin Fiore, *The Medium is the Massage* (Penguin, Harmondsworth, 1967), n.p.

49 See Goosse, *Néologie française*, p. 47.

50 Orwell, *Nineteen Eighty-Four*, p. 244.

51 Christian Moncelet, *Mots croasés* (Bof, Le Cendre, 1978), p. 6.

52 Alain Finkielkraut, *Ralentir! mots-valises!* (Seuil, Paris, 1979), n.p.

53 Cannon, 'Blends in English', pp. 736–7.

54 Ibid., p. 750.

55 Algeo, 'Where do all the new words come from?' p. 271.

56 I will, however, look at accidental blends later, in discussing lapsus.

57 Eric Hoffer, *The Ordeal of Change* (Harper & Row, New York, 1964), p. 14.

58 Sade, quoted in Geoffrey Gorer, *The Life and Ideas of the Marquis de Sade* (Peter Owen, London, 1962), p. 153.

59 Roland Barthes, *Sade, Fourier, Loyola* (Seuil, Paris, 1971), p. 87.

60 Gershon Legman, *The Limerick* (Panther, London, 1977), p. 36.

61 Jean-Paul Clébert, *La Vie sauvage* (Denoël, Paris, 1953), p. 218.

62 Evert Van Der Starre, 'Sally Mara romancière? exercices de style', *Temps mêlés*, 150 + 20–21 (1983), pp. 99–100.
63 Clive Hart, *Structure and Motif in 'Finnegans Wake'* (Faber, London, 1962), p. 154ff.
64 Céline, *Bagatelles pour un massacre*, p. 61.
65 'Petit dictionnaire des mots retrouvés' (by M. D., P. de L. and R. de R.), *Nouvelle Revue Française*, 292 (1938), pp. 100, 102.
66 Valerie Adams, *An Introduction to Modern English Word-Formation* (Longman, London, 1973), p. 149.
67 Gilbert Salmon, 'Qu'est-ce qui fait néologiser l'écrivain?', *Bulletin de la Faculté des Lettres de Mulhouse*, XI (1980), p. 80.
68 Mencken, *American Language*, p. 559, quoting W. D. Whitney, *The Life and Growth of Language* (Appleton, New York, 1897), p. 113, and Paul Shorey, *Academy Papers* (American Academy of Arts and Letters, New York, 1926), p. 149.
69 Quoted in Algeo, 'Blends, a Structural and Systemic View', p. 52.

CHAPTER 18   CONTROLLED APPELLATIONS

 1 See Stephen Heath, 'Ambiviolences: notes pour la lecture de Joyce', *Tel Quel*, 51 (1972), p. 72.
 2 See *Puns*, p. 38.
 3 Carroll, *Annotated Alice*, p. 263.
 4 John Algeo, 'The Acronym and its Congeners', in *The First Lacus Forum 1974*, eds Adam and Valerie Makkai (Hornbeam, Columbia, SC, 1975), p. 218.
 5 Examples from Safire, *New Language of Politics*, p. 5.
 6 Algeo, 'The Acronym', p. 232.
 7 Souriau, 'Sur l'esthétique des mots et des langages forgés', p. 22.
 8 Quoted in Migliorini, *Contribution of the Individual to Language*, p. 16.
 9 Quoted in Widal, 'Pour une physiologie du néologisme', p. 359.
10 Pearsall Smith, 'Needed Words', p. 325.
11 See Guilbert, *La Créativité lexicale*, p. 47.
12 For this area, see Frank Close, 'Pions, leptons, quarks: the language of physics', *Times Higher Education Supplement*, 13 April 1984, p. 13, and the follow-up letter from T. S. Harriss, 4 May 1984, p. 2. 'Quark' comes from James Joyce, *Finnegans Wake*, p. 383: 'Three quarks for Master Mark!'
13 Bolton, *The Language of '1984'*, p. 168.
14 Etiemble, *Le Jargon des sciences* (Hermann, Paris, 1966), pp. 89–91.
15 Ibid., p. 99.
16 Arthur G. Kennedy, 'Hothouse Words Versus Slang', *American Speech*, 11 (1927), pp. 417–24.
17 Examples from Keith Foley, letter of 1 May 1987.
18 Raymond Queneau, *Zazie dans le Métro*, p. 92.
19 René Bertelé (ed.), *Henri Michaux*, rev. edn (Seghers, Paris, 1965), p. 21.
20 Matthews, 'The Art of Making New Words', p. 64.
21 Fritz Spiegl, *In-Words and Out-Words* (Elm Tree, London, 1987), p. 97.
22 Rogers 'The *OED* at the turning-point', p. 489.

23 Allen Walker Read, 'The Sources of Ghost-Words in English', *Word*, 29 (1978), p. 96.

24 Ibid., p. 97.

25 Makkai, *Idiom Structure in English*, p. 81.

26 Stéphane Mallarmé, letter of 3 May 1868, to Lefébure, quoted in Guy Michaud, *Mallarmé* (Hatier-Boivin, Paris, 1953). The original title of the poem was 'Sonnet allégorique de lui-même' (Tautegorical Sonnet).

27 Michel Riffaterre, *Semiotics of Poetry* (Indiana University Press, Bloomington, 1978), p. 18.

28 Ibid.

29 A. Smythe Palmer, *The Folk and Their Word-Lore* (Routledge, London, 1904), p. 9.

30 Ogden Nash, 'The Rhinoceros', *Family Reunion*, (Dent, London, 1966), p. 71.

31 See Clark and Gerrig, 'Understanding Old Words with New Meanings', p. 599; and Herbert H. Clark, 'Making Sense of Nonce Sense', in *The Process of Language Understanding*, eds G. B. Flores d'Arcais and R. Jarvella (Wiley, Chichester, 1983), p. 299.

CHAPTER 19   HIGH NEOLOGISM

1 Emily Dickinson, an untitled poem, in *Poems*, eds Bianchi and Hampson (Cape, London, 1937), p. 4).

2 Keith Foley, letter of 1 May 1987.

3 Michel Riffaterre, *La Production du texte* (Seuil, Paris, 1979), p. 61.

4 Francis Ponge, *Méthodes* (Gallimard, Paris, 1971), p. 75.

5 Valéry, 'L'Idée fixe', p. 234.

6 Balzac, who appropriated the particle *de*, quoted in Rheims, *Le Dictionnaire des mots sauvages*, p. 18.

7 Salmon, 'Qu'est-ce qui fait néologiser l'écrivain?', p. 79, conflating his figures and those of Rheims (pp. 15–16).

8 Rogers, 'The *OED* at the turning-point', p. 488.

9 Ezra Pound, *Literary Essays*, ed. T. S. Eliot (Faber, London, 1963), pp. 33, 25.

10 Jules Laforgue, *Lettres à un ami, 1880–1886* (Mercure de France, Paris, 1941), pp. 64–5.

11 Respectively from these poems and prose writings: 'Grande Complainte de la ville de Paris', 'Complainte des nostalgies préhistoriques', 'Complainte à Notre-Dame des soirs', 'Complainte des voix sous le figuier bouddhique', *Revue Indépendante*, 5, 1888, p. 1, 'Lohengrin' (twice), 'Préludes autobiographiques'.

12 Vladimir Markov, *Russian Futurism: A History* (University of California Press, Berkeley, 1968), p. 93.

13 Marc Angenot, 'Le Paradigme absent', *Poétique*, 33 (1978), pp. 75–7.

14 Quoted in Angenot, 'Fonction linguistique et subversion littéraire', *Revue de l'Université de Bruxelles*, 3–4 (1976), p. 232.

15 Queneau, *Bâtons, chiffres et lettres*, p. 25.

16 Respectively in: *Les Enfants du limon* (Gallimard, Paris, 1938), p. 69; *Les Oeuvres complètes de Sally Mara* (Gallimard, Paris, 1962), p. 46; *Loin de Rueil* (Gallimard, Paris, 1976), p. 24; and *Les Fleurs bleues*.

17 Queneau, *Petite Cosmogonie portative* (Gallimard, Paris, 1950), p. 84.
18 See Claude Daubercies, *Le Jeu de mots chez Raymond Queneau*, Diplôme d'Etudes Supérieures, Lille University, 1960, p. 81.
19 Queneau, *Zazie dans le Métro*, pp. 108, 160, 150.
20 John Donne, 'To the Countess of Bedford', *The Complete English Poems*, ed. A. J. Smith (Penguin, Harmondsworth, 1977), p. 231.
21 James Joyce, *Finnegans Wake*, p. 120. Further references are bracketed in the text.
22 Samuel Beckett, in *Our Exagmination* ..., p. 15.
23 Robert McAlmon, ibid., p. 110.
24 Stuart Gilbert, ibid., p. 57.
25 James Joyce, *Stephen Hero*, eds J. J. Slocum and H. Cahoon (New Directions, Norfolk, Conn., 1963), p. 30.
26 Margot C. Norris, 'The Consequences of Deconstruction: A Technical Perspective of Joyce's *Finnegans Wake*', *ELH*, 41, 1 (1974), p. 142.
27 Joyce, *Finnegans Wake*, pp. 181, 424.
28 See Stephen Heath, 'Ambiviolences'.
29 Anthony Burgess, *Joysprick*, p. 136.
30 Michel Butor, 'La traduction, dimension fondamentale de notre temps', *James Joyce Quarterly*, 4 (1967), p. 216. Butor's italics.
31 McLuhan, *From Cliché to Archetype*, p. 9.
32 Leonard Forster, *The Poet's Tongues: Multilingualism in Literature* (Cambridge University Press, 1970), p. 77.
33 Geoffrey Hartman, *Beyond Formalism* (Yale University Press, New Haven, 1970), p. 343.
34 Bryant, 'Blends are Increasing', p. 184.
35 Adams, *Introduction to Modern English Word-Formation*, p. 159.
36 According to A. Walton Litz, *The Art of James Joyce* (Oxford University Press, 1961), pp. 91–2.
37 Steiner, *Language and Silence*, p. 51.
38 Bazin, *Le Matrimoine*, p. 198.
39 Arthur Rimbaud, letter to Professor Izambard of 25 August 1870, at the time of the Franco-Prussian War.
40 Francis Ponge, *Le Parti pris des choses* (Gallimard, Paris, 1967), p. 33.
41 Ogden Nash, *Candy is Dandy* (Methuen, London, 1987), p. 223.
42 Edmond de Goncourt, quoted in Rheims, *Dictionnaire des mots sauvages*, p. 394.
43 Salmon, 'Qu'est-ce qui fait néologiser l'écrivain?', p. 77.
44 Ibid., pp. 73–4.
45 Quoted in Wentworth, *Blend-Words*, p. 10.
46 Algeo, 'The Acronym', p. 232.

CHAPTER 20 LOOKING ROUND THE BEND

1 Eve V. Clark, 'The Young Word Maker: A Case Study of Innovation in the Child's Lexicon', in *Language Acquisition: The State of the Art*, eds Eric Wanner and Leila R. Gleitman (Cambridge University Press, 1982), p. 424.
2 Bréal, *Semantics*, p. 268.

3   Gaston Ferdière, 'Les "Mots-valises" et le Wonderland de l'enfance', *Temps Modernes*, 86 (1952), p. 941.

4   Maria Yaguello, *Alice au pays du langage* (Seuil, Paris, 1981), p. 29.

5   Hugh W. Buckingham and Andrew Kertesz, *Neologistic Jargon Aphasia* (Swets & Zeitlinger, Amsterdam), p. 13.

6   Gaston Ferdière, 'Les Mots-valises', *Cahiers du Sud*, 287 (1948), p. 31.

7   See François, *La Langue postclassique*, p. 1161.

8   Guiraud, *Les Locutions françaises*, p. 90.

9   Henri Michaux, *Connaissance par les gouffres* (Gallimard, Paris, 1967), p. 128.

10 Michaux, postface to *Mes Propriétés*, in *La Nuit remue* (Gallimard, Paris, 1967), p. 195.

11 Ibid., p. 194.

12 Almuth Grésillon, 'Le Mot-valise: un "monstre de langue"?', in *La Linguistique fantastique*, eds S. Auroux et al. (Denoël, Paris, 1985), pp. 254, 258.

13 See E. Bleuler, *Dementia praecox* (International University Press, New York, 1950), p. 152.

14 Jean-Pierre Brisset, *Le Mystère de Dieu est accompli*, ed. P. Cullard (Navarin, Paris, 1983), p. 72. For further details on Brisset, see my *Puns*, pp. 113–17.

15 Brisset, *La Grammaire logique* (Baudoin, Paris, 1980), p. 114.

16 Leiris, *Langage tangage*, p. 30.

17 See Jean Bobon and Jaroslav Stucklik, 'Les "druses" écrites et dessinées (Kontaminationen, blendings); pathogénie de certains néomorphismes', *Acta Neurologica et Psychiatrica Belgica*, 6 (1960), pp. 530–35, 544.

18 Roger Cardinal, 'Image and Word in Schizophrenic Creation', *Forum for Modern Language Studies*, IX, 1 (1973), p. 109.

19 Léon-Paul Fargue, *Espaces* (Gallimard, Paris, 1929), p. 101.

20 Quoted in Wentworth, *Blend-Words*, p. 94.

21 Coined by Christine Brooke-Rose in an interview with David Hayman and Keith Cohen, *Contemporary Literature*, 17 (1976), p. 9.

22 From my colleague, Geoffrey Strickland.

23 Twain, *Notebooks*, p. 374.

24 Jane Grigson, letter of 8 October, 1986. Much the same, she feels, applies to cocktails.

25 Jencks and Silver, *Adhocism*, p. 192.

26 Francis Ponge, *Pièces* (Gallimard, Paris, 1962), p. 186.

27 Makkai, *Idiom Structure in English*, p. 159.

28 Dwight Bolinger, *Aspects of Language* (Harcourt, Brace & World, New York, 1968), p. 103.

29 Jean Aitchison, *Words in the Mind* (Blackwell, Oxford, 1987), pp. 82, 168.

30 Freud, *The Psychopathology of Everyday Life*, tr. A. Tyson (Penguin, Harmondsworth, 1975), p. 100. He refers to similar findings in his *Interpretation of Dreams*.

31 See Victoria A. Fromkin (ed.), *Speech Errors as Linguistic Evidence* (Mouton, The Hague, 1973), p. 15, and *Errors in Linguistic Performance: Slips of the Tongue, Ear, Pen, and Hand* (Academic, New York, 1980).

32 Ferdière, 'Notes préliminaires sur les "Portmanteau words"', p. 966.

33 Burrhus Frederick Skinner, *Verbal Behaviour* (Methuen, London, 1957), p. 297.

34 Charles Hockett, 'Where the Tongue Slips There Slip I', in *To Honor Roman Jakobson*, ed. Morris Halle (Mouton, The Hague, 1967), p. 935. The *NED* gives the date of 1881 for 'blunderful'.

35 Samuel Taylor Coleridge, *Miscellaneous Criticism*, ed. T. M. Raynor (Constable, London, 1936), p. 173.

36 Randle Cotgrave, *A Dictionarie of the French and English Tongues* (Scolar, Menston, 1968 (1611)), n.p.

37 These four examples from Advanced Level and University Finals papers.

38 I toyed with calling this book *Higher Platitudes*.

39 Souriau, 'Sur l'esthétique des mots et des langages forgés', p. 23.

40 Bolinger and Sears, *Aspects of Language*, p. 248.

41 Bolinger, *Language*, p. 42.

42 George Orwell, letter to Richard Rees, in *Collected Essays*, vol. 4, p. 533.

43 Read, 'The Sources of Ghost-Words', p. 99.

44 W. H. Auden, 'The Truest Poetry is the Most Feigning', *Collected Poems*, p. 470.

45 Ogden Nash, 'If a Boder Meet a Boder, Need a Boder Cry? Yes?', *There's Always Another Windmill*, p. 69.

46 Eco, *Faith in Fakes*, p. 11.

47 Pound, 'Then and Now', p. 13.

48 F. Gohin, *Les Transformations de la langue française pendant la deuxième moitié du XVIIIe siècle* (Belin, Paris, n.d.), p. 42.

49 Henri-Pierre Jeudy, 'Essais sur la néologie', *L'Homme et la Société*, 28 (1973), p. 130.

50 Grandjouan, *Les Linguicides*, p. 4.

51 Michel Foucault, *Raymond Roussel* (Gallimard, Paris, 1963), p. 223.

52 Bréal, *Semantics*, p. 268.

53 Eve V. Clark, 'The young word-maker', p. 393.

CHAPTER 21   CODA: WHEN ALL IS SAID AND DONE

1 Jean Paulhan, 'La Rhétorique renaît de ses cendres', *Oeuvres complètes*, (Cerde du livre précieux, Paris, n.d.), vol. 2, p. 159.

2 Shakespeare, *King John*, IV, 2, 30–1.

3 Jean-Paul Sartre, *Réflexions sur la question juive* (Gallimard, Paris, 1962), p. 21.

4 Camus, *La Chute*, p. 13.

5 Ludwig Wittgenstein, *Philosophical Investigations*, tr. G. E. M. Anscombe (Blackwell, Oxford, 1953), p. 34.

6 Browne, *The Major Works*, p. 200.

7 Bertrand Russell, quoted in W. H. Auden, *A Certain World* (Faber, London, 1971), p. 333.

8 G.-Th. Guillebaud, *Leçons d'à peu près* (Bourgois, Paris, 1985).

9 Michel Tournier, 'L'Espace canadien', *La Nouvelle Critique*, 105 (1977), p. 52. For further details, see my article 'Approximating Man'.

10 Shakespeare, *Twelfth Night*, III, 1, 14–15.

11 I owe this nice polarity to Michael Edwards.

12 Browne, *The Major Works*, p. 60.

13   Robert Graves, 'The Climate of Thought', *Selected Poems*, p. 129.
14   Hugh Kenner, 'The *Portrait* in Perspective', in *Joyce's 'Portrait'*, ed. Thomas Connolly (Peter Owen, London, 1967), pp. 34–5.
15   Keith Foley, letter of 1 May 1987.

Bibliography

This bibliography, reduced from one several times as long, contains the items I found most useful. Others of interest can be found in the Notes.

Adams, V., *An Introduction to Modern English Word-Formation*, Longman, London, 1973.

Albalat, A., *La Formation du style, par l'assimilation des Auteurs*, Colin, Paris, 1901.

Algeo, J., 'Blends, a Structural and Systemic View', *American Speech*, 52, 1–2 (1977), pp. 47–64.

Algeo, J., 'The Taxonomy of Word Making', *Word*, 29 (1978), pp. 122–31.

Algeo, J., 'Where do all the new words come from?' *American Speech*, 55 (1981), pp. 264–77.

Amossy, R. and Rosen, E., *Le Discours du cliché* CDU/SEDES, Paris, 1982.

Bagnall, N., *A Defence of Clichés*, Constable, London, 1985.

Bate, W. J., *The Burden of the Past and the English Poet*, Chatto & Windus, London, 1971.

Bauer, L., *English Word-Formation*, Cambridge University Press, Cambridge, 1983.

Bechtel, G. and Carrière, J.-C., *Dictionnaire de la bêtise*, rev. edn, Laffont, Paris, 1983.

Bengtsson, S., *La Défense organisée de la langue française*, Almqvist & Wiksells, Uppsala, 1968.

Berrey, L. V., 'Newly-wedded Words', *American Speech*, 14, 1 (1939), pp. 3–10.

Bloom, H., *The Anxiety of Influence*, Oxford University Press, New York, 1973.

Bolinger, D., *Language: The Loaded Weapon*, Longman, London, 1980.

Bolton, W. F., *The Language of '1984'*, Blackwell, Oxford, 1984.

Booth, T. Y., 'The Cliché: A Working Bibliography', *Bulletin of Bibliography and Magazine Notes*, 23 (1960), pp. 61–3.

Brown, C. F., *Star-Spangled Kitsch*, Universe, New York, 1975.

Brunot, F. et al., *Histoire de la langue française des origines à nos jours*, Colin and CNRS, Paris, 1905→

Bryant, M. M., 'Blends are Increasing', *American Speech*, 48–9 (1973–4), pp. 163–84.

Burgess, G., *Are You a Bromide?*, Huebsch, New York, 1908.

Buyssens, E., 'Tautologies', *La Linguistique*, 6, 2 (1970), pp. 37–45.

Cannon, G. 'Blends in English Word Formation', *Linguistics*, 24, 4 (1986), pp. 725–53.

Champion, S. G., *Racial Proverbs*, Routledge, London, 1938.

Compagnon, A., *La Seconde Main, ou le travail de la citation*, Seuil, Paris, 1979.

Corbeil, J.-C., 'Aspects du problème néologique', *La Banque des mots*, 2 (1971), pp. 123–36.

Curtius, E. R., *European Literature and the Latin Middle Ages*, tr. W. R. Trask, Routledge & Kegan Paul, London, 1953.

Deroy, L., *L'Emprunt linguistique*, Belles Lettres, Paris, 1956.

Dierickx, J., 'Les "mots-valises" de l'anglais et du franglais', *Revue des Langues Vivantes*, XXXII, 5 (1966), pp. 451–9.

Diki-Kidiri, M., Joly, H. and Murcia, C., *Guide de la néologie*, Conseil international de la langue française, Paris, 1981.

Duneton, C., *Parler croquant*, Stock, Paris, 1982.

Dupriez, B., *Gradus: les procédés littéraires*, Union Générale d'Editions, Paris, 1980.

Eco, U., *Faith in Fakes*, tr. W. Weaver, Secker & Warburg, London, 1986.

Etiemble, R., *Parlez-vous franglais?*, Gallimard, Paris, 1964.

Etiemble, R., *Le Jargon des sciences*, Hermann, Paris, 1964.

Ferdière, G., 'Les "Mots-valises" et le Wonderland de l'Enfance', *Temps Modernes*, 86 (1952), pp. 937–60.

Ferdière, G., 'Notes préliminaires sur les "Portmanteau words" de Lewis Carroll', *Acta Neurologica et Psychologica Belgica*, 57 (1957), pp. 993–1003.

Fernando, C. and Flavell, R., *On Idiom*, Exeter Linguistic Studies 5, University of Exeter, 1981.

Finkielkraut A., *Ralentir! mots-valises!*, Seuil, Paris, 1979.

Finnegan, R., *Oral Literature in Africa*, Clarendon, Oxford, 1970.

Flaubert, G., *Correspondance*, Conard, Paris, 1927.

Flaubert, G., 'Dictionnaire des idées reçues', in *Bouvard et Pécuchet*, ed. C. Gothot-Mersch, Gallimard, Paris, 1979.

Genette, G., *Palimpsestes*, Seuil, Paris, 1982.

Goosse, A., *La Néologie française aujourd'hui*, Conseil international de la langue française, Paris, 1975.

Gourmont, R. de, 'Le Cliché', in *Esthétique de la langue française*, Mercure de France, Paris, n.d.

Gourmont, R. de, *Le Problème du style*, Mercure de France, Paris, 1907.

Guilbert, L., *La Créativité lexicale*, Larousse, Paris, 1975.

Guiraud, P., 'Néologismes littéraires', *La Banque des mots*, 1 (1971), pp. 23–8.

Guiraud, P., *Les Locutions françaises*, Presses Universitaires de France, Paris, 1961.

Haig, S., *Flaubert and the Gift of Speech*, Cambridge University Press, Cambridge, 1986.

Herschberg-Pierrot, A., 'Problématiques du cliché: sur Flaubert', *Poétique*, 43 (1980), pp. 334–45.

Hudson, K., *The Language of Modern Politics*, Macmillan, London, 1978.

Hutcheon, L., *A Theory of Parody*, Methuen, London, 1985.

Jacobs, N. J., *Naming-Day in Eden*, Gollancz, London, 1958.

Jencks C. and Silver, N., *Adhocism*, Anchor, New York, 1973.

Jenny, L., 'Structure et fonctions du cliché', *Poétique*, 12 (1972), pp. 495–517.

Joscelyne, A., 'French Language Planning, 1966–1986', *Language Monthly*, 36 (1986), pp. 28–30.

Kapferer, J.-N., *Rumeurs*, Seuil, Paris, 1987.

Kellett, E. E., *Literary Quotation and Allusion*, Heffer, Cambridge, 1933.

Kettridge, J. O., *French Idioms and Figurative Phrases*, Routledge, London, 1939.

Lakoff, G. and Johnson, M., *Metaphors We Live By*, Chicago University Press, Chicago, 1980.

Lawrence, J., *Mix Me a Metaphor*, Gentry, London, 1972.

Lawrence, J., *Unmentionables and Other Euphemisms*, Gentry, London, 1973.

Lechner, Sister J. M., OSU, *Renaissance Concepts of the Commonplaces*, Greenwood, Westport, Conn., 1974.

Lerner, L. D., 'Cliché and Commonplace', *Essays in Criticism*, VI, 3 (1956), pp. 249–65.

Levine, J. S., 'Originality and Repetition in *Finnegans Wake* and *Ulysses*', *PMLA*, 94, 1 (1979), pp. 106–20.

Lindey, A., *Plagiarism and Originality*, Harper, New York, 1952.

Lippman, W., *Public Opinion*, Macmillan, New York, 1947 (1922).

Loomis, C. G., 'Proverbial Phrases in Journalistic Word Play', *Western Folklore*, 23 (1964), pp. 187–9.

Macdonald, D. (ed.), *Parodies*, Faber, London, 1960.

Macdonald, D., *Against the American Grain*, Gollancz, London, 1963.

McLuhan, M., *From Cliché to Archetype*, Viking, New York, 1970.

Makkai, A., *Idiom Structure in English*, Mouton, The Hague, 1972.

Marchand, H., *The Categories and Types of Present-Day English Word-Formation*, C. H. Beck'sche, Munich, 1969.

Martin, A., *The Knowledge of Ignorance*, Cambridge University Press, Cambridge, 1985.

Martinet, A., 'Les Puristes contre la langue', *Le Français sans fard*, Presses Universitaires de France, Paris, 1969.

Matthews, B., 'The Art of Making New Words', *Unpopular Review*, IX (1918), pp. 58–69.

Mead, L., *Word-Coinage*, Crowell, New York, 1902.

Mencken, H. L., *The American Language*, Kegan Paul, London, 1936 (Supplement 1, 1945 and 2, 1948).

Merton, R. K., *On the Shoulders of Giants: A Shandean Postscript*, Free Press, New York, 1965.

Michaels, L., and Ricks, C. (eds), *The State of the Language*, University of California Press, Berkeley, 1980.

Migliorini, B., *The Contribution of the Individual to Language*, Clarendon, Oxford, 1952.

Moncelet, C., *Essai sur les mots-croasés*, Bof, Le Cendre, 1978.

Mormile, M., *La 'Néologie' révolutionnaire de Louis-Sébastien Mercier*, Bulzoni, Rome, 1973.

'La Néologie lexicale', *Langages*, 36 (1974).

'Le Néologisme dans la langue et dans la littérature', *Cahiers de l'Association Internationale des Etudes françaises*, 25 (1973).

Ong, W. J., *The Presence of the Word*, Yale University Press, New Haven, 1967.

Ong, W. J. 'Commonplace Rhapsody: Ravisius Textor, Zwinger and Shakespeare', in *Classical Influences on European Culture, AD 1500–1700*, ed. R. R. Bolgar, Cambridge University Press, Cambridge 1976, pp. 91–126.

Ong, W. J., *Orality and Literacy*, Methuen, London, 1982.

Orwell, G., 'Politics and the English Langauge', *Collected Essays, Journalism and Letters*, Penguin, Harmondsworth, 1970, vol. 4.

Partridge, E., *A Dictionary of Clichés*, Routledge & Kegan Paul, London, 1950.
Partridge, E., *A Dictionary of Catch Phrases*, Routledge & Kegan Paul, London, 1977.
Paulhan, J., *Les Fleurs de Tarbes, ou la Terreur dans les lettres*, Gallimard, Paris, 1973 (1941).
Pennanen, E., 'Current Views on Word-Formation', *Neuphilologische Mitteilungen*, 1–2, xxxiii (1972), pp. 292–308.
Perrin-Naffakh, A.-M., *Le Cliché de style en français moderne*, Université de Lille III, 1985.
Pietra, R., 'Lieux communs', *Littérature*, 65 (1987), pp. 96–108.
Pope, A., *The Art of Sinking in Poetry*, ed. E. L. Steeve, Russell & Russell, New York, 1968 (1952).
Postman, N. et al. (eds), *Language in America*, Pegasus, New York, 1969.
Pound, L., *Blends: Their Relation to English Word-Formation*, Winter, Heidelberg, 1914.
Praninskas, J., *Trade Name Creation*, Mouton, The Hague, 1968.
Quemada, B. et al., *Matériaux pour l'histoire du vocabulaire français*, Didier, Paris, 1970→
Reboul, O., *Le Slogan*, Complexe, Brussels, 1975.
Reboul, O., 'Le Slogan et les fonctions du langage', *Le Français dans le monde*, 143 (1979), pp. 21–6.
Redfern, W. D., *Puns*, Blackwell, Oxford, 1984.
Rees, N., *The Joy of Clichés*, Macdonald, London, 1984.
Rey, A., 'Néologisme: un pseudo-concept?', *Cahiers de Lexicologie*, 28, 1 (1976), pp. 3–17.
Rheims, M., *Le Dictionnaire des mots sauvages*, Larousse, Paris, 1969.
Ricks, C., *The Force of Poetry*, Clarendon, Oxford, 1984.
Riffaterre, M., *Essais de stylistique structurale*, Flammarion, Paris, 1971.
Riffaterre, M., *La Production du texte*, Seuil, Paris, 1979.
Roback, A. A., *A Dictionary of International Slurs*, Sci-Art, Cambridge, Mass., 1944.
Roberts, M. H., 'The Science of Idiom', *PMLA*, LIX, 1 (1944), pp. 291–306.
Rogers, J., *The Dictionary of Clichés*, Ward Lock, London, 1986.
Rogers, P., 'Swift and the Revival of Cliché', in *The Character of Swift's Satire*, ed. C. Rawson, Associated Universities Presses, London, 1983, pp. 203–26.
Rosen, R. D., *Psychobabble*, Wildwood House, London, 1978.
Ruthven, K. K., *Myth*, Methuen, London, 1976.
Sabin, M., *The Dialect of the Tribe*, Oxford University Press, New York, 1987.
Safire, W., *The New Language of Politics*, Random House, New York, 1968.
Salmon, G., 'Qu'est-ce qui fait néologiser l'écrivain?' *Bulletin de la Faculté des Lettres de Mulhouse*, XI (1980), pp. 73–88.
Sartre, J.-P., *L'Idiot de la famille*, Gallimard, Paris, 3 vols, 1971–2.
Schneider, M., *Voleurs de mots*, Gallimard, Paris, 1985.
Smith, L. P., *Words and Idioms*, Constable, London, 1925.
Sontag, S., 'Notes on Camp', *Against Interpretation*, Eyre & Spottiswoode, London, 1967.
Souriau, E., 'Sur l'esthétique des mots et des langages forgés', *Revue d'Esthétique*, 18 (1965), pp. 19–48.
Spitzer, L., 'The Individual Factor in Linguistic Innovations', *Cultura Neolatina*, 16, 1 (1956), pp. 71–89.

Stein, G., *English Word-Formation over Two Centuries, Tübinger Beiträge zur Linguistik, 34*, Tübingen, 1973.

Swift, J., *Polite Conversation*, ed. E. Partridge, Deutsch, London, 1963.

Tauli, V., *Introduction to a Theory of Language Planning*, Almqvist & Wiksells, Uppsala, 1968.

Thompson, P. and Davenport, P., *The Dictionary of Visual Language*, Penguin, Harmondsworth, 1982.

Trescases, P., *Le Franglais vingt ans après*, Guérin, Montreal, 1982.

Valéry, P., 'L'Idée fixe', in *Oeuvres*, ed. J. Hytier, Gallimard, Paris, vol. 2, 1960.

Wentworth, H., *Blend-Words in English*, Ph.D., Cornell University, 1954 (microfilm).

White, H. O., *Plagiarism and Imitation during the English Renaissance*, (Harvard University Press, Cambridge, Mass., 1935.

Widal, P., 'Pour une physiologie du néologisme', *Meta*, 18 (1973), pp. 355–64.

Yates, F. A., *The Art of Memory*, Routledge & Kegan Paul, London, 1966.

Young, E., *Conjectures on Original Composition*, ed. E.J. Morley, Manchester University Press, Manchester, 1918 (1759).

Zijderveld, A., *On Clichés: The Supersedure of Meaning by Function in Modernity*, Routledge & Kegan Paul, London, 1979.

Index

Academies 30, 102, 189, 191, 193, 198
acronyms 149, 207, 228–30
Adam 182, 227
Adams, Valerie 225–6
  Addison, Joseph 191
  adhocism (recycling, *bricolage*,
  rejasing) 2, 20, 58, 81, 95, 113–14,
  116–17, 149, 150–1, 164, 173, 175,
  177, 205, 222, 247
adjectives 104
advertising 101, 115, 117, 120–1,
  151, 167, 208, 221, 222, 234
Aitchison, Jean 248
Albalat, Antoine 10
Algeo, John 185, 207, 216, 223, 224,
  228–9, 240
Allen, Woody 176
allusion 62, 76
Americanisms 191, 197, 198, 200, 213,
  214
Amossy, Ruth and Rosen, Elisheva 34,
  63–4, 140, 178
Ancients and Moderns 30, 32–3, 80,
  163, 191
Angenot, Marc 236
animals 50, 52, 56, 60, 67, 87, 120, 153,
  264n.
anti-intellectualism (mindism) 138, 142,
  150
approximation 2, 176, 221, 254–6
Aragon, Louis 90, 147, 155, 158, 277n.
archaisms 181, 187, 192, 194, 205, 209,
  211, 212, 214, 251
Aristotle 27
Ascham, Roger 27
atopy 28
Attridge, Derek 286n.
Auden, W. H. 88, 144, 250

automatism (inertia) 7, 18, 36, 89, 111,
  129, 130–2, 135, 168, 170, 224

back-formation 209, 228, 243
Bacon, Sir Francis 32, 34
Bagnall, Nicholas 149, 157, 161, 173
Baldick, Chris 149–50
Bally, Charles 140–1
Balzac, Honoré de 44, 88, 158, 235
Barfield, Owen 61, 209–10
Barthes, Roland 4, 19, 67–8, 72, 81–2,
  89, 107, 111, 112, 120, 135, 136, 140,
  157, 162, 172, 225
Bate, Walter J. 163
bathos 97, 108
Baudelaire, Charles 44, 49, 67, 140,
  142, 145, 155, 160–1
Bazin, Hervé 184, 239
Beauvoir, Simone de 60, 122, 182
Beckett, Samuel 45, 159, 196, 238
Bergson, Henri 21, 132
blends (portmanteaux, melds) 2, 62, 95,
  115, 180, 181, 185, 205, 206, 207,
  208, 216–26, 227, 237, 238, 239,
  246, 247–9, 251
Bloom, Harold 29
Bloy, Léon 54–6, 57, 63, 97
Bolinger, Dwight 4, 14, 15, 16, 130,
  131, 177, 247, 250
Bootle *see* Liverpool, and die
Börne, Ludwig 12–13, 69
Borges, Jorge Luis 70, 92
borrowings (loan-words) 149, 180, 181,
  183, 185, 187, 188, 189, 191, 194,
  195, 198, 201, 202, 207, 209, 210,
  211, 212, 213, 214
Bréal, Michel 9, 214–15, 221, 241, 252
Brenan, Gerald 142, 276n.

Brisset, Jean-Pierre 243–4
bromide 153–4
Browne, Sir Thomas 3, 88, 254, 255
Burgess, Anthony 91, 114, 204, 238
Burgess, Gelett 153–4, 205

Cabrera Infante, Guillermo 166, 169, 181
calques (and false friends) 181, 211, 212
Camus, Albert 18, 19, 49, 95–6, 100, 104, 106, 157, 162, 176, 254
Canada 202
cannibalization 164
Cardinal, Roger 163, 244
Carroll, Lewis 56, 60, 153, 217, 227, 248–9
Casablanca (archetypal film) 174
Céline, Louis-Ferdinand 10–11, 92, 206, 216, 225, 235, 237, 240
Chesterton, G.K. 92, 125
children (and coinages) 38, 185, 241
circumlocutions 31, 100–1, 125, 165, 192, 208, 239
classicism 27–46, 56, 66, 168, 188, 189, 191, 235
clichés *see* coinages
clichés (mine, *passim*)
clichés and coinages (loose connections) 54, 56–7, 65, 77, 92, 149, 162–3, 178, 179, 180–2, 186, 190, 193, 194, 196–7, 208, 211, 223, 253, 254, 256
coinages *see* clichés
Coleridge, Samuel Taylor 29, 150, 249
Colton, Rev. Caleb 32, 66, 68, 86
commercialese 14
commonplace-books 80
Compagnon, Antoine 74–6, 78, 111, 206n.
compound-words 139, 194, 201, 207, 220, 221
computers 52, 95, 135, 181, 202–3, 229, 230
consensus 16–25, 153

dandyism 107, 145, 155, 161
defamiliarization 16, 208, 211, 219, 238, 239, 247
déjà vu 36–7, 39, 68, 93, 130, 134
dialectisms 187, 205, 212, 231
Dickens, Charles 99, 100

dictionaries 81, 202, 250, 251
Diderot, Denis 9, 21, 45, 86, 87, 93, 120, 132–3, 192, 244
Disraeli, Isaac 119, 200, 240
Du Bellay, Joachim 38, 201
Duchamp, Marcel 147–9
Duneton, Claude 10, 200, 201, 213

Eco, Umberto 86, 93, 95, 151–2, 174, 251
Edinburgh, Philip Duke of 232
education 8–15, 27–8, 65, 104, 124, 141, 155, 172–3, 177, 195
Eliot, T.S. 34, 35, 36, 38, 86, 143, 175, 236
Emerson, Ralph Waldo 29, 77, 159–60, 172
Enright, D.J. 26, 95, 267n.
eroticism 225
Etiemble, René 136, 212–13, 230–1
etymology 23, 91, 127, 136, 195, 209, 210, 227, 251
etymology of 'cliché' and 'stereotype' 8
etymology of 'neologism' 183
euphemisms 67, 98–100, 116, 129, 147, 157, 192, 211, 225, 228
exaggeration 7, 98, 100, 101, 106, 127, 196, 208
exegesis 78–9, 190
existentialism 2, 122

fashion (and vogue-words) 19, 20, 38, 145, 156, 187, 199
Ferdière, Gaston 221, 241, 242, 249
Flaubert, Gustave 12, 19, 21, 24, 42, 44–52, 55, 56, 57, 61, 62, 63, 67, 69, 82, 86, 88, 97, 98, 120, 133–4, 141, 142, 150, 158, 161, 166, 169, 177, 182, 209
Foley, Keith 171, 187, 204, 231, 234, 281n., 284n.
forgery 85, 88–9, 94, 151, 181, 204
formulae 15, 109, 116, 122, 141, 150, 169
Fowler, H.W. 128, 157, 191
franglais 195, 212–13
free indirect speech 63, 267n.
Freud, Sigmund 12–13, 69, 83, 91, 139, 172, 208, 248, 266n., 269n.

Gardner, Philip (unnamed in text)1

Gaulle, Charles de 105–6, 197, 220
generalization 33, 119, 138, 140, 155, 176
Genette, Gérard 32, 58–9, 76, 85, 88–9, 90–1, 231
gestural clichés 144
Gide, André 60, 67, 112, 161, 162
glossolalia 244
God 85, 106, 182, 205, 268n.
Goethe, Johann Wolfgang von 29, 41, 162
Goncourt, Edmond and Jules de 29, 88, 185, 206, 240
Gourmont, Rémy de 22, 30, 68, 155–6, 197
Gracián, Baltasar 76, 227
graffiti 144–5, 167, 216
Graves, Robert 65, 141, 204
Grigson, Jane 247 and n.
Guiraud, Pierre 22, 127, 139, 141, 162, 188, 243

hacking (and piracy) 17, 80, 82, 95
Haig, Stirling 63, 108, 274n.
Heraclitus 82, 183
Hitler, Adolf 110, 112, 136
Hollywood 143, 150
Homer 36, 39, 94, 104, 221
howlers 49, 53, 164, 249–50, 264n.
Hugo, Victor 29, 43, 95, 194, 198
humour 153, 175, 225, 230
hybrids 216, 219, 222–3, 224, 236, 253; *see also* monsters
hyphens 220–1

iconoclasm 225
idée fixe 234
idioms 49, 77, 116, 121, 125–8, 140, 168, 169, 176, 211
idiots savants 62
imitation 6, 8, 11, 27, 47, 58, 66, 70, 85–88, 91, 92, 93, 132, 139, 209, 227
impersonal pronouns 24
impersonation 6, 70, 85, 88
influence 29, 91
inkhorn terms 212, 231–3, 242
intertextuality 17, 77, 91
Ionesco, Eugène 20, 44, 60–1, 128, 161–2
Irish Bulls 44, 103–4, 250, 255
irony 20, 42, 54, 63, 100, 120, 125, 141, 167–8

Jacob, François 164
James, Henry 48, 51
Japan, 38, 77, 94
jargon 13–15, 99, 109, 115, 128, 182, 190, 196, 225, 231
Jencks, Charles and Silver, Nathan 167, 205, 247
Jiménez, Juan Ramón 262n.
jingles (and doggerel) 60, 115, 116, 125, 145, 150
Johnson, Samuel 29, 35
Joscelyne, Andrew 198, 283n.
journalism 152–3, 222, 235
Joyce, James 29, 57–8, 91, 92, 105, 157, 163, 171, 172, 223, 225, 238–9, 244, 248

Kapferer, Jean-Noël 24–4, 259n.
Keaton, Buster 164
Kellett, E. E. 76, 77, 90
Kenner, Hugh 51–2, 97, 222, 287n.
kitsch (and camp) 61, 150–2, 174
Ku Klux Klan 111, 209, 222

La Bruyère, Jean de la 28, 29, 157, 190, 192
Lacan, Jacques 71, 172, 266n.
Laclos, Pierre Choderlos de 64, 163, 190
Laforgue, Jules 236
Lamb, Charles 11, 32
Larbaud, Valery 138–9, 197
Lautréamont, Comte de 28, 89, 94, 147
Lawrence, Jeremy 99
Lechner, Sister Joan Marie 28
Legman, Gershon 169, 268n.
Leiris, Michel 205, 219, 244
Lerner, Laurence 7, 26, 35, 39–40, 104, 152
Lindey, Alexander 78, 85
Lippmann, Walter 135, 162
litotes 7, 11, 100–1, 106, 147, 157, 190, 196, 208
Liverpool 1, 3, 183

Macdonald, Dwight 12, 89, 171
McLuhan, Marshall 42, 58, 82–3, 173, 174, 223, 239
Mallarmé, Stéphane 107, 143, 197, 232, 234, 240, 289n.
markers (for clichés) 63, 153, 177

Marx, Karl 33, 50, 102
Matthews, Brander 185, 189, 232
Maverick, Maury 15
maxims (and epigrams) 81, 111, 120, 141, 168
memory (and amnesia) 68–9, 79, 92n, 93, 155, 160, 163
Mencken, H. L. 13, 183, 195, 196, 214, 226
mental illness (and clichés) 59, 125, 126, 131, 135
mental illness (and coinages) 183, 241–6
mentalities 138
Mercier, Louis-Sébastien 193–4
Merton, Robert K. 33, 76
metaphor 43, 88, 90, 101–2, 111, 125, 128, 130, 152, 167, 168, 173, 175, 178, 180, 182, 195, 234
Migliorini, Bruno 185, 207
mishearing 166, 241, 249
misspelling (creative) 208–9
Molière 133, 214
Mona Lisa 147, 151
monsters (neologisms as) 180, 237, 246–7
Montaigne, Michel de 8, 28, 29, 66, 70, 74–5, 76, 79, 88, 94, 111, 188
Mormile, Mario 283n.
Musset, Alfred de 53

names (nicknames) 227
Napoleon 23, 144
Nash, Ogden 53, 94, 104, 205, 232–3, 251
neologisms (mine) 28, 73, 104, 106, 132, 138, 170, 181, 184, 192, 196, 220, 225, 227, 232, 236, 238, 239, 246, 256
Nietzsche, Friedrich 29, 87, 137, 181, 182
Nodier, Charles 70, 85, 194
nonce-words (hapax) 131, 181, 232–3, 234, 238
nothing 38, 44, 51, 56, 73, 115, 158

O'Brien, Flann (Myles na Gopaleen) 63, 153
obvious 107, 115, 177
officialese 22, 45
Ong, Walter 28, 80, 104, 124–5

oral cultures 123–5
originality 31, 33, 34, 55, 58, 66, 76, 77, 83, 85, 86, 112, 159–63, 174
Ortega y Gasset, José 92, 130
OULIPO 36, 168
oxymoron 45, 62, 75, 103, 107, 114, 150, 151, 209, 223

Palmer, A. Smythe 209, 214, 232
Paracelsus 205
paradox 32, 82, 107, 120
parody 1, 36, 62, 84, 85, 89–90, 122, 144, 149, 164
Partridge, Eric 4, 14, 19
Pascal, Blaise 41, 74, 106, 161
Pasternak, Boris 31–2
pastiche 1, 84, 85, 88–9, 149, 159, 164
Pataphysics 93
Paulhan, Jean 22, 39, 63, 82, 123, 141, 156–7, 175–6, 253
phatic speech (and chatter) 22, 23, 56
Pietra, Régine 158–9
plagiarism 17, 19, 27, 29, 32, 33, 57, 65–74, 76, 78, 79, 83, 85–96, 115, 139, 159, 163, 164, 176, 193, 207, 211, 226, 229
platitude 45, 50, 51, 55, 97–8
Plato 255
play 225–6
politics (and clichés) 24, 52, 62, 67, 103, 111, 112–13, 115, 131, 167
politics (and neologisms) 194, 224
pomposity 44, 101, 112, 131, 158
Ponge, Francis 97, 117, 235, 239, 247
Pope, Alexander 61, 97, 116, 171, 187
popular culture 42, 149–50
Porter, Cole 149
Pound, Ezra 236
Pound, Louise 208, 209, 251
preciosity 30, 189, 192, 239
propaganda 24, 45, 112–13
Proust, Marcel 21, 44, 50, 68, 70, 73, 76, 88, 92, 200, 283n.
proverbs 3, 81, 109, 110, 116–17, 119–25, 127, 128, 135, 168, 169, 170, 173, 176, 189
psychobabble 14–15
puns 2, 17, 33, 42, 49, 69, 71, 76, 99, 100, 114, 125, 127, 135, 166, 167,

169, 170–2, 176, 186, 195, 200, 202, 204, 208, 215, 216, 218, 219, 224, 225, 236, 237, 250, 251, 254, 255

Queneau, Raymond 13, 39, 44, 48, 56–7, 59, 77, 99–100, 129, 168, 169, 200, 213, 219, 228, 231, 236–7, 285n.
quotations 28, 41, 47, 72, 74–8, 82, 90, 117, 205

Rabelais, François 41, 45, 77, 188, 206
racism 23, 134, 136–8, 189, 197, 214–15, 216
ready-mades 59, 119, 147–9, 153, 164, 181
Reboul, Olivier 110–16, 119, 141
Redfern, Angela (as author) 174
redundancy 22, 31, 104, 105, 107, 108, 128, 141, 158
repetition 8, 50, 57, 60, 75, 104, 105, 106, 112, 115, 121, 128, 131, 142, 144, 145, 175, 177, 253
resistance (to clichés) 18–19, 61, 157
resistance (to neologisms, purism) 180, 184, 187–203, 208, 210, 212, 214–15, 235, 251–2
rhetoric 3, 8, 11, 27–8, 57, 75, 80, 100, 104, 110, 137, 156, 178, 218, 255
rhymes (and rhyming slang) 101, 121, 128–9, 152, 175, 221, 232, 249
rhythms 42, 60, 109, 128, 129, 175
Ricks, Christopher 18–19, 113–14, 171, 174
Riffaterre, Michel 31, 158–9, 193, 232, 234
Roback, A. A. 136–7, 138, 276n.
Rogers, Pat 168, 202, 235
romanticism 27, 28, 32, 33–40, 42, 46, 55, 93, 194
Rosenberg, Harold 142–3
Rousseau, Jean-Jacques 7, 29, 86, 160, 189–90, 192
Roy, Claude 121–2
rumour 23–4

Sabin, Margery 43, 76, 120, 139–40, 160
St Jerome 55, 138
Salmon, Gilbert 240
Sarraute, Nathalie 59–60

Sartre, Jean-Paul 48, 49–50, 59, 63–4, 67, 72, 82, 95–6, 101, 111, 122, 144, 160, 223–4, 247, 253, 259n., 263n.
Schneider, Michel 19, 32, 39, 42, 67, 68, 69, 70, 71–2, 74, 82, 83, 84, 85, 86, 91, 93, 96, 141, 159, 177
scientific coinages 217, 229–31
science-fiction (and neologisms) 236
sentimentality 97, 145, 150
Shakespeare, William 42–3, 47, 58, 120, 124, 253, 255
Shlovsky, Viktor 41, 165
silence 23, 50, 55, 63, 143, 158, 161, 177
Silone, Ignazio 74, 166
slang 191, 196, 205, 226, 237
slips 63, 103, 127, 130, 136, 181, 247–50
slogans 13, 17, 99, 109–17, 120–1, 152, 168, 170, 215, 217
Smith, Logan Pearsall 125–6, 191, 195, 207, 229
social cement (clichés as) 16–25, 174, 176
Sontag, Susan 61, 105
sources 79–81, 91
Souriau, Etienne 130, 204, 229
Spinoza 47, 184, 185, 206
Spitzer, Leo 117
Steiner, George 36, 73, 83, 239
Strickland, Geoffrey 36, 158, 246, 258n.
stupidity 46–57, 62, 134
surrealism 58–9, 82, 123, 143, 145, 151, 168, 225, 236, 242, 265n.
Swift, Jonathan 77, 102, 168, 191, 220, 228
synthetic languages 202, 238–9

Textor, Ravisius 80–1, 104
Thatcher, Margaret 112
Thompson, Philip and Davenport, Peter 145, 147
Thoreau, Henry David 18, 160
Time 221–2, 223
topoi (loci, commonplaces) 27–8, 32, 33, 35, 46, 54, 68, 80, 81, 159
Tournier, Michel 31, 62, 134, 200, 220–1, 255, 265n., 287n.
trade-names 229
translation 138–9
truisms 104–7, 114, 126, 206, 253

Twain, Mark 74, 165
twists (of clichés and proverbs) 60, 95,
    107, 115, 122–3, 126, 151, 153,
    165–70, 173, 182, 205

Valéry, Paul 26, 34, 35, 134, 143, 162,
    235
Vallès, Jules 9, 10, 107, 140, 166, 231
visual clichés 67, 144–52
visual neologisms 244–6
Voltaire 62, 93, 95, 192

weasel words 98

Wellerisms 122
Wellington, Arthur Duke of 109
Wentworth, Harold 218
White, Harold O. 66
women (and feminism) 2, 35, 136,
    137–8, 150, 167, 182, 185, 207, 241–2
Wordsworth, William 43, 90, 94

Yates, Frances 68–9
Young, Edward 34, 94

Zijderveld, Anton C. 18–19, 150, 169,
    173